Time and Eternity

Cornell Studies in the Philosophy of Religion

EDITED BY WILLIAM P. ALSTON

God, Time, and Knowledge
  by William Hasker

*On a Complex Theory of a Simple God: An Investigation in Aquinas'
Philosophical Theology*
  by Christopher Hughes

Time and Eternity
  by Brian Leftow

Theology in the Age of Scientific Reasoning
  by Nancey Murphy

The Nature of God: An Inquiry into Divine Attributes
  by Edward R. Wierenga

Brian Leftow

Time and Eternity

Cornell University Press, Ithaca and London

First published 1991 by Cornell University Press.
ISBN 0-8014-7522-8
International Standard Book Number 0-8014-2459-3
Library of Congress Catalog Card Number 90-55890
Printed in the United States of America
*Librarians: Library of Congress cataloging information
appears on the last page of the book.*

For Denise

Because joy comes in jars.

Contents

Preface   xi

1 *Introduction*   1

2 *Some Working Assumptions*   6

Reality Has a Modal Structure *6*
Possibilities Come in World-Sized Clumps *7*
Only Actually Existing Entities Have Attributes *9*
There Are Absolute Modal Facts *10*
The Logic of Absolute Modality Is S5 *13*
Some Modal Claims Have Sufficient Warrant to Deserve Belief *14*
Time Can Be Viewed as Tensed or as Tenseless *17*
The Primary Occupants of Time Are Not Things *18*
We Can Speak Affirmatively and Literally of God *18*

3 *The Possibility of the Timeless*   20

Is the 4D Universe Timeless? *21*
Would a Second Time Series Be Timeless? *21*
Motion and Spatially Continuous Paths *23*
Continuous Paths, Single Spaces, and Single Times *24*
One Space, Two Times *26*
Indirect Evidence *28*
God and Multiple Times *29*
Timeless Space *31*
The Necessity of Time: Hartshorne *34*
God and the Necessity of Time *35*
The Contingency of Time *36*
Numbers and Mathematical Truths *40*

4 *The Logic of Eternity*   50

Truth and Timelessness: Eternity as a Date *50*
Applications *52*

An Objection   55
A Reply Rejected   57
A Second Proposal   58
A Third Proposal   60
Eternity and Tense   61
Timelessness and Alethic Modality   63
Eternity, Simplicity, and Absolute Necessity   66
Eternity and Uniqueness   71
The Position to Date   72

5   Augustine: Eternality as Truest Existence   73
Timelessness and Being TI   76
Two Problems   80
Genuineness of Existence   81
Genuine Existence   83
Genuine Presentness and Augustine's Position   89
Degreed Existence and Tenseless Time   91
Unity and Existence   92
An Argument for Degreed Existence   95
How Many Degrees?   96
The Superior Reality of the Timeless   97
Existence, Unity, and Augustine's Position   99
Greatest Unity and Its Marks   99
Dream and Reality   100
Continuity   105
Coherence   106
Explicability   106
Intersubjectivity   107
"Hardness"   108
Inclusiveness   109
Dream, Reality, and Augustine's Position   110
The Importance of the Timeless   110

6   Boethius: Eternity as Duration   112
Eternity in the Consolation of Philosophy   113
Eternity in De Trinitate   119
QTE and the Stump-Kretzmann View   123
Fitzgerald's Critique   123
The Stump-Kretzmann Response   125
Eternity and Divine Simplicity   134
On Behalf of a Partless Extension   137
Eternity and the Experienced Present   143
Is Eternity Timelike or Spacelike?   144
Vale et Salve   146

7   The Roots of Eternity   147
Points, Lines, and Eternity   147
Eternity and Divine Simplicity   150
Eternity as an Answer to Abstractness   157

8   *Boethius: Foreknowledge, Eternity, and Simultaneity*   159
    Stump and Kretzmann on Time and Eternity   *164*
    The Relativity of Simultaneity   *165*
    The Stump-Kretzmann Definition   *167*
    Can Events Be Temporally Present in Relation to Eternity?   *167*
    Questions of Interpretation   *168*
    Discrete Times and Eternity   *175*
    Incommensurable Times and Eternity   *175*
    Another Approach   *177*
    Other Problems   *178*
    A Historical Footnote   *181*

9   *Anselm: Eternity and Dimensionality*   183
    Anselm on Time and Eternity   *184*
    Eternity in the *Monologion*   *185*
    Causal Presence   *187*
    Why Temporal Omnipresence?   *191*
    Omnipresence and Omniabsence   *194*
    God's Presence in Time   *199*
    Simplicity and Temporal Omnipresence   *203*
    Intrinsic Eternity   *209*
    Eternity in the *Proslogion*   *210*
    Anselm's Later Work on Time and Eternity   *212*

10 *A Theory of Time and Eternity*   217
    An Anselmian Advantage   *217*
    From God's Spacelessness to Creatures' Timelessness   *222*
    A Medieval Objection   *228*
    An Objection: Does Occurring in Eternity Entail Tenseless Time?   *230*
    An Objection: Must Whatever Occurs in Eternity Be Eternal?   *235*
    Time and Eternity   *238*
    Eternity and Tense   *241*
    An Objection: Is Eternal Presence Otiose?   *243*
    Applications   *244*

11 *Timelessness, Freedom, and Foreknowledge*   246

12 *A Case for God's Timelessness*   267
    Timelessness and Infinite Time   *267*
    Timelessness and Infinity   *270*
    Timelessness and Necessary Existence   *270*
    Timelessness and Spatiality   *271*
    Timelessness and Omnipotence   *273*
    Timelessness and the Modal Status of Time   *273*
    Timelessness and the Creation of Time   *273*
    Timelessness and the Creation of the Universe   *275*
    Timelessness and the Beginning of Time   *275*
    Timelessness, Creation, and Providence   *277*

Timelessness as Metaphysically Superior to Temporality *278*
Timeless Life and Time's Tooth *278*
Timelessness and Perfect Knowledge of the Past *279*
Timelessness, Freedom, and Foreknowledge *280*
Timelessness, Omniscience, and Divine Dialogue *280*
Timelessness and God's Foreknowledge of His Own Acts *281*
The Road Ahead *282*

13   *Timelessness and Personhood*   283

Mind and Time *283*
Understanding and Time *285*
Creation and Timelessness *290*
Sustaining and Timelessness *291*
Intentional Action and Timelessness *295*
Passage, Power, and Timelessness *297*
Some Other Mental Concepts *298*
Timelessness and Freedom *299*
Immutability and Timelessness *302*
Change of Will *302*
Change of Property *309*

14   *Time, Actuality, and Omniscience*   313

The Metaphysical Argument Stated *315*
Recasting the Argument *317*
Must God Know Whatever We Know? *321*
How God Perceives Present-Actuality *327*
Another Version *330*
The Anselmian Approach *332*
Factual Omniscience *335*

15   *Omniscience, Change, and Epistemic Indexicals*   338

What Can the Blind Know about Colors? *339*
Omniscience and What the Blind Can't Know *342*
Knowledge of Change *342*

16   *Timelessness and Religious Experience*   349

Does Perception Locate the Perceived in Time? *349*
A Second Argument against Observing the Timeless *355*

17   *Vale et Salve*   360

References   363

Index   373

Preface

This book seeks to defend the claim that God is timeless, that is, exists, but exists at no time. One thing it suggests is that there is more than one conception of a timeless God and a timeless God's relation to time. I have my favorite among them, and I attempt to recommend it. But I have also tried to show how alternate conceptions might handle various problems and to point out the merits of these conceptions. My hope is that if my particular version of God's timelessness and a timeless God's relation to time does not prove appealing, some other version mentioned here will.

This book has benefited from the counsel of many. William Alston gave generously of his time to improve the paper that was its root, then provided detailed and extremely helpful comments on the entire manuscript. William Hasker's comments also led to improvements, as did Eleonore Stump's treatment of the first half of the book. Robert O'Connell and Margaret Walker provided useful comments on the Augustine chapter. These colleagues have my sincerest thanks. Audiences of the American Philosophical Association, the Society of Christian Philosophers, the New Jersey Regional Philosophical Association, and the International Patristic, Medieval, and Renaissance Conference heard earlier versions of some of this material. I cannot individually acknowledge all their contributions (save perhaps for some remarks of Philip Quinn), but I thank them all.

On a more personal level, I must thank four people. Dick Trammell was my first philosophy prof, and his friendship and professional example have much to do with my being in philosophy at all. Paul Vinroot and Doug Steele have provided consistent reminders that there is more to life than philosophy. No words can adequately say my thanks to and for my wife Denise. This book is for her.

Let me also thank my parents, Barbara and Alvin Leftow, for their many kindnesses, and particularly their affectionate interest in my admittedly esoteric endeavors.

Finally, some professional debts. Some matter in this book has appeared in other venues: a bit of Chapter 2 in "A Modal Cosmological Argument," *International Journal for Philosophy of Religion* 24 (1988), 159–188; a bit of Chapters 2 and 10 in "Aquinas on Time and Eternity," *New Scholasticism* 64 (1990), 387–399; much of Chapter 6 in "Boethius on Eternity," *History of Philosophy Quarterly* 7 (1990), 123–142; most of Chapter 7 and some of Chapter 8 in "The Roots of Eternity," *Religious Studies* 24 (1989), 189–212; parts of Chapter 9 in "Anselm on Omnipresence," *New Scholasticism* 63 (1989), 326–357; most of Chapters 8 and 10 in "Eternity and Simultaneity," *Faith and Philosophy* 8 (1991); and most of Chapter 14 in "Time, Actuality, and Omniscience," *Religious Studies* 26 (1990), 303–322. My thanks to the editors of these publications for their permission to use this material.

BRIAN LEFTOW

Ossining, N.Y.

Time and Eternity

[1]

Introduction

The Western religions all claim that God is eternal. This claim finds strong expression in the Old Testament, which is common property of Jews and Christians and well-respected by Moslems:

Before the mountains were born or you brought forth the earth and the world, from everlasting to everlasting you are God . . .
A thousand years in your sight are like a day that has just gone by, or like a watch in the night.[1]

In the beginning you laid the foundations of the earth, and the heavens are the work of your hands.
They will perish, but you remain . . . the same, and your years will never end.[2]

Such passages seem to say that God's being eternal is His enduring forever through time: that God is "timeless" in that His life is temporally infinite and so not "contained" or limited by time.[3] But for a

1. Psalm 90:2, 4, New International Version.
2. Psalm 102:25–27, NIV.
3. That may be Aristotle's view of eternity; see *Physics* IV, 12–14, and the discussion of them in Richard Sorabji, *Time, Creation, and the Continuum* (Ithaca, N.Y.: Cornell University Press, 1983) (henceforth *TC&C*), pp. 125–127. Martha Kneale expresses this idea clearly: "If there is an eternal object, e.g., God . . . then since He is *at* all times, He is not *in* time, but this is not to be confused with saying that He does not exist at any time, i.e., not yesterday, today or tomorrow . . . Timelessness is lack of limitation of existence in time; it is not failure to exist at all times" ("Eternity and Sempiternity," in Marjorie Grene, ed., *Spinoza* (New York: Doubleday, 1973), p. 232).

variety of reasons, Western religious thinkers have often not been content with this view of God's eternity. They have claimed instead that God's being eternal or timeless is his existing without in any way being in time—that though God exists, there is no time at which He exists, and He does not exist before, during, or after any time. As Anselm puts it, addressing God in the *Proslogion,* "none of your eternity is past as if it now did not exist, and none of it is future as if it did not exist yet. Therefore it is not the case that you existed yesterday or will exist tomorrow. Instead, yesterday, today, and tomorrow, you exist. Or better, neither yesterday nor today nor tomorrow do you exist, but you simply exist, beyond every time. For yesterday, today, and tomorrow exist only in time."[4] Henceforth I take the claim that God is timeless in the second way, as asserting that God is in no way in time. We will see that within the theological tradition that concerns us, "God is eternal" asserts that God is in no way in time and also entails two other claims, that God is metaphysically "simple" and that God is alive.

The claims that God is timeless or eternal are standard features of late-classical and medieval philosophical theology. They are prominent in discussions of the relation of God's foreknowledge to human freedom, and their consequences pervade traditional accounts of other kinds of divine knowledge, of God's will, and of God's relation to the world. But their chief importance lies not in what they imply for other attributes and issues but for what they say in themselves. As we will see, the medieval theologians who developed doctrines of God's eternity held that eternality is the distinctive mode of God's life and experience—that the claim that God is eternal, properly understood, tells us as much as we can know about what it is like to be God. That God is eternal has entailments both for what God is not and for what God is. As we have seen, it entails that God is not temporal. It entails that God *is* in full possession of the whole extent of His life at once: in Boethius' famous phrase, on which I dwell at length, an eternal being possesses all at once and perfectly the fullness of an illimitable life. So an examination of the concept of eternity promises to repay our efforts with a better understanding of the history of philosophical theology and with insight into the concept of God.

The doctrine of divine timelessness was a nearly unchallenged

4. "An de aeternitate tua nihil praeterit ut iam non sit, nec aliquid futurum est quasi nondum sit. Non ergo fuisti heri aut eris cras sed heri et hodie et cras es. Immo nec heri nec hodie nec cras es, sed simpliciter es extra omne tempus. Nam nihil aliud est heri et hodie et cras quam in tempore." Anselm, *Proslogion,* in Franciscus Schmitt, ed., *S. Anselmi: Opera omnia* (Edinburgh: Thomas Nelson, 1946) (henceforth *Opera*), vol. 1, chap. 19, p. 115, ll. 10–14.

orthodoxy for the millennium between Athanasius and Duns Scotus. Today the claim that God is temporal enjoys nearly as universal an acceptance among philosophers and theologians. Nelson Pike expresses a prevalent judgment: "Plato (probably) thought that the things of ultimate value are eternal in the sense of timeless. But Plato was not a Christian—nor can I think of any reason why a Christian should accept Plato's judgment on this matter without careful consideration of how it relates to the broad Christian tradition concerning the nature of God . . . the doctrine of God's timelessness entered Christian theology (only) because Platonic thought was stylish at the time and because the doctrine appears to have considerable . . . systematic elegance."[5] The claim that God is timeless is widely considered to be at best needless and outmoded metaphysical baggage, and at worst incompatible with such central theistic claims as that God is omniscient, that God is an agent or a person, and that God can act in the world. Recent philosophers and theologians tend to think that anything that could count as *God*—as the living, loving person whom the Old and New testaments depict as in dialogue with creatures in history—must be in time. Their message is that the deity of atemporalists is too remote and impersonal to be God. Yet medieval philosophers and theologians tended to think that anything that could count as *God*—as the transcendent, perfect source of all that is other than Himself— could not be in time. The medievals would say that the deity of the temporalists is too small or too creaturelike to be God. Another reason for interest in the claim that God is timeless, then, is that it is a point of conflict between apparently divergent visions of the nature of God. Any reason to opt for or against this claim could be a reason to emphasize one or the other basic picture of the divine.

This book's aim is to articulate and defend the claim that God is in no way in time. If God is not *in* time, of course, one must wonder what his relation to time is. Thus my second aim is to clarify the relations between a timeless being and temporal beings: between time and eternity. I begin by identifying and sketching arguments for some working assumptions, chiefly concerning the nature and logic of possibility (Chap. 2). With these given, my project unfolds in three stages.

I first articulate the claim that God is timeless. I do so in three ways. First, in Chapter 3, I display possible and (I argue) actual examples of timeless beings. Second, in Chapter 4, I set out precisely some abstract, formal aspects of what one asserts when one calls something timeless or eternal, and I show what semantic machinery one needs to make

5. Nelson Pike, *God and Timelessness* (New York: Schocken, 1970), pp. 189–190.

sense of talk about timeless or eternal beings. Third, I build up the concrete content of the claim that God is timeless through analytic historical studies of three major proponents of divine timelessness. I begin with Augustine (Chap. 5), whose thought about God was the foundation of medieval philosophical theology through the time of Aquinas. Augustine's thought about divine eternity lets us see the broader metaphysical context and (some of) the religious importance of the claim that God is timeless. I contend that Augustine's claim that timeless beings are "more real" than temporal makes good sense and is surprisingly plausible, and I show that this claim, if true, provides reason to want to say that God is timeless.

I move then to Boethius, whose treatment of God's eternity became arguably the most important text for medieval discussion of the subject. Boethius' thinking (and Stump and Kretzmann's recent treatment of it) let us focus on the nature of eternity itself and broach the problem of eternity's relations to time.[6] I argue that there can be such a thing as an atemporal duration and that eternity as Boethius conceives it is one (Chap. 6). I also show that Boethius' concept of eternity was shaped by his doctrine of divine simplicity and commitment to the claim that God is alive (Chap. 7). In the end, however, I do not opt to defend a durational view of eternity. I also critique Boethius' ideas about time-eternity relations as reconstructed by Stump and Kretzmann (Chap. 8). From Boethius I move to Anselm (Chap. 9). Discussing his position permits me to formulate my own concept of time–eternity relations; I argue that temporal things exist not only in time but also in eternity and that this is the key to the relations of time and eternity (Chaps. 10–11).

It is widely thought that there are no good reasons to claim that God is timeless. So once I have set out what it is for God to be timeless, I move to the second stage of my project and develop some arguments for God's timelessness. These arguments are at once reasons to want to claim that God is timeless and reasons to think that God is in fact timeless. I argue that the doctrine of divine timelessness is a consequence of many claims theists wish to make, including the claims that God exists necessarily, that God does not exist in space, that God is omnipotent, and that God is the creator of time (Chap. 12).

A great many recent thinkers have contended that nothing timeless can qualify for the title "God." As I argue that God is timeless, the third stage of my project is to defend the claim that a timeless being can

6. Eleonore Stump and Norman Kretzmann, "Eternity," *Journal of Philosophy* 79 (1981), p. 429–458.

be God against their objections. In doing so, I also seek to flesh out a picture of the sort of being a timeless God would be. Some writers have urged that nothing timeless can be personal, because no timeless being can have knowledge or be an agent. So I devote a chapter (13) to arguing that a timeless, changeless being can know, will, and act. Some writers have averred that even if a timeless being can be personal, such a being cannot be God, because no timeless being can be omniscient. Thus I spend two chapters (14–15) discussing what a timeless being can know and arguing that such a being can be omniscient. Finally, some writers have argued that a timeless being cannot be experienced. If this is true, then since theists claim to be able to experience God, theists must reject the claim that God is timeless. So I argue in Chapter 16 that experience of a timeless God is possible. This last argument may in addition open up one further way to support the claim that God is timeless. Whatever the value of religious experience as evidence for the claim that God exists, if one already believes that there is a God, it is surely rational to take at least some apparent experiences of God as evidence about His nature. Now it is perhaps not impossible that religious believers and mystics have experiences that they take to be of a timeless divine reality (though it is far from clear just what it could be to experience something to be timeless). If such experiences occur, then, the argument of this chapter gives religious believers some reason to take them at face value and so some reason to treat them as evidence that God is timeless.

[2]

Some Working Assumptions

Like any other large-scale philosophical project, this book rests on some philosophical views that it cannot completely justify. Let me at least identify them and briefly suggest some reason to consider them plausible.

Reality Has a Modal Structure

It seems, preanalytically, that there are modal truths. Consider the thesis that human beings cannot survive a week without oxygen. This proposition essentially involves modality of some sort, for "cannot" is an ineliminable part of it. Yet this proposition has a strong claim to be true. Efforts to show that the truth of modal claims is based purely on convention seem to me unsuccessful; conventionalism about modality appears false. Thus I would argue that realism about modal truth is as well or ill founded as realism about nonmodal truth. That is, in whatever sense there are facts about how things are and are not, there also are facts about how things can and must be.

My talk of facts and states of affairs here and elsewhere is just a façon de parler; I intend no ontological commitment. In continuing this façon de parler, I speak of facts as rendering propositions true or false. I do not presuppose that propositions and facts are "isomorphic" or that propositions "picture" facts. I do, however, speak of truths corresponding to facts. I mean no more by this talk than that (a) truth conforms to Tarski's schema, i.e., that "Fa" is true iff Fa, and that (b) truths have *truthmakers*, i.e., for every true proposition P, there exists at least one entity or complex of entities P* such that necessarily, P is true if P* exists. The claim that truths have truthmakers asserts only that the world somehow determines truth-values. This claim is neutral between theories of truth. Correspondence theories can say that what determines truth-value is that with which a proposition corresponds. Coherence theories can say that what determines truth-value is the set of propositions coherence with which qualifies P as true. Antirealist theories assert that truth-values are determined, e.g., by what an ideal community of inquirers would eventually find it most rational to believe. These theories can say that what determines truth includes, e.g., the beliefs that would be formed by the ideal community. They can say, for instance, that the truth of P is determined by whatever attributes of actual things determine the truth of the subjunctive conditional "were an ideal community of inquirers to pursue their inquiries without temporal limit, they would in the end come to believe P." Even a conventionalist about necessary truth can affirm that even necessary truths have truthmakers. The conventionalist can just say that what determines the truth of a necessary P includes the relevant decisions of the language-using community. Moreover, saying only that the world somehow determines truth-values makes no statement as to *how* the world does this. Thus it does not commit one to any claims about terms' references or sentences' interpretations.[1]

Possibilities Come in World-Sized Clumps

It is possible, in some sense, that Ronald Reagan serve a third term as president of the United States. But were Reagan to serve a third term, this could not be all that occurred. Reagan either would or would not continue to be over six feet tall, the sun either would or would not continue to rise, and so on: one wants to say that for every proposition one could express, that proposition would be or become true or false as the world history containing Reagan's third term unfolded. Thus what truly are possible are not single discrete states of affairs (henceforth SOAs), such as Reagan's serving a third term. Rather, what are possible are various world histories containing that SOA. Reagan's serving a third term is the intersection of a set of possible world histories, each of which (one wants to say) is complete in the sense of determining for every proposition P whether P or not-P is true in that world history.

---

1. Thus this claim circumvents Quine's indeterminacy of reference argument and Putnam's treatment of sentences' interpretations. My treatment of the truthmaker assumption owes much to John Post, *The Faces of Existence* (Ithaca, N.Y.: Cornell University Press, 1987), chap. 1.

There is only one universe. But that universe has and has had an infinity of possible histories, each differing from all the rest. Philosophers call a possible world history a possible world.

It is common to say that a possible world suffices to determine the truth-value of every proposition at that world. This further suggests that a possible world is in some sense a "complete" possibility. One might therefore want to hold that a possible world is a set of (say) SOAs which, for every SOA P, contains P or contains not-P. But arguably, one cannot hold this, at least if SOAs correspond one-to-one with truths. For if one says this, then possible worlds exist iff there are sets of all truths which would be true in certain circumstances. The claim that there are such sets generates Liarlike and set-theoretic paradoxes.[2] Still, if one wants a set-theoretic account of possible worlds, one has several options. One can, for instance, just deny that SOAs correspond one-to-one with truths.[3] Again, one can take a possible world to be a complete, consistent set of *atomic* SOAs, i.e., an arrangement of particulars and attributes which for every atomic proposition "Fa" suffices to verify or falsify Fa.[4] One can say that if a world W contains the SOA that Fa, "Fa" is true in W, and continue from there:

i. if W does not contain Fa, "Fa" is false in W and "~Fa" is true in W.[5]

ii. if W contains Fa and contains Fb, "Fa·Fb" is true in W; otherwise "Fa·Fb" is false in W.

iii. if W contains Fa or contains Fb or both, "Fa ∨ Fb" is true in W; otherwise "Fa ∨ Fb" is false in W.

iv. if W does not contain Fa or contains Fb or both, "Fa ⊃ Fb" is true in W; otherwise "Fa ⊃ Fb" is false in W.

2. See Patrick Grim, "Some Neglected Problems of Omniscience," *American Philosophical Quarterly* 20 (1983), 265–276; "There Is No Set of All Truths," *Analysis* 44 (1984), 206–208; "Logic and Limits of Knowledge and Truth," *Nous* 22 (1988), 341–367; and "Truth, Omniscience, and the Knower," *Philosophical Studies* (1988), 9–41.
3. I do so in Chapter 14.
4. What follows is indebted to Michael Pendlebury's "Facts as Truthmakers," *Monist* 69 (1986), 177–188.
5. The truthmaker assumption requires that "~Fa" have a truthmaker. The truthmaker of "~Fa" if W is actual, I suggest, is just the fact that the members of W exhaust the actual world. For if the SOA that Fa is not a member of W, this is so necessarily, and so necessarily, if the members of W exhaust the actual world, "~Fa" is true. The fact that W's members exhaust the actual world is not itself a member of W. W includes only atomic SOAs, and the fact that W's members exhaust the actual world is a fact that involves quantification over SOAs: it is the fact that for all x, if there exists a y that is identical with x, then y is a member of W. But though this fact is not a member of W, it will obtain if W is the actual world.

If one is willing to treat quantified sentences as infinite conjunctions or disjunctions, then (ii) and (iii) provide truth- and falsity-conditions for quantified propositions as well. If one rejects this treatment of quantified propositions, one can instead assert these:

    v. if W contains at least one SOA of an x being Φ, then "(∃x)(Φx)" is true in W; otherwise "(∃x)(Φx)" is false in W.

    vi. if no particular involved in an SOA W contains fails to be Φ, then "(x)(Φx)" is true in W; otherwise "(x)(Φx)" is false in W.

Given (i)–(vi), one can, of course, recursively define truth-conditions for conjunctions and disjunctions of quantified propositions, multiply quantified propositions, etc. So a world taken as a complete set of positive atomic facts does suffice to verify or falsify all indicative propositions.[6] Further, if among the propositions this world verifies are (say) statements of natural laws, and such statements entail counterfactuals, this world will be complete with respect to all such counterfactuals. It is not clear that such a world would be complete with respect to all counterfactuals. I have, for instance, made no provision for claims about what free agents would do in counterfactual situations. But as there is room for doubt about whether such claims *have* truth-values,[7] it is not clear that I need to do so. Given this notion of a possible world, one can construct the usual modal semantics, taking possibility (in a set of worlds) as truth in at least one world (of the set) and necessity (in a set of worlds) as truth in all worlds (of the set). Though I speak of possible worlds as sets of facts and SOAs, this book does not require this particular theory of possible worlds. Any theory compatible with my assumption that there are real modal facts and with the next assumption will do.

Only Actually Existing Entities Have Attributes

I make the "actualist" assumption that only existing things have attributes. For it seems plausible that nothing has attributes unless it exists to bear them. This does not entail that propositions such as "there could be a man not identical with any man who ever actually

---

6. One would have to complicate all this to deal adequately with tense. As I seek only to indicate the general direction of a way around the set-of-all-truths problem, I forebear doing so.

7. See, e.g., Robert M. Adams, "Middle Knowledge and Evil," *American Philosophical Quarterly* 14 (1977), 109–117; William Hasker, *God, Time and Knowledge* (Ithaca, N.Y.: Cornell University Press, 1989), pp. 22–52.

exists" are all false or truth-valueless. The assumption entails only that this truth's truthmakers do not involve any possible but nonactual men. There are many other ways to understand such truths. One can, for instance, say that they are true because no genuine kind (including the kind "male human") places limits on the number of particulars that exemplify it, and so however great the number of men who at some time actually exist, there can always be more.

My "actualist" assumption extends to modal attributes. When I say, for instance, that a certain attribute is exemplifiable, I do not mean that in some nonactual possible world, something exemplifies that attribute. I instead mean that that attribute actually exists and actually bears a modal attribute, that of being possibly exemplified. For it is plausible that what a thing *can* be is determined by its actual character; thus many philosophers argue that a chemical's dispositional properties (e.g., its propensities to combine with other chemicals in new compounds) are determined by its nondispositional properties (e.g., its molecular structure). Things that do not actually exist have no actual character to determine their modal attributes. Thus it seems reasonable to say that they have no modal attributes.[8]

There Are Absolute Modal Facts

"Absolute modality" is what Alvin Plantinga calls "broadly logical" modality and Saul Kripke calls "metaphysical" modality.[9] It is easier to suggest what absolute modality is by examples than to say what it is explicitly. Absolute modality is most like logical modality. Truths that are logically necessary are also absolutely necessary, and like logical falsehoods, claims that are absolutely-necessarily false are also false with every other sort of necessity. Moreover, it is likely that many philosophers who have spoken in terms of logical modalities have really meant to be discussing absolute modalities. But absolute and logical modalities are distinct, for at least three reasons.

First, all logically necessary truths are truths of logic, i.e., truths

8. "Actualism" is currently a topic of intense debate. For criticism of it, see, e.g., John L. Pollock, "Plantinga on Possible Worlds," in James Tomberlin and Peter van Inwagen, eds., *Alvin Plantinga* (Dordrecht: Reidel, 1985), pp. 145–186; Nathan Salmon, "Existence," in James Tomberlin, ed., *Philosophical Perspectives I: Metaphysics* (Atascadero, Calif.: Ridgeview, 1987), pp. 49–108.

9. Alvin Plantinga, *The Nature of Necessity* (New York: Oxford University Press, 1974), chap. 1, passim; Saul Kripke, "Naming and Necessity," in Donald Davidson and Gilbert Harman, eds., *Semantics of Natural Language* (Dordrecht: Reidel, 1972), pp. 253–355.

such that every proposition with their logical form is true. But some absolutely necessary truths are not truths of logic. Nonlogical absolutely necessary truths include truths of set theory and mathematics, and such truths as that red is a color, that all human beings are animals, and (perhaps) that nothing is red and green all over at once.

Second, some logically possible propositions are not absolutely possible. This follows from the first difference. That is logically possible whose contradiction is not logically necessary. "Red is a color" is not logically necessary; not every proposition with its logical form is true. Thus "red is not a color" is logically possible, though it is absolutely impossible.

Third, absolute modality is a kind of objective modality, as versus merely epistemic or conceptual modality. To claim that a SOA is epistemically possible is to claim that it is not known not to be possible (in some other sense of "possible"). To claim that a SOA S is conceptually possible is to claim that within a certain system of concepts, it is a permissible move to assert that S. Logical possibility is a sort of conceptual possibility: it is conceptual possibility within the system of the concepts of logic. To say that a SOA is objectively possible is to speak not of whether it can be conceived or believed to be possible but of whether it really is possible, independent of systems of concepts or languages or states of any believer. Of course, if a SOA is logically or conceptually impossible, it will also be objectively impossible. Whatever one's concept F, nothing can be both F and ~F.

Now it may be the case that some absolute possibilities are not conceptually possible. But this is not to say that some absolute possibility may be conceptually impossible. What I mean is this. Only those SOAs actually are conceptually possible which actual conceptual schemes permit us to assert. There is no guarantee that actual human conceptual systems permit us to assert all the facts there can be. So there may be absolute possibilities that we lack the resources to describe or assert. But this is the only sense in which an absolute possibility can fail to be conceptually possible, and it does not amount to an absolute possibility's being conceptually impossible. Logical or conceptual impossibility are infallible signs of objective impossibility.

Still, they are *only* signs of it. Objective impossibility does not *consist in* logical or conceptual impossibility. Rather, we can define the objective modalities this way:

vii. SOA S is objectively possible = df. some world-sized set of facts all of which can be actual at once includes S or verifies the claim that S.

viii. SOA S is objectively necessary = df. no world-sized set of
facts all of which can be actual at once fails to include S or
verify the claim that S.

There are several kinds of objective modality. To be physically possible, I suggest, is to be objectively possible given actually obtaining
physical law. To be *absolutely* possible, I suggest, is to be objectively
possible with no such restriction as "given actual physical law"—that
is, no restriction that makes the set of absolutely possible worlds appear a proper subset of the set of objectively possible worlds. To put it
another way, every other sort of objective possibility adds to the re-
quirements for possibility some requirement beyond what is required
for being absolutely possible. To be physically possible, for instance, a
world must be absolutely possible *and* compatible with actual physical
law.

Thus we can define absolute possibility this way:

ix. S is absolutely possible = df. S is objectively possible without
restriction.

As a consequence of (ix), absolute possibility is the sort of objective
possibility with the widest extent. That is, any state of affairs objectively possible in any other sense is also absolutely possible, but it may
be that some absolutely possible states of affairs are not objectively
possible in any other way.[10] Thus the set of worlds objectively possible
in any other way is at least a subset and perhaps is a proper subset of the
set of absolutely possible worlds.[11] Also, given (ix), absolute possibility is the barest, minimal sort of objective possibility. Given (ix),
every objectively possible world is absolutely possible; the absolutely
possible worlds are all the possible worlds there are. Hence it is (so to
speak) true by definition that facts of absolute possibility are the universe's basic, final facts of possibility.

We can define absolute necessity thus:

x. S is absolutely necessary = df. no absolutely possible world
fails to include S or verify the claim that S.

10. For all we know, of course, only physically possible states of affairs are absolutely
possible. If this is so, physical possibility is a merely vacuous restriction of absolute
possibility. But it would take some doing to establish this. The *concept* of absolute
possibility permits it to extend beyond physical possibility, and so there is some presumption that it does so.

11. Should set theory preclude speaking of the collection of absolutely possible
worlds as a set, one can make appropriate verbal alterations here.

Since the absolutely possible worlds are all the worlds there are, an absolutely necessary fact, as such, obtains in all objectively possible worlds. By contrast, a physically necessary state of affairs, as such, obtains only in possible worlds whose physical laws are identical with those of our world. Thus for every other sort of objective necessity, the set of worlds in which facts thus necessary obtain is a subset and perhaps a proper subset of the set of worlds in which absolutely necessary facts obtain. Absolute necessity, then, is the sort of objective necessity with the widest extent. Every absolutely necessary fact is also (for instance) physically necessary, since it obtains in all worlds with the appropriate physical laws. But perhaps not every physically necessary fact is absolutely necessary; perhaps some physical necessities do not obtain in other possible worlds.

To qualify as absolutely necessary, a fact must obtain in all objectively possible worlds, not just in some. Thus (so to speak) it is harder for a fact to qualify as absolutely necessary than to qualify as necessary in some other way. Thus, too, absolute necessities are absolutely unavoidable. No objectively possible world escapes their sway. In this sense, absolute necessity is the strongest sort of objective necessity.

The Logic of Absolute Modality Is S5

The distinctive feature of the S5 system of modal logic is that it incorporates a complete invariance of possibility. In S5, whatever is possible in any possible world is possible in all; nothing is possibly but not actually possible. For this reason, S5 has a strong claim to express the logic of absolute modality.

Let me argue this. As was just mentioned, facts of absolute possibility compose the final framework of possibility. For a framework of possibilities to be the final one, all possibilities it allows must be actual possibilities. For suppose that we say that A is a framework of possibility and that in A, P is possibly possible but not possible. Then the framework A of possibilities, of which P is not actually a member, is not final. Rather, there must be behind A another framework of *possible* possibilities, of which A is one possible realization and a framework including P would be another. This further framework, then, must be the final framework of possibility. Thus the final framework of possibility must be such that whatever is possibly possible is actually possible. This is true only in logical systems containing S4. S5 is one such system.

Why opt for S5 rather than some other S4-containing system? Here is one way to think about this. That some particular, Porky, has an attribute, pighood, is absolutely possible just in case in some absolutely possible world, Porky *is* a pig. Thus if one pictures all possible worlds somehow spread out to conceptual view, to ask whether possibly Porky is a pig is in effect to ask whether in any of these worlds there is a fact or complex consisting of Porky and pighood. To say that there is such a complex is to say that possibly, Porky is a pig. In effect, then, the question of whether Porky can be a pig is a question of whether Porky can "fit together with" pighood to compose a complex. Now if the shapes of pieces of a jigsaw puzzle remain constant, so does the answer to the question "can they be put together?"—the answer does not vary no matter how much one varies the rest of the puzzle. Porky and pighood can be said to have invariant "shapes." Their "shapes" are their essential traits, the traits that make them themselves. These are constant; in every world in which each is itself, it has these traits. But then one expects that whether Porky and pighood can fit together to form a complex will also remain constant, no matter how else the contents of a world vary. That is, the answer to the question "can they be put together?" remains the same, no matter what possible world they are situated in. If this is so, then if "Porky is a pig" is possible in one world, it is possible in all. This reasoning applies to any state of affairs whatever. Hence all absolute possibility is world-invariant. But only S5 embodies the complete world-invariance of possibility. So S5 must be the logic of absolute modality.[12]

Some Modal Claims Have Sufficient Warrant to Deserve Belief

Different sorts of evidence warrant the asserting of modal and non-modal claims. One can directly observe what is actually the case. One cannot directly observe that a SOA is possible or necessary, though observational evidence can be used to back claims of possibility or necessity. Still, I suggest that though the *kind* of evidence one needs to warrant a modal claim differs from the kind one needs to warrant a nonmodal claim, one can in principle have as much evidence for a modal claim as for almost any nonmodal claim. At the moment, I have much better evidence for the proposition that human beings cannot

---

12. This conclusion can be disputed, as in Robert M. Adams, "Actualism and Thisness," *Synthese* 57 (1981), 3–42; Hugh Chandler, "Plantinga and the Contingently Possible," *Analysis* 36 (1975–76), 106–109; Nathan Salmon, *Reference and Essence* (Princeton, N.J.: Princeton University Press, 1981), pp. 229–252; Salmon, "The Logic of What Might Have Been," *Philosophical Review* 98 (1989), 3–34. Again, here I am only indicating what my assumptions are. A full defense of them must await another occasion.

survive a week without oxygen than I have for any number of non-modal claims about Alpha Centauri or other distant objects.

Just what sort of evidence backs modal claims, and how it does so, are surprisingly untouched topics. But one claim on which I want to insist is that if "S" is a logically consistent proposition, this is (defeasible) reason to assert that it is absolutely possible that S. Kripke and Putnam have made familiar the thought that the content of our concept of some attribute need bear little relation to the real nature of that attribute. If this is so, the fact that (say) two concepts are cosatisfiable is not much guarantee that one and the same entity can have the attributes of which they are concepts. But though I cannot defend this claim here, I suspect that there cannot be absolutely *no* connection between concept and attribute. If a concept does express something of an attribute's nature, though, then the fact that one and the same entity can satisfy two concepts is some positive reason, however slight, to believe that the attributes these concepts express are coexemplifiable.

Let "S" name some state of affairs whose possibility we want to assess. Clearly, the best warrant for a claim that S is possible is knowledge that S is actual. But we also find warrant for a claim that S is possible in the actuality of states of affairs other than S. For instance, we believe that *ceteris paribus,*

> 1. confidence that S is possible should increase the greater the proportion of S's components that are known to be or have been actual.[13]

For the more of S's components we know to be or have been actual, the greater our assurance that none of S's components is individually such as to preclude S's being possible. We often accord weight to arguments based on (1). Suppose, for example, that we read a science-fiction tale filled with species of animals never found on earth, and we ask ourselves how likely it is that such species of animals could really exist. One way we answer this question is by seeking properties the supposed extraterrestrial species have in common with species that have existed on earth. For we reason that the more such properties the alien animals have, the more likely it is that such animals can occur.

We also find it reasonable that *ceteris paribus,*

> 2. the more S is like some past or present state of affairs, the more confidence we should have that S is possible.

---

13. We know an attribute to be actual if we know that it has an instance.

Resemblance between states of affairs is a matter not just of common components but also of their arrangement. Arrangement of components obviously would be a relevant consideration in assessing the claim that our science-fictional animals are possible. For even if there have been sloths with three toes and sloths with four, we will not grant that there could be a sloth all of whose feet are both three- and four-toed at once. This principle seems too basic to our thinking to allow of much justification. When we call it reasonable, perhaps what we mean is that anyone who did not accept it would not count as what we call rational.

We also believe that

> 3. the greater the agreement of impartial thinkers that S is possible, the more reason we have to believe that S really is possible.

This is a "realist" principle that assumes that whatever mechanism accounts for the forming of modal beliefs is generally reliable and does not vary between individuals. We need not worry here about what that mechanism may be. The fact is that we are realists in this sense in our attitudes toward almost any sort of belief, unless and until we find out that the belief-forming mechanism in question either is unreliable or varies among individuals.

It also seems reasonable that *ceteris paribus,*

> 4. confidence in S's possibility should increase the less definite the description of S we consider.

For the less definite the description, the fewer its entailments, and the fewer S's entailments, the less opportunity there is for them to conflict with those of other actual or possible states of affairs. Also,

> 5. the fewer S's components, the fewer the opportunities for them to come into conflict among themselves or with other states of affairs, and so the more confidence is warranted in the claim that S is possible.

Further,

> 6. if S's possibility follows from or is rendered probable to some degree by a well-justified theory, confidence of an appropriate degree that S is possible is warranted.

No doubt there are other principles governing possibility-claims. I mention these six only to foster confidence that not everything goes in making modal claims—that some of them can be seen to be epistemically respectable. My argument at various points turns on claims that states of affairs are or are not possible. I do not always explicitly justify these claims. But where they are not argued, it is sometimes because the application of some of the foregoing principles to back them is obvious.

Time Can Be Viewed as Tensed or as Tenseless

We have two distinct ways of speaking about temporal facts. One way involves the system of verb tenses, which relates events, processes, etc., to the times of sentences' utterance. Present-tensed propositions have a variety of uses, but in one central sort of use, a present-tensed claim that P ("the baby is crying") entails that P is the case at the time the claim that P is made.[14] In one central use, a future-tensed claim that P (as in "he will learn to read") entails that P will take place after the claim that P is made. Such tensed utterances thus can cease to be true; "he will learn to read" ceases to be true when this process is no longer in the future. Tenseless utterances, on the other hand, cannot cease to be true. If we ignore the tensed use of "is" which grammar enforces, "Queen Elizabeth's coronation was earlier than the Falklands War" expresses a truth that will be true for all time after the Falklands War.

Tensed theories of time take tensed speech about time, and its associated ceasings to be true, as revealing time's inmost nature. Tenseless theories of time accord tenseless speech about time this role. This leads the theories to disagree at several points. Tensed theories hold that tensed propositions change truth-value because the events of which they speak come and cease to exist. According to tensed theories, there is a great difference between present and future events: present events exist, and future events do not. According to tenseless theories, both present and future events exist: present events exist now, and future events also exist, but at a later location in time. In tensed theories, that future events do not now exist entails that future events do not exist. In tenseless theories, "future events do not now exist" does not entail that future events do not exist. Instead, that proposition merely notes that future events exist at a temporal location that is later than the location of its utterance.

14. This is not always the case. For instance, we sometimes say such things as that (P) Aquinas argues that God exists. (P) is in the "historical present tense" and does not entail that Aquinas is arguing this when (P) is asserted.

Tensed and tenseless theories differ sharply over the "passage" of time as well. If future events are in no way actual while still future, their becoming present changes these events' ontological status, lending them an actuality they had lacked as future and rendering true propositions that previously were false or truth-valueless. Accordingly, tensed theories hold time's "passage" to be a genuine feature of objective reality, e.g., the becoming actual of nonactual future events. On the other hand, if future events are already fully real, their becoming present does not alter their ontological status. In tenseless theories, then, time's "passage" lends future events no actuality that they did not have as future. Thus in tenseless theories, time's "passage" is not a feature of objective reality, but is instead a feature of human perception. For tenseless theories, that time passes means only that in some mysterious way, our perceptions and/or our perspectives alter, so that events that could not be experienced at t because they exist later than t somehow come within the scope of possible experience. Still, though there is no passage between tenseless-theory times, tenseless theories can and do affirm that if temporal point t is earlier than temporal point t + 1, what occupies t does so earlier than what occupies t + 1. Tenseless theories do not assert that the universe exists "all at once." All actual things are equally tenselessly actual, but this does not entail that they in any sense exist simultaneously, for simultaneity must involve something more than mere coactuality.

This book does *not* assume that either a tensed or a tenseless view of time is correct. Some philosophers have argued that the claim that God is timeless is incompatible with a tensed view of time. I contend that they are wrong, but in asserting this I do not implicitly or explicitly endorse a tensed theory.

The Primary Occupants of Time Are Not Things

"Fido at 7:00" is not a sentence. "Fido exists at 7:00" is, as are "Fido breathed at 7:00" and "Fido was barking at 7:00." What we primarily speak of as located at times, then, are states (e.g., of existence), events, processes, and the like. I take it that these *are* what are primarily located at times, and that things involved in these states—particulars like Fido, etc.—are located at times because their states, etc., are. I refer to the entities we primarily speak of as located at times as *temporal relata*.

We Can Speak Affirmatively and Literally of God

This claim was widely rejected in the Middle Ages by "negative theologians," who held that only those humanly formulable propositions that are denials can be literally true of God. In differing ways Aquinas and Duns Scotus defended literal affirmative talk of God. In our own day positivists of various stripes have denied it. Richard Swinburne has defended it on the assumption that God is temporal.[15] More to the present point, William Alston has persuasively argued in a pair of important papers that we can speak affirmatively and literally of God even if God is timeless.[16] I take it, then, that we can.

One other matter deserves mention. Some who will read this book are Christians and may wonder whether the claim that God is timeless is compatible with the claim that God was incarnate in Jesus Christ. Reading below that whatever is timeless is necessarily so, they may ask whether a timeless God could become a man with a location in time. I do not discuss this question. But let me note here that the claim that a God who is necessarily timeless became a temporal man is neither harder nor easier to understand than the claim that a God who is necessarily omniscient became a fallible, humanly ignorant man or the claim that a God who is necessarily omnipotent and everlasting became a man of limited power who died.[17] If so, the Incarnation is no more and no less an objection to the doctrine of divine timelessness than it is to the doctrines of divine omnipotence and omniscience. So too, if (as I argue) the doctrine of divine timelessness is not intrinsically problematic, it does not add to the burden a defender of the Incarnation must bear.

15. Richard Swinburne, *The Coherence of Theism* (New York: Oxford University Press, 1977), part 1, passim.
16. William Alston, "Functionalism and Theological Language," and "Divine and Human Action," in William Alston, *Divine Nature and Human Language* (Ithaca, N.Y.: Cornell University Press, 1989), pp. 64–102.
17. I owe this point to Eleonore Stump.

[3]
The Possibility of the Timeless

If God is timeless, God exists, but exists at no time. Thus God bears no temporal relation to any temporal relatum—God does not exist or act earlier than, later than, or at the same time as any such thing. If God is timeless, such truths as "God exists" are timeless truths: though they are true, they are not true at any time.[1] We are not disposed to recognize the existence of timeless realities. Current common sense tends to materialism, and material entities are solidly spatiotemporal. Still less do we incline to grant that there are timeless truths. "True, but not true at any time" has a flavor of contradiction about it. We therefore must ask: Can there be timeless beings? Can there be timeless truths? The two questions are, of course, connected. Many who have argued that there are timeless truths have found this claim important because they believed that the truthmakers of such truths are timeless beings.

Only if there can be timeless beings and truths can the claim that God is timeless be possibly true. Further, if there can be such things, giving an account of them will help us to envision the timelessness of a timeless God and so will forward our project of understanding the claim that God is timeless. Let us, then, examine some candidate timeless truths and timeless beings.

---

1. Martha Kneale suggests an alternate account of timeless truths. On her view, they are those that can be expressed in sentences involving neither tenses nor dates ("Eternity," p. 234). There can be truths about purely temporal entities which are timeless in Kneale's sense, e.g., "if anything is a lion, it is an animal." Truths timeless in the text's sense must be truths about timeless beings.

Is the 4D Universe Timeless?

John Post has recently argued that the universe, viewed as extended in four dimensions (one of them temporal), is not in time.[2] Clearly, the universe so viewed is not a continuant through time: continuants are objects extended in only three dimensions. Further, if the 4D universe is the whole of physical reality, then the 4D universe includes space-time itself. If it does, then if the 4D universe is in time, time itself is in time. But the whole of time does not have a date; this is one reason that the question "when is time?" is bizarre.[3] As this is so, time is not "in time" in the sense of having a datable location in time. Still, I do not think this lets us conclude that the universe viewed in 4D, or time, is timeless. "Time exists" is true at all times rather than at no time. So is "The universe exists," if the existence of time constitutes or at least entails the existence of a universe. Further, "time now exists" and "the universe now exists" are alike true; time exists now insofar as part of it (or a cut along its continuum) exists now, and the universe exists now insofar as a space-time slice or cut of it now exists. Finally, one can sensibly call the universe and the whole of time temporally simultaneous with themselves. None of these things holds of beings timeless in our sense.

Would a Second Time Series Be Timeless?

If our own time series or universe are not timeless beings, perhaps a second time series or universe would at least be significantly like a timeless being. Some philosophers have argued that there could be at least two discrete temporal series.[4] Let us say that if one moment is earlier or later than or simultaneous with a second, the two moments are temporally connected. Then two discrete temporal series would be two series of moments, A and B, such that every moment in A is

---

2. Post, *Faces*, pp. 144–145.
3. Ibid.
4. For defense of the possibility of discrete temporal series, see Richard Swinburne, "Times," *Analysis* 25 (1964), 185–191, and "Conditions for Bi-temporality," *Analysis* 26 (1965), 47–50; Martin Hollis, "Times and Spaces," *Mind* (1967), 524–536, and "Box and Cox," *Philosophy* 42 (1967), 75–78; Norman Swartz, "Spatial and Temporal Worlds," *Ratio* 17 (1975), 217–228; W. H. Newton-Smith, *The Structure of Time* (London: Routledge and Kegan Paul, 1980), pp. 79–95. For the case to the contrary, see Anthony Quinton, "Spaces and Times," *Philosophy* 37 (1962), 130–147; Richard Swinburne, *Space and Time* (New York: Macmillan, 1968), 198–207; E. M. Zemach, "Many Times," *Analysis* 28 (1968), 145–151; L. Falkenstein, "Spaces and Times: A Kantian Response," *Idealistic Studies* 16 (1986), 1–11.

temporally connected with every moment in A, every moment in B temporally connected with every moment in B, yet no moment in A is temporally connected with any moment in B. So if there is a second time series, something exists that has no temporal location in or temporal relations to our own time series. We could call such a time series *extrinsically* timeless. Though it would be internally temporal, it would be related to our own time series as a timeless being would.[5] If a second time series is possible, nothing in the relations of a timeless being to time can be reason to deny that a timeless being is possible.

Can there be a second time series? There is no contradiction in supposing that there are two temporal series. That "a second discrete time series exists" is not a contradiction is a genuine though defeasible reason to claim that possibly such a series exists. Some might assert that we could never have evidence that a second time series exists and that this defeats the claim that a second time series is possible. But I do not think that its being impossible to have evidence of a second time series would be reason to deny that possibly a second time series exists. I am realist enough not to be disturbed by the thought that possibly there is a state of affairs for the obtaining of which we can have no evidence; I know of no good reason to believe that necessarily, human beings can have evidence of the existence of whatever can exist. Still, let us ask anyway whether it is possible to have evidence that a temporal series other than one's own exists.

Suppose, as is plausible, that it is a necessary truth that temporal cause-events occur at the same time as or earlier than or (if backward causation is possible) later than temporal effect-events. If temporal cause and effect must be temporally connected, no event in one temporal series can have effects in another series. For if this is so, then if event E in A causes event E* in B, it follows that E is temporally connected with E* and so that A and B are not discrete after all. Nor if this is so can one remember any events from a second discrete temporal series if one somehow finds oneself there, causelessly, and then causelessly returns. For a mental event E is a memory of some other event E* only if E* is among the causal conditions of E. Thus any event of remembering must be temporally connected with any event it recalls. So no evidence of the existence of a second temporal series could

5. A second universe or time series was first used to model claims about an extrinsically timeless being in Brian Leftow, "Simplicity and Eternity" (Ph.D. diss., Yale University, 1984), pp. 146–148. The strategy has since reached print in Herbert Nelson, "Time(s), Eternity, and Duration," *International Journal for Philosophy of Religion* 22 (1987), 3–7.

take the form either of memories of living in that series or of effects of that series' events in this series.

But the claim that one could somehow causelessly find oneself in a second temporal series is in any event dubious. For it is not physically possible that a material object make the transition from one time series to another. Let me show this.

Motion and Spatially Continuous Paths

A material object moves from one place to another only if its constituent matter traverses a continuous sequence of places between those places. This does not entail that the object itself makes the trip. It could be that only its parts do, as when one disassembles a bicycle and then reassembles it in another place. It also could be that only its constituent matter makes the trip, if, e.g., *Star Trek*'s transporter beam is possible. Still, the spatial motion of a macrophysical parcel of matter is always over some sort of continuous spatial path. We can see this if we suppose that a macrophysical parcel of matter M moves from place P1 to place P4 without following a continuous spatial path. Iff this is so, there is an interruption somewhere in M's P1–P4 path; somewhere between P1 and P4, there are two points P2 and P3 such that M "jumps" from P2 to P3 without occupying any continuous sequence of places between them. For convenience, let us suppose that this "jump" is the only discontinuity in M's path. If the instant at which M reaches P2 = the instant at which M reaches P3, then M is wholly in two discrete places at once. This cannot be.[6] Hence there is some gap of time between M's arrival at P2 and M's arrival at P3. During this temporal gap, there is no place M is. For ex hypothesi the jump from P2 to P3 is the only jump in M's path. But if M were at some place P5 between being at P2 and at P3, either M would jump from P2 to P5 or M would jump from P5 to P3, or the P1–P4 path would be continuous, counter to our original assumption that M makes one jump, that from P2 to P3.

Now if M is a macrophysical parcel of matter, then if there is a time at which M is not any place, at that time M does not exist. Accordingly, such a parcel of matter follows a discontinuous spatial path only if it

6. If time travel is possible, then in a *sense*, M can be in two places at once. For M can be in P1 at t2, then reach t3 and thence travel back to t1 and move to P2 by t2. But this is not being in two places at one and the same time *on M's own timeline*. The text denies only that M can be in two places at one time on M's own timeline.

ceases to exist and then pops back into existence some time later.[7] But macrophysical parcels of matter just do not do this. That they do not seems to be a natural law. Hence no parcel of matter follows a discontinuous spatial path; this likely is so by physical necessity.

Continuous Paths, Single Spaces, and Single Times

We have seen that moving macrophysical matter follows a continuous spatial path. Any transition from one distinct place to another is a case of spatial motion. Hence if any matter were to be first in one time series and then in another, there would be a continuous spatial path from the one series to the other. Now if there is a continuous spatial path from one place to another, the two are parts of a single larger space. For a path is continuous only if between any two points on the path there is another point also on the path. If spatial points P_1 and P_2 exist in discrete spaces, there is no space between them—since if there were, they would be spatially connected and so not in discrete spaces. Thus any purported path from P_1 to P_2 would contain two points, P_1 and P_2, such that between them would be no other point of space. That is why no such path can be continuous. But if any path between points in discrete spaces is discontinuous, then any continuous path links only points in the same space.

Current physics overwhelmingly confirms the claim that "time" and "space" just name abstracted aspects of a single reality, space-time. This claim entails that if two spaces are part of a larger space, they have the same time, the time of that space-time of which these spaces are abstracted aspects. My argument, then, is this: any transition of a material object from place to place is a case of spatial motion. The spatial motion of a material object must follow a continuous spatial path. Continuous spatial paths link places within the same space. Places within the same space are within the same time series. Hence any places our bodies can visit share the same time with our present place. It is not physically possible that our bodies make a trip from one time to another. Hence it is physically possible that we visit another time only if we are disembodied Cartesian egos or Platonic souls. Now the

---

7. It will not do to say that M "ceases to exist" only in the sense that it is disaggregated into smaller parcels and M "pops back" only in the sense that it is regrouped as a parcel. For we have not stipulated that M is a nonscattered parcel; in the preceding argument, we can allow that if various disjoined subparcels of M followed individually continuous paths from P_1 to P_4, this would count as M following a continuous path from P_1 to P_4. As we allow this, M "pops out of existence" only if at least one subparcel of M goes from being something to not being anything, i.e., complete nonexistence.

claim that there are such things at all is hard to maintain. But the claim that *we are* not persons but egos or souls is even harder to support. Accordingly, it seems that we cannot visit another time.

This reasoning may seem to involve a question-begging step. For the argument that discontinuous paths are not possible depended crucially on the claim that if a parcel of matter's path is discontinuous, there is a time at which it is at no place. But (one might suggest) suppose that the discontinuity involved is that of causelessly "jumping" from one discrete space-time to another. In this case a parcel of matter follows a discontinuous spatial path, but there is no time at which it is not at any place, because "between" space-times there is no time. Consider, however, the career of a material object M that jumps from space-time 1 to space-time 2. Even if times within space-times 1 and 2 are not temporally connected, times within M's career surely must be.[8] For if (say) a human body's history contained temporally disconnected episodes, during those episodes that body would not be older or younger than it is at any other time, and this just seems impossible. But now consider M's last moment in space-time 1 and M's first moment in space-time 2. Either they are or they are not the same moment in M's history. If they are, M is wholly at two discrete places at one and the same instant of its history. This surely is impossible. If they are not, then there are times in M's career that fall "between" space-times. This is at best mysterious. Further, whatever these times are, at these times M again occupies no space. So arguably, at these times M does not exist: and if M does not, what reason can we have to call these times portions of M's career? Thus specifying that the discontinuity in M's career arises "between" space-times does not really alter the argument.

Let me add two final points. First, even the supposition that a soul or ego moves from one time series to another faces a severe difficulty. We have suggested that if events in time series are causally connected, the time series are temporally connected. If this is true, no soul-event in

8. That all times in a material object's career must be temporally connected does not entail that any space-times the object occupies must be so. Consider the individual timeline of Herman, and say that Herman undergoes event E1 at time t in space-time 1 and event E2 at time t* in space-time 2, and E2 is later on Herman's timeline than E1. In this case t* is later on Herman's timeline than t, but because of the relativity of simultaneity (to be discussed later), it does not follow that t* is later than t in any other sense. Intuitively, if Herman enters space-time 2 from without, Herman can enter space-time 2 at any point in its history. If Herman's entering space-time 2 effects any objective correlation between the times of space-time 1 and space-time 2, then what 1-times are earlier than what 2-times depends on Herman's arbitrary choice of a point of entry. This is absurd. It is as if whether the Battle of Borodino preceded Napoleon's exile on Elba were up to us.

series 2 could be causally connected to any soul-event in series 1. No experience, thought, or knowledge acquired in series 1 could carry over to or in any way influence the soul's life in series 2. Is it at all plausible that two soul-careers so completely disjoined could be phases of the same career? Second, if the claim that all moving macrophysical material objects follow continuous spatial paths is absolutely rather than just physically necessary, it is not just physically but absolutely impossible that a macrophysical material object visit a second space.

One Space, Two Times

If no macrophysical object can visit a second space, a macrophysical material object can visit another time only if possibly one space exists in two discrete time series. Now though the existing of one space in two time series is not physically possible, it may be absolutely possible, if the traits of our space-time are not absolutely necessary traits of time and space. If this *is* absolutely possible, there are perhaps two ways in which we can exist in two discrete times series without being mere souls. For the same place could exist within two separate time-streams if time at some point "divided" at that place into two streams or if that place always existed in two streams without having divided, i.e., if that place existed in two series of times which never coincided.[9]

Let us first consider the division of time. If this occurred, then perhaps an object existing at the place of the division would ipso facto exist in two time streams. Say that time divides at t. One could say that one of the resulting streams is identical with the time stream up till t. In this case, an object would come to exist in two streams only if it existed in both streams that exist after t. One could also say that neither resulting stream is identical with the time stream up till t. In this case, an object would come to exist (or at least have existed) in two streams if it existed in only *one* post-t stream. For it would have existed in one stream up to t and then in a second distinct stream after t.

Still, it may be impossible for time to divide. For if time divides, at least one of the resulting time streams must be nonidentical with the time stream that exists before the divide, else no division will have occurred. Time streams (as versus phases of time streams) are noniden-

---

9. According to Quentin Smith, some physicists claim to have evidence that time actually has divided ("A New Typology of Temporal and Atemporal Permanence," *Nous* 23 [1989], 311). Swinburne envisions time dividing in "Times" and "Conditions for Bi-temporality." He later abandoned the claim that this is possible in *Space and Time.* Newton-Smith considers the division of time but is unsure whether it is possible (*Structure of Time,* pp. 92–95).

tical only if they are temporally discrete. Hence at least one of the time streams resulting from the divide cannot be called later than the dividing-event. Moreover, it cannot be that the dividing-event caused this stream to exist. For if it did, then by the absolute necessity that temporal cause and effect be temporally connected, the dividing-event would be temporally connected with the first event in the new series, and so the new series would not be discrete from the old. But if the new series is not later than the earlier series and is not caused by any event in it, why should we say that it represents a division of the old series, rather than just a discrete time series with no relation to the old series?

Further, even if a material object such as a human body can exist in two time series, it might not be possible for us to have evidence that a division of time at one place had occurred. For it could be that any discontinuities in our experience large enough to give us warrant to suppose that we are suddenly in a second discrete time series would also be large enough to give us warrant to say that we are suddenly in a second discrete space, and if two spaces are discrete, no single place exists in both. So to envision a circumstance in which we could have evidence of a second time stream, we should perhaps think not of time as dividing at some point but of one space as existing in two discrete time series that at no point merge.

But it is not clear that this is even possible. For if one space thus exists in two discrete time series, there is an entity that has phases of its history during which it is not as old as, older than, or younger than it is at some other phases in its history (since the time coordinates of the phases are not temporally connected). This does not seem possible. For the same reason, it does not seem possible that any material object thus exist in two discrete time series.

Another argument also yields that conclusion that no material object can exist in two discrete time series that never merge. All material objects (save *perhaps* the universe) begin to exist. But an object's beginning of existence can occur in only one time series. For if a beginning of existence occurs in two time series, it occurs at two different times. (Were this not so, the time series would not be distinct.) If beginnings of existence occur at different times, they are distinct events. Hence if an object begins to exist in each of two time series, it begins to exist twice. But no object can begin to exist twice. Hence any object that begins to exist exists in two nonmerging time series only if it begins to exist only in one of them and in the other one exists beginninglessly. But of no material object other than perhaps the universe is it plausible to say that it could exist beginninglessly in any time series. Moreover, if no material object that is part of our universe can also exist beginninglessly in another time series, our universe cannot so exist in one either, even if it had no beginning. For if none of an object's parts exists in a time series, that object does not exist in that time series.

Finally, it is plausible that the matter of which any material object is constituted must have a spatiotemporally continuous history. But a history is spatiotemporally continuous only if every event in it is temporally connected with every other. If this is so, then any material object that exists in one time series is distinct from any object existing in another. Further, if space is a system of relations between material objects, then if the same material objects cannot exist in two time series, the same space cannot. It appears, then, that a space existing in two times would have to be an absolute space and a Newtonian space (i.e., one that is not just three abstracted dimensions of a four-or-more-dimensional space-time continuum).

Suppose, then, that some such space exists in two times in some possible world. Even so, it does not seem possible that a conscious being exist in two discrete time series without ever making a transition between them. For this is possible only if conscious beings can have mental episodes that are not temporally connected with any of their other mental episodes. But we cannot even imagine what it would be to have a thought that was not earlier or later than any of our other thoughts. So even if in some absolutely possible world one place exists in two time streams and even if we are souls, we could not gain evidence of the existence of a second discrete time series by living in one at that place. Further, if we are not souls and if our attribute of being human (and so embodied) is essential to us, then since no human body can exist in two time series, we cannot exist in a second time series at all.

Indirect Evidence

Another possible source of evidence for a second time series might be the characteristics or effects of an event that caused the second series to exist. Specifically, someone could suggest that perhaps as our knowledge of the traits of the Big Bang grows, we might come to see that the properties of that event could best be explained by saying that it led to the formation not just of our space-time, A, but of at least one more discrete space-time, B. But if cause and effect must be temporally connected, then if the Big Bang caused A and B, the Bang is temporally connected to both series and so located in both. Every event in every temporal series is temporally simultaneous with itself. So if the

Big Bang caused both A and B, there is an event in series A (the Bang) which is A-simultaneous with an event in series B (the Bang), and so A and B are not discrete temporal series. Instead, they are disjoint portions of one single space-time with a rather odd topology.

God and Multiple Times

So far, nontheistic scenarios have not yielded a sure way to gain evidence that a second time series exists. But things change if we bring God into the picture. Let us suppose that God exists in our time series. A God who exists in our time series could not create a second time series. For if God creates at time t, what God creates begins to exist at time t. So if God exists at t in time series A and at that point creates series B, B begins to exist at t: the first moment of B is simultaneous in A with a moment in A, and so A and B are not discrete. I cannot see at all how a temporal God who had not created it and was altogether causally insulated from it could know that a second temporal series existed. If He could not know this, He could not reveal it. But God's ways are inscrutable; perhaps a temporal God could know this, and then if He had also established a record as a reliable teller of truths to people in A, His revealing to them that B exists would be a good reason for them to believe that B exists. Hence perhaps we could learn that a second time series exists if a temporal God existed.

Keith Ward suggests that if we alter our picture of His relation to time, a temporal God *could* create multiple time series:

> God can create different . . . space-time systems which cannot be spatially or temporally related to one another. He will relate himself to each of those systems, in such a way that he will exist simultaneously with each event in each system, as it occurs. But those different time sequences will not be temporally relatable to each other . . . God is temporal, in that he does some things before he does others; and in changing, he projects his being along one continuous temporal path. But there may be many such paths . . . in different universes . . . which are not absolutely correlatable with each other. So God must be conceived as moving along all such paths, as existing in a number of different times. To the extent that this is so, there cannot be causal relations between those times, for each such point of correlation would establish a simultaneity. We may speak of God, then, not just as temporal but as multitemporal.[10]

10. Keith Ward, *Rational Theology and the Creativity of God* (Oxford: Blackwell, 1982), p. 166.

If what Ward suggests is possible, it strengthens our case that a temporal God could reveal the existence of a second time series. Now Ward does not picture a God who is located in one temporal series creating another. He seems rather to suggest that the divine act of creating is not located in any time series, and yet once these series are created, God's existence (if not His creative act) is located in all of them and so is (multi)temporal. Let us ask whether Ward's alternative is possible.

Either the very same divine events, states, and processes are located in more than one temporal series on Ward's scenario or they are not. If they are, then (say) God's knowing that He is God is a state obtaining in A whose obtaining is A-simultaneous with the obtaining of a state (itself) in B. But again, if a state in B is A-simultaneous with a state in A, the two series are not discrete after all. On the other hand, if the very same state of God is *not* located in more than one temporal series, then on Ward's account, God's mind contains multiple tracks of conscious thoughts, intentions, etc., such that no mental item on one track has any causal influence on a mental item on any other track (since if one did, the items would be temporally connected and so would temporally connect their temporal series). This does not seem possible; why would such a congeries count as one mind? Suppose Ward were to reply that these add up to God's mind because God alone has privileged access to them all—that God alone is aware "from within" of (say) divine intending I in series A and divine intending I* in series B. We would then have to ask about the relation between God's awareness of I and God's awareness of I*. On Ward's theory, surely these awarenesses are caused by I and I*.[11] They therefore are temporally connected with I and I*. But are the awarenesses themselves temporally connected? I cannot conceive that they are not, for I cannot conceive of one mind having two nonsimultaneous experiences neither of which is earlier than the other. But if they are connected, then so are I and I* and so then are A and B. Thus I submit that A and B can remain discrete only if God never has access to the A- or the B-strand of divine mental life. But if God is not aware "from within" of (say) the B-strand, and cannot be aware of it so long as A and B are discrete, how can one maintain that the A- and B-strands contain conscious states of the same mind? So I conclude that Ward's alternative is no alternative at all, and a temporal God cannot create multiple time series.

11. This is likely "on Ward's view" because Ward allows that God has many distinct states of awareness. Doctrines of divine simplicity such as Aquinas' affirm that God has only one state of awareness (see, e.g., *Summa contra Gentiles* I, 45). If this is so, God's awareness of His awareness = His awareness, and so it is false that the one causes the other.

On the other hand, if God is timeless and (as argued later) His creating time does not locate Him in time, then He can create in eternity both A and B without its following that any moment in A is temporally simultaneous in A or in B with any moment in B. For on this assumption neither God nor His acts of creating are or become located in either temporal series. If God can create a second time series, He can know that a second one exists and so can reveal this. So if a timeless God were to establish a record as a reliable teller of truths to denizens of A, and then were to reveal B's existence to the A-dwellers, the A-dwellers would have good reason to believe that B exists.

So there could perhaps be these two ways to obtain evidence that a second temporal series exists. There may be still others. But as stated above, even if none turned out to be possible, I would not for that reason conclude that no second time series is possible. I take it, then, that such a series is possible and so that it is possible that an extrinsically timeless being exist.

A being is *intrinsically* timeless iff it does not "contain" time, i.e., does not endure through time. If there are events without duration, they are intrinsically timeless even if they are located in time. But arguably, if there is a distinct event that is my beginning to write this chapter, it is a nonenduring or "point" event. For it does not take time to begin to write, and it makes no sense to ask how long I have been beginning to write. We can certainly conceive that events of beginning exist. There seems no contradiction or other impossibility in this. Moreover, arguably, there *are* such events, for many events we hold to occur are really of this kind. For instance, we believe that we win races. But the moment of winning a race is the moment when it begins to be true that one has won. Winning is a beginning and so more generally is every achievement: one learns at the moment when it begins to be true that one has learned, one spots a target at the moment when it begins to be true that one sees it, and so on. If any of these things really happen, then, there are events of beginning. So we have reason to consider an intrinsically timeless entity possible. The question, then, is whether something both extrinsically and intrinsically timeless is possible.

Timeless Space

If space existed but time did not, space would be both extrinsically and intrinsically timeless. I will now argue that it is possible that there be no time or temporal things. Then I will show that this entails that there could be timeless truths and give reason to say that there could be a timeless space, or at least a timeless extensive continuum.

One can argue that time and temporal things can fail to exist by appealing to the absolute possibility that space-time (that of which time is just an aspect) has a beginning. This does seem possible; to say that space-time can begin is just to say that there could be an event or a point in space-time than which no event or point is earlier, and this claim seems consistent. Further, the currently favored Big Bang cosmology can be read as implying that the universe not only can but did have a beginning.[12] On current views, space-time is itself part of the universe, being either a system of relations between physical objects or an independent physical something.[13] So then, on the Big Bang view (on one reading), space-time itself had a beginning. If space-time even possibly begins or ends, one wants to say, space-time does not exist of necessity. Nor then does time. Nor then do temporal things.

One could object to this argument as follows. Any object that does not exist at all moments of time ipso facto exists contingently: there are times when it actually does not exist, and so it possibly does not exist. But time exists at all moments of time. Suppose, then, that time has a first or a last moment. This will *not* entail that there is a time at which time does not exist. Time still exists at all moments of time. Nor is there anything before or after time, for relations of before and after can link only times or relata in time. So we cannot appeal to any timeless "period" outside time at which it would then be true that time did not exist. So it can seem that even if time has a beginning and an end, this does not rule out time's existing necessarily. By similar reasoning, one can contend that any object that must exist at every moment of time could exist necessarily.

One can reject this rejoinder, however. Let "T" denote the actual series of times, which on the present assumption has a first and last member. It would not be plausible to say that there necessarily are no times other than those actually included in T. So it seems possible that there have been a minute before the first minute actually included in T—that time have lasted a minute longer than it actually has. If this is so, then possibly there is a time at which T does not exist. For T exists only at times it contains, and if this further minute existed, it would be beyond the boundaries of T. An analogue to this argument will apply to every time series with at least one endpoint. One also can extend this argument to deal with time series without endpoints. For suppose that

12. It can also be read as allowing that before the Bang there was another universe, which had contracted into the single infinitely dense mass-point from which the Bang erupted, and so on back ad infinitum.
13. On space-time as a component of the physical universe, see Post, *Faces*, pp. 118–128.

time consists of a series of at least $\aleph_0$ minutes before and after an arbitrary time t. Then the series of minutes is of the order-type $\omega^* + \omega$: it can be mapped 1:1 onto the series of positive and negative whole numbers,

$$\ldots\, -3,\ -2,\ -1,\ 0,\ 1,\ 2,\ 3 \ldots$$

But even so, there can be minutes outside this series, since as Cantor showed, there are infinities greater than $\aleph_0$. In fact, there can be a series of order-type $\omega^* + \omega^* + \omega + \omega$.[14] Such a series maps 1:1 onto this number series:

$$\ldots\, -6,\ -4,\ -2 \ldots -5,\ -3,\ -1,\ 0,\ 1,\ 3,\ 5 \ldots 2,\ 4,\ 6 \ldots$$

Since one can continue to add ω^*s and ωs to time's order-type indefinitely, if infinite times exists, it exists contingently, no matter which order-type one chooses.

To argue in a second way the contingency of time and the temporal, let us consider the propositions that temporal things exist and that time exists. These propositions do not appear to be necessarily true. After all, "no time exists" and "no temporal things exist" do not appear to be contradictions or to conflict directly or indirectly with any clearly necessary truth. Many philosophers deny that *any* existential statement is necessarily true. Of those who grant necessary existentials, most limit them to abstract truths such as "there is at least one prime number between 1 and 10," truths that seem to refer to abstract entities.[15] Neither "temporal things exist" nor "time exists" seems an abstract truth of this sort. For one thing, physical events are relevant to the truth of these two propositions, but at least on the face of it, physical events are not relevant to the truth of abstract truths like "there is at

14. I owe this point to Smith, "A New Typology," pp. 314–319.
15. I stress "seem"; I am not committing myself at this point to an ontology of abstract entities. As to what an abstract entity *is:* the abstract-concrete distinction is rather hard to make clear. Perhaps one can say no more about it than that concrete objects are objects relevantly like shoes, ships, and sealing wax, and abstract objects are objects relevantly like points, planes, and properties. The only universally accepted dictum on the subject, to my knowledge, expresses a sufficient condition for concreteness: an object is held to be concrete if it is possibly a direct terminus of a causal relation.
Talk of necessary existentials raises the question of whether God's existence is necessary. I turn to this question in the next chapter. I would be prepared to argue, though, that God can exist necessarily only if He shares some significant abstract-entity features. Peter van Inwagen makes a powerful case that purely concrete entities cannot exist necessarily in his "Ontological Arguments," *Nous* 11 (1977), 375–396.

least one prime number between 1 and 10." For another, neither "time exists" nor "temporal things exist" seems even prima facie to refer to any abstract entity. Temporal things are clearly concreta. One can argue that time is concrete if one accepts Michael Dummett's suggestion that whatever one can point to directly is concrete and his further claim that using such phrases as "the space that now contains me" or "the time that now contains me" is one form of direct pointing.[16] But even without this, talk of time is just talk of space-time under a particular aspect, and space-time is concrete: it is, for example, the sort of thing one can sensibly say the Big Bang causes to exist. So if there are any necessary existentials, "time exists" and "temporal things exist" do not seem to be among them.

A third argument for time's contingency arises from the fact that time is a physical reality, if perhaps not strictly speaking a physical *thing*. A physically empty world is conceivable and so seems possible. So both the claim that some particular physical reality exists necessarily and the claim that there necessarily is some physical reality or other appear false.

The Necessity of Time: Hartshorne

Of course, that a claim appears false hardly entails that nobody has made it. Charles Hartshorne has maintained for years that time and some physical universe or other necessarily exist. But Hartshorne in fact derives this claim only with the aid of a strange modal thesis, that "possibility and necessity are . . . *modi* of time and process. That is necessarily which is always; that happens of necessity which never fails to happen; that exists or happens contingently which exists or happens only at, during or after a particular or limited time."[17] If always P entails necessarily P, then since at every time there is time, "time exists" is a trivially necessary truth. Moreover, if one adjoins to this a relational theory of time, on which there is no time unless there are temporal events, it will follow that a universe of temporal events exists necessarily. But Hartshorne's claim that "always" entails "absolute-

---

16. Michael Dummett, *Frege: Philosophy of Language,* 2d ed. (London: Duckworth, 1981), chap. 14, passim.

17. Charles Hartshorne, *Creative Synthesis and Philosophical Method* (London: SCM Press, 1970), p. 133. See his "Real Possibility," *Journal of Philosophy* 60 (1963), 593–605. Hartshorne represents an ancient tradition in matters modal. For this modal theory in Aristotle, see Jaakko Hintikka, *Time and Necessity* (New York: Oxford University Press, 1973). For its fate in later Greek philosophy, see Michael White, *Agency and Integrality* (Dordrecht: Reidel, 1985).

necessarily" will appeal to few. There is now a certain quantity Q of mass-energy in the universe. Given the conservation laws, perhaps there has always been and will always be Q mass-energy in the universe. But as there is no contradiction in supposing there to always be Q + 1 instead, most contemporary philosophers and scientists suppose that even now, that Q + 1 has always been the amount of mass-energy in the universe is absolutely possible. Yet on Hartshorne's account, it is absolutely impossible that the universe ever have had Q + 1 mass-energy—as impossible as it is that 2 + 2 = 5. A modal theory that cannot accommodate our intuition that there is a difference in modal status between "the universe has Q + 1 mass-energy" and "2 + 2 = 5" is surely not acceptable.

God and the Necessity of Time

Theists could commit themselves to the necessity of time's existence without recourse to Hartshorne's modal theory. Suppose that some theist holds that there necessarily is a God and that necessarily, God is temporal.[18] These two claims can both be true only if time exists of necessity. So such a theist would have to hold that time exists necessarily. I argue shortly that nothing can be contingently temporal. If, as I claim, whatever is temporal is necessarily temporal, then theists would commit themselves to the necessary existence of time merely by maintaining that God exists necessarily and is temporal.

This theistic position has unpleasant consequences in light of contemporary physics. Contemporary physics treats time as one more extensive dimension in addition to the dimensions of space (whatever else time may be). Now whatever is located in one dimension is ipso facto located in all other dimensions of the same continuum. Thus imagine a two-axis coordinate system, representing a two-dimensional geometry, and a point P within this system. If one adds a third axis to the system, P acquires a third coordinate, just because the system now has a third axis. In doing this, one in effect embeds the first two dimensions within the third dimension; whatever is located in the first

18. Keith Ward has explicitly taken this position (see *Rational Theology*, pp. 44, 163). A great many other contemporary theists are committed to it. For many theists endorse the claim that necessarily, there is a God and at least one of the following: (a) necessarily, a God is or has a mind, and necessarily, a mind is temporal; (b) necessarily, a God is omniscient, and necessarily, only a temporal being is omniscient; or (c) necessarily, a God is an agent who acts in history, and necessarily, only a temporal being is an agent who acts in history. Claims (a)–(c) entail that necessarily, a God is temporal—as do other conjunctive claims endorsed by critics of divine timelessness.

two will also have a location in the third. The same will hold for any higher number of dimensions; as a rule, something is located in one dimension of a geometry if and only if it is located in all. So if it is correct to represent time as another dimension, it follows that whatever in time is also in space: *only spatial things are temporal*. Note that I am not claiming that this conclusion holds in all possible worlds. Perhaps there is a possible world in which time is *not* a fourth dimension of a physical geometry. If so, perhaps in this world there are spaceless temporal things. But regardless, if God is in the time of our world, God is also in space. Any object with a space-time location is a physical object. Hence if the time in which God exists is the same physical time in which we exist, then God is a physical object with a spatial location. Theists affirm (with good reason) that God is nonspatial and non-physical. Hence theists should reject the claim that God is temporal and with it the present reason to hold that time exists necessarily. Non-theists, of course, would not find this route to time's necessity in any way appealing. For even those irenic agnostics disposed to grant that possibly God exists would not concede enough for the present argument's purposes. Only if God is not just possible but necessary and therefore actual does the conclusion that time exists necessarily follow.

Now the temporalistic theist is not without a response to this. William Hasker has suggested that "the time in which God is is not a fourth dimension of an extensive continuum."[19] If God's time ≠ the ordinary physical time in which we dwell, a temporal God need not be spatial. By the same token, if God's time ≠ our time, our time can be contingent even if God is necessarily temporal and necessarily existent. I discuss below this proposal to posit a second, divine time. For now it is enough to note that in rejecting the claim that God is in space, the temporalist also rejects the claim that our time exists necessarily.

The Contingency of Time

It appears, then, that we have no good reason to think that our time exists necessarily and some reason (though not overwhelming reason) to think that our time exists contingently. As we will later find reason to reject the claim that God inhabits a discrete, necessarily existing divine time, let us simplify the discussion and simply say that on balance, it seems that any time exists contingently. Since there are temporal things only if there is time, it thus is also contingent that temporal things exist. It follows that "time does not exist" and "no

19. William Hasker, personal correspondence, June 27, 1989.

temporal things exist" are only contingently false—and so are possibly true. Let us now ask just how these sentences could be true (or express truth). To do so we need some understanding of what truth is.

Theories of truth can be sorted as realist and antirealist. Antirealist theories of truth define truth in a way that links it with the possibility of knowledge, verification, or awareness. Antirealists say such things as that a proposition P is true iff a community of ideal inquirers, given unlimited time to inquire, would in the end affirm P, or that P is true iff it would in the end be verified. Realists, by contrast, hold that truth is independent of all such matters, that it consists in something like correspondence with a reality independent of all verification and belief-justifying procedures (save when the truth in question *concerns* verification and belief-justifying procedures).

Let us ask how an antirealist could give an account of the truth-conditions of "time does not exist" and "no temporal things exist." If antirealism *cannot* generate possibly obtaining truth-conditions for these claims, then antirealists must call them necessarily false even though they are in fact contingent, and so these claims' being possibly true constitutes a good reason to reject antirealism. But antirealism pays a heavy price to explain these claims' truth-conditions. Suppose, for instance, that a Peircean or Sellarsian antirealist argues that "P is true" = df. an ideal community of inquirers, undertaking unlimited inquiry, would in the end affirm P. "Time does not exist" and "no temporal things exist" could be known to be true only by a timeless ideal inquirer (or community of inquirers)—one that exists, but exists at no time. A timeless ideal inquirer (or community of inquirers) could not *come* to know that these things are true. This would be a change in its cognitive state, and as we will see, a timeless being cannot change. Hence there could be a timeless ideal inquirer or community of inquirers only if it timelessly possessed all the knowledge at which a temporal ideal community of inquiry would eventually arrive—namely, all knowledge of the sort such a community would seek.

So it would appear that antirealists can accept that "time does not exist" and "no temporal things exist" are contingently false only by accepting that possibly there is an individual or community that is both timeless and nearly omniscient. Surprisingly, then, one cannot reject at once the claim that there are necessary existential truths, a realist theory of truth, and the claim that possibly there is a timeless nearly omniscient mind or community; the Humean position that denies all three is inconsistent. In any event, for antirealists, "time does not exist" and "no temporal things exist" are timeless truths if they are true: they are true but not true at any time. Realist accounts of these claims' conditions of truth are simpler, on the surface.[20] Realists can just say that "time does not exist" and "no temporal things exist," if true, are true by corresponding with a language- and mind-independent reality. But if these claims are true in this way, then in language- and mind-independent reality, no times or temporal things exist. Hence these claims, if true, are true but not true at any time. Accordingly, for realists, too, "time does not exist" and "no temporal things exist" are timeless truths if they are true. As these claims are possibly true, possibly there are timeless truths.

These would be negative timeless truths. But it seems at least conceivable, and so prima facie possible, that there be positive timeless truths. Physicists disagree about the number of dimensions space-time involves. It is common to say that there are just four dimensions, but some propose as many as eleven.[21] In any event, there does not seem to be any good reason to hold that necessarily, any extensive continuum has four or more dimensions. It is conceivable and mathematically describable that there be a strictly three-dimensional continuum. One could think of such a continuum as a space not accompanied by a time. For even if the existence of space physically necessitates the existence of time, it just does not seem that the existence of space *entails* the existence of time. (This entailment could fail even if, as Kant thought, we could not *represent* to ourselves a spatial world without representing to ourselves a temporal world.)[22] This is reason to consider a space without time possible. If such a space is possible, "a space exists" is possibly a positive timeless truth (though in fact it is true at all times), and a strictly three-dimensional space-time is a possible timeless and non-abstract entity. Note that even though "a space exists" is actually a temporal truth and possibly a timeless truth, it does not follow that space is actually temporal but possibly timeless. Even if "a space exists" is possibly a timeless truth, it may be that our actual space and any other possible extensive continua are necessarily temporal or neces-

---

20. This may be true *only* on the surface; there are well-known problems in fleshing out the correspondence-relation realists employ. But for a powerful proposal that avoids them, see Post, *Faces,* chap. 1, passim.

21. See Robert Geroch, "Space-Time Structure from a Global Viewpoint," in R. K. Sachs, ed., *General Relativity and Cosmology* (New York: Academic Press, 1971), pp. 71–103. "Superspace" theorists go so far as to suggest that space-time is infinite-dimensional.

22. Kant held that time is "the form of inner sense" and so that we cannot conceive of any atemporal reality. This is a good case of confusing a property of a conceiving with a property of its content. A three-dimensional space-time would simply be a set of space-time points which permits only two sorts of line perpendicular to any line. The conception is mathematically clear; if Kant meant to deny that timeless space is conceivable, he was just wrong.

sarily timeless. For it could be that "a space exists" is possibly a timeless truth not because our space (or any other) is temporal but possibly timeless, but because our necessarily temporal space exists contingently and a timeless space could exist in its stead.

The case of space is a bit more complex than I have so far indicated. For it could be that despite our initial impression, the existence of space *does* entail the existence of time. But suppose that this is so. Since Minkowski, it has become common to treat space and time as abstracted aspects of a four-dimensional continuum, space-time. In Minkowskian terms, then, space without time would be in effect a continuum of only three dimensions. Continua of fewer than four dimensions are mathematically describable. So we would not want to conclude from space's entailing time that no such continua are genuinely possible. We would want to say, rather, that while an extensive continuum's having three dimensions does not entail its having a fourth, a continuum's having a spatial dimension does entail its having a temporal dimension. But if this is so, then no matter how many dimensions an extensive continuum has, one of its dimensions qualifies as spatial only if another of its dimensions qualifies as temporal. If space entails time and continua of fewer than four dimensions are possible, then, the concepts of space and time are correlative: just as being tall entails being taller than some other person, and so entails being unlike some other person in a way which entails that that other person is not tall, being spatial entails being unlike some other dimension in a way which entails that that other dimension is temporal.

Now if the existence of space entails the existence of time, no space is possibly a timeless object and "a space exists" is not possibly a timeless truth. But a 3D continuum may still be a timeless, nonabstract entity, and "a 3D continuum exists" may still be possibly a timeless truth. For there is no necessity that any dimension of a continuum qualify as temporal *or* spatial. On Minkowski's view, for instance, there are no spatial or temporal dimensions in space-time, strictly speaking. There are only four space-time dimensions, some of which we usually *treat* as spatial and one of which we usually *treat* as time. I take it, then, that even if space entails time, we still have examples of a possible positive timeless truth and a possible timeless entity.

So far, then, I have argued that timeless truths and entities are possible if time does not exist. Can there also be timeless truths and beings if time *does* exist? Some writers suggest that even if a timeless being can exist if there is no time, there can be no such thing as a timeless being that *coexists* with time.[23] Swinburne, for instance, reasons that even if a

23. See Smith, "A New Typology," pp. 325–326.

God apart from a world would be timeless, still if "God coexists with
the world and in the world there is change . . . there is a case for
saying that God continues to exist for an endless time rather than that
he is timeless. In general that which remains the same while other
things change is not said to be outside time, but to continue through
time."[24] I now argue that timeless beings and truths can coexist with
time.

Numbers and Mathematical Truths

Mathematical truths have been the most popular candidates for timeless truths that can coexist with time.[25] Numbers, whatever else they
are, are the truthmakers of mathematical truths. So among those who
hold that mathematical truths are timeless, numbers have been a popular candidate for timeless existence. For instance, William Kneale notes
that

> an assertion such as "There is a prime number between five and ten" can
> never be countered sensibly by the remark "You are out of date; things
> have altered recently." And this is the reason why the entities discussed
> in mathematics can properly be said to have a timeless existence. To say
> only that they have a sempiternal or omnitemporal existence (i.e. an
> existence at all times) would be unsatisfactory because this way of talking
> might suggest that it is at least conceivable that they should at some time
> cease to exist, and that is an absurdity we want to exclude.[26]

Norman Malcolm, Nelson Pike, Richard Sorabji, Grace Jantzen, and
John Post make similar remarks.[27]
    Now if one says, e.g., that there still is a prime number between five
and ten, a listener will indeed take there to be some point to this claim

24. Richard Swinburne, "The Timelessness of God," *Church Quarterly Review* 166
(1965), 331; see also William L. Craig, "God, Time, and Eternity," *Religious Studies* 14
(1978), 501–503. A like point is implicit in the distinction of two ways to be temporal in
Delmas Lewis' "Eternity Again," *International Journal for Philosophy of Religion* 15 (1984),
73–79, and Nicholas Wolterstorff's "God Everlasting," in Steven Cahn and David
Shatz, eds., *Contemporary Philosophy of Religion* (London: Oxford University Press,
1982), pp. 77–98.
    25. Though less remarked on, logical truths should enjoy a similar status.
    26. William Kneale, "Time and Eternity in Theology," *Proceedings of the Aristotelian
Society* 61 (1960–61), 98.
    27. Norman Malcolm, "Anselm's Ontological Arguments," in Alvin Plantinga, ed.,
The Ontological Argument (New York: Doubleday, 1965), p. 144; Pike, *God*, pp. 12–13;
Sorabji, *TC&C*, p. 133; Grace Jantzen, *God's World, God's Body* (Philadelphia: Westmin-
ster Press, 1984), pp. 46–47; Post, *Faces*, pp. 145–146.

and so infer that it could be otherwise on other days; if it cannot, why distinguish the particular *time*? But that "there still is a prime number between five and ten" thus *conversationally implies* that things could be otherwise does not mean that it strictly speaking *entails* it.[28] If "there still is . . . " does not entail that things can be otherwise, that things cannot be otherwise does not falsify it and so does not entail that mathematical truths are timeless or that numbers exist timelessly. Again, that the number seven exists timelessly is not the sole possible explanation for the "is there still . . . " question's being out of court. The number seven's being necessarily omnitemporal or necessarily existent would explain this equally well. Many philosophers do in fact view mathematical truths as omnitemporally rather than timelessly true. Martha Kneale, for instance, writes that "all that is meant by calling mathematical truths timeless is that there is no point in asking when two and two are four in the way that there is point in asking when the daffodils are in bloom. But this does not mean that it is not the case that two and two are four today . . . were four yesterday and . . . will be four tomorrow."[29] Kneale adds that she "would go so far as to say that it is true that today two and two have been four for a day longer than they were yesterday" but admits that this last claim is a bit bizarre.[30]

Kneale is correct; this last claim seems odd. The oddity is not just that (given special relativity) if numbers exist at times, they also have locations in space and turn out to be concrete physical objects. I believe that the oddity is also that if today two and two have been four for a day longer than they were yesterday, the number two has aged a day. Numbers just do not seem to be the sort of thing that can grow older. There are theories of number on which numbers *are* the sorts of things that can age, e.g., the theory that numbers are just humanly created concepts. But this does not so much suggest that numbers do age after all as suggest that these theories are false. This is not just because aging is a biological process and numbers are not alive. The oddity remains

28. To say that a proposition P conversationally implies a proposition Q is to say, roughly, that even if P does not entail Q, the asserting of P in an ordinary conversational situation will lead an ordinarily competent hearer who believes the speaker to be prepared to affirm Q. Ordinarily competent hearers who are being charitable assume that what their interlocuters say has a point. So in the case in the text, it is because there is no point to the claim that "there still is . . ." if there cannot fail to be such a number that a hearer will gather that things could be otherwise.

29. Martha Kneale, "Eternity," p. 231. See also, e.g., Steven Davis, *Logic and the Nature of God* (Grand Rapids, Mich.: Eerdmans, 1983), pp. 15–16, and Wolterstorff, "God Everlasting," p. 80.

30. Martha Kneale, "Eternity," p. 231.

(though it is lessened) even if we subtract all biological implications of aging, leaving only the bare acquiring of later and later dates. Perhaps the roots of this sense of oddity are an intuition that numbers are the sort of things that in no way change, and the thought that acquiring a later date is or supervenes on a change of some sort.

If numbers cannot age, they cannot exist *at* times. For things that exist at a time t either first exist at t or have existed for some time before t. If a number has existed for some time before t, it has grown older for that period of time. Yet the claim that two begins to exist is strange. For we have good reason to think that whatever begins to exist exists contingently: time itself seemed the only possible exception, and we showed that it in fact is not. Now if there were no number two, it would not be possible that there be collections with two members. Hence if there contingently is a number two, there is a possible world in which it is not absolutely possible that there be two distinct things. But in S5, all true claims of absolute possibility are true in all possible worlds. So since in our world it is possible that there be two-membered collections, this is possible in all worlds. This is possible iff there is a number two (whatever it is). So there necessarily is a number two: in every world, there is some entity that in that world is the number two.[31] And so the number two does not begin to exist. Similar reasoning will rule out the claim that the number two ceases to exist. Thus it seems that the number two does not exist *at* any time.

Still, this is not a decisive argument. Merely to acquire a later date, remaining in all other respects the same, is a paradigmatic case of what ordinary language would call mere endurance without change. Hence one could perhaps contend that this sort of change is not *really* a change. If it is not, perhaps our intuition that it is odd to say that a number grows older is not well founded and can be disregarded. It would be clear that growing older involved some real change if it were clear that the "passing" of time, just by itself, involves some real change, of the sort that Richard Taylor has called "absolute becoming,"[32] and that the subject of this change is not some independent entity called time, but instead every entity that exists while time passes. But this is something that only tensed theories of time affirm, and in this book I am not supposing either a tensed or a tenseless theory of time.

A more persuasive argument may begin from a claim already ar-

31. I put the conclusion thus because it has not been shown that the same entity is the number two in all worlds. If the number two is (say) a class of two-membered classes, then different such classes are the number two in different worlds, because different pairs populate different worlds.

32. Richard Taylor, *Metaphysics*, 3d ed. (Englewood Cliffs, N.J.: Prentice-Hall, 1983), pp. 71–79.

gued, that in the actual world, whatever is temporal is spatial.[33] For whatever is spatial and temporal is a possible terminus of causal relations and so is a concrete entity. It is strongly counterintuitive to speak of causal relations with numbers, and numbers are paradigm examples of abstract entities. Hence at least in the actual world, it seems, numbers (whatever they are) exist timelessly.

Further, it is plausible that whatever is timeless in our possible world and relevantly similar worlds is necessarily timeless, and whatever is temporal in such worlds is necessarily temporal. For an entity is contingently temporal only if it is temporal in some possible world and not temporal in some possible world. Now in no possible world can a timeless thing become temporal or a temporal thing become timeless. An entity is timeless in a world W only if in W that entity exists, but exists at no time—i.e., only if its existence is not located at any point in time. Hence any entity that at some time t is temporal in W is always temporal in W, for at any other time it remains true that this thing's existence is located (inter alia) at t. So the same object can be timeless and can be temporal only if it is timeless in one possible world and temporal in another.

But this is not possible if the object is timeless in our world or one whose space-time shares the traits of ours. For if we are dealing with a pair of possible worlds whose space and time share the traits of our own, temporal and timeless beings will have properties of such very different *kinds* as to make a transworld identification of such beings implausible. For instance, in such possible worlds, every temporal thing is spatial and every atemporal thing is aspatial—and so the difference between temporal and atemporal things is as great as that between spatial and spaceless entities, or concrete and abstract entities, or physical and nonphysical entities. But this difference is great enough virtually to ensure nonidentity. For we would not credit a claim that the same individual is a property in one world and a podiatrist in another. Suppose on the other hand that only one world of a pair has a space-time relevantly like ours. A being which in this world is not in time or space still cannot be in time but not space in the other world. For the difference between these states is still as great as the difference between abstract and concrete. Hence whatever is timeless in our world or relevantly similar worlds is necessarily timeless, and whatever is temporal in such worlds is necessarily temporal.[34] This has a corollary. Since any necessary being exists in all worlds (given S5), any necessary

33. Temporalistic theists may add "except God" if they wish. Again, I discuss below their proposal that God is in time but not in ordinary physical time.
34. Temporalistic theists need not demur, since they can hold that God is necessarily temporal but contingently related to *physical* time.

being exists in our world. So any necessary being that is actually timeless is necessarily timeless.

Could any individual of any sort be timeless in one possible world
and temporal in any other possible world? Intuitively, this does not
appear possible. Timelessness and temporality are two radically different modes of being. If something is timeless, it does not change and its
existence is not divided into earlier and later phases. If something is
temporal and exists for more than a moment, it likely does change, and
its existence must have earlier and later phases; we will see still other
differences between temporal and timeless existence below. So again,
temporal and timeless beings will have to have properties so radically
different as to make transworld identification of such beings implausible. The greater these differences, then, the more plausible it is that
whatever is timeless is necessarily so.

Another, more persuasive argument that numbers are actually timeless entities begins from a thesis just argued, that there necessarily are
numbers. This surely entails that

> MT. Mathematical truths have the modal status of absolute
> necessity.

For it is incontestable that mathematical truths cannot be false, and if
this is so, they can fail to be true only if they can be truth-valueless in
virtue of the nonexistence of the numbers they concern. If that argument for (MT) does not seem persuasive, one can construct another.
For it seems literally inconceivable that it fail to be true that $2 + 2 = 4$;
it seems that if this is possible, *anything* is possible. Such modal intui-
tions are not indefeasible and are not universally shared. But they are
the best guides we have to whatever the real modal facts are, and it is
legitimate to trust them until given good reason not to trust them.
Hence it is legitimate to affirm the absolute necessity of mathematical
truth. But if mathematical truths are necessarily true, they have truthmakers in every possible world.

Does absolutely necessary truth entail timeless truth? Martha Kneale
has argued that on the contrary, necessary truth entails everlasting truth
and so temporal truth.[35] Working with the putative necessary truth
that God exists, she reasons this way:

> 1. "God exists" is necessarily true.   premise.
> 2. "God exists" is not everlastingly
>   true.   hypothesis for
>   reductio.

---

35. Martha Kneale, "Eternity," p. 235.

3. Necessarily, if "God exists" is not
   everlastingly true, there is a time
   at which it is not true.   premise.
4. If there is a time at which "God
   exists" is not true, possibly "God
   exists" is not true.   instance of modal rule.
5. Possibly "God exists" is not true.   2–4, HS, MP.
6. Necessarily, if "God exists" is
   necessarily true, then "God
   exists" is not possibly not true.   instance of modal rule.
7. It is not the case that possibly
   "God exists" is not true.   1, 6, MP.
8. "God exists" is everlastingly true. 1–7, RAA.

Paul Helm has replied in effect that the proposition that (3) claims to be
necessary is not necessary and that therefore (3) is not true.[36] For if

9. there is no time,

"God exists" is not everlastingly true and yet there is no time at which
it is not true. So as (9) is possible, the contained proposition in (3) is
possibly false. But this won't do. For all Helm has said, it could still be
necessarily true that

3a. if "God exists" is not everlastingly true, either there is no time
    or there is a time at which "God exists" is not true.

If (3a) is true, then given that in fact there is time, the argument still
goes through. An advocate of divine timelessness in particular must
grant (3a). For the atemporalist holds that "God exists" is true, but true
at no time. So as far as the atemporalist is concerned, if "God exists" is
timelessly true, it is not everlastingly true. If it is timelessly true,
further, then either there is no time or any time at all is a time at which
it is not true. Thus the doctrine of divine timelessness seems to entail
(3a). Worse, from (3a) one can reason as follows:

10. if "God exists" is not everlastingly
    true, then if there is time, there is
    a time at which "God exists" is
    not true.   3a, df. of "⊃"

36. Paul Helm, "Timelessness and Foreknowledge," *Mind* 84 (1975), 520. Helm's
actual claim is that (2) and (3) do not entail (4). But they need not; Kneale's point is
rather that (4) is a conceptual truth that enables one to move from (2) and (3) to (8).

11. if "God exists" is not everlastingly
true, then if possibly there is
time, possibly there is a time at
which "God exists" is not true   10, modal rule.

(11) creates as much trouble as (3a), without even requiring us to affirm that time exists.

I suggest, therefore, that the problem in Kneale's argument lies with (4). (4) actually *begs the question* against the claim that necessary truths are timeless. For if a necessary truth is timeless, it is not the case that if there is a time at which "God exists" is not true, then possibly "God exists" is not true. What is true is rather that

4a. if there is a time at which "God exists" is not true, then either "God exists" is necessarily true, but true at no time, or possibly "God exists" is not true.

(4) presumes that the only alternatives to truth at all times are truth at some times and falsity at others, or truth at no time and falsity at all. It thereby begs the question against the claim that there is another alternative, truth not at any time. If God exists necessarily and is timeless, at every moment it is correct to say that God exists, but false that God exists *then*. In the same way, were it correct to say that a second time series exists, it would be false to say that it exists *then* (since if it exists then, its existence has a location in our time series, and so the second series is not discrete from ours).[37] Given that only (4a) rather than (4) is defensible, neither (3a) nor (11) need trouble one who wants to deny that necessary truth entails temporal truth.

Let us deny this, then. The second premise of our argument for the timelessness of numbers is that

ET. the existence of time is contingent.[38]

This chapter's third section developed several reasons to believe (ET). There is reason, then, to consider both (MT) and (ET) true. But if both are true, it follows that there is a possible world in which all mathematical truths are true even though time does not exist. So mathe-

37. I discuss the tense of the verb in "God exists" in the next chapter.
38. Strictly speaking, (ET) should claim that space-time exists contingently. I continue to speak of separate time and space where doing so can simplify the argument and where the character of space-time as distinct from separate space and time does not affect the argument.

matical truths are at least possibly timeless truths. Moreover, if this is so, numbers, whatever they are—the truthmakers of mathematical truths—can exist even if time does not exist. Now we have already argued that whatever is timeless in our actual world (or relevantly similar worlds) is necessarily timeless. If we let "NT" symbolize the claim that numbers are timeless, that is, we earlier argued that

12. NT → □NT,

and we have just shown that

13. ◊NT.

Given these claims, we can argue as follows:

14.	(NT → □NT) → (◊NT → ◊□NT)	instance of modal rule.
15.	◊NT → ◊□NT.	12, 14, MP.
16.	◊□NT.	13, 15, MP.

(16) entails NT in the Brouwer system of modal logic and entails □NT in S5. So depending on the system of modal logic one adopts, one can show that numbers are timeless or that they are necessarily timeless, given only that they are possibly so, as (MT) and (ET) entail, and that space-time has its actual character.[39]

Given (MT) and (ET), further, if numbers *are* located in time, then, they are so only if time exists, and so only if they are related to temporal entities (minimally, to time itself). Numbers are located in time, that is, only if coexisting with time or with a certain sort of time entails that they exist at times.[40] We have already seen that coexisting with time does not necessarily locate numbers in time, for we have seen that numbers are timeless even though they do coexist with our actual time. But perhaps other sorts of time are possible. Perhaps there can be a time which is not a dimension of an extensive continuum also including spatial dimensions, and perhaps the existence of such a time would lessen the plausibility of (12) and so weaken the argument just completed. So let us now ask whether coexisting with any other sort of time may locate numbers in time.

---

39. The latter claim supports (12).

40. Swinburne seems to say much the same about God in the passage quoted at the end of the section entitled, "The Contingency of Time."

Things can have earlier and later phases of existence only if time exists, for a thing can have earlier and later phases of existence only if it exists at at least two times. So if a number's existence has earlier and later phases, it has them only in worlds in which time exists. If a number exists and time does not, the number's existence has no phases ordered as earlier and later. Now if A's existence has no earlier and later phases and B's does, A and B differ in many ways. For instance, B is such that (*ceteris paribus*) some of its states can occur later than others, but A is not. Further, B is such that (*ceteris paribus*) some of its states can have ordinary causal relations to others, but A is not. If perchance B and A are both personal, B can deliberate about its future and remember its past, whereas A can do neither, an inability that entails many other differences in the mental lives of A and B. Again, if one adopts a tensed theory of time, B's existence is appropriately imaged by a line, different parts of which successively stand under the "spotlight" of actuality, whereas A's existence is appropriately imaged as a point. Within a tensed theory, that is, some of B's existence is past and some future, but none of A's is either. If one adopts a tenseless theory of time, one can say that B's duration or temporal extension has parts and A's does not. For these reasons, if B has earlier and later phases of existence and A does not, A and B differ really and intrinsically.

Thus if coexisting with temporal things made numbers have earlier and later phases of existence, coexisting with temporal things would make numbers really and intrinsically different than they would otherwise be. But it does not seem reasonable to suppose that merely coexisting with changing, temporal things effects a real intrinsic difference in numbers. Merely coexisting with a thing does not make *me* really and intrinsically different in any way, for instance. Other things really change me only if they causally interact with me. Changing, temporal things in no way causally interact with numbers. So coexistence with temporal things should affect numbers only with respect to properties supervening on noncausal relations with other things—properties appropriately called purely extrinsic. The property of having earlier and later phases is not one of these. As we have seen, having or lacking this property makes things differ intrinsically. Nor does this property supervene on relations with other things; a thing can have earlier and later phases of existence even if it is the only thing in existence. If coexisting with time or temporal things cannot affect numbers really and intrinsically, then whether or not time exists, numbers do not have earlier and later phases of existence. More generally, what is timeless remains timeless whether or not time exists. Thus if any sort of time exists and numbers exist, numbers are absolutely timeless: they exist, but exist at no time. But of course, if time does not exist and numbers exist, numbers also are absolutely timeless. Necessarily, time exists or time does not exist. Hence in every possible world, numbers are timeless. Numbers are not just timeless, but necessarily so.

This chapter's argument can be extended to any other truthmakers of absolutely necessary truths. So it seems that all such entities are actually and necessarily atemporal. Timeless entities exist, whether or not God exists or is timeless. But even if one denies that timeless entities exist, this chapter's arguments have given reason to believe that such entities can exist. Thus one cannot rule out the claim that God is timeless on the ground that nothing can be timeless. Further, one can use the natures of such entities as numbers to get an initial handle on what a timeless God might be like. Finally, this chapter has given reason to say that if God is timeless, coexisting with time does not make Him temporal.

The Logic of Eternity

The last chapter argued that there can be truths that are not true at any time and a being that exists, but does not exist at any time. Both claims still have an air of paradox. The rest of this book seeks to flesh out an understanding of what is involved in God's existing, but not existing at any time. This chapter, though, tries to shed some light on how it can be that "God exists" is true, but not true at any time. If we can do this, it will not just advance our understanding of divine timelessness. It will also provide another argument that there actually is a timeless entity. For if "God exists" is true, but not true at any time, then

> T. "God exists" is true, and yet for any t, "God exists at t" is false.

If only temporal things exist, (T) is inconsistent. That is, if only temporal things exist, then whatever exists exists at some time or other, and so "God exists" materially implies that for some t, God exists at t. So if (T) is consistent, then by *modus tollens* it is false that only temporal things exist.

This chapter argues that (T) is consistent. It also investigates the logical status of the claim that God is timeless.

Truth and Timelessness: Eternity as a Date

Let us first see just what it is for a truth to be true, but not true at any time. To do so, let us say that in each possible world, correlated with each time is a set of propositions true at that time.[1] We can call these the truths indexed to that time, and their set the time's T-set. These truths need not explicitly incorporate a date to be indexed to that date. As long as they are in fact true at a time, they are indexed to that time. By talking of truth at times, I do not mean to assert that truth is tensed rather than tenseless. If truth is tenseless, the same truths are true at all times, and if truth is tensed, what is true may vary by time. Nor do I mean to say that truth at a time is a primitive predicate in terms of which we should define truth simpliciter. I believe that my argument is neutral on this matter.[2]

If there are T-sets, there also may be truths that are not members of any T-set. If there are such truths, a set of these truths exists. Let us say that just as T-sets correlate with times, this further set, if it exists, correlates with a further timeless but timelike locus to which one can index the truth of propositions. We can call this locus eternity. We can say, then, that eternity is like one more "time" in addition to all times: all truths that are not indexed to any time are automatically indexed to the "time" that is no time, the null time, eternity. The absence of tense in a truth is a fact about its tense, a fact that could be recorded by the use of a special tense-operator expressing tenselessness. So, too, the absence of a date for a truth is a fact about its indexing to a date, a fact that could be recorded by the use of a special "null date." Eternity is this null date.

This treatment of eternity is perhaps adumbrated in Boethius' claim that "our now makes time as if it were running along . . . but the divine now, remaining, and not moving, and standing still, makes eternity."[3] For calling eternity a "now" models it on a time, an instant. Again, that eternity is logically a time may also help to explain the fact that even theists who uphold divine timelessness and the creation of time itself persist in speaking of God as existing "before" the world and time. "Before" is a temporal relation. Where there is no time, there are no relations of before and after. Thus strictly speaking, there can be no

1. Sometimes different sets are correlated with the same time in different possible worlds.

2. I do suggest that if a proposition is true yet not true at any time, we can define another "time," eternity, such that the proposition is true at that "time." But this hardly amounts to a proposal to define unindexed in terms of indexed truth; the claim that something is true iff it is true at some t makes no assertion about the order of analysis between truth and truth at t.

3. "nostrum nunc quasi currens tempus facit . . . divinum vero nunc permanens neque movens sese atque consistens aeternitatem facit." Boethius, *De Trinitate,* chap. 4, in H. F. Stewart and E. K. Rand, eds., *Boethius: The Theological Tractates* (New York: G. P. Putnam's Sons, 1926), chap. 4, p. 20, ll. 72–74.

such thing as a period "before" God created time. But if theists sense that logically, eternity is *as if* another time, it is understandable that they would speak of eternity as if it were a time "before" the first moment of time.

This treatment of eternity as a "time" makes formal sense of timeless truth (and correlated timeless existence) using only the notions of a time, a set, and a truth, and the set-theoretic relation "is not a member of." Of course, even if we have a formally coherent account of this, another sort of question remains: how can it happen that any truth satisfies this account? We tackle this question shortly.

Applications

Even this bare, abstract understanding of the nature of timeless truth can let one block specious arguments against the claim that a timeless God coexists with time. William Craig asks:

> If God sustains any relations to the world, does this not imply that he exists in time? . . . Aquinas attempted to solve this problem by arguing that while creatures are really related to God, God sustains no real relation to creatures . . . this doctrine is singularly unconvincing. It is system-dependent upon regarding relation as an accident inhering in a substance . . . if we reject the Aristotelian metaphysical doctrine of substance and accidents, then it seems foolish to say that God is not really related to the world as Creator to creature. If God is really related to the world then it seems most reasonable to maintain that God is in time subsequent to creation.[4]

I have already argued against a similar claim made by Swinburne. But the nature of timeless truth lets us abort Craig's argument without invoking either Aristotelian metaphysics or the previous chapter's reasoning. Whether or not time exists, we can say, "God exists" fails to be a member of any T-set. This is an entirely coherent claim; sets can contain or fail to contain anything whatever. So whether or not time exists, one can say, God remains timeless.

Again, the logical point that eternity is a "time" can aid insight into the relations between eternity and time. Intuitively, one would say that events or states A and B are *temporally contiguous* just in case either A and B overlap temporally or there is no time between the existing or occurring of A and the existing or occurring of B. But on this account, it would turn out that no nonoverlapping events or states are con-

---

4. Craig, "God, Time, and Eternity," p. 502.

tiguous. For time is a continuum, and therefore between any two distinct times there is an infinity of distinct times. Thus if two events or states do not overlap temporally, an infinity of distinct times divides them. So a more adequate definition might be this:

> A and B are temporally contiguous = df. either A and B overlap temporally or every time between an arbitrary point in A's duration and an arbitrary point in B's duration is included in A's duration or B's duration.

This is a reasonable definition. It calls temporally contiguous all and only the pairs of events or states in the same temporal series which one would intuitively expect, it avoids problems with the continuum, and yet its requirement of inclusion in A's or B's duration captures the idea that A and B directly abut without overlapping. But this definition has two surprising consequences.

First, it entails that if there are two discrete temporal series, A and B, then every point in A is temporally contiguous with every point in B, and every point in B is temporally contiguous with every point in A, though not all points in B are temporally contiguous with all points in B and not all points in A are temporally contiguous with all points in A. For if A and B are discrete, there is no temporal path from the one to the other: were there a temporal interval linking the two, they would not be discrete time series, but would instead be two periods within a single temporal series. But if there is no temporal path between A and B, there are no times between A and B and so no times between them that are not included in their durations. Thus every time between an arbitrary point in A's duration and an arbitrary point in B's duration is included in A's duration or B's duration. I think we can just accept this result and perhaps even use it as an alternate definition of temporal discreteness. For if two time series are temporally discrete, there *can't* be any time between and linking their times. But one cannot even imagine what that is not a time could occur between and link times. Thus there can be nothing at all between the times of discrete temporal series, and so it is intuitively apt to speak of them as directly abutting one another, i.e., as contiguous.

Second, if eternity is a "time," our definition of temporal contiguity applies to its relations to time. Our definition of temporal contiguity entails that if A is a temporal series and B is eternity, then every point in A is temporally contiguous with every point in B, and every point in B is temporally contiguous with every point in A, and every point in B is temporally contiguous with every point in B. For there can be no time "between" time and eternity, and a fortiori no time between different "points" in eternity itself. We can accept this result, I think. We will see Anselm claim that an eternal deity is temporally omnipresent, meaning by this that an eternal deity, though existing *at* no time and not at the same time as any temporal event, is yet intimately *with* all events at all times. We can use the present result to give an account of this intimate temporal omnipresence.[5]

The claim that eternity stands in relations of temporal contiguity with times is liable to attract this sort of counterargument: "You say that eternity is contiguous with times because there is no time between eternity and any time. But by the same token, there is no time between the color yellow and the number three. Are you therefore going to say that the color yellow is temporally contiguous with the number three?" This sort of objection is misplaced. Yellow and three satisfy our definition of temporal contiguity only if either they overlap temporally or every time between an arbitrary point in yellow's duration and an arbitrary point in three's duration is included in yellow's or in three's duration. But as they are usually conceived, yellow and three do not overlap temporally and neither are nor have durations. If the usual view of yellow and three is correct, then, they cannot stand in the relation of temporal contiguity as defined here. If someone does claim that yellow and three have durations, then for this person there should be no further oddity in applying our definition of temporal contiguity to them, and for others, the oddity will lie not in applying the definition but in the claim that yellow and three have durations.

We will see in Chapter 6 that one can conceive eternity to be a duration. But one need not do so to sustain the claim that it is temporally contiguous with times. For we have seen that logically speaking, eternity is a date, a "time" or point in time. It is a *locus* to which one can index propositions' truth and (as will emerge) to which the tense-system can relate the present. One can view a duration as an interval of dates. Conversely, one can view a date as a degenerate duration, a "point-thick" duration or duration which does not endure. A degenerate duration is a duration, logically speaking. So eternity *can* stand in relations of temporal contiguity, per our definition, and such inappropriate entities as yellow and three cannot do so unless they have durations.

5. Note that God's being temporally contiguous with every event does not entail that His existence is in any sense *simultaneous* with any event. Events or states can be contiguous which are not simultaneous.

An Objection

The account of the first section is open to a simple but powerful objection. It is this: here and now, one can say "God exists." If one does, presumably, the proposition "God exists" exists now. If it exists now and is true, then surely it is true now. But then "God exists" is a part of this moment's T-set. So either God is not timeless or our account of timeless truth is incorrect.

Responding to this objection affords us a chance to flesh out our account of timeless truth. One response begins by noting that there are logical similarities between moments of time and possible worlds.[6] Being actual entails existing at *this* possible world, whatever else it entails; one need not say that this is *all* it entails to grant that actuality has an indexical aspect. Similarly, being present entails existing at *this* time, whatever else it entails. Being alethically necessary = existing at all possible worlds. Being temporally necessary, or omnitemporal, is a matter of existing at all times. Both worlds and times are consistent; no inconsistent sets of propositions are true at either. It is not wholly implausible, then, to take a moment of time as an analogue to a possible world.[7]

Now on certain views of propositions, a proposition can describe a possible world truly without being true *in* that possible world.[8] A singular proposition is a proposition about just one individual, e.g., "Spot is a dog." According to one theory, singular propositions contain as constituents not items that refer to their subjects, but their subjects themselves.[9] On this view, Spot himself is a constituent of

6. Possible-worlds semantics assumes that whatever is possible is actual at some world. The parallel thesis that would let times perform all semantic functions of possible worlds would be that whatever is possible is actual at some *time*. Aristotle may well have held this thesis and so used times as possible worlds; see Hintikka, *Time and Necessity*. M. J. White has traced this thesis' semantic role in Aristotle and in later Hellenistic philosophy in his *Agency and Integrality*. White contends that some Hellenistic philosophers did in fact use times as today's semanticists use possible worlds.

7. I owe the preceding points to Edward Zalta, "On the Structural Similarities of Worlds and Times," read at the American Philosophical Association Pacific Division meeting, San Francisco, April 1987. My treatment was developed independently of the brief statement of a similar idea in Helm, "Timelessness and Foreknowledge," pp. 518–519.

8. See, e.g., Robert M. Adams, "Actualism and Thisness"; Christopher Menzel, "On Set-Theoretic Possible Worlds," *Analysis* 46 (1986), 68–72.

9. See, e.g., David Kaplan, "Dthat," in P. Cole, ed., *Syntax and Semantics: Pragmatics* (New York: Academic Press, 1978), vol. 9; John Perry, "The Problem of the Essential Indexical," *Nous* 13 (1979), 9–10. One can also find the view in the early Russell and the writings of Hector-Neri Castañeda.

"Spot is a dog." Now a proposition exists only if its constituents exist. So if this theory is true, then if an individual does not exist in a possible world, neither do any singular propositions about that individual. On this theory, that is, if Spot does not exist in possible world W, neither "Spot is a dog" nor "it is not the case that Spot is a dog" exists in W. We are assuming that only existing entities have attributes. If this is so, then if a proposition does not exist, it does not bear a truth-value. Thus in W there are no truths or falsehoods about Spot. In W it is neither true nor false that Spot is a dog.

All the same, if Spot does not exist, it is not the case that Spot is a dog. We *know* that in W it is not the case that Spot is a dog. One may well wonder how this can be if in W "it is not the case that Spot is a dog" is neither true nor false. The answer, I suggest, is that *we* consider W from a cognitive perspective that includes more than W. For convenience, let us say that in our world Spot exists and so propositions about Spot exist. [10] If this is so, we can know that in W it is not the case that Spot is a dog. Though "it is not the case that Spot is a dog" is not true *in* W, it truly describes W, and we can know it on the basis of W, for as we have the appropriate concepts and information, we can infer its truth from what is the case in W.

These claims about propositions serve only to illustrate the distinction between truly describing a possible world and being true in a possible world. One need not accept them to grasp the distinction and see that it is intelligible. Let us now apply this distinction (but *not* the theory of propositions) to the case of "God exists." As Spot was not available in W to render claims about him true or false, if God is timeless, God is not available at any time to verify or falsify claims. As W was nonetheless such that Spot did not exist, every time is nonetheless such that God timelessly exists. As we could know that Spot did not exist in W because we knew facts about worlds other than W, we can know at t that God timelessly exists because we know facts about a time other than t, the "time" of eternity. Now in the case of Spot, what we knew was a fact about the world W. So on this model, if one now knows that God exists, what one knows is a fact about the present moment: one knows that the present moment is such that God exists. But if God is timeless, "God exists" is not true *at* the present moment, since God does not exist in the present moment. Thus this statement is not a member of the present moment's T-set.

---

10. This theory raises interesting questions about fictional reference. As I cannot pursue them, I assume that there really is a Spot to avoid them.

One cannot take "time does not exist" or "a three-dimensional space-time exists" as a fact about any moment of time. For if these claims are true, there is no time. But these claims could be not just true descriptions of but true during the "time" that is eternity. Moreover, we are not seeking an understanding of how these particular claims can be timelessly true. We seek only to grasp how "God exists" can be timelessly true rather than true at the time at which we token it. Thomas Aquinas may implicitly understand the timeless truth of "God exists" in just this way. For Thomas calls God everlasting even though he clearly considers God timeless.[11] This could be just sloppiness. But it could also be a recognition of the fact that every moment is such that God timelessly exists.

A Reply Rejected

Yet the last section may not provide an adequate account of talk about a timeless God. For on this account, if it is now t, "God exists" asserts that t is such that God timelessly exists: "God exists," tokened at t, asserts that at t, God timelessly exists. So on this account, if "God exists" is true, t exists. But a defender of divine timelessness who asserts that God exists means to assert something that would be true even if time did not exist. Further, if God is timeless, the claim "God exists" is about an entity outside and temporally unrelated to our time. This is why a timeless God would be related to our time like a second discrete time series. But if a second time series exists, then even if we token at t "a second time series exists" and this claim is true, this claim is not true *at t*. For if "a second time series exists" were true *at* a time in our time series, the two series would not be discrete. This would be because SOAs in one series could then cause SOAs in another, and causally linked SOAs are temporally connected. Arguing this requires two premises.

We can begin toward the first by noting again that all points in a second time series are contiguous with any time t in our time series. So if "a second time series exists" is true at t, so too are the claims "moment m of the second series exists," "moment n of the second series exists," "event E1 that occurs at moment m occurs," and "event E2 that occurs at moment n occurs." For m, n, E1, E2, and the entire time series have the same relation to t. If this relation makes it the case that "a second time series exists" is true at t, it validates the other claims as

11. See, e.g., *Summa contra Gentiles* (henceforth *SCG*) I, 15.

well. Thus we have our first premise: if "a second time series exists" is true *at* a time t in our series, every truth about that second series is true at t.

My second premise is that

> C. if (i) A causes P to be true, and (ii) P entails Q, and (iii) Q's truth is not a precondition of A's being able to cause P to be true, and (iv) had P not been true, Q would not have been, then A causes Q to be true.

(C) seems almost self-evident. But then let us suppose that some action of A in a second time series S1 causes P to be true. Let Q be the proposition "P is true in S1." Then it is clear that Q satisfies (i)–(iv) and so that A causes Q to be true as well. Suppose now that "S1 exists" is true at t in our own time series. Then per the first premise, Q is true not just in S1 but also in our own time series, at t, and is caused to be true in our own time series *by A's action of causing P to be true in S1*. Thus a SOA in our time series, the SOA that Q is true, causally depends on a SOA in the other series. But then the two time series are causally connected, hence temporally connected and hence not two. So as our first response to the objection of the third section entails that truths about a timeless God are true at t, we must reject it.

A Second Proposal

Our second response to the objection begins by rejecting its key inference. We have seen that if we token at t "a second time series exists," and this is true, it does not follow that this is true at t. So too, the mere fact that the statement "God exists" is true and is made at t does *not* entail that the statement is true at t. In the same way, that a television screen is green and is dim does not entail that it is dimly green. A screen *can* be both green and dim because it contains a dim green glow. But it can also be so because it contains two distinct glows, one on the left which is green and bright and one on the right which is red and dim. In the latter case, the screen is green and dim but not dimly green.[12] In fact, often one absolutely *cannot* infer a statement affirming an adverbially modified predicate ("is dimly green," "exists at t") from one affirming two predicates ("is green and dim," "exists, and is said to exist at t"). A patch of paint may be square and red but

12. I owe this illustration to unpublished work by Toomas Karmo.

cannot be squarely red or redly square. "Square" and "red" cannot modify one another in this way, for being square is not a way to be red, nor is being red a way to be square.

Given the difference between affirming two predicates and affirming a single adverbially modified predicate, one would expect "P is true at t" to make a different claim than "P is true and is tokened at t." It does in fact do so. To explicate the difference between these two claims, let us begin from something unproblematic: some truths are true at a time t in virtue of truthmakers that exist at t. If at t Spot is a dog, "Spot is a dog" is one such truth, and we might emphasize its status by saying "it is now true that Spot is a dog." There are also truths that are true at a time in virtue of truthmakers that exist or did exist or will exist, but do not necessarily exist at that time. "Caesar crossed the Rubicon" is true, but it is not true because Caesar's crossing exists now. Rather, it is true because in the past, Caesar *did* cross the Rubicon.

Consider the claim "it is now true that Caesar crossed the Rubicon." This claim is not false, strictly speaking, but it does seem odd or out of place. I suggest that it seems out of place *because* the truthmaker of "Caesar crossed the Rubicon" is in the past; as this is so, there just seems to be no point to emphasizing the "now." (The oddity here is akin to that attending the claim "today 2 + 2 = 4.") If this explanation is correct, then the ordinary-language function of the locution "it is now true that . . ." is to indicate that what makes the claim in question true exists or occurs now. If this is the case, then perhaps we should treat "it is at t true that . . ." or "it is true at t that . . ." as a sort of generalization of "it is now true that . . ." That is, perhaps we should consider them locutions indicating that what makes the claim in question true exists or occurs at t.

If this account is acceptable, then the difference between "P is true at t" and "P is true and is tokened at t" is clear. For the former implies and the latter does not imply that P's truthmaker exists at t. (If this is so, the latter does not imply the former either, since if it did, the latter *would* entail that P's truthmaker exists at t.) If this is the difference between them, then clearly only the latter is appropriate to discourse about a timeless God. Also, if there is such a difference between the two, (T) may be consistent (if we exclude eternity from the values of "t"). For if being true and tokened at t does not entail being true *at t,* then it is not clear why being true and tokened at t must entail being true at some time or other. What reason can one have to affirm this entailment which will not beg the question against the claim that there can be timeless entities?

A Third Proposal

Another approach to the issue of truth and truth at t will yield a stronger argument that (T) is consistent. The following definitions seem reasonable:

> A exists during t = df. A's existence is located in time, and t is one of its temporal locations.
> P is true during t = df. a truthmaker of P exists during t, P exists during t, and P bears the attribute of truth during t.

Given these definitions, we can say that

> P is true *at* t = df. a truthmaker of P exists, but not necessarily during t, P exists during t, and P bears the attribute of truth during t.

In terms of these definitions, our earlier examples suggest that "Spot is a dog" is true during t and "Caesar crossed the Rubicon" is true at and not during t. On this account of truth at t, if "God exists" is true, and is tokened at t but is not true at t, then either "God exists" exists but does not bear the attribute of truth during t or "God exists" does not exist during t. The former alternative seems unattractive; it would require theists to affirm that no claims made about God in time are true. The latter, more radical alternative is more promising.

On this alternative, we can say this. If a token of "God exists" exists at t, this does not entail that the proposition itself exists at t. Rather, only the token does.[13] This token is a token of a proposition that bears the attribute of truth, but not the attribute of truth at t. The proposition, not the token, is strictly speaking the bearer of truth. We say that my token of "God exists" is true only to speak loosely of the fact that this token is a token of a true proposition. But the proposition (as distinct from the token) does not itself exist at t. The proposition that God exists is timeless, as is any proposition whose truthmakers involve only timeless entities. This proposition exists only at the "time" of eternity. With eternity as a value of t, this proposition's truth is truth during t.

This story about the proposition "God exists" does not seem in any obvious way inconsistent. But if it is not inconsistent, then it gives us a

13. Thus either a type is a timeless exemplar that tokens "imitate," a sort of Platonic Form, or the sense in which a type is present in its token is such as to block this inference.

way to make sense of the claim that "God exists" is true, but not true at any time. It therefore suggests that (T) is consistent (if we exclude eternity from the values of "t").

Eternity and Tense

In his treatise on divine foreknowledge, Anselm of Canterbury suggested that to speak correctly of eternity might require a special tense: "eternity has its own simultaneity in which exist all things which are at the same place and time and all things which are diverse in place and time . . . the apostle spoke in the past tense of even things which are future . . . due to the lack of a verb signifying [this] eternal present . . . for things which are temporally past are in all ways immutable, after the likeness of the eternal present."[14] Several centuries later, Luis de Molina granted a special eternal tense in the course of commenting on Aquinas, noting that "the verbs that we use as copulas in propositions signify, in addition to their principal significatum, a certain duration as the measure of the truth of those propositions. For if the verb is present-tense, it consignifies present duration; if past-tense, past duration . . . present duration . . . can be of two types, namely the present time . . . or eternity, which is always present . . . propositions can have [a] sense such that the verbs . . . consignify . . . an always present eternity."[15] Molina traces the idea to Augustine, Boethius, and Aquinas as well as Anselm and notes its adoption by such later medievals as Richard of Middleton, John Capreolus, Francisco Ferrariensis, and Cajetan.[16]

I believe that Anselm, Molina, and the rest were correct: proper discourse of the eternal requires its own peculiar tense. The need for this arises from the fact that eternity is a locus logically like a time. We use the system of tenses to relate times or timelike loci to sentences' times of utterance; for instance, using the present tense often indicates that that of which one speaks is going on while one speaks. Eternity is a "time" not temporally simultaneous with any time, for if it were, it

14. "Habet aeternum suum simul in quo sunt omnia quae simul sunt loco vel tempore, et quae sunt diversis in locis vel temporibus . . . apostolus . . . illa etiam quae futura sunt praeteriti verbo temporis pronuntiavit . . . propter indigentiam verbi significantis aeternam praesentiam . . . quoniam quae tempore praeterita sunt, ad similitudem aeterni praesentis omnino immutabilia sunt." Anselm, De concordia, I, 5, in Opera, vol. 2, p. 254, ll. 13–22.
15. Luis de Molina, De concordia, pt. IV, tr. Alfred Freddoso (Ithaca, N.Y.: Cornell University Press, 1988), disp. 48, pp. 101, 103.
16. Ibid., pp. 98, 99, 103, 104.

would be in time rather than apart from time. If eternity has this status, then no ordinary tense relates our times of utterance to eternity. Nor can we infer from this that talk of the eternal is tenseless. What is true tenselessly is true at all times.[17] What is true in eternity is true, but true at no time. To speak of what is the case in eternity, then, one must distinguish an eternal-present tense in addition to present, past, and future tenses.

Strictly speaking, then, in such claims as "God is timeless," the verb is neither ordinarily tensed nor tenseless, but eternal-tensed. Moreover, if God is timeless, all strictly true statements that are about God alone (including "God exists") must be in this tense. Using the eternal-present tense indicates that that of which one speaks is the case, but is not the case before, during, or after one's speaking. This description of the eternal-present tense does not distinguish between a tense appropriate to events in a temporal series discrete from ours and a tense appropriate to events in eternity. But this is as it should be, since both a second time series and an eternal being are extrinsically timeless. A second time series would be intrinsically temporal, as an eternal being would not. But even so, we could not use different tenses to refer to events that in a second time series are past, present, or future. For we have no temporal relations (save vacuous contiguity) to events in a second time series. These events are not past, present, or future in relation to our present. But the system of tenses relates events only to our present—for instance, we use the past tense to speak of events that are past in relation to us.

Granting an eternal-present tense would have some impact on the rest of tense logic, as for that matter would granting the possibility of alternate temporal series. For instance, it is an accepted thesis of tense logic that for all P, P entails that presently-P, where the present in question is the present of this temporal series. If either a second temporal series or a timeless being is possible, this thesis is false. Something unwieldy and disjunctive might have to take its place, e.g., that P entails that presently-P or discrete- or eternal-presently-P. But in most cases, it will be easy to rule out the irrelevant disjuncts, and so the overall impact on tense logic will be minor. Theists may well find this small complication of their tense system worthwhile. Below, I further develop the rationale of an eternal tense and show that the point that eternity requires its own tense can help one to defend a Boethian resolution of the problem of freedom and foreknowledge.

17. Thus if eternal truth were tenseless truth, the concept of timeless truth would be otiose—all we would need to speak of is omnitemporal truth. See Martha Kneale, "Eternity," passim.

Timelessness and Alethic Modality

In his *God and Timelessness,* Pike assumes that "timelessness is an essential property of any individual possessing it."[18] The previous chapter's argument sought to validate Pike's assumption, contending that timelessness is *de re* necessary to whatever has it. The introduction's citation of scriptural sources makes it plausible to claim that for Western theists, "God is eternal" is *de dicto* necessary, i.e., necessarily true because being eternal (however one interprets it) is one of the requisites for deity. Thus the claim that God is timeless turns out to be necessary *de dicto et re.* If God is timeless, then necessarily, God is necessarily timeless.

Some writers contend that what exists timelessly must exist with absolute necessity. Malcolm, for instance, reasons that "from the supposition that it could happen that God did not exist it would follow that if He existed, He would have mere duration and not eternity . . . If a thing has duration then it would be merely a contingent fact . . . that its duration was endless . . . If something has endless duration it will make sense (although it will be false) to say that it will cease to exist."[19] Malcolm's point appears to be that something exists in time iff it exists contingently, whence it follows that whatever is timeless exists necessarily. Again, Martha Kneale, examining the concept of eternity, finds absolutely necessary existence to be one of its notes and then goes so far as to suggest that "the notion of timelessness is otiose and could well be allowed to collapse . . . into . . . that of necessity."[20]

Malcolm and Kneale are continuing an ancient tradition. Spinoza, for instance, wrote, "By eternity I mean existence itself, insofar as it is conceived necessarily to follow solely from the definition of that which is eternal . . . Existence of this kind is conceived as an eternal truth, like the essence of a thing."[21] Existence that follows solely from a thing's definition is, of course, conceptually and so absolutely necessary existence, of the sort the ontological argument ascribes to God. Thus Spinoza seems simply to equate eternal existence and necessary existence. Spinoza's phrasing recalls Plotinus' treatment of eternity:

eternity . . . is the life . . . of real being . . . true being is never not being . . . If, then . . . its "is" is the truest thing about it, and itself, and

18. Pike, *God,* p. 28.
19. Malcolm, "Anselm's Arguments," p. 144.
20. Martha Kneale, "Eternity," p. 234.
21. Spinoza, *Ethics,* tr. R. Elwes (New York: Dover, 1955), Bk. I, Def. 8 (plus explanation), p. 46.

this in the sense that it is by its essence or its life, then again there has come to us what we are talking about, eternity. But when we use the word 'always' and say that it does not exist at one time but not at another, we must be thought to be putting it this way for our own sake . . . For existing is not one thing and always existing another, just as a philosopher is not one thing and the true philosopher another . . . So . . . "always" is applied to "existing" . . . so [that] the "always" must be taken as saying "truly existing."[22]

To equate existing, true existing, always existing, and eternal existing as Plotinus does is practically to say that eternal existing is "existence itself," the real, genuine form of existence. The claim that an eternal being "*is* by its essence" seems to mean that it has the necessary existence of which Spinoza speaks, though one should be hesitant in affirming that two writers separated by more than a millennium have the same modal concepts.[23] Thus Plotinus, too, seems to equate eternal existence and necessary existence (as he conceives it).[24]

Though it recalls Plotinus' phrasing, Spinoza's thinking far more likely derives from Maimonides, whose *Guide for the Perplexed* also equates eternal existence and (his concept of) necessary existence, stating that "absolute existence includes the idea of eternity, i.e., the necessity of existence."[25] But the ultimate source of the belief that eternity and necessary existence are connected is Greek, and Hellenic rather than Hellenistic. Parmenides' One exists necessarily and is timeless, and to Parmenides, nothing else "really" exists at all.[26] To Plato, the Forms alone exist necessarily and timelessly. For each, then, something is timeless iff it exists necessarily. Aristotle, too, connected eternity and

22. Plotinus, *Enneads* III (Cambridge: Harvard University Press, 1980), tr. A. H. Armstrong, chap. 7, pp. 313–315.

23. This raises an intriguing question. In Plotinus' cosmology, Nous, the eternal being, is not the supreme being. Rather, Nous is ontologically inferior to the absolutely simple One. We may presume, then, that the One has a mode of reality superior to eternal or necessary existence: and Plotinus in fact says repeatedly that the One is "above Being," i.e., above that of which necessary existence is the truest form. What, then, can the One's mode of reality be? I discuss what is in effect an answer to this question in "God and Abstract Entities," *Faith and Philosophy* 7 (1990), 193–217.

24. Thus when Augustine and Boethius argue that God is both simple and eternal, they deliberately combine in a single concept of God characteristics Plotinus considered not only distinct but incompatible. Some have wondered whether the resulting amalgam is self-consistent. We will meet some of their worries later.

25. Moses Maimonides, *The Guide for the Perplexed*, tr. M. Friedländer (New York: Dover, 1956), I, chap. 63, p. 95.

26. For discussion of the eternity of Parmenides' One, see Sorabji, *TC&C*, pp. 98–107.

his concept of necessity, arguing in detail in *De caelo*, I, 12 that whatever exists eternally exists necessarily. Aristotle thus went beyond his predecessors in providing a rationale for the coupling. But Aristotle did not mean by "eternity" what his predecessors did. Rather, he seems to use the term "eternal" to express what we have called everlasting or omnitemporal existence. Repeatedly in *De caelo*, I, 12, he pairs eternal existence with existence through all of infinite time, and noneternal existence with coming and ceasing to be. Again, Aristotle writes in *De gen. et corr.* II, 11 that "what is of necessity coincides with what is always, since that which must be cannot possibly not be. Hence a thing is eternal if its being is necessary and if it is eternal, its being is necessary."[27] So far, then, it seems that Aristotle ties necessity and everlastingness. When he comes in the *Physics* to discuss what it means for a thing to be in time, he concludes that for a thing to be *in* time is for it to be *contained by* time, i.e., to not last for the whole of time.[28] Thus again, on Aristotle's view, an eternal being, a being not in time, is a being of infinite temporal duration.[29]

Does existing timelessly—in our sense, not Aristotle's—truly entail existing necessarily? That depends on what one means by "necessarily." In *De caelo*, Aristotle takes existing necessarily to be existing ingenerably and incorruptibly, i.e., being unable to come or cease to exist.[30] A timeless being cannot begin or cease to exist. For if it did, its beginning and ceasing to exist either would or would not have a date in time. If its beginning or ceasing were dated, this being's existence would have a first or last moment. Whatever has a first or last moment of existence is located in time. On the other hand, if this being's beginning or ceasing were not dated at any time, it would be dated at the "time" of eternity.

On the present account, a timeless being exists at no time, but only at the "null time," eternity. Hence whatever is true of that being alone must be true only at that "time." For any x, if x comes to be or ceases to be, then at one time "x exists" is true and at some other time "x does not exist" is true. These cannot both be true at the same time. If all truths about a timeless being are true only at the single "time" of eternity, then if a timeless being began or ceased to exist, "it exists" and

27. 338a1–4. Cf. also *An. Post.* I, 8 75b24–26, see 73a28–29, 73b26–27.
28. *Physics* IV, 12, 221a17–31.
29. So to the extent that later authors drew on Aristotle to support the claim that eternal existence entails necessary existence, they muddied the discussion. One possible example of such muddiness is Bonaventure, *QD de mysterio Trinitatis*, q. 5, a. 1.
30. *De caelo* I, 12, passim.

"it does not exist" would both have to be true at one "time." So a timeless being cannot come to be or cease to be.

Someone who rejects my treatment of eternity as logically a "time" might reject this last argument. But if one rejects the claim that eternity is a "time," one must also reject my suggestion that there is a distinct eternal tense, for if eternity is not a timelike locus that can stand in a peculiar relationship to our present, there is no rationale for such a tense. If one rejects an eternal tense, one also must reject a discrete-present tense, since as we have seen, from our perspective there is no difference between the two. If one rejects both eternal- and discrete-present tenses, then claims about a timeless being alone must be either tenseless or in an ordinary tense. Now if a timeless being ceases to exist, both "a timeless being exists" and "no timeless being exists" are somehow true. What is tenselessly true is true at all times. So if both claims are tenselessly true, both are true at all times, which is impossible. If only one is tenselessly true, then both are true at some time, which is impossible. If both statements are ordinarily tensed, this supposedly timeless being is temporal, for its beginning and ceasing to exist can be located in our past, present, or future. Hence again, a timeless being cannot cease (or begin) to exist. A timeless being must have the sort of necessary existence for which Aristotle argued.

Still, this does not render the existence of a timeless being absolutely necessary. What we have shown is that no possible world can include both the existing and the not-existing of a timeless being. But this does not entail that there cannot be two distinct possible worlds, one of which includes the existing of a timeless being and the other of which does not include it. I believe that on the concepts of *eternity* developed by Boethius and some other major Christian medievals, being eternal does entail existing with absolute necessity. But this turns out to be so not because eternity entails timelessness, but because of the connection between this concept of eternity and these writers' doctrines of divine simplicity.

Eternity, Simplicity, and Absolute Necessity

The claim that God is eternal is logically like the claim that some being is temporal. To say that a being is temporal is not so much to ascribe to it an attribute as to ascribe to it a *way* or *mode* of *having* attributes, or of existing. A temporal being has attributes and exists at times. An eternal being does not have attributes or exist at times; being eternal and being temporal are mutually exclusive modes of being. I argue later that eternity is in fact the mode of being appropriate and unique to a simple being. For now, let us premise the result of this argument and say that

    1. for all x, if x is eternal, x is simple.

(1) will allow us to show that whatever is eternal exists with absolute necessity. First, though, we must say a bit about the doctrine of divine simplicity.

Most mainstream medievals held that God is metaphysically simple. Despite differences in philosophical vocabulary, the vast majority of them meant the same thing by this claim. Writers with differing philosophical resources available had different ideas about what sorts of metaphysical distinctions or complexity the world contained. But to say that God is metaphysically simple is to say that whatever such sorts of distinction or complexity there are, none is to be found in God. So differences in writers' stocks of distinctions and modes of complexity do not entail differences in their doctrines of divine simplicity.[31]

The claim that God is metaphysically simple asserts that God exemplifies no metaphysical distinctions of any sort. This means, for instance, that whether or not it is true that God is good, if God is simple, it is false that God is the subject of a distinct attribute, goodness. Rather, if God is simple, "God is good" is true because of precisely the same SOA making "God is God" true, and this "SOA" contains no components or complexity of any sort. To put it another way, if God is simple, that in God which makes it correct to call Him good is in no way distinct from that which makes it correct to call Him God.

We give the name "goodness" to that in a thing which makes it correct to call it good. So we can rephrase our example this way: if God is simple, then God is identical with goodness, or with His goodness. (We will see below that the difference does not matter.) More generally, if God is simple, then for all F, if God is really F, God is identical with Fness. The qualification "really" alludes to the common distinction between real and "mere Cambridge" attributes. Examples of real attributes include being red, round, and smart. Examples of mere Cambridge attributes include being envied by the mob and being thought about by Ronald Reagan. One could say that whereas real attributes really are attributes of their subjects, mere Cambridge at-

---

31. This is not quite right, but the further precisions needed do not affect the point that all the writers concerned here have the same doctrine of divine simplicity. I hope to offer a fuller account in this book's sequel, *Divine Simplicity*.

tributes are merely shadows cast on their subjects by real attributes of other subjects: it is because Ronald Reagan has the real attribute of thinking of me that I have the merely Cambridge attribute of being thought about by Ronald Reagan. No generally recognized criterion for sorting attributes as "real" or "mere Cambridge" exists. But the two sorts of attribute clearly differ, and it is clear in most cases which attributes are of which sort.

Having real attributes involves some sort of real complexity. A human being is in reality a much more complex sort of entity than a round, red afterimage, and one can represent this complexity by saying that human beings have many more real attributes than afterimages. It seems intuitively, though, that I do not become any the more complex really if first one person, then another, and then a whole crowd begin to think about me. That only real attributes entail real complexity is the reason the doctrine of divine simplicity identifies God with only His real attributes. Having distinct mere Cambridge attributes would not import any real complexity into the divine being.

If God is simple, all statements about God are true or false in virtue of the same SOA, and this SOA involves no metaphysical complexity. It may, however, involve what one could call *theological* complexity. Boethius, Anselm, Aquinas, and most other major Latin medievals were orthodox Christians. They therefore were Trinitarians, holding that God's intrinsic reality includes three objectively distinct divine Persons, and so had to worry about whether the Trinity and total divine simplicity are compatible. Aquinas meets this concern by saying (in effect) that he maintains only God's *metaphysical* simplicity.[32] That is, on Aquinas' view, God is simple relative to the distinctions metaphysics is equipped to make, and yet Trinitarian theology affirms that God is complex relative to further distinctions theology alone is equipped to draw.

But let us leave Trinitarian considerations aside. The doctrine of divine simplicity just presented seems to have a bizarre consequence. If God is identical with an attribute or attributes, does it not follow that He is an attribute or some other sort of abstract entity? Aquinas explicitly affirms that a simple God appears abstract at *ST* Ia 13, 1 *ad* 2, noting that names "which are given to signify simple forms signify something not as subsisting in itself but as that by which something exists, just as 'whiteness' signifies as that by which something is white . . . because God too is simple . . . we ascribe to Him abstract

32. Again, I hope to discuss this in *Divine Simplicity*.

names to signify His simplicity."[33] For Thomas, "whiteness," an abstract name, signifies not something that exists independently, an Aristotelian substance, but an attribute, by having which a substance is
white. Thomas insists that because He is simple, we at times must,
e.g., call God not just good but goodness, giving Him an abstract
"name" appropriate to an attribute. Evidently, then, Thomas thinks
that God's simplicity renders Him significantly attributelike.

It would, however, be a bit hasty to conclude forthwith that a simple
God just is an attribute or is attributelike in respects that rule out His
being personal.[34] If God = goodness, then where one might have
thought that there were two subjects of predication, God and goodness, there is just one. This one subject has all the attributes God really
has and all the attributes goodness really has. But it does not necessarily have any particular subset of the attributes we thought goodness
(or God) to have before hearing that God = goodness. Thomas' God
may be in some ways attributelike, but we are not forced to say that He
is an attribute or other abstract entity. We could just as easily say that as
God = His attributes, all talk of divine attributes is just an abstract way
to speak about the simple yet nonabstract being that is God, or say that
the case of a simple being is like a quantum mechanical "two model"
situation, in which some x is incompletely yet truly known when
described either as God or as goodness. (Aquinas would likely say the
latter.)[35] The mere truth of the statement that God = goodness does
not settle the matter.

There will be more to say about simplicity and abstractness below.
For now, though, let us show that a simple being has at least one
attribute usually associated with (some) abstract entities, that of existing with absolute necessity if at all. To show this, we need only a
definition and two uncontroversial premises. The definition is that

   D. an individual essence of an individual x = df. an attribute that
       x exemplifies in every possible world in which x exists and
       that nothing other than x exemplifies in any possible world.

33. "Quae autem imponuntur ad significandas formas simplices significant aliquid
non ut subsistens sed ut quo aliquid est, sicut albedo significat ut quo aliquid est album.
Quia . . . et Deus simplex est . . . attribuimus ei nomina abstracta ad significandam
simplicitatem ejus." *ST* Ia 13, 1 *ad* 2, in *Summa theologiae* (New York: McGraw-Hill,
1964–), vol. 3, p. 50.
34. As does Alvin Plantinga, *Does God Have a Nature?* (Milwaukee: Marquette University Press, 1980), pp. 27–47.
35. See *ST* Ia 13, 1 *ad* 2, and *ST* Ia 13, 9.

By definition, a simple being is identical with its attributes. Thus necessarily,

> 2. for all x, if x is simple, x = x's individual essence.

Now if x is possible in a world W, then x's individual essence is exemplifiable in W, for this is just what it is for x to be possible in W. As we are assuming actualism, we are taking it that only entities exist-ing in W have attributes in W. Accordingly, if x's individual essence has in W the attribute of being exemplifiable, x's individual essence exists in W. The upshot is that

> 3. for all x and all worlds w, if x is possible in w, x's individual essence exists in w.[36]

(2) and (3), conjoined, entail that

> 4. for all x and all worlds w, if x is simple, then if x is possible in w, x exists in w.

In S5, absolute possibility does not vary over possible worlds; whatever is possible in one is possible in all. So if S5 gives the logic of absolute possibility, then

> 5. for all x, if x is simple, then if x is possible, x exists in all possible worlds.

(1) and (5) conjoined entail that

> 6. for all x, if x is eternal, then if x exists in one possible world, x exists in all.

Via the doctrine of divine simplicity, eternal existence does entail abso-lutely necessary existence. It is not clear that merely *timeless* existence entails necessary existence, for it is not clear that necessarily, every timeless being is a simple being. We can conceive of apparently time-less beings that are in various ways complex, e.g., propositions that contain many constituents, sets that contain many members, and the

---

36. Note, incidentally, that via (2) and (3), the doctrine of divine simplicity generates its own version of the ontological argument. For a brief development of this argument, see my "Individual and Attribute in the Ontological Argument," *Faith and Philosophy* 7 (1990), 235–242.

deities of many theologies. If these things do not even possibly exist, then in fact, timelessness entails simplicity. But we have no space to try to show that they do not. Further, we can conceive of apparently timeless beings that exist contingently, e.g., sets with contingent members or singular propositions as conceived in the theory discussed at this chapter's outset. Perhaps singular propositions do not have the nature we have discussed, and perhaps sets are not truly timeless. But again, we do not have the space to discuss these things and so cannot conclude that timelessness entails necessity.

Eternity and Uniqueness

Given the connection between eternity and simplicity, we can also show that there necessarily is at most one eternal being. This is so because there can be at most one simple being. For suppose that there are two actual simple beings, A and B. Then A is simple and also has whatever attribute or set of attributes suffices for identity with A. Now the attribute of simplicity either is or is not identical with the attribute or attributes sufficient for identity with A. If it is, and B is simple, then B = A, and we have only one simple being. If it is not, then A is not simple, and as B alone is simple, we again have only one simple being. We can go even further. If it is absolutely possible that there is a simple being, A, then

7. possibly the attribute of simplicity = the attribute of identity with A.

Attribute–identities are absolutely necessary. Hence (7) entails that

8. possibly, necessarily the attribute of simplicity = the attribute of identity with A.

We are assuming that S5 gives the logic of absolute modality. It is a theorem of S5 that possibly necessarily P entails necessarily P. Hence (8) entails that

9. necessarily the attribute of simplicity = the attribute of identity with A.

So it is not even possible that there be a simple being not identical with A. Thus if there is an eternal being, it is not even possible that there be an eternal being not identical with that being. On the other hand, if there is no eternal being, then because an eternal being exists in all possible worlds if in any, there can be no eternal being in any possible world. So to speak, at most one possible individual is eternal, and even that one is possibly so only if it is actually so.

The Position to Date

The conclusions so far reached about eternity and about timeless beings add up to this position. A timeless being is related to time as a second time series would be. It does not exist earlier, later than, or at the same time as anything. Nor are truths about it alone true at any time. For just this reason, one can call a timeless being immediately contiguous with every time and every temporal thing: timelessness carries with it a peculiar sort of omnipresence to time. Yet despite its temporal omnipresence, one cannot use any ordinary tense to speak of a timeless being, nor can one in strict propriety speak of it tenselessly. Rather, proper discourse of a timeless being requires a discrete- or eternal-present tense. I have suggested that a timeless being exists at a "time" because it exists at eternity: eternity, the null date, is the "date" at which it has attributes and exists. Thus I have called eternity logically a "time" even though it has no temporal properties. Finally, I have argued that "x is timeless" is a claim necessary *de dicto et re* and that eternity (as distinct from timelessness) entails absolutely necessary existence and absolute uniqueness.

[5]

Augustine: Eternality
as Truest Existence

Having completed the formal preliminaries, let us put flesh on the concept of eternity. Augustine's thinking was the core that determined the broad outlines of all that later medieval philosophical theology made of the concept of God. So Augustine's thought about eternity is an appropriate place to begin our investigation.

Augustine's thinking was shaped by a basic conviction of the Neo-Platonic metaphysics he absorbed before his conversion to Christianity, that "true" existence is immutable existence:

> That which is changed does not retain its own being, and that which can be changed, even if it is not actually changed, is able not to be that which it had been. For this reason, only that which not only is not changed, but also is even unable to be changed in any way, is most truly said to be.[1]

> Being is a name for immutability. For all things that are changed cease to be what they were, and begin to be what they were not. Nobody has true being, pure being, real being except one who does not change . . . What does "I am who am" mean but "I am eternal . . . I cannot be changed"?[2]

---

1. "Quod enim mutatur non servat ipsum esse, et quod mutari potest, etiamsi non mutetur, potest fuerat non esse: ac per hoc illud solum quod non tantum non mutatur, verum etiam mutari omnino non potest, sine scrupula occurrit quod verissime dicatur esse." Augustine, *The Trinity*, Bk. V, ii, 3, Benedictine text, in *Oeuvres de Saint Augustin* (Paris: Desclée de Brouwer, 1955)(henceforth *Oeuvres*), vol. 15, p. 428.

2. "Esse, nomen est incommutabilitatis. Omnia enim quae mutantur desinunt esse quod erant et incipiunt esse quod non erant. Esse verum, esse sincerum, esse germanum non habet nisi qui non mutatur . . . Quid est, Ego sum qui sum, nisi . . . Aeternus sum . . . mutari non possum?" Augustine, Sermon 7, 7, in J. P. Migne, ed., *Patrologia Latina* (Paris, 1841), vol. 38, p. 65.

God . . . truly exists because he is unchangeable.[3]

Augustine asserts not just that immutable objects are "most truly said to be" but that changeable objects are less truly said to be, declaiming, "What is that which exists? That which is eternal. For what is always different does not exist, because it does not remain: not that it wholly does not exist, but it does not exist in the highest way."[4] So like his Neo-Platonist mentors, Augustine held that

    1. Existence is a matter of degree.

As will emerge, (1) need not mean that there is a status between existing and not existing. It does, however, entail that some objects do not truly exist and yet are not simply nonexistent in the way fictional or dream objects are: "God so exists that compared with Him, things which were made do not exist. If they are not compared with Him, they exist, since they are from Him. But if they are compared, they do not exist, because to exist truly is to exist immutably, which He alone is."[5] "We cannot say that what does not remain exists, nor can we say that what has come and is passing does not exist."[6]

    If "being is a name for immutability," then "being" *means* immutability, and to have maximal-degree or truest existence includes being maximally immutable, or unchangeable in all respects. Augustine states that "to exist truly is to exist immutably." So for Augustine, to exist truly *includes* existing immutably, which is existing and being unable to change with respect to existing, i.e., unable to cease to exist. Let us say that something that is maximally immutable and exists immutably is totally immutable, or TI. Then Augustine holds not just that whatever has truest existence is TI but that the predicate "has truest existence" includes in its meaning "is TI." Thus, according to Augustine, "one should say to exist most highly what . . . cannot in any

---

    3. "Deus . . . vere . . . est, quia incommutabilis est." Augustine, *The Nature of Good*, 19, in *S. Aur. Augustini: Opera omnia* (Paris: Gaume Fratres, 1836)(henceforth *Opera*), vol. 8, p. 780.
    4. "Quid est quod est? Quod aeternum est. Nam quod semper aliter atque aliter est, non est, quia non manet: non omnino non est, sed non summe est." Augustine, *Commentary on Psalm 121*, 5, 6, *Opera*, vol. 4, p. 1978.
    5. "Ita enim ille est, ut in ejus comparatione ea quae facta sunt, non sint. Illo non comparato sunt, quoniam ab illo sunt: illi autem, comparata, non sunt, quia verum esse incommutibile esse est, quod ille solus est." Augustine, *Commentary on Psalm 134*, 4, *Opera*, vol. 4, p. 2130.
    6. "nec esse possumus dicere quod non stat, nec non esse quod venit et transit." Augustine, *Commentary on Psalm 38*, 7, *Opera*, vol. 4, p. 446.

part cease to exist or be changed . . . *for the signification of this word* *["existence"] includes 'a nature remaining in itself and having itself immutably.'*"[7] For present purposes, though, we need ascribe to Augustine only a weaker claim to which his meaning-claim commits him, that

> 2. For all x, x has highest-degree existence iff x is TI.

Augustine holds that necessarily, if something is eternal, it is maximally immutable, affirming that "even if something lives forever, still, if it is changeable, it is not properly called eternal."[8] Beyond this, Augustine thinks that if something is eternal, its existence has no endpoints.[9] If this is so, then an eternal individual can cease to exist only if it can first be eternal, then become temporal, and *then* cease to exist. But becoming temporal would be a change, and an eternal being cannot change. So even though, strictly speaking, ceasing to exist is not a change, Augustine also holds that necessarily, if something is eternal, it exists immutably. Thus Augustine holds that necessarily, if something is eternal, it is TI.

Augustine also affirms, "What is unchangeable is eternal, for it always exists in the same state."[10] But we have already seen that nothing is eternal unless it exists immutably. So we can infer that for Augustine, whatever is immutable and exists immutably—i.e., is TI—is eternal. We will see that when a writer such as Augustine asserts that something is eternal, he asserts not just that it is timeless but that it is simple. But if we ignore divine simplicity for now, we may say that in Augustine's eyes.

> 3. for all x, x is timeless iff x is TI.

(2) and (3) together yield

> 4. for all x, x is timeless iff x has highest-degree existence.[11]

---

7. "Hoc enim maxime esse dicendum est quod . . . quod nulla ex parte corrumpi ac mutari potest . . . Subest enim huic verbo manentis in se atque incommutabiliter sese habentis naturae significatio." Augustine, *The Ways of the Church*, II, i, 1, *Opera*, vol. 1, p. 1157. Emphasis mine.

8. "etsi semper aliquid vivat, tamen si mutabilitatem patiatur, non proprie aeternum appellatur." Augustine, *Eighty-Three Different Questions*, q. 19, *Oeuvres*, vol. 10, p. 68.

9. Augustine, *Civitas Dei*, bk. XI, chap. 11.

10. "Quod incommutabile est aeternum est: semper enim ejusdem modi est." Augustine, *Eighty-Three Different Questions*, q. 19, *Oeuvres*, vol. 10, p. 68.

11. (4) includes the claim that for all x, if x is timeless, x has highest-degree existence. This can seem false; are timeless truths "as real as" God? Part of the reason

In conjunction with the claim that temporal things exist, (1) and (4) entail

> 5. temporal existence is a status "between" highest-degree existence and nonexistence.

Augustine, then, holds (1)–(5). What do (1)–(5) mean? Why does Augustine believe these strange things? Is there any truth to (1)–(5)? These are the questions this chapter tries to answer.

Timelessness and Being TI

As we can discuss (3) without broaching the broader metaphysical considerations that occupy the rest of this chapter, let us turn to it first. (3) is a conjunction of

> 3a. for all x, if x is TI, x is timeless, and
> 3b. for all x, if x is timeless, x is TI.

(3b) appears clearly true. For we have seen that a timeless being cannot cease to exist and so exists immutably. Again, if something changes, first it satisfies a predicate, then it satisfies that predicate's complement: for instance, when a man's face goes pale, first he satisfies "is not pale-faced" and then he satisfies "is pale-faced." One and the same thing can satisfy a predicate and its complement only if it exists at at least two times, satisfying the predicate at one and the complement at the other. So whatever changes must exist at at least two times. A timeless being exists, but exists only at one "time," eternity. Thus a timeless being cannot change.

Let us turn to (3a). (3a) is true if

> 3c. for all x, if x is immutable, x is timeless,

since whatever is TI is immutable. But (3c) is questionable. Being unchangeable in all respects does not entail not coming or ceasing to exist, as these are not changes. An object changes at t only if it is in one

---

Augustine is willing to affirm (4), I believe, is that in his view there can be only one truly timeless entity, namely, God. (2) includes the claim that for all x, if x is TI, x has highest-degree existence. This, too, can seem false, as timeless truths are TI. Again, Augustine may be willing to affirm this because he thinks that only God is truly TI; if God is the creator of all that is not somehow an aspect of Himself and can annihilate whatever He can create, only God and things that are somehow aspects of God are TI.

state up to t and in a different state from t on. But an object that begins
to exist at t was in no state prior to t, as it did not exist then, and an
object that ceases to exist at t is in no state from t on, as it does not exist
then. Hence being immutable is compatible with coming or ceasing to
exist. This is reason to think it possible that something come or cease
to exist and yet neither change nor be able to change while it exists. But
what comes or ceases to exist does so at some time and so exists in
time. Thus we have reason to think that (3c) may be false. Further, we
have reason to think that (3c) *is* false. For we have already spoken of a
temporal yet immutable kind of entity, events of beginning. Beginnings take place at times but cannot be temporally extended or continue; an event of beginning *cannot* last. Thus a beginning cannot extend over two discrete times, and so a beginning cannot change. Such
an event is located in time and yet immutable. We have seen that there
are in fact events of beginning. Accordingly, something can be immutable and yet be temporal. Thus it seems that (3c) is false.

Aquinas affirms (3c), stating that "being eternal follows from immutability . . . Hence since God is maximally immutable, it supremely
belongs to Him to be eternal."[12] He backs (3c) by claiming that
"time . . . is just the measure of motion by before and after . . . Those
things are said to be measured by time which have a beginning and an
end in time . . . because in everything which is moved there is a beginning and an end."[13] "Time measures not only actually changed things,
but also changeable things. Hence it not only measures motion, but
also rest, which is the state of a thing which is naturally movable but is
not actually being moved."[14] Thomas' view is that as only things that
do or can change are "measured" by time, what cannot change is not
"measured" by time, and so is timeless.[15] Now a "measure" is a met-
ric, a way of charting relations among things. So Thomas claims in
effect that time is a system of relations among things that possibly or

12. "Ratio aeternitatis consequitur immutabilitatem . . . Unde cum Deus sit maxime immutabilis sibi maxime competit esse aeternum." Aquinas, *ST* Ia 10, 2, in T.
McDermott, ed., *Summa theologiae* (London: Blackfriars, 1964), vol. 2 (henceforth *Summa*, vol. 2), p. 138.

13. "tempus . . . nihil aliud est quam numerus motum secundum prius et posteri-
us . . . Item, ea dicuntur tempore mensurare quae principium et finem habent in tempore . . . et hoc ideo quia in omni eo quod movetur est accipere aliquod principium et
aliquem finem." Aquinas, *ST* Ia, 10, 1, in *Summa*, vol. 2, p. 136.

14. "Tempus enim mensurat non solum quae transmutantur in actu sed quae sunt
transmutabilia. Unde non solum mensurat motum sed etiam quietem quae est ejus
quod natum est moveri et non movetur." *ST* Ia 10, 4 *ad* 3, in *Summa*, vol. 2, p. 136.

15. For Thomas' taking "motion" or "movement" as terms for change generally, see
ST Ia 2, 2.

16. *ST* Ia 10, 5. The qualification "by natural means" takes into account Thomas'

actually change and (as he makes clear elsewhere)[16] possibly cease to exist by purely natural means. We noted earlier that the primary occupants of time are not things. So we can rephrase Thomas' claim this way: time is a system of relations between the changes of things that can cease to be by natural means, and things are *in* time derivatively, standing in temporal relations if and only if they possibly undergo changes that stand in these relations.[17] This is certainly a reasonable claim, though it would be simpler and more plausible to say that time is a system of relations between *all* changes. But if we grant Thomas' claim or its simpler counterpart, the move from immutability to timelessness is easy. For an immutable being is precisely one that does not possibly change in any respect. Therefore, such a being lacks the prerequisite for standing in temporal relations and so is timeless.

Thus Thomas' argument that immutability entails timelessness seems valid. But one cannot judge it sound. One of Thomas' key premises is that

6. a thing is in time only if it possibly changes.

If there are events of beginning, (6) is false. If we accommodate this by weakening (6) to

6a. a thing is in time and noninstantaneous only if it possibly changes,

(6a) will not yield the conclusion that what cannot change is atemporal. Further, suppose that one countered this problem by arguing that there cannot be a real instantaneous event. This would preserve (6), but (6) is equivalent to the conclusion Thomas seeks, that a thing is unchangeable only if it is not in time. So as Thomas offers no real independent backing for (6), to judge Thomas' argument sound would beg the question at issue.

Paul Helm argues that whether or not immutability entails time-

---

distinguishing of a third mode of being, aeveternity, lying "between" temporality and eternality. An aeveternal being does not possibly cease to exist by natural means (ibid.), but as in Thomas' eyes God can annihilate all nondivine beings (see *ST* Ia 104, 3), it would be false to say that aeveternal beings are distinguished from temporal beings because the latter can and the former cannot cease to exist.

17. Thomas' Aristotelian predilection for tracing everything back to concrete material things keeps him from putting it this way. But his claim is expressly modal. In explaining why time measures rest as well as motion, he asserts that time measures the changeable whether or not it is actually changing. This is equivalent to saying that a thing exists in time iff it possibly undergoes an appropriate sort of change at some time.

lessness, God's being immutable would entail God's being timeless: "A God who acts but is immutable . . . must be timelessly eternal, since any action in time (as opposed to an action the effect of which is in time) presupposes a time before the act, and a time when the act is completed, and thus presupposes real change."[18] Helm's argument is this:

7. Necessarily, if anything is God, it acts.
8. Necessarily, every temporal act is of finite duration. Therefore
9. Necessarily, every temporal agent changes in every act from acting to not-acting or vice versa. Therefore
10. Necessarily, if God is temporal, God changes. Therefore
11. Necessarily, if God does not change, God is not temporal. Therefore
12. Necessarily, if God cannot change, God cannot be temporal.

But (8) and (9) seem false, and it also seems that (8) does not entail (9). Suppose that God is temporal and exists at every moment of time, and that at every moment, God sustains a universe in existence. In this case, if time had no first moment, neither did God's sustaining a universe, and if time will have no last moment, God will never cease to sustain a world. I find nothing incoherent or absurd in the claims that some deity is omnitemporal and everlastingly has sustained and will sustain a world. If these claims are consistent, it appears that (8) is false: possibly some temporal agent performs an act of infinite duration. Moreover, (9) too is false, for in this case God never changes from not sustaining to sustaining the world or vice versa. False also is the weaker claim that

9a. Necessarily, a temporal agent changes at some time (if not in every single action),

for it is not hard to fill out the claim that God is everlasting and everlastingly sustains the world in a way that shields God from all real change. Finally, (8) does not entail (9). A change occurs at t only if the object that changes was in one state until t and is in a different state from t on. So if an object begins to perform a certain act at its first moment of existence, its doing that is not a change in it. For like reasons, if that object continues to perform its act for its whole duration, then ceases to exist, its ceasing to do that act is not a change in it. Now it seems possible that there be a thing that performs just one act,

18. Paul Helm, *Eternal God* (New York: Oxford University Press, 1988), p. 90.

performs that act at every moment it exists, and exists for a finite time. But if this is possible, then even if every temporal act were of finite duration, a temporal agent could still act without changing from acting to not-acting or vice versa. That is, even if (8) were true, (9) could be false.

Since we have no clearly sound argument for (3c) and have a strong argument against (3c), it appears that (3c) is false. But if (3c) is not available to back it up, there so far seems little reason to believe (3a). It certainly seems imaginable that something endure changeless throughout the length of time, and so we have reason to call this possible. But if this can happen in one possible world, perhaps it could happen that some temporal entity endure changeless in every world in which it exists. For perhaps some entity can exist only in a literally unique set of possible circumstances—i.e., in one possible world—and perhaps in these circumstances, it is changeless throughout its existence. Hence it appears that something temporal and permanent could be immutable. Again, it is not obviously unreasonable to hold that an immutable permanent thing that coexisted with changing, temporal things would thereby be enmeshed in time. So though (3b) is clearly true, (3a) remains in doubt. Let us now turn to (1) and (2).

Two Problems

One initial difficulty Augustine faces is that speaking of existence as a matter of degree is just bizarre. Logicians gloss such questions as "do Fs exist" as "is there at least one F." For any F, the question "is there at least one F" admits only a straight yes-or-no answer. There can be no such thing as greater or lesser degrees of there being one of anything. This is so even if the concept of an F is vague, and so (as some writers argue)[19] the statement "there is an F here" admits of truth-values between 0 (false) and 1 (true). I am not at all sure what it could mean to say that this statement has (say) a truth-value of .5. But if it would mean that there is a half an F here, this would just entail that the answer to "is there at least one F" is a straightforward no. If it would mean that there is an F here with half-strength existence, this would just entail that the answer to "is there at least one F" is a straightforward yes. If it would mean that an F is halfway to being here, this would just entail that the answer to "is there at least one F" is no, not yet.

Augustine's second problem is that even if one is willing to play

---

along with the degree-of-reality game, one will likely resist his conclusions. Augustine ascribes higher-degree existence to the immutable and timeless, lower to the changeful and temporal. Further, for him, immutability and timelessness are marks of higher-degree existence. This cannot but seem strange to us. Surely, we reason, concrete material things that one can touch and see and alter are "really real," and the Platonist's abstractions are at best pale and ghostly, impoverished entities barely real at all.

Still, these problems are not insurmountable. Even if "is there at least one" admits only a yes-or-no answer, one can nuance such an answer. One can reply "yes, but barely," write yes boldly or faintly, or speak it loudly or softly. If the appropriate conventions exist, these nuances can be informative. So perhaps such nuances can let us speak of degrees of existence without having to say that "is there at least one" admits answers other than yes or no, or that there are truth-values between 0 and 1. Perhaps what writers like Augustine mean by allowing degrees of existence is not that one existing object has more existence than another or that one true assertion of existence is truer than another, but that one object has more intense, full, or genuine existence than another, or that one assertion of existence is better founded than another. As for the second problem, the considerations that led Neo-Platonists to speak of existence as degreed have become unfamiliar to us. So it is only to be expected that resurrecting them may challenge our initial opinions about the superior reality of the concrete. I now develop three ways to understand degrees of existence.

Genuineness of Existence

We do use a degreed idea of *reality* in everyday contexts: for instance, we distinguish "a real man" from those less manly. In such cases, degrees of reality are degrees of genuineness. If we call John Wayne a real man and say that Caspar Milquetoast is not much of a man, we say that both are men, but one is more truly, fully, or intensely masculine than the other. Let us note two things about such cases. First, we call one man more genuinely a man than another in accord with definite criteria of manliness, e.g., hairiness of chest or depth of voice. If we did not have such criteria, we would not know what we were saying in calling one man more manly than another. Talk of being more truly a man may even be just a shorthand for judgments in accord with these criteria; perhaps we could eliminate this talk in favor of comparisons of chest hair, vocal timbre, and so on. Second, that someone is a more genuine man the more he is like a fully genuine man looks like a conceptual truth. This truth renders the fully genuine man a paradigm for the less genuine man, and the less genuine man a mere approximation to the most.

The claim that timeless beings have higher-degree existence than temporal could assert that they are more real than temporal beings, i.e., could mean that in some way, timeless beings are more genuine than temporal. If it is true that John Wayne is more genuinely a man than Caspar Milquetoast, this is because for some range of attributes F that are relevant to masculinity, John Wayne is more genuinely, fully, or intensely F than Caspar Milquetoast. Might Augustine mean by "timeless beings are more existent than temporal beings" that for some range of attributes F in respect of which one can compare timeless and temporal beings, the timeless being always turns out to be the more genuine F?

This proposal would not get Augustine far. There are few if any attributes possessed by both timeless and temporal things. According to Plato, temporal particular triangles are called triangles because they "imitate" a timeless exemplar, the Form of triangle.[20] But are Plato's Form of triangle and particular triangles all alike triangles? Do they share triangularity, and can they be compared with respect to it? Plato himself learned that this assumption is rife with paradox.[21] Even if we assume that the Form of F is an F, though, it will not follow that Forms are more real Fs than particulars. If a human being is by nature alive, and the Form of Humanity is not alive, then even if in some strained sense the Form is human, it is hard to see how the Form is more genuinely human than the particular. Moreover, Augustine says that timeless things are more real than temporal *precisely because* they are timeless, or because they have whatever underlying feature accounts for their timelessness. But this is not what we would expect him to say were he comparing the attributes of temporal and timeless beings. For it would seem fairer to say that if a timeless Form of humanity is human at all, it is so despite rather than because of its timelessness.

Still, even if the timeless and the temporal share nothing else, they share existence.[22] I therefore suggest that when Augustine says that timeless beings have higher-degree existence than temporal beings, his claim is that timeless existence is more genuinely existence than temporal, that timeless beings exist more genuinely than temporal ones, and that temporal ones exist at all only insofar as they exist like timeless

20. See, e.g., Plato, *Phaedo*, 74–78e.
21. See Plato, *Parmenides*, passim.
22. Which according to many philosophers is not an attribute.

ones.[23] Plato expressed this thought when he wrote that time is "a moving image of eternity," created to be as like eternity as a noneternal duration could be.[24] Under the influence of Augustine and Plato, Boethius put it this way:

> Eternity . . . is the perfect possession all at once of interminable life . . . The infinite changing of things in time is an attempt to imitate this state of presentness of a changeless life, but since it cannot equal that state, it falls from changelessness into change, from the simplicity of the present into the infinite quantity of past and future . . . by the very fact that it is impossible for its existence ever to come to an end, it does seem in some measure to emulate that which it cannot fulfill or express. It does this by attaching itself to some sort of presence in this small and fleeting moment, and since this presence bears a certain resemblance to that abiding present, it confers on whatever possesses it the appearance of being that which it imitates.[25]

We can judge one man more a man than another because we have criteria by which to judge manliness. So to speak of a more real *mode of existence,* we also need criteria of genuineness. One's criteria of more genuine manhood presumably are rooted in one's view of the nature and function of masculinity; it is because of what one thinks it is to be a man that one judges men to be more manly the more (say) they are like John Wayne. So Augustine's criterion of being more genuinely existent will be rooted in his understanding of what it is for something to exist.

Genuine Existence

Augustine holds a tensed theory of time, on which only presently existing beings exist and only presently exemplified attributes are exemplified. He makes this plain in such passages as these: "How then

23. I discuss shortly just how there can be resemblance with respect to existence.
24. Plato, *Timaeus,* 37c–d, tr. Benjamin Jowett, in Edith Hamilton and Huntington Cairns, eds., *Plato: The Collected Dialogues* (Princeton, N.J.: Princeton University Press, 1961), p. 1167.
25. "Aeternitas . . . est interminabilis vitae tota simul et perfecta possessio . . . Hunc enim vitae immobilis praesentarium statum infinitus ille temporalium rerum motus imitatur cumque eum effingere atque aequare non possit, ex immobilitate deficit in motum, ex simplicitate praesentiae decrescit in infinitam futuri ac praeteriti quantitatem . . . hoc ipso quod aliquo modo numquam esse desinit, illud quod implere atque exprimere non potest, aliquatenus videtur aemulari alligans se ad qualemcumque praesentiam huius exigui volucrisque momenti, quae, quoniam manentis illius praesentiae quandam gestat imaginem, quibuscumque contigerit id praestat ut esse videantur." Boethius, *Philosophiae consolationis,* V, prose VI, in Stewart and Rand, eds., *Boethius,* ll. 9–11, 40–53, pp. 400, 402. Tr. partly that of V. E. Watts.

can these two times, the past and the future, exist, when the past now does not exist and the future does not yet exist? . . . The past now does not exist, and the future does not yet exist. Therefore we should not say 'It is long,' but we should say of the past 'It was long' and of the future 'It will be long.' "26 "Everything past now does not exist, everything future does not yet exist, therefore nothing past and nothing future exists."27 For Augustine, then, genuine existence is present existence. Boethius picks up on this. For him, time imitates eternity (and so is a mode of existence) only insofar as it is present, and time falls short of imitating eternity (and so fails to be a mode of existence) insofar as it fails to remain present.

In asserting that timeless existence is more genuine than temporal, then, Augustine and Boethius assert that timeless beings are more genuinely present in eternity than temporal ones are in time. One can show this to be a reasonable claim given only a tensed theory of time and an uncontroversial account of what it is to be temporal.

To be temporal is either to exist for only a moment, as does an instantaneous event, or to exist for an extended period of time. There is no past or future within the span of an instantaneous event. But something is an instantaneous temporal event iff it has a past or a future in the sense (and only in the sense) that other events and states are past or future to it. Other events and states are past or future to a temporal continuant's existence. But something is a temporal continuant iff in addition, at any moment, some of its span of duration is only past or only future. Now on a tensed theory of time, to exist = to be present. Thus for such a theory, if a timeless being exists, it ipso facto is in some sense present. But if a being is present and also has a portion of its duration as past or future or has events or states in its past or future, it is temporal. Hence a timeless being exists in a present to which nothing is past or future, and within its duration nothing is past or future. If this is so, then arguably, timeless beings are more genuinely present than temporal beings: for they are present without taint of past or future.

One can argue in a second way that timeless beings are more genuinely present in eternity than temporal ones are in time. Whatever is timeless is changeless. If a being is changeless, that of it which is

<hr/>

26. "duo ergo illa tempora, praeteritum et futurum, quomodo sunt, quando et praeteritum iam non est et futurum nondum est? . . . praeteritum enim iam non est et futurum nondum est. non itaque dicamus: longum est, sed dicamus de praeterito: longum fuit, et de futuro: longum erit." Augustine, *Confessions*, XI, 14–15, *Oeuvres*, vol. 14, p. 300, #275, ll. 22–24, and #276, ll. 8–11.

27. "Omne praeteritum jam non est, omne futurum nondum est, omne igitur et praeteritum et futurum deest." Augustine, *Eighty-Three Different Questions*, q. 17, *Oeuvres*, vol. 10, p. 66.

present is qualitatively identical with that of it which exists at any other time: it never was or will be other than it is.[28] Thus an unchanging being is fully present in that its entire character is manifest in its present existence—in fact, all that it ever is is fully present throughout its existence. A changing thing was or will be other than it now is. Hence its character is less than fully present at any moment—at no one moment does it have at once all the attributes it ever will have. Thus in this sense the changing thing itself is less than fully present. Moreover, if a thing is changeable, its actual attributes do not exhaust its character; it can come to have attributes that it does not ever actually have. So in a second way, the full character of such a being is not fully present at any one time. Thus an immutable thing is in this way more fully present than a changeable thing. For as there is nothing that an immutable thing can come to be, there is nothing that an immutable thing can come to be which is not manifest in its present state.

Let us call this kind of presence *character-presence*. That an immutable thing has maximal character-presence will not yield the claim that maximal presence is timeless presence. For immutability does not entail timelessness, and a necessarily instantaneous temporal being (such as a beginning) also has maximal character-presence: something that can exist only for an instant has in that instant all the attributes it can ever come to have. Thus one must bring in a second sort of presence, *existential presence*. This is the sort involved in the thought that something that is gone as soon as it arrives is "scarcely present at all." If this thought is true, it is false that instantaneous beings can be in all senses as fully present as noninstantaneous beings. Also, if there is this second sort of presentness, maximal presentness consists of the conjunction of the maxima of character- and existential presence (if both have maxima).

28. Since I am trying to build up an understanding of presentness that will let us compare the presentness of timeless and temporal beings, it is important to phrase the implications of presentness in ways that can apply to both timeless and temporal things. Thus I speak, e.g., of that of it which exists "at any other time." Yet my "canonical" view of timelessness rules out any claim that timeless beings exist at times or that truths about them are true at times. One can rephrase the text's claim in a way that will apply both to temporal beings and to timeless beings so understood. If one assumes that truth is tensed, i.e., that in some cases the set of true statements which one can make about some being now ≠ the set one can make about it at other times, then the rephrasing can be, "If a being is changeless, the set of true statements which one can make about it now = the set of true statements which one can make about it at any time." This rephrasing is canonical because it does not imply that the true statements we make now are true now. (It does *allow* this, though, and so applies to both timeless and temporal things). As such talk is awkward, I have spoken and will continue to speak as I do in the text. But all such claims can be canonically rephrased, and I am committed to the truth only of their canonical rephrasings.

Augustine does seem to think that a thing is not very genuinely present at t if at t it exists and is ephemeral, and is most present at t only if it exists at t and exists permanently after t: he insists, for instance, that "we cannot say that what does not remain exists."[29] Augustine's claim might be that being existentially more present = being more permanent. But arguably, it is instead that one perhaps-defeasible indicator of a greater degree of existential presence at t is a greater degree of permanence after t. For Augustine, I suggest, greater permanence is a mark of greater presentness and so of more genuine existence.

To begin to explore Augustine's claim, let us consider this analogy. One cannot observe at t which of two people before one at t is wiser at t. But by asking them questions or watching their actions over time, one may come to know that one was a good deal wiser than the other at t. Sometimes—e.g., in dealing with a dispositional quality—one can see how fully or intensely two particulars have a quality at t only by seeing the extent to which they manifest the characteristic effect of that quality after t. Now suppose that presence is something that admits of degrees. One can observe in one moment—say, just after t—that something is not present at t or that something is present at t, i.e., present in *some degree or other*. But one cannot observe in one moment just after t the precise degree of something's existential presence at t; it is not even clear what it would mean to say that one so observes this. If the most we can observe in one moment just after t is that a thing is present at t in some degree or other, only evidence from times still later than t can provide a basis for determining the degree of presence a thing had at t.

Augustine evidently takes greater permanence after t as the characteristic effect of truer presence at t. He may have found reason to do this in an Aristotelian dictum that became common classical coin. In *De interpretatione*, Aristotle writes that what is, necessarily is, when it is, "necessarily" bearing the sense of "fixedly" or "unalterably."[30] One can read this dictum *de dicto* or *de re*, i.e., as

13. fixedly, what is, when it is, is,

or as

14. what is, when it is, is fixedly.

---

29. Augustine, *Commentary on Psalm 38*, 7, *Opera*, vol. 4, p. 446. Again, in the quoted text of Boethius, time fails to imitate the "true existence" of the eternal precisely because it passes, and time imitates eternity just insofar as it is permanent, i.e., permanently passing.

30. Aristotle, *De interpretatione* I, 9, 19a23.

The Aristotelian dictum was usually invoked to explain a sense in which what is present is beyond an agent's control.[31] (13) will not perform this role, but (14) will. Thus (14) is likely what the dictum means. (14) is a reasonable claim. If a fact is already established and present, it is too late to prevent its obtaining. For us it is as fixed and unalterable as the past; it can no longer be affected. We can affect only whether it continues to be a fact.

Let us suppose that Augustine believed (14). Fixity is a degreed concept; some facts are more fixed than others. So perhaps Augustine holds that presentness is degreed because he connects an entity's presentness and the fixity of its existing. That is, perhaps Augustine reads (14) as

> 14a. what is present, to the extent that it is present, is present fixedly.

If (14a) is true and some present facts are more fixed than others, it is not unnatural to infer that some present facts are more present than others and that a present entity is more truly or intensely present the more fixedly it exists.[32] Further, fixity has the logic of a dispositional property. In effect, the fixity with which a thing exists is or is manifest in the thing's disposition to remain in existence for certain periods. Hence like a person's wisdom, it is a quality whose degree at t can be judged only by the appropriate behavior after t. Moreover, the more fixed a thing's existence is in the nature of things, the more immune to alteration the thing's existence is and the harder it should be to dislodge the thing from existing. The harder a thing's existence is to dislodge, other matters being equal, the longer the thing will exist, or so one would think a priori. Thus the fixity metaphor yields a rationale for Augustine's grading of things' existential presence according to how permanent they are.

Moreover, maximal fixity is immutable existence. This might seem false; it might seem that a necessarily existent being is as such more firmly fixed in existence than one that exists contingently and immutably.[33] For an immutably but not necessarily existent being cannot cease to exist, but still might simply have failed to exist and so (one might argue) is less firmly "rooted" in reality than one that could not have

31. Much later, Aquinas used it this way, at *ST* Ia 14, 13 *ad* 2.
32. (14a) does not license the argument "the facts about the past are unalterable; therefore they are present." For (14a) ranks only present facts.
33. Arguably, Augustine lacked the modal apparatus to distinguish necessary from immutable existence. (A good account of related inadequacies in late-classical modal theories is White, *Agency and Integrality*.)

failed to exist. But the difference between necessary and immutable existence, though real, is irrelevant. To say that a thing's existence is maximally fixed is to say that its existence is maximally rooted in the actual history of the world, i.e., that it exists in all possible continuations of any past segment of the world's history. An immutably existent being exists in all worlds that continue any past segment of the world's history and so in all worlds in which any segment of that history exists. Hence any world in which a necessarily existent being would exist and an immutably existent being would not is a world in which no segment of the world's past history would exist. But such worlds are irrelevant to the evaluation of fixity *in the sense of rootedness in actual history*. So the existence of a necessary existent is no more fixed *in this sense* than that of something that exists immutably. If maximal fixity = immutable existence, then the fixity metaphor yields a rationale for Augustine's belief that something has the maximum degree of presentness only if it exists immutably.

All this gives us some reason to think that the fixity metaphor may lie at the back of Augustine's mind. All the same, the fixity metaphor is dispensable, for we can render in literal terms the facts one uses it to report. Given the sense of (14), an existing thing is fixed in existence to the extent that it is beyond agents' power to affect. Moreover, when Augustine speaks of change in the texts quoted at the chapter's outset, he speaks of it in the *passive* voice, as *being* changed. In Augustine's eyes, it seems, things that change are *made* to change. As a first approximation, then, we could say that

> 15. x is more fixed in existence than y = df. existing causes and conditions within and without x and y tend against y's longer-continued existence more than they do against x's.

That is, the more the forces at play tend toward eliminating y, then the longer the period one considers, the less likely it is that y continues to exist for that whole period and so (moving again into metaphor) the looser y's purchase on existence. We can gloss "tending against" in this way: a cause or condition tends against x's existence if the obtaining of such causes or conditions makes it less probable that x-like entities exist. Existing causes and conditions alone determine how probable a certain outcome is. Hence given this gloss, the mention of causes and conditions in (15) is superfluous, and we can replace (15) with

> 16. x is more fixed in existence than y = df. x's longer-continued existence is more probable than y's.

Now (16) might need some tinkering to become truly acceptable. But even in this simple form, it lets us draw a conclusion we seek. For whatever the precise repairs it may need, they will likely not affect the point that being such that one's longer-continued existence is probable has an intrinsic maximum, namely, being such that for any period and any variation of conditions during that period, one's passing out of existence during that period has a 0 probability.[34] Now (16) or some similar claim will yield a criterion for a greater degree of existential presence. Thus if one accepts the fundamental connection between presence at t and endurance beyond t, one can put such a criterion in literal probabilistic terms. One can also derive the conclusion that greatest fixity in existence is immutable existence, for to exist immutably = to be such that in any possible variation of present or later circumstances over any period, one's passing out of existence during that period has a 0 probability.

We have found, then, that if there are two sorts of presentness, character- and existential presence, maximal presentness is the conjunction of their intrinsic maxima. Something has maximal character-presence, I have suggested, iff it is completely immutable. Something has maximal existential presence iff its existence is maximally fixed, and maximally fixed existence, I have suggested, is immutable existence. Hence something has maximal presence iff it is TI. We have already seen that if something is timeless, it is TI. Thus if something has maximal presence iff it is TI, we again have the conclusion I first argued by appeal to the "purity" of a timeless being's presentness, that if something is timeless, it has highest-degree or most genuine presence and so is more genuinely present than any temporal being.

Genuine Presentness and Augustine's Position

Let us apply all this to Augustine's (1)–(5). I have suggested that one can make sense of taking presentness as degreed by distinguishing degrees of fixity among present facts. This degreed notion of presentness is intelligible. So, too, is the typical claim of the tensed theory of time, that presentness = existence. If presentness is degreed and presentness = existence, existence is degreed, i.e., (1) is true. So (1) is

---

34. If one said instead "such that for any period, one's continuing to exist during the whole period has a 1 probability," it would follow that a timeless being is not at all fixed in existence, for a being that is outside time cannot continue to exist—only temporal things continue. At every moment, however, the claim that the probability that a timeless being pass out of existence at that moment is 0 is true, as such a being cannot pass out of existence. So this phrasing lets (15) and (16) apply to a timeless entity.

intelligible, following as it does from intelligible premises. Moreover, if the degreed notion of presentness is intelligible, nothing hinders our applying it. We can speak this way if we choose, and the more this way of speaking seems to capture real and interesting distinctions, the more reason we have to adopt it. If we do adopt it, then any reasons to think that presentness = existence are reasons to accept (1). (1), then, is not just intelligible but has some degree of support, since there are reasons to accept tensed theories of time, which involve the claim that presentness = existence, and to speak of presentness as degreed.

Now accepting (1) on such grounds would not commit us to a continuous or even a very finely graduated "scale of being." So far, our "scale of being" contains only three grades, the highest, the lowest (nonexistence), and a "between" occupied by temporal things. There is reason to find finely graduated "scales of being" suspect. If such a scale existed, its existence might entail that such claims as "aardvarks exist more than escalators" or "one elephant exists more than another" are true. If they are true, these claims are in principle intelligible. But these claims do not appear intelligible, nor therefore intelligible in principle. So to the extent that a finely grained scale of being might seem to involve them, these claims' unintelligibility is reason to think that no such scale exists. But a scale of being as coarsely grained as ours incurs no such problems, and so fear of its consequences is no reason to shy away from (1).

Let us turn to (2). By working with our degreed notion of presentness, we have found that something has maximal presentness iff it is TI. If existence = presentness, then highest-degree existence = maximal presentness. So if we grant that existence = presentness, Augustine is correct that

   2. for all x, x has highest-degree existence iff x is TI.

We saw above that (3b) is true. Now (4) is a conjunction of

   4a. for all x, if x is timeless, x has highest-degree existence, and
   4b. for all x, if x has highest-degree existence, x is timeless.

Conjoined, (2) and (3b) yield (4a). If (1) and (4a) are true, then so is (5). Thus reasoning about genuine presentness seems to support at least part of Augustine's views of timeless beings and highest-degree existence.

Degreed Existence and Tenseless Time

So far I have argued on Augustine's behalf in Augustine's terms, i.e., on the assumption of a tensed theory of time. Many philosophers now reject such a theory, holding instead that time is tenseless. So a question arises: can one support Augustine's tie of highest-degree existence and timelessness given a tenseless theory of time? The answer, I think, is that one can. I offered (1) some support by noting that if presentness is degreed and presentness = existence, existence is degreed. On a tenseless theory of time, existence = presentness *or* pastness *or* futurity. If one of the disjuncts of the latter disjunctive property is degreed, so is the property as a whole. For a degreed property is in effect a determinable property with determinates that differ from one another along a scale of degrees. Temperature, for instance, is a degreed and determinable property, and so to have a temperature is to have some determinate temperature, 10 Farenheit, 11 Farenheit, or so on. If so, the disjunctive property of having a temperature or a dog is also a degreed determinable. To have it is to be at 10 Farenheit or have a dog or be at 11 Farenheit or have a dog and so on. Accordingly, if presentness is degreed, so is presentness *or* pastness *or* futurity. Our support for (1), then, does not essentially depend on a tensed theory of time. Rather, regardless of one's view of time, if one finds it plausible to say that presentness is degreed, one has reason to accept (1).

My argument for (2) had two premises, that

17. for all x, x has maximal presentness iff x is TI, and that
18. existence = presentness.

(18) is, of course, distinctive of tensed theories. But a slight alteration yields a claim acceptable to tenseless theorists. The tenseless theorist will not grant that whatever exists at t is present at t. Tenseless theorists hold instead that whatever exists at t is present or past or future at t. For instance, suppose that the first moment at which x is ever present is t + 1. If this is so, at t, x is future. On a tenseless theory, to exist at t = to be present or past or future at t. So on such a theory, if at t x is future, "x exists" is tenselessly true at t: on a tenseless theory, "x exists" can be true at times at which it is never true that x is present. We can express this by saying that on a tenseless theory, things can exist at t without having their existence located at t. But if we say this, it follows that at t, anything whose existence is located at t is present at t, and even that

19. at t, existence located at t = presentness located at t.

Our argument for (17) depended on the notions of character-presence and existential presence, but *not* on a tensed-theory interpretation of these notions or of fixity in existence. Thus a tenseless theorist can grant (17). If (17) is true, then so is

20. at t, for all x, x has maximal presentness located at t iff x is TI located at t.

But (19) and (20) give us

21. at t, for all x, x has maximal existence located at t iff x is TI located at t.

As "t" is just some random time, it is appropriate to prefix (21) with "for all t." The result is a tenseless-theory version of (2). The argument for (3b) did not depend on a tensed theory of time. If (3b) is true, then so, presumably, is

3d. for all x, if x is timeless located at t, x is TI located at t.

But we can argue (3d)'s truth independently. For either "is timeless at t" expresses a satisfiable predicate or it does not. If it does not, the antecedent of (3d) will always be false and so the conditional will always be true. If it does, it does so only because we allow eternity as a value for t, since eternity is the only "time" at which something can be timeless. So if it is satisfiable at all, the predicate is satisfiable only by a timeless being. We have seen that whatever is timeless is TI. So (3d) is true whether or not "is timeless at t" is satisfiable. Given the tenseless-theory version of (2) and (3d), one can arrive at suitably qualified versions of (4a) and (5). Thus although Augustine developed his views in the context of a tensed theory of time, they do not depend essentially on one.

Unity and Existence

Being TI seems a mark rather than a feature constituting highest-degree existence. For the claim that something is TI merely says what it is *not* and does *not* do. Presumably, something is TI because it has some other, positive trait. The positive trait in virtue of which a thing is TI would be a more plausible candidate for a feature constituting highest existence. I now suggest that the highest-degree existence of which being TI would provide a mark consists in a greatest inner unity.

Aristotle holds that "being and unity are the same and are one thing in the sense that they are implied in one another as principle and cause are . . . the two things are not separated either in coming to be or in ceasing to be."[35] Aristotle may not have had a degreed concept of existence in view in writing this. But someone with a degreed concept of existence, reading that being and unity "are not separated either in coming to be or in ceasing to be," might naturally infer that something comes to have a greater or lesser degree of being iff it comes to have a greater or lesser degree of unity. Thus we find Plotinus writing that "because what the soul seeks is the One . . . it must withdraw from . . . objects of the lowest existence and turn to those of the highest . . . it must again become one. Only thus can it contemplate . . . the One . . . As we turn toward the One we exist to a higher degree, while to withdraw from it is to fall."[36] In Plotinus' eyes, that is, as the soul turns to the One, it becomes more one and for just that reason exists to a higher degree.

Augustine writes in a similar vein that "to the extent that they exist, things can be called similar to unity . . . moreover things exist to the same extent that they are like the source of unity."[37] Let me make three points about this claim. First, as things resemble unity insofar as they are one, Augustine is endorsing Plotinus' way of tying existence and unity. Second, as resemblance is a degreed concept, Augustine like Plotinus is allowing that there are various degrees of unity to which correspond various degrees of existence. Third, unlike Plotinus, Augustine holds that the greatest possible unity coincides with the greatest possible existence.[38] For Augustine, "one should say to exist most highly what always has itself in the same way, what is in all ways like itself."[39] The claim that something is "in all ways like itself" asserts that this thing is homogenous, that in it are no parts or other aspects whose content is distinct from that of their whole. This is true only of something with no proper parts or other distinguishable aspects, something wholly simple in the sense sketched earlier. A simple being is maximally one. Nothing in it is apart or disconnected from anything

35. Aristotle, *Metaphysics* IV, 2, 1003b24–32.
36. Plotinus, *Ennead* VI 9 [9], 3 and 9. Tr. of Elmer O'Brien in his *The Essential Plotinus* (Indianapolis: Hackett, 1980), pp. 76–77, 85.
37. "Caetera illius unius similia dici possunt inquantum sunt . . . intantum autem sunt, inquantum principalis unius similar sunt." Augustine, *On True Religion, Opera*, vol. 1, p. 1242.
38. For Plotinus, the One is not a being but "above being." See *Ennead* V, passim.
39. "Hoc enim maxime esse dicendum est quod semper eodem modo sese habet, quod omnimodo sui simile est." Augustine, *The Ways of the Church*, II, i, 1, *Opera*, vol. 1, p. 1157.

else in it, since nothing in it is even distinct from anything else in it. Further, this maximal unity is also maximally maintained, for as we noted earlier, a simple being is as such wholly immutable and cannot cease to exist. Now if a simple being has the greatest possible unity, then when Augustine assigns highest-degree existence to a simple being, he asserts that maximal unity and maximal existence are coexemplified. Thus like Plotinus, Augustine uses a degreed concept of existence, but like Aristotle, Augustine sees degree of existence and degree of unity as always in tandem.

Now Augustine could be asserting that existence and unity are distinct but covariant, degree of one being a sign of degree of the other. I suggest, however, that Augustine intends the stronger claim that to exist *is* to exemplify a kind of unity, and I also suggest that this claim is plausible. In truth, many things exist if and only if they exemplify a characteristic unity. My table exists only so long as its parts are joined together as table parts should be. As the table is gradually disassembled, losing its unity, it becomes ever more unclear that the table still exists—though to say this is not as yet to say that it exists less and less. Now unity is a paradigmatic degreed concept. One political party can be more unified than another, a psyche can be more or less unified, and so on. If we focus on examples in which existence and unity are clearly tied, we see that it seems natural to treat existence as also degreed.

Such examples include entities that are organized systems of subentities. A nation, for instance, can cease to exist gradually as its distinctive national unity erodes. Consider the gradual decay of law, order, and nationhood in Lebanon over the last decades. Is there still a nation of Lebanon? It is hard to know how to answer this; neither yes nor no seems clearly appropriate. It *does* seem appropriate to say something like "yes, but it *barely* exists at all." That is, it seems that Lebanon exists, but not as fully as other nations. Lebanon, one feels, is a nation gradually fading out of existence, existing ever less until at last it will be no more. One feels this precisely because the sort of systemic unity characteristic of functioning nations is gradually passing away.

The example of Lebanon suggests that things can exemplify their characteristic unity in varying degrees. If a particular A is an organized system of subthings or elements, the existing of A = there being a certain sort of unity among A's elements or parts. So if this unity decreases—i.e., if the elements come to deviate more from the patterns of relation which constitute this unity—so ipso facto does A's existence.

An Argument for Degreed Existence

The case of Lebanon suggests a brief argument for the general de-greedness of existence:

22. Existence = there being the unity of a system (i.e., certain parts' standing in certain relations).
23. There being the unity of a system is degreed.
24. Existence is degreed.

(22) and (23) entail (24) via the indiscernibility of identicals, and (23) is true. So the key premise of this argument is (22). Can (22) be true? The thought of existence being a form of unity should not be strange. Wang's Law, a logical truth, states that

25. $(x)((Fx) \equiv (\exists y)(Fy \cdot (y = x)))$.

Many philosophers in effect take Wang's Law to suggest a definition of existence, that existence is being identical with something, or

26. existence $= (\lambda x)(\exists y)(y = x)$.[40]

Now identity is a form of unity. It is numerical unity, the unity of a thing with itself.[41] So contemporary philosophers already countenance one definition of existence in terms of unity; (22) is just another, in terms of a different unity.

Now (22) is true only if necessarily, every existing thing is a system of some sort of parts or elements. But this latter may not be true. For perhaps some form of atomism is possible, i.e., perhaps there can be indivisible ultimate material entities not composed of further material parts. Again, perhaps there can be discarnate minds. Such minds could be viewed as systems of mental entities, and perhaps some of the latter mental entities might lack more basic mental constituents. Moreover, we have argued that some nonspatial, nontemporal abstract entities exist, and perhaps abstract entities have no parts of any sort. Thus (22) is arguably false. Still, unless some form of atomism is true, every material thing from the universe down to quarks is a system of distinct

---

40. See, e.g., Nathan Salmon, "Existence," pp. 62–67.
41. See Aristotle, *Metaphysics*, V, 6, 1016b32, and Francisco Suarez, *Disputationes Metaphysicae*, Disp. VII, sec. 3, #2, in Francisco Suarez, *Opera Omnia* (Paris: Vives, 1856–66), vol. 25.

material parts or elements. Thus unless there are atoms and in addition
no objects other than atoms truly exist, even if (22) is false, still

> 22a. many material things are systems, and necessarily, for all x, if
> x is a system, x's existence = there being the unity of a
> system.

As I find it implausible to claim that only atoms exist, I will take it that
(22a) is true. Now if in (22a) the existence of x is not a particular case of
existence, x's existence, but existence simpliciter, we can conclude
forthwith that existence = there being the unity of a system and so is
degreed per our earlier argument. But perhaps x's case or state of
existence ≠ existence simpliciter. Perhaps x's case or state of existence
is instead an entity distinct from x and from existence and involving
both as constituents of some sort. Still, on this reading it remains true
that a case or state of existence is at least sometimes a degreed case or
state. I believe that this conclusion would be strong enough to satisfy
Augustine and verify an appropriately altered version of (1), for on the
present reading, we never deal with existence apart from any case or
state of existence.

How Many Degrees?

Granting that existence is degreed does not require us to grant that
something can exist to some degree between 1 and 0 or that "it exists"
can have a truth-value between 1 and 0. Let us rather say that if A exists
in any degree, A does exist, and so "A exists" has truth-value 1.[42] To
suggest otherwise would be to make a very unintuitive claim, that our
ordinary view that existence-claims are either wholly and simply true
or wholly and simply false is incorrect. We can say rather that if A
exists, A exists in some degree, but the ordinary claim "A exists" does
not represent this degree and its truth does not fluctuate with this
degree. One *could* symbolize degree of existence by entering "1" in the
truth-value column in ever-lighter inks. As a system decays, it gradually "fades out" of existence, and the fadeout of the "1" could provide
an almost comically apt way to represent this. Moreover, that the
correct entry remains "1"—i.e., that whatever exists in any degree
does exist simpliciter—would help to explain why most philosophers

---

42. Someone concerned to allow for degree-of-truth solutions to sorites problems
could say more cautiously that if "A exists" has some intermediate truth-value, this is
not due to A's existence being degreed in the sense now under discussion.

just do not notice the phenomenon of degreed existence. One could use this device to represent a continuous scale of degrees with which things have the unity that is their existence. But I will not use it so. I will instead keep to our simple scale relating the timeless and the temporal.

Not only can things exemplify their characteristic unity in varying degrees, but it also makes sense to say that some things by nature are more unified in some respects than others. No nation can attain the unity of purpose and action manifest in the agency of a single individual. Thus a person is a "tighter" unity than a country, even if the characteristic unity of a nation has its own positive qualities (e.g., the richness and complexity that come from integrating such divergent components). If existence and unity are covariant, then we might want to make a further judgment: perhaps persons are "more real" than nations. This might explain or at least be connected with the fact that persons are more unambiguously sources of what goes on in the world. But I will not attempt to rank kinds of thing on a Great Chain of Being. Again, I will keep to our simple scale relating the timeless and the temporal. Let us turn to this scale.

The Superior Reality of the Timeless

Augustine thinks that any spatiotemporal object will have a low degree of existence:

> Corporeal beauty is the lowest beauty because it cannot have all its parts at once, but while some things give place and others succeed them, they complete the number of temporal forms in a single beauty. But all this is not evil because it passes away. For so also a verse is beautiful in its own way although two syllables can in no way be spoken at once.[43]

> Who will dare, after due consideration, to call any body truly and simply one? All are changed by passing from form to form or from place to place, and consist of parts each occupying its own place, through which they are divided in diverse spaces. True and primary unity is not perceived by the fleshly eye or any bodily sense, but by the intellect.[44]

43. "corporum pulchritudo. Nam ideo extrema est quia simul non potest habere omnia, sed dum alia cedunt atque succedunt, temporalium formarum numerum in unam pulchritudinem complent. Et hoc totum non propterea malum, quia transit. Sic enim et versum in suo genere pulcher est, quamvis duae syllabae simul dici nullo modo possint." Augustine, *On True Religion, Opera*, vol. 1, p. 1228.
44. "audeatque dicere, cum diligenter consideraverit, quodlibet corpus vere ac simpliciter unum esse; cum omnia vel de specie in speciem, vel de loco in locum transeundo

For Augustine, an object is temporal iff it is changeable.[45] Thus these texts speak not just of changeable but of spatiotemporal objects. If Augustine thinks that degree of existence varies with degree of unity, we can see why he downgrades spatiotemporal existence. Any extended spatiotemporal object is as such a *scattered* object. It is a union of many loosely joined but discrete spatial parts that can easily come apart. Thus its spatial unity is tenuous. Again, such an object's duration is dribbled out to it one instant at a time. Thus its unity over time never really exists at all, given Augustine's commitment to the sole reality of the present and the obvious truth that a unity over time is a relation among past, present, and future phases of a duration. Platonist cosmology would provide a further sense in which the intrinsic unity of a spatiotemporal thing is low. For in a Platonist system, a spatiotemporal thing is just an organization of bits of matter in the Receptacle, a scattered object that is one not intrinsically but only insofar as these bits are under the influence of an abstract Form and thereby constitute an imperfect image of it. (One could make a like point via the ontological commitments of some contemporary physical theories: for the Receptable substitute space-time, and for the Form substitute a mathematically formulable law of behavior.) By contrast, an object beyond space and time is not composed of scattered parts, cannot come apart spatially, and has its duration all at once, at eternity: no phase of its existence is earlier than any other, for its existence has no phases at all. So it is hardly surprising that Augustine sees timeless, spaceless objects as intrinsically more unified than spatiotemporal objects. But then this is another reason for him to say that nonspatiotemporal objects have a greater degree of existence than ordinary physical objects.

---

mutentur, et partibus constent sua loca obtinentibus, per qua in spatia diversa dividuntur? Porro ipsa vera et prima unitas non oculis carneis neque ullo tali sensu sed menta intellecta conspicitur." Augustine, *On True Religion, Opera*, vol. 1, p. 1236.

45. Augustine believes (3). (3) is equivalent to

    T1. for all x, x is not timeless iff x is not TI, and so to

    T2. for all x, x is temporal iff x can change or can cease to exist.

Augustine also asserts that nothing can cease to exist unless it can change (*Confessions* XII, 11). Thus (T2) in his view collapses into the text's claim. Augustine also says some things that appear inconsistent with the text's claim. For instance, in *Confessions* XII, 12, he speaks of a creature that is forever unchanged but changeable as "eternal." But his next sentence goes on to call this same entity immutable, thus apparently contradicting himself. A charitable reading requires us to say that Augustine means something different in his first and second assertions. But then we ought similarly to say that this changeable creature is not "eternal" in the very sense in which a purely unchangeable being is either. I suspect that allied distinctions between Augustine's strict and looser uses of terms for timeless or eternal existence can preserve the claim that for Augustine, something is changeable iff it is temporal.

Existence, Unity, and Augustine's Position

Let us now see how the claim that existence = the obtaining of a certain sort of unity affects (1)–(5). Clearly, if this is so, (1) is true. Again, if this is so, then (2), (4), and (5) are equivalent to

2a. for all x, x has highest-degree unity iff x is TI,
4c. for all x, x is timeless iff x has highest-degree unity, and
5a. temporal existence is a status "between" highest-degree unity and nonexistence.

Now we are operating with an existence scale of only three positions, lowest (which is already taken by nonexistence), highest, and middle. Hence if the timeless ranks higher than the temporal, this suffices to place it in the highest spot. Since it appears that timeless entities do have greater inner unity than temporal entities, then, (4c) appears true. So then does (5a). (2a) is a conjunction of

2b. for all x, if x has highest-degree unity, x is TI, and
2c. for all x, if x is TI, x has highest-degree unity.

(4c) and (3b) jointly entail (2b). (4c) and (3a) jointly entail (2c), but since (3a) remains dubious, so must (2c).

Greatest Unity and Its Marks

I have suggested that highest-degree existence = the obtaining of a certain sort of unity. Since the obtaining of a unity ≠ being TI, it emerges again that being TI is at best a mark rather than a feature constituting highest-degree existence/unity. If (4c) is true and (3a) is false, being TI is not an infallible mark of highest unity. All the same, it does flow from that unity. As we observed earlier, for Augustine, the highest degree of unity is that of a simple being. We have seen that a simple being exists immutably. Further, it is clear that a simple being must have all of its attributes immutably. For if something changes, it ceases to have some features while retaining others. If this is so, there is a real distinction between the features it loses and the features it keeps, and so the thing is not simple. Thus being TI flows from highest unity as Augustine sees it. But one need not appeal to the doctrine of divine simplicity to argue the connection between highest unity and being TI. For our scale of existence contains only three positions, nonexistence, highest-degree existence, and what lies between them. Hence any feature that makes one broad kind of object more one than another suffices to put that kind into the highest position and to explain TI's status as a mark if being TI is connected with having that feature.

One such feature is lacking spatial parts. As we have seen, it is plausible that any object without spatial parts has a greater inner unity than any object that has such parts. In conjunction with the claim that there really are no such entities as geometric points, i.e., entities with spatial location but no spatial extension, this generates one possible explanation of the markhood of being TI. For if there are no points, anything located in space has spatial parts. If the special theory of relativity is true, then whatever is located in time is located in space. Accordingly, whatever has no spatial parts has no spatial location and so no temporal location. Whatever has no location in time is TI. Thus being TI flows from the sort of inner unity that involves having no spatial parts.

Dream and Reality

So far we have spoken of the marks of higher existence and of that in which higher existence consists. But we can approach degrees of existence in yet a third way. This approach will perhaps suggest the difference in attitude toward an object which a claim that that object has higher-degree existence should inspire. In *Republic* V, Plato speaks of people who do not believe in Forms as asleep and dreaming, and taking for real objects things that are just figments of their dreams.[46] This suggests an analogy: Forms are real, or exist, in comparison to ordinary material objects as ordinary material objects are real, or exist, in comparison to the objects we meet in dreams. Augustine, I suggest, envisions a similar analogy when he writes that "compared with [God], things which are, are not. If He is not compared with them, they are, because they are from Him. But compared with Him, they are not, for to be truly is to be immutably, and this He alone is"[47] Note the structural similarity of Plato's and Augustine's cases. Each writer twice asserts the obtaining of a dyadic relation, "____ is real as versus ____": for instance, a material object is called real as versus a dream object but unreal as versus a Form. (One could as easily take the dyadic relation to be "____ exists as versus ____." I do not because this locution is somewhat more jarring.) If we take this as equivalent to twice

46. Plato, *Republic*, V, 476c–d.

47. Augustine, *Commentary on Psalm 134, 4, Opera*, vol. 4, p. 2130. For the Latin, see n. 5 above.

applying a monadic predicate, "___ is real," we take their claims to be contradictory. For then we take them to be calling one and the same object real (when compared with a dream object) and unreal (when compared with a Form or God). If we keep the dyadic relation in view, the natural thing to say is that as "___ is real as versus ___" is transitive, in applying it twice they establish a *scale of reality* (or existence), on which kinds of objects are ranked:

Form	God
material thing	material thing
dream object	dream object

I suggest that another rationale for talk of degrees of existence is precisely that Platonists of any stripe (including Augustinian) find that they must apply a relation "___ is real as versus ___" in more than one case. For as we have just seen, doing so establishes a scale of reality. Establishing a scale of reality gives one reason to treat "___ is real" as a degreed predicate, i.e., as such that one object can be more real than another. For what does a position on a scale of reality connote if not having greater or lesser reality?

We ourselves are prepared to operate with a scale of reality, though we do not notice it. First, we use the predicate "___ is real as versus ___." J. L. Austin has noted that "real" is essentially a *contrastive* term. To say of a duck that it is a real duck, for instance, is precisely to compare it implicitly to other things that are not real ducks and say that it is not like these.[48] In other words, we not only use the dyadic predicate "___ is real as versus ___," we cannot do without it; it is what we are really using on many occasions when we *think* we are deploying the monadic "___ is real." Second, we use this predicate to distinguish not just, e.g., real ducks from wooden ducks but also real ducks from their images in dreams, dream ducks. Third, we use the predicate to distinguish not just real *ducks* but real *beings,* for if we distinguish a real from a dream duck, we have ipso facto distinguished a real from a dream being, though not under that description. If, then, we were to find a reason to say of some further sort of duck that it is real as versus an ordinary material duck, we would have in fact established a scale of reality.

Let us ask how we distinguish real from dream objects. We will find that there are certain standards that for any F let us distinguish a real

48. J. L. Austin, *Sense and Sensibilia* (New York: Oxford University Press, 1964), p. 70. I owe this reference to Margaret Walker.

from a dream F. We will see that it is because what we ordinarily call waking objects satisfy these standards better than what we ordinarily call dream objects that we call the first real and the second unreal, or the first waking objects and the second dream objects. Suppose we then found a third realm of objects, Xs, which satisfied the standards even better than material objects do. We would then have two alternatives. We could conclude that after all, material objects are not real. But this would wipe out the significant difference we all acknowledge between dream and material objects. Our second option would be to establish a scale of reality and say in effect: dream objects are unreal in comparison with ordinary objects, and ordinary objects are unreal relative to Xs. If we establish a scale of reality, we give sense to talk of degrees of reality. We make it possible to explain the contrast of degree of reality as just like the one we make between dream and real objects.

I suggest in addition that once we have found our standards of reality, timeless objects will appear real as versus temporal objects. I thus suggest that relative to the standards of relative reality we do in fact have, Augustine's judgment about the relative reality of the timeless and the temporal is correct. If Augustine is correct, then, we will be able to say that the timeless is to the temporal as real objects are to dream objects, and so that the attitudes appropriate to timeless entities are to the attitudes appropriate to temporal entities as the attitudes appropriate to real things are to the attitudes appropriate to things in dreams.

Note first that we *do* in fact have a distinction to make between dream objects and physical objects. We say that physical objects are real and dream objects are not. If this were all there was to it, then there would be no distinction to make, because there would not even prima facie be two sets of objects to distinguish. But the griffin I dreamed of did exist in my dream; had I dreamed a zoological survey, the survey would have been incomplete without mentioning the griffin. We say that a dream griffin is only a part of my dream, an intentional content of a mental state I had, not a distinct object on its own. But this is what we say once we're awake and adult and sure that the griffin is not real. Children are sometimes scared to go to sleep, for fear that they will meet again the same monster they dreamed last night—a belief that entails that (according to the child) the monster has enough reality and self-identity to survive from one dream to the next. Again, while we dream, the griffin seems quite real, save in dreams when we know we're dreaming. So if we are not sure whether we are awake, we are not sure whether the griffin is real.

Thus there are states of mind (if only childish or confused states) in which we admit two sorts of griffins, dream and waking griffins. Only on reflection do we say that dream griffins aren't really griffins, but just parts of mental images. We know that only objects met in waking experience are real. This, however, does raise a question: given that we have two sets of experiences (waking and dream) and in them meet two sets of objects (waking and dream), how do we decide which of our experiences are the waking ones or, equivalently, which are the experiences that reveal really real objects? To put it another way, how do we select, among the various griffins experience might present, the ones that are real and met while awake?

There is in truth a decision in this, unnoticed though it be. We know this both because we can point to states of mind in which this decision does not seem to have been made and because some cultures deny the Western claim that the series of experiences that we Westerners identify as waking experiences are in fact the ones that reveal the world's true contents. In some Native American religions, for instance, it is thought that only in dreams and drug-induced dreamlike states do we pierce the veil of illusion that is ordinary life to confront directly what things really are: dreams are revelations of reality. In these systems of thought, when we think we are awake, we are really asleep, and only in certain dreams do we waken. We do not agree with the Native Americans. So there is a judgment that we make and they do not. It is worth asking: by what standards do we make this judgment? How would we justify it? Again, we have all heard of the Chinese philosopher who dreamed that he was a butterfly and who on awakening felt unsure whether he was a philosopher dreaming of being a butterfly or a butterfly dreaming of being a philosopher. It is worth asking: why are we so sure that we know how to answer his question?

Obviously, we never suspend judgment on the question of which experiences are the waking ones and try to decide this question explicitly. But why, then, are we so sure which experiences are wakeful and reveal real things? The answer is surely that we tacitly use certain standards of what is real to decide just this. We did not step back outside experience and decide reflectively to adopt these standards. We grow up having no question what sort of object is real and which is not, and so we in effect use these standards unquestioningly to decide what sort of object is real. For this reason, these standards define what reality means for us. It may even be that our concept of a real being just is the concept of a being that satisfies these standards. For these reasons, I do not know how well we could justify these standards for ascribing reality. We could not justify our criteria for ascribing the predicate "___ is a dog"; they are just how we do use the word. The same may be so with our criteria of reality.

To uncover our standards of reality, I propose a thought experiment. I will try to show under what conditions we would become unsure which experiences revealed the real world, the ones we ordinarily call dreams or the ones we ordinarily call waking experiences. If we can describe such conditions, the difference between dreams that can perhaps convince us of their reality and dreams that cannot will show our reality-standards in action.

Imagine the following. Starting tomorrow, every person on earth sleeps exactly twelve hours a night. Every person on earth begins to dream continuously for those twelve hours: each person has a single dream lasting all twelve hours, and each such dream contains no internal gaps. As each dream ends, each dreamer dreams of preparing for bed, going to bed, and falling asleep. Each night's dream is in certain broad ways continuous with the dreams of prior nights: for instance, each dream begins with awakening in the same bed in which last night's dream had one falling asleep, and so on. People begin frequently to meet people during waking hours whom they had seen during sleep (and vice versa) and discover that both parties have basically the same memories of what went on during their dreams. Further, as the contents of the dreams are discussed, it emerges that the dreams fit together into a broadly consistent world story. In these dreams, we are all three-headed Martians, living our daily lives on the red planet and meeting, recognizing, and conversing with each other in our Martian guises. This continues, unvarying, for several years, during which time our Martian personas gradually acquire apparent memories of having been Martians for the full duration of our past lives and of having had similarly consistent dreams of being one-headed Earthlings, meeting, recognizing, and conversing with our Martian friends in this strange monocranial guise. After several years, would it not begin to seem unclear whether we were really Earthlings dreaming we were Martians, or really Martians dreaming we were Earthlings—that is, when we were really awake and when we were really asleep?

I submit that it would. It seems to me that in this case, in which our dream lives would become much like our waking lives in the respects mentioned, the criteria whose satisfaction convinces us that our waking lives are real would be as well satisfied by our dream lives, leading to a confusion over just which life was real (or whether perhaps both were).

I suggest that the reality criteria internal to our very concept of reality include continuity, coherence, explicability, intersubjectivity, "hardness," and inclusiveness.

Continuity

Continuity is order between episodes. Ordinary dreams "jump" from one scene to the next, with no felt transition between them. So ordinary dream objects suddenly disappear and rarely appear. Ordinary dream objects almost never continue between dreams or from one night's dreaming to the next. Dreams ordinarily break off suddenly when we wake, and when we next dream, there is almost never a sense of picking up where the last dream left off, still less of one dream and then the next as episodes in a single ongoing history.

Our experience of waking life almost always traces a continuous progress from one episode to the next. So, too, does our experience of waking objects. When our experience of these objects has gaps in it, it mostly picks up where it left off: unless Mom throws our old toys away overnight, they are there for us in the morning. In short, there are strong connections between episodes of experience of objects of the waking world; these experiences are easily construed as episodes in a continuing history. Episodes with objects in our dream world are connected weakly and infrequently or not at all. Note that in my Earthling–Martian example, I took care to make the dream world as continuous as the real world, and this contributed strongly to the impression that after a while, we would not know whether we were Earthlings or Martians.

We find objects of what we ordinarily call waking life real because (inter alia) episodes of experiencing them are strongly continuous and connectible. We find these objects identical over different episodes (inter alia) because these continuities suggest this identity as a natural interpretation. A timeless object is immune to real change. Hence experience with such objects, if any, would be even more strongly continuous and connectible and would more strongly suggest the objects' identity over episodes. Moreover, if we came to know that these objects were immutable, we would know that any differences in our experience of them were our contribution, not the objects'.

Let us turn now from continuity of experience to continuity of the object experienced. We call material objects identical over episodes because the phases of their careers are strongly similar and their changes make a smooth, continuous pattern. The relation between episodes of a timeless being's career is not just similarity but identity, the intrinsic maximum of similarity. The timeless being we meet now is not just a slightly altered version of the one we met before; it is absolutely self-same whenever met.

Thus relative to the standard of continuity, timeless objects appear real as versus temporal objects, just as temporal objects appear real relative to dream objects. Further, the timeless scores higher on the scale of continuity precisely because it is timeless.

Coherence

Coherence is order within episodes. Within each episode, our experience of waking objects is stable and orderly. They hang together to form a single world where a single set of laws obtains. Ordinary dream objects are more prone to wild fluctuations of character. Even the basic laws of our ordinary dream worlds vary with the dream; in one and the same dream, some cows fly and some cows can't. Note again that in my Earthling-Martian example, part of what generated confusion about our real identity was that I made the dream world as coherent as the waking world.

Now timeless beings are absolutely changeless. So in themselves, timeless objects are absolutely stable. Hence they have an even greater coherence than the objects of the waking world of stable laws and regular changes, for any apparent changes they undergo in our experience are guaranteed to be the results of our input, not theirs. So again, on the standard of coherence, timeless objects appear real as versus temporal objects, just as temporal objects appear real relative to dream objects. Again, the timeless scores higher on this scale precisely because it is timeless.

Explicability

A world is explicable iff its objects' behavior can be rationally explained. Within the waking world, objects display regular patterns of behavior, which lead us to form justified expectations about their future behavior, let us discover laws of their natures, and so generate explanations of what they do. Ordinary dream objects display fewer such regularities. Also, the properties of objects other than ourselves which we perceive in our waking experience sometimes explain the properties of objects other than ourselves which we perceive in our dreams (as in Freud). The reverse does not occur. Bad dreams may make us grouchy, and so one can perhaps say that they give us a real dispositional property, that of (an elevated degree of) irritability.[49] But this is not a case of dream objects causing waking objects other than ourselves to have a real property that they would not otherwise have, the property of being apt to cause us irritation: the change is in us, not in our world. Psychoanalysis may probe our dreams to explain features reality appears to us to have (e.g., the apparent sexual attractiveness of some inappropriate object). But psychoanalytic explanations do not explain the way waking-world objects appear by the properties of dream objects. Instead, they seek a common waking-world psychological cause of both phenomena. Thus it seems that the properties of objects (other than ourselves) of our waking world cause the properties of objects (other than ourselves) of our dream world, but not vice versa.

Clearly, if an object can undergo no change at all, we can have maximally justified expectations about its future behavior. Further, according to Platonism, we can explain the traits of temporal objects by appealing to those of timeless objects, but not vice versa. So again, the timeless appears real as versus the temporal.

Intersubjectivity

Intersubjectivity is perhaps our most important criterion of reality. If I see a pink elephant and nobody else does, the weight of others' testimony will convince me that I am deluded. If many people claim to see one, then though I do not, eventually they may convince me that one is there. My dream objects are private to me; nobody else can check on them or corroborate my experience of them. That nobody else can see my dream dog and all can see my waking dog helps to convince me that the waking dog is real (or, equivalently, that the one I call the waking dog *is* the waking dog). Conversely, if people in my dream world consistently corroborated my experience of dream objects, and people in my waking world systematically failed to, I could perhaps become greatly confused. One feature of my Earthling-Martian example was that objects in the two sorts of experience appeared to be equally accessible intersubjectively in two ways: my fellow Martians seemed to perceive public objects of the Martian world pretty much as I did and also seemed to perceive the objects of my Earthling dream world.

Augustine seems to believe that timeless entities are intersubjectively

49. I owe this point to Eleonore Stump.

accessible in a way temporal entities are not. In *De Trinitate* IX, he asserts that we know necessary truths by some sort of direct intuition of the timeless exemplars that temporal things imitate, and he expressly says of such knowledge that in contrast to other sorts, one "sees a thing in the truth itself, in such a way that another person can also gaze upon it."[50] We can perhaps explain the superior accessibility Augustine ascribes to these truths in this way: our view of physical objects depends on our perspective, our physical position in relation to them. Thus we the more easily pass false judgments on them.[51] Physical perspective is irrelevant to acknowledging such truths as that $2 + 2 = 4$. Anyone who persistently gets this wrong is subject not to a bad perspective, but to a radical failure of his conceptual equipment. Note that on this account, necessary truths' superior accessibility is guaranteed by their independence of reference to perceptual and temporal particulars.

Now here a defender of the temporal could interject: but do not truths of logic and mathematics face a parallel problem of perspective? After all, one's conceptual scheme determines which such truths one acknowledges or can acknowledge. Whether we agree with this objector or with Augustine on the superior accessibility of the timeless depends on our epistemology. Is there a realm of objective truth which all can grasp regardless of their conceptual scheme (i.e., their particular "perspective" on this realm of truth)? If so, then most likely mathematical and logical truths—timeless truths—make up the largest part of it, thus validating Augustine's intuition that the timeless is more accessible intersubjectively than the temporal. If timeless truths have this special status, further, it may be because their relative independence of temporal objects removes them from the ambit of most of our interpretive equipment. But regardless, we can see at least that realists about necessary truth have reason to say that the timeless is more accessible intersubjectively than the temporal, whereas antirealists can perhaps say no worse than that the two are on a par in this respect.

"Hardness"

"Hardness" is the characteristic of resisting one's wishes and agency. Dream objects sometimes are outside the control we exert in dreams; at

---

50. "videat; aliud autem in ipsa veritate, quod alius quoque possit intueri." Augustine, *The Trinity*, IX, vi, 9, *Ouevres*, vol. 16, p. 92. See more generally IX, vi–vii, 9–12.

51. This phrasing is deliberate. Augustine would not say, as Plato would, that in cases, e.g., of optical illusion we are *deceived by* physical objects; see, e.g., *Against the Academics*, III, x–xi, 23–26; *On True Religion*, xxxiii, 61–62; xxxvi, 67.

other times, though, we have superhuman powers in dreams and can mold entire worlds to our will. The objects of ordinary life are consistently of greater hardness; most of our circumstances in life are largely beyond our control. What we cannot control, we cannot believe that we have created: thus it is that solipsism is so very unintuitive. Thus we favor the claim that what we come to call the objects of our waking world are the real ones.

Now timeless entities are absolutely beyond our control. As they are termini of no direct causal relations, nothing we do can affect them. I suggest, therefore, that if there are timeless realities, they are "harder" than the temporal objects that we can with effort mold to our will, and so again emerge as more real than temporal objects.

Inclusiveness

One of a pair of worlds is inclusive if it includes the other. If world A includes world B and not vice versa, we want to call B the less real or unreal world. When I wake, I can remember my dream world, and so my waking world includes my dream world. When I dream, I rarely if ever explicitly remember my waking life and remember it as a waking life. Thus the world of my waking experience includes my dream world, but my dream world does not include my waking world. Again, we can sometimes control the contents of (what we come to call) our dreams from (what we come to call) our waking states; for instance, some people can virtually guarantee that they will have nightmares by concentrating on a monster movie. We cannot at all control the contents of (what we come to call) our waking experience from within (what we come to call) our dreams. If one can control objects in world A from world B, B in a sense includes A. In two ways, then, what we come to call the waking world includes what we come to call the dream world, but not vice versa. So it is easier to knit together a single life-story including the two sorts of experience by taking the perspective that what we call waking life is the real one and that the other world we visit is merely a dream: and for this reason, inclusiveness becomes a criterion of reality. Note again that part of the confusing effect of my example was my stipulating that the Earthling and Martian worlds were equally inclusive, each able to see the other as a dream episode within itself.

We shall see below that the criterion of inclusiveness favors the superior reality of the timeless. For I argue that in a way, time exists in eternity and not vice versa. Further, though it is clear that temporal objects cannot control or even causally affect timeless ones, I argue that

God is timeless and so that a timeless being affects all and controls some temporal beings.

Dream, Reality, and Augustine's Position

The distinction between dream and reality is a distinction between degrees of existence, for when we decide which objects are dream objects, these are at once demoted to the lowest point on our ontological scale and called nonexistent. If existence = the exemplifying of a unity, the distinction between dream and reality is also a distinction between lesser and greater inner unity. But this is trivially true, for what does not exist has no unity at all. Thus it appears that the dream-reality distinction gives a further perspective on the very concepts we have been developing. By examining the way we distinguish dream from reality, we have uncovered six criteria of higher reality. All apply to the case of the temporal and the timeless. Four clearly dictate taking the timeless to be more real than the temporal, and I argue that a fifth, inclusiveness, also favors this conclusion. None cuts in the opposite direction; one either favors the timeless or puts it on a par with the temporal. I suggest, then, that if the dream-reality understanding of degrees of reality is at all on target, talk of such degrees makes sense, and such Platonists as Augustine may actually have a strong case for the superior reality of the timeless.

The dream-reality approach gives us another reason to consider (1) both intelligible and true. Further, since we are operating with only our simple scale of existence, by giving us reason to say that timeless and TI realities have a higher degree of existence than temporal realities, this approach gives us reason to affirm (2) and (4). Now if (2) and (4) are both true, then so is (3). We have already seen that if there are temporal things, (4) implies (5). So this approach seems to validate the whole of Augustine's position; if we accept it, as I suggest that we should, we wind up committed even to (3a).

The Importance of the Timeless

Let us note in closing what difference in one's attitude toward timeless and temporal realities (if one recognizes both) this ought to make. Our attitude to ordinary material objects and dream objects is just this: material objects are the real and important ones, the ones we need to take seriously in our plans and aspirations. Dream objects are just the idle playthings of our mind's distraction; they do not matter. Even if we had to have dreams involving certain sorts of dream objects to survive (e.g., dream food, drink, and clothing), it would be a mistake to think that dream objects were more valuable and important than real material ones. In the same way, the Platonist can urge, even if we must live and move and have our being in the ordinary material world, concerned with ordinary human cares, it would be a mistake to think that this world is what is truly important and valuable or that our best life would be one that rested here. Martha Nussbaum has recently argued at length that certain "fragile" earthly goods are of most importance for human life.[52] If in fact timeless objects have the highest degree of existence, this is false. So given the tie between timelessness, highest existence, and highest importance or value, we can perhaps begin to appreciate the experiential and religious importance of the claim that God is timeless.

52. Martha Nussbaum, *The Fragility of Goodness* (New York: Cambridge University Press, 1986).

[6]

Boethius:
Eternity as Duration

The history of philosophical theology has the shape of an hourglass. The subject flourished in the academies of late antiquity. With the rest of the humanities, it was caught up in the collapse of Roman civilization and dribbled down to the Middle Ages through comparatively few sources. Later, the field was reborn from these sources and flourished anew. Where the concept of eternity is concerned, Augustine and Boethius were the hourglass's neck. The study of Augustine as anthologized in Peter Lombard's *Sentences* was the meat of theological education well into the 1300s, and most treatments of eternity for long after that included discussion of Boethius' definition of the concept. If we want to examine the concept of eternity mainstream medievals developed, then, we must deal with Boethius.

As the first chapter noted, many ancient and contemporary authors have seen eternity as everlasting duration through time. Others liken eternity to a static, durationless instant, a timeless *nunc stans*. Boethius appears to be among these, writing in his *De Trinitate* that "our now, as if running along, makes time and sempiternity; the divine now, permanent, not moving and standing still, makes eternity."[1] A now is an instant of time; thus Boethius models eternity explicitly on a "motionless," "standing" instant. Yet when he defines eternity explicitly, Boethius writes that "eternity . . . is the complete possession all at

---

1. "nostrum nunc quasi currens tempus facit et sempiternitatem, divinum vero nunc permanens neque movens sese atque consistens aeternitatem facit." Boethius, *De Trinitate,* chap. 4, in Stewart and Rand, *Boethius,* p. 20, ll. 72–74.

once of illimitable life."[2] This definition is on its face puzzling. To say that a life occurs all at once suggests that it is instantlike. Yet that a life is "illimitable" naturally suggests that it endures forever in time. Perhaps Boethius wrote misleadingly, wavered between different views of eternity, or was just inconsistent.[3] In a well-known article, Eleonore Stump and Norman Kretzmann have suggested that there is another possibility.[4] On their view, when Boethius seems to waffle between talk of a durationless now and talk of everlasting duration, he is actually trying to communicate a single thesis, that eternity is "atemporal duration." This chapter argues that Stump and Kretzmann are right about Boethius, though not for the reasons they give. Stump and Kretzmann have recently tried to defend the concept of atemporal duration against an attack by Paul Fitzgerald.[5] I suggest that their defense is inadequate, then offer a different defense and a different view of atemporal duration.

Eternity in the *Consolation of Philosophy*

Stump and Kretzmann focus their discussion on this text from Boethius' *Consolation of Philosophy*:

> Eternity . . . is the complete possession all at once of illimitable life. This becomes clearer by comparison with temporal things. For whatever lives in time proceeds as something present from the past into the future, and there is nothing placed in time that can embrace the whole extent of its life equally. Indeed, on the contrary, it does not yet grasp tomorrow but yesterday it has already lost, and even in the life of today you live no more fully than in a mobile, transitory moment . . . [A temporal thing's] life may be infinitely long, but it does not embrace its whole extent simultaneously . . . Therefore, whatever includes and possesses the whole fullness of illimitable life at once and is such that nothing future is absent from it and nothing past has flowed away, this is rightly

2. "Aeternitas . . . est interminabilis vitae tota simul et perfecta possessio." Boethius, *Philosophiae consolationis*, V, prose VI, in Stewart and Rand, *Boethius*, p. 400, ll. 9–11. Tr. of Eleonore Stump and Norman Kretzmann.
3. Thus William Kneale, "Time and Eternity," p. 99; Martha Kneale, "Eternity," pp. 230–231; Swinburne, *Coherence of Theism*, pp. 218–221; Sorabji, *TC&C*, pp. 108–113; Robert Cook, "God, Time, and Freedom," *Religious Studies* 23 (1987), 81.
4. Stump and Kretzmann, "Eternity," pp. 429–458.
5. Eleonore Stump and Norman Kretzmann, "Atemporal Duration," *Journal of Philosophy* 84 (1987), 214–219 (henceforward "AD"). They are responding to Paul Fitzgerald, "Stump and Kretzmann on Time and Eternity," *Journal of Philosophy* 82 (1985), 260–269 (henceforward "SKTE").

judged to be eternal, and of this it is necessary both that being in full possession of itself it be always present to itself and that it have the infinity of mobile time present to it.[6]

Boethius explains his definition of eternity by describing ways things live. So for him, eternality (being eternal) is a way something lives; a thing is eternal if it is alive and lives at once the whole of its life. By contrast, Boethius states, if any x lives and is located in time, that x does not live at once the whole of its life. This entails that an eternal being is not located in time.

Boethius' claim that if any x lives and is located in time, that x does not live at once the whole of its life is false if there is an instantaneous living being. Such a being would be located at a particular instant in time and so temporal. Yet it would live all of its life at once, because it would live at that one moment the sole moment of its life. So to maintain his claims, Boethius must deny that there are any instantaneous living beings. Now we would ordinarily consider this denial plausible; living, we think, involves processes that take time. But if we say or imply that living takes time, we make it difficult to claim (as Boethius wants to) that timeless beings can be alive. So there is a tension between two parts of Boethius' position, for the chief plausible reason to deny that there are instantaneous living beings would also be a reason to deny that there are timeless living beings—eternal beings, in Boethius' sense.

This tension might be a reason for Boethius to emend some part of his position. At least one possible emendation would preserve all that Boethius wants to say here. Suppose that as Stump and Kretzmann say, Boethius does think of an eternal life as a sort of extended life. If this is so, all he really must contrast eternal life with is temporally extended life. So Boethius can avoid the whole question of instantaneous living

---

6. "Aeternitas . . . est interminabilis vitae tota simul et perfecta possessio, quod ex collatione temporalium clarius liquet. Nam quidquid vivit in tempore id praesens a praeteritis in futura procedit nihilque est in tempore constitutum quod totum vitae suae spatium pariter possit amplecti. Sed crastinum quidem nondum adprehendit hesternum vero iam perdidit; in hodierna quoque vita non amplius vivitis quam in illo mobili transitorioque momento . . . Non enim totum simul infinitae licet vitae spatium comprehendit . . . Quod igitur interminabilis vitae plenitudinem totam pariter comprehendit ac possidet, cui neque futuri quidquam absit nec praeteriti fluxerit, id aeternum esse iure perhibetur, idque necesse est et sui compos praesens sibi semper adsistere et infinitatem mobilis temporis habere praesentem." Boethius, *Philosophiae consolationis*, V, prose 6, in Stewart and Rand, *Boethius*, p. 400, ll. 9–18, 22–31. Tr. of Eleonore Stump and Norman Kretzmann, "Eternity," p. 430. I have added one line of the original text to what Stump and Kretzmann translate.

beings and simply say that eternal life, which is a form of extended life, is lived all at once, whereas temporal extended lives are not.

An eternal being is not located in time, then. Neither is an eternal life, for it cannot be the case both that time exists and that there exists in time a limitless life lived all at once.[7] The reason is this. Suppose that a temporal being lives at once that of its life which is at $t + 1$ and that of its life which occurs at an earlier time t. Something temporal can at once live life-at-t and life-at-$t + 1$ only if its living is temporally simultaneous with both t and $t + 1$. If its living is so, then t and $t + 1$ are simultaneous, counter to our original assumption. If an eternal being exists in time, it exists forever, as otherwise its duration will not be "limitless." Therefore, if an eternal being exists in time, all moments of time are simultaneous—which is to say that time, taken as a tissue of relations of earlier and later, does not exist. Hence if time exists, then if there is an eternal being, its life must lack temporal location. Boethius clearly believes that an eternal God coexists with temporal creatures. Thus he is committed to denying his God's life location in time.

According to Stump and Kretzmann, the quoted text also depicts eternal life as having an "infinite duration."[8] Stump and Kretzmann offer five arguments for this reading. They are that (i) the Platonist authors by whom Boethius was influenced took the concept of eternity in this way, (ii) Boethius speaks of eternal life as a "fullness," (iii) Boethius speaks of an eternal present as "remaining" or "enduring," (iv) in De Trinitate, Boethius says that an eternal God "is always," and (v) Boethius' claim that an eternal life is unlimited is most naturally read as a claim that an eternal life "lasts forever." Let us examine these arguments.

Argument (i) is weak by itself. Even if Plato and Plotinus took eternity as atemporal duration (a debatable claim)[9] and Boethius is in

7. To claim that an eternal being's life is located in time is not necessarily to claim that that being is so; see the next chapter.

8. Stump and Kretzmann, "Eternity," p. 432.

9. Sorabji has recently argued that Plato and Plotinus do not take eternity to be atemporal duration (TC&C, pp. 98–130). He contends that Plato wavers inconsistently between taking eternity as unextended timelessness and taking it as extension throughout everlasting time (pp. 108–112) and that though Plotinus mostly speaks of eternity as timelessness, he "often slips back into ways of talking which suggest that the eternal enjoys duration" (p. 114). But Sorabji also claims not to understand Kretzmann and Stump's distinctive concept of eternity (p. 101 n. 14). This concept involves both timelessness and everlasting duration. So Sorabji is defenseless against the claim that Kretzmann and Stump's (or another durational) concept of eternity really is there in Plato and Plotinus, and Sorabji does not see it because (by his own admission) he does not understand it. Moreover, if (as I argue) a durational concept of eternity is coherent,

general influenced by both, we can assert that he was influenced by them *in his concept of eternity* only if we have independent reason to think that Boethius too takes eternity to be atemporal duration. But (ii)–(v) do not provide such reason. As Fitzgerald notes, we can take Boethius' talk of "remaining," "enduring," "always," and "limitlessness" in at least two ways.[10] God's duration could be *in se;* He could literally endure. But God's duration could be merely *quoad nos.* Talk of God existing "always," "limitlessly," etc. could just be metaphor for the fact that God exists in a single unextended *nunc stans* while all time goes by—that at every time, it is correct to say that God exists. Finally, talk of God's fullness could be a way to assert God's lack of all duration. Boethius may be saying that rather than having His life spread out and so "diluted," God has His life all-together, compact and replete.[11] Thus I suggest that Kretzmann and Stump's (ii)–(iv) are inconclusive. This renders (v) inconclusive as well, since what we make of the other phrases Boethius applies to eternity should determine whether we accept the "natural" reading of Boethius' talk of limitlessness.

There are, however, three relevant aspects of Boethius' text which Stump and Kretzmann do not discuss. I think that these tilt the balance in favor of divine atemporal duration.

vi. Boethius says of an eternal being that "nothing future is absent from it, and nothing past has flowed away." One can read this phrase in at least two plausible ways. On the first reading, Boethius' phrase means that

1. an eternal being has a past and a future of its own, as temporal beings do, but does not lose its past and does not have its future yet to come.

---

charity would dictate ascribing it rather than inconsistency to Plato and Plotinus. Sorabji may even inadvertently aid Kretzmann and Stump's historical case for their reading of Boethius. For he cites texts from Boethius' contemporary Philoponus which seem (to this reader) to evince an atemporal-duration view of eternity (pp. 117–118). Now Philoponus had the same philosophical sources as Boethius and may even have studied with him under the same teachers. So if an atemporal-duration concept of eternity is present in Philoponus, this makes it a bit more probable that Boethius himself would have arrived at such a view.

Although I do not think that Sorabji carries the day against Stump and Kretzmann, I am undecided as to whether they are correct in their claim about Plato and Plotinus. Plotinus, for instance, seems in *Ennead* III,7 quite at pains to deny that eternality involves any kind of extension. But on the other hand, if it does not, then how does his Nous' mode of being differ relevantly from that of the One?

10. Fitzgerald, "SKTE," p. 265.

11. As Boethius was influenced by Augustine, it is germane to recall here the Parmenidean overtones Augustine packs into his description of eternal existence.

On this reading, then, an eternal being's life is a timelike extension. On the second reading, the past and future that are present to an eternal being are not its own, but those of temporal beings, as the claim that it has "the infinity of mobile time present to it" suggests. On the second reading, then, Boethius' phrase means only that

> 2. an eternal being is somehow copresent with the whole of time.

This second reading lends itself to two different spatial metaphors. Perhaps

> 2a. an eternal God is copresent with the whole of time in the way the unextended center point of a circle is equally present to all points on its circumference.

For Boethius compares an eternal God to the center point of a circle earlier in the *Consolation*.[12] Or perhaps

> 2b. an eternal God is copresent with the whole of time by His life's being stretched out alongside it.[13]

(1) and (2b) fit together naturally. As the text seems genuinely ambiguous, this "fit" establishes some presumption that Boethius meant (2b) or (1): it would have been easier for him to fail to distinguish (2b) from (1) than to conflate (2a) and (1). Both (2b) and (1) commit Boethius to divine atemporal duration.

vii. According to Boethius, an eternal being "embrace[s] its whole extent simultaneously." One expects that a being that embraces its whole extent has an extent to embrace. But contemporary logic would let one say that a being without an extended life lives its whole extension at once.[14] If Herman has no extended life, no two portions of an extended life are both Herman's and not lived by Herman simultaneously. On a now-orthodox treatment of conditionals, this entails the material conditional "(x)(y)(if x and y are portions of Herman's extended life, Herman lives x and y at once)."

Still, astute logician though he was, Boethius is not likely to have accepted this claim about conditionals. We take the conditional "$(x)(Fx \supset Gx)$" as equivalent to "$(x) \sim (Fx \cdot \sim Gx)$" partly to *deny* existential

12. Bk. IV, chap. 6.
13. Without referring to Boethius, Stump and Kretzmann offer this as their best spatial metaphor for eternity in "AD," p. 219.
14. Stump and Kretzmann make a similar point, "Eternity," p. 432.

import to universally quantified conditionals. The Aristotelian logic Boethius knew steadfastly *ascribed* existential import to universal conditionals.[15] Thus Boethius' talk of "embracing its whole extent" likely implies in his eyes that an eternal being has a duration or extension. For Boethius, I suggest, the material conditional "(x)(y)(if x and y are portions of Herman's extended life, Herman lives x and y at once)" is true only if Herman does in fact have an extended life. This in turn suggests that we read Boethius' contrast of eternity with time in this way: a temporal being that lasted forever would not enjoy its whole unending life at once, whereas an eternal being lasts forever, literally, and does enjoy its whole unending life at once.

viii. Following Plato's *Timaeus*, Boethius calls the endless changing of the temporal universe "an attempt to imitate this state of presence of unchanging life," explaining that "by the very fact that it is impossible for its existence ever to come to an end, it does seem in some measure to emulate that which it cannot fulfill or express."[16] Boethius asserts, that is, that the everlastingness of the universe's existence is (part of) what makes it an imitation of eternal life.[17] The *everlastingness* of the

15. See, e.g., *An. Pr.* I, 2, 25a9.
16. "Hunc enim vitae immobilis praesentiarium statum infinitus ille temporalium rerum motus imitatur . . . hoc ipso quod aliquo modo numquam esse desinit, illud quod implere atque exprimere non potest." Boethius, *Philosophiae consolationis*, V, prose 6, in Stewart and Rand, *Boethius*, p. 402, ll. 40–42, 47–49. Tr. by V. E. Watts, in *Boethius: The Consolation of Philosophy* (Harmondsworth: Penguin Books, 1969).
17. Stump and Kretzmann suggest (e.g., at "Eternity," p. 433 n. 10) that Aquinas understands eternity the way they say Boethius does. But note that for Aquinas, time reveals more about God, the sole eternal being, by the fact that it is not necessarily everlasting: see *ST* Ia 46, 1 *ad* 9. Further, though Aquinas adopts Boethius' language for and definition of eternity, and uses his simile of the center point and the circle at *SCG* I, 66, this really counts for little. Aquinas often uses others' language to express his own rather different ideas; this is a facet of the medievals' peculiar way of dealing with *auctoritates*. A telling example in this context is the very unBoethian freight Thomas loads onto Boethius' distinction of *esse* from *id quod est*. So it is at least arguable that Aquinas did not in fact agree with Boethius. One text that points to this is *In I Sent.* d. 8, q. 2, a. 1, *ad* 6: "duratio dicit quamdam distensionem ex ratione nominis: et quia in divino esse non debet intelligi aliqua talis distensio, ideo Boetius non posuit durationem, sed possessionem . . . illud enim dicimus possidere quod quiete et plene habemus; et sic Deus possidere vitam suam dicitur, quia nulla inquietudine molestatur." ("Duration" is said to be a certain distension by the meaning of the name: and because in God's being nothing should be understood as a distension, therefore Boethius does not say "duration," but "possession" . . . we say ourselves to possess what we have quietly and fully, and so God is said to possess His life, because it is molested by no inquietude.) I owe my awareness of this text to Nelson, "Time(s)."
Still, the slightly later text quoted in the last section of Chapter 8 is more naturally read as involving an extensional view of eternity: there Thomas first speaks of a temporally extended observation of a road, then says that God's eternal "seeing" is as if this

universe is a quality of its duration. If the universe's duration is like eternity in virtue of a quality of that duration, it is natural to infer that eternal life is a form of duration. For if eternity involved no duration, being everlasting would make the universe's existence less rather than more like eternity. A durationless present instant would be a better temporal analogue to a durationless eternal present than would an everlasting temporal duration.

Given my (vi)–(viii), Stump and Kretzmann's (i)–(v) can perhaps be taken to provide additional confirming evidence that for Boethius, eternity is atemporal duration. I submit that the balance of the evidence favors this claim.

Eternity in *De Trinitate*

What, then, is atemporal duration? Boethius explains in his *De Trinitate* that "God is said to always exist . . . as if he had existed in all the past, exists in all the present and will exist in all the future . . . but he 'always exists' in that for him 'always' has to do with present time . . . Our now, as if running along, makes time and sempiternity. The divine now, permanent and not moving . . . makes eternity."[18] As time "runs along," instants of time are successively present, and so time itself is present—not as a whole, but because a point in the temporal continuum is present. Whereas time is always present, eternity is a present-always: somehow all of it, not just an instant of it, is always present.[19] The now of time "runs along" in that ever-later temporal positions successively are "now." The now of an eternal life does not run along, then, because in such a life there is no succession between earlier and later positions: all "has to do with present time."

There are at least two ways an eternal life could contain no succes-

---

whole extended observation occurred at once. Further, that time reveals more about God by not being everlasting than it would by being everlasting does not entail that time would not reveal more about God's *eternity* by being everlasting. On balance, then, Thomas may at the outset of his career have denied that eternity is a duration or significantly durationlike, but if he did, he shifted to a durational view by the time of his *Quaestiones de Veritate.* He seems to have retained a durational view of eternity thereafter; see, e.g., the texts from *ST* Ia 10 cited in Chapter 7.

18. "de deo dicitur 'semper est'" . . . quasi omni praeterito fuerit, omni quoquomodo sit praesenti est, omni futuro erit . . . Semper enim est, quoniam semper praesentis est in eo temporis . . . nostrum nunc quasi currens tempus facit et sempiternitatem, divinum vero nunc permanens neque movens sese atque consistens aeternitatem facit." Boethius, *De Trinitate*, chap. 4, in Stewart and Rand, *Boethius*, p. 20, ll. 64–66, 69–74. Tr. partly Stump and Kretzmann's.

19. Cf. Plutarch, "Single, He has completed 'always' in a single now." *On the E at Delphi*, 393 A–B, tr. in Sorabji, *TC&C*, p. 121.

sion. It could be that an eternal life contains no succession because it contains no earlier and later positions. This is Stump and Kretzmann's reading: "Because an eternal entity is atemporal, there is no past or future, no earlier or later, within its life; that is, the events constituting its life cannot be ordered sequentially from the standpoint of eternity."[20] On the other hand, it could also be that an eternal life contains earlier and later points, but with no succession between them. In the *De Trinitate* text just quoted, Boethius contrasts eternity with time taken as involving a "moving now," i.e., time as tensed. Perhaps, then, Boethian eternity is like an extension in tenseless time.[21] Perhaps, that is, it involves earlier and later, and yet none of it "passes away" or is "yet to come," as tensed theories say that phases of time do. If this is so, then an eternal being could be one that somehow lives at once ("*tota simul*") all moments of a life whose moments are ordered as earlier and later. This second concept of eternal life renders it a bit more like a life in time, by asserting that it contains earlier and later positions. So let us call eternality so conceived Quasi-Temporal Eternality, or QTE.

The life of a being with QTE is an extension in which positions are ordered as earlier and later. Yet none of it "passes away" or is "yet to come," as we think happens with temporal lives. This likens extension in QTE to an extension in tenseless time. Because of this, it may also make eternal life sound more like an extension in space than like a life in time; "tenseless" theories of time, which deny that time literally "passes away" or is "yet to come," are sometimes accused of "spatializing" time. But if the charge of spatializing time accuses one of denying all significant difference between time and space, the tenseless theorist of time is not guilty. The tenseless theorist can, for instance, note that space and tenseless time have different relations to spatiotemporal particulars. The same concrete particular thing can be wholly present at many points along the extensive dimension of tenseless time, as I am wholly present at 1 P.M. and at 1:01 P.M. Concrete particular things cannot be wholly present at any point along a spatial extension. For every spatial concrete particular is spatially extended and so covers more than a single point in space. That tenseless time does and space does not permit concrete particulars full location at a point is a large difference between the two. Again, I can be wholly present at many points in tenseless time at the same place, but I cannot be wholly

20. Stump and Kretzmann, "Eternity," p. 434. It will emerge that in fact, eternity as Stump and Kretzmann conceive it contains no distinct positions at all.

21. Tenseless views of time were formulated in sources to which Boethius probably had access. See Paul Plass, "Timeless Time in NeoPlatonism," *Modern Schoolman* 55 (1977), 1–19.

present at many points in space at the same time. We will see below that in these respects, a life with QTE is more like a duration through tenseless time than it is like an extension through space.

A being with QTE which has experience always changelessly experiences the full extent of its duration. If it did not always changelessly experience whatever it experiences, its experience would change, and so it would change, and so it would be temporal rather than eternal. If its experience did not always encompass the whole of its duration, in a clear sense it would be false that "nothing future is absent from it and nothing past has flowed away." The character of a QTE-being's experience may point to an underlying difference between the way beings with QTE and temporal beings occupy their durations.

We can see this deeper difference if we recall Boethius' claims that "there is nothing placed in time that can embrace the whole extent of its life equally" and that an eternal being "includes and possesses the whole fullness of illimitable life at once."[22] It *could* be that in denying that a temporal being can "embrace the whole extent of its life," Boethius speaks only of the quality of experience of a temporal being with experience. But this would leave him no account of the difference in mode of being between a QTE-being and a temporal being without experience. So it is more charitable to assume that Boethius is speaking of relations between the segments of temporal things' durations and affirming that things' earlier temporal stages are not temporally simultaneous with their later stages. If we make this assumption, Boethius' contrasting point about QTE is that despite the fact that eternal point e + 1 is later than eternal point e, since an eternal being exists "*tota simul*," what occupies e does so simultaneously (in some nontemporal sense of simultaneity) with occupying e + 1.

This being so, a QTE-being always occupies its full duration at once; there cannot be a part of its duration which is divided from any other part of it as "not yet" or "no longer." To put it another way, even though points within QTE are ordered as earlier and later, no segments of it are past or future in relation to any others, where being past or future entail, in addition to being earlier or later, that some segments of QTE have ceased to be lived or are not yet lived. (Thus, again, an extension in QTE is like a temporal extension in tenseless time.) This difference lies beneath and helps to explain the fact that temporal subjects have experiences sequentially and subjects with QTE have them all at once. As a life with temporal extension can be divided into "not yet" and "no longer," it can contain a sequence of many discrete experiences. As a life with QTE cannot, it cannot contain a sequence of many discrete experiences. Even though such a life is extended, its whole extension must be lived at once or not be lived (and so not be of that life) at all. One may well wonder how segments of a life can be genuinely earlier and later and yet simultaneously lived. One can answer this question on the basis of a complex set of distinctions between different kinds of actuality and simultaneity, which will be set out later.[23] But let me make at least one point dialectically. One problem tenseless theories of time have is accounting for the apparent change in our experience. On a tenseless theory of time, in a strong sense, nothing happens and nothing changes: time does not pass, and events do not become actual with the onrush of ever-new time. Rather, things just *are*, in frozen stasis at various temporal coordinates. If this is so, though, whence do we derive the illusion of time's passage, and why are we not aware of the whole of our experiences at once? If I am not aware of the whole of my life at once, is there not some real change in my awareness, a passage of my awareness from past to present to future in some sense that a tenseless theory cannot allow? It seems intuitively that there is. But if God's eternity is QTE, this problem does not arise, because though QTE is *like* life in tenseless time, God enjoys the whole of His life *totum simul*. In a sense, then, if a tenseless theory of time is true, it is easier to understand the living and experiencing of a God with QTE than to understand our own.

Now to affirm both that points within a QTE-being's life are earlier or later than one another and that they are lived at once sounds like a flat contradiction. Again, if points within a QTE are ordered as earlier and later and yet no part of QTE is "not yet" or "no longer," QTE is a single extended present *containing* earlier and later points. This, too, sounds impossible; surely, one wants to say, if eternal point e is eternally present and eternal point e + 1 is in any way later than e, e + 1 is eternally future. Further, the claim that there cannot be a part of a QTE which is divided from any other part of it suggests that a QTE, though extended, lacks parts. This claim also sounds flatly contradictory, as does the claim that an extension containing distinct points contains no distinct parts. I argue below that none of these claims is impossible. This argument also suggests how an extension can contain distinct points yet lack parts.

23. In terms of these later distinctions, segments that are ordered as earlier and later and so not B-simultaneous (or not in an eternal analogue of B-simultaneity) can nonetheless be A-simultaneous.

QTE and the Stump-Kretzmann View

Read either as Stump and Kretzmann suggest or as QTE, Boethian atemporal duration is a limitless timelike extension. But it is a time*less* extension. This may be because an eternal life does not contain relations of earlier and later (Stump-Kretzmann). Or it may be because an eternal life contains these relations, but without succession between them, without "not yet" or "no longer" (QTE). Both the Stump-Kretzmann and the QTE readings of Boethian eternity have disadvantages. We have seen the problems the QTE reading faces. The Stump-Kretzmann reading makes it hard to see in what sense an eternal life is extended or is a *timelike* extension (as is implied in calling it a *duration*). Arguably, what contains distinct points, but not points ordered as earlier and later, may be an extension but lacks the traits distinctive of *temporal* extension, and what contains no distinct points is not an extension at all.

The rest of this chapter develops an objection to the Stump-Kretzmann reading of Boethius, then tries to give an account of QTE and answer the questions raised about it. My goal henceforth is both philosophical and historical. I try to show that QTE is a possible sort of duration, and this has a historical implication. For if both the Stump-Kretzmann view and the theory of QTE could be found in Boethius' text, charity dictates ascribing to Boethius the philosophically most viable concept of eternity. I want to suggest that this is the concept of QTE and so suggest that QTE is Boethius' concept of eternity.

Fitzgerald's Critique

Fitzgerald has recently argued that there cannot be any such thing as an atemporal duration.[24] A duration is a sort of extension. According to Fitzgerald, if atemporal duration is "an extensive mode of being (and) not pointlike," it must meet three conditions: "First, two distinct particulars can both have [this] kind of extension . . . Second . . . there must be different . . . subphases of [eternal] duration . . . one cannot have literal infinite duration without ordered, finitely extended sub-phases . . . Thirdly, by having different positions along the extensive dimension in question, two qualitatively identical particulars can be numerically distinct."[25] Fitzgerald's conditions on extensionhood seem to be that

24. Fitzgerald, "SKTE."
25. Ibid., pp. 262–263, 264.

      3. necessarily, any kind of extension contains distinct positions,
      4. necessarily, any kind of extension has parts or subphases, and
      5. necessarily, any kind of extension is such that two distinct
         particulars can have it.

(3) and (4) are distinct conditions and would be so even if it were the
case (as I will deny) that necessarily, something satisfies (3) if it satisfies
(4). They are distinct because points in or along an extension are not
parts of that extension. For it seems possible that lines intersect without
sharing a part. But if points are parts, this is impossible. Again, it
seems plausible that for all x, if x is part of finite extension E, then E
minus x is shorter than E including x. But if points are parts, this is
false. Finally, only if points are not parts can QTE contain distinct
points but no distinct parts, as I will argue that it does.

    Fitzgerald's backing for (3)–(5) is that every extension with which
we are acquainted meets them. Fitzgerald's mention of "order" brings
in a fourth condition, which he thinks any extension must meet to
count as a sort of duration, i.e., as a timelike rather than spacelike
extension. This is that

      6. necessarily, any duration has an intrinsic order among its
         parts.

Plausibly, time has an intrinsic direction and therefore has an intrinsic
order between its various phases. Time's intrinsic direction is from
earlier to later. To be a segment of time thus involves being earlier or
later than other segments of time and/or containing relations of earlier
and later; it involves having a place in a series of time segments ordered
intrinsically by these relations and/or being such a series. There is no
comparable intrinsic direction or order to space. Hence any extension
that fails (6) is to this extent more like space than like time.

    Fitzgerald argues that the Stump-Kretzmann conception of atem-
poral duration fails to meet conditions (3), (4), and (6). If in an eternal
life there is no earlier or later, there is no intrinsic ordering relation or
direction between "parts" of eternal duration, counter to (6). If so, it
seems that eternal life cannot be a duration, even if it is an extension.[26]
Again, Fitzgerald notes that Stump and Kretzmann question whether
the idea of parts of eternal duration makes sense.[27] This contravenes

---

26. Sorabji has offered the same argument (*TC&C*, p. 111), and related points are
made in Nelson, "Time(s)," pp. 16–17.
27. Fitzgerald, "SKTE," pp. 263–264.

(4). Moreover, says Fitzgerald, if all in an eternal life is present, there are no distinct positions within eternal duration; thus eternal duration runs afoul of (3).[28] (Also, though Fitzgerald does not bring this out, we will see that on Stump and Kretzmann's view, eternity fails [5].) Thus Fitzgerald concludes that Stump-Kretzmann eternity cannot be a duration or an extension, but must be something pointlike. According to Fitzgerald, "timeless duration" is an incoherent concept.

The Stump-Kretzmann Response

Stump and Kretzmann grant that eternity as they conceive it fails Fitzgerald's conditions but contend that this just doesn't matter.[29] Fitzgerald, they argue, has modeled his conditions for durationhood closely on temporal duration. But "atemporal duration is the genuine, paradigmatic duration of which temporal duration is only the moving image . . . any instance of which is correctly called duration only analogically, since it is only a partial manifestation of the paradigmatic, genuine duration."[30] In short, being eternal is radically unlike being temporal, but that doesn't entail that eternal beings lack true duration—rather, it entails that temporal beings do. This response is faithful to the Platonist-influenced metaphysical tradition Stump and Kretzmann are defending: one can imagine Augustine arguing in the same way about eternal versus temporal existence.[31] But arguably, the move concedes too much. Stump and Kretzmann grant that eternal duration is so radically unlike temporal that

7. if eternal duration is a true duration, temporal duration is not.

(7) entails another conditional, that

8. if temporal duration is a true duration, eternal duration is not.

(8) will cause Stump and Kretzmann trouble, for there is a good case to be made that temporal duration is a true duration.

Temporal duration is the only duration of which we have any experience. Our concept of duration is built on this experience; the only concept of duration we have to work with is the one relative to which

---

28. Ibid., p. 263. Sorabji makes the same point when he asks, "if the present *endures* . . . how are we to understand endurance without a past or future?" (*TC&C*, p. 100).
29. Stump and Kretzmann, "AD," esp. pp. 216–217.
30. Ibid., p. 219.
31. This is not to say that Augustine considers eternal existence an extension.

temporal duration counts as a genuine duration. One could almost say that "time" is just what we mean by "duration," for one can substitute "time" or constructions containing it for "duration" in most ordinary contexts. Given our concept of duration, then, we cannot but affirm that time is a true duration: time is the paradigmatic example of what we mean by a duration.

If time is a true duration and (8) is true, it follows that eternity is not a true duration. So to avoid this conclusion, one must deny (8) or deny that time is a true duration. Now Stump and Kretzmann would likely not want to withdraw (8). For one thing, the logic of Platonism favors (8). As R. E. Allen argued in a classic essay, the Platonic paradigm of F is not literally an F at all, but merely some abstract particular with a causal role relative to Fs, which is called F equivocally—which is to say that it is called F although it has none of the attributes by which ordinary Fs deserve to be called Fs.[32] So according to the Platonist tradition in which Stump and Kretzmann stand, the paradigm of duration is so unlike ordinary (temporal) duration that if ordinary temporal duration is a duration, paradigmatic duration is not. Further, if time and eternity are *not* so unlike as to warrant (8), it is reasonable to expect that if both are durations, both will satisfy some selection of Fitzgerald's (3)–(6). But again, for Stump and Kretzmann, eternity satisfies none of (3)–(6). Thus Stump and Kretzmann would likely stick to their guns, retain (8), and continue to deny that time is a true duration.

Given our argument that time *is* a true duration, there seems only one way to make this denial at all plausible. Stump and Kretzmann could say that though we so understand the term "duration" that it is correctly applicable to temporal duration, we have no idea at all of what it really means. More precisely, Stump and Kretzmann could say that the understood meaning of "duration," the meaning that is "in the head," has no content at all in common with the contribution of "duration" to the truth-conditions of sentences containing it. If this is true, then even if eternity is not a duration in the sense of a genuine example of what we mean by the term "duration," it can still be a true duration. For it can still be the case that "eternity is a duration" would appear true to us in a language whose understood meanings adequately expressed (as ours do not) the real truth-conditional contributions of the terms in this English sentence. Allowing a complete divorce of understood meaning and truth-condition contribution thus would let Stump and Kretzmann preserve the claim that eternity is the Platonic para-

32. R. E. Allen, "Participation and Predication in Plato's Middle Dialogues," in Gregory Vlastos, ed., *Plato I: Metaphysics and Epistemology* (Garden City, New York: Doubleday, 1971), pp. 167–183.

digm of duration, that of which temporal duration is merely the moving image.

Still, this move faces difficulties. Is it really at all plausible that we have absolutely no idea what we are talking about when we use the term "duration"? If we know that true duration really is nothing at all like what we mean by duration, why call eternity a sort of duration at all, given what we cannot but mean by that word?[33] If the content we attach to the term "duration" has nothing to do with the term's truth-conditional contribution, then why do we even *care* to call eternity a duration? If we do not know what we "really mean" by saying this, what interest can attach to saying it? Fully adjudicating this would take us deep into the theory of meaning, but I suspect that one cannot in the end accede to so great a distance between what is "in the head" and what is in reality. If one cannot, one cannot preserve both the radical unlikeness of time and eternity Stump and Kretzmann concede and the claim that eternity is literally any sort of duration. Boethian eternity must fulfill at least some of (3)–(6) to be a duration. If it does not, it is not one.

Now the foregoing rests on a particular interpretation of (7). We have taken (7) to say in effect that

    7a. if eternity is a true duration, temporal duration is not a duration.

That is, we have taken Stump and Kretzmann's claim that "atemporal duration is . . . genuine, paradigmatic duration . . . temporal duration . . . is correctly called duration only analogically" as a claim that atemporal duration really is duration, and temporal duration is not really duration but is at most like duration in some ways. But a second reading of (7) is available. We can take (7) as

    7b. if eternal duration is a metaphysically paradigmatic duration, temporal duration is not a metaphysically paradigmatic duration.

The consequent of (7b) does not entail that temporal duration is not a duration at all. Nor does it entail that time is not a good or paradigmatic example of what *we* mean by duration. It entails only that in some metaphysical ranking scheme other than the ordinary one that

---

33. To reason "any true duration is nothing at all like what we mean by duration; eternity is nothing at all like what we mean by duration; therefore eternity is a true duration" would of course be to commit the fallacy of affirming the consequent.

makes time a paradigm of duration, time is not as good an example of a duration as some other durations.[34] Still, if both eternity and time are durations, then either they share some common attributes relevant to being durations or they do not. If they do not, they are both *called* durations due to likenesses not reducible to identities of attribute, and arguably once more, time is not a duration, but is just like one in some ways. If time and eternity do share relevant common attributes, it is not clear what these could be or how they can outweigh the difference between time and eternity with respect to (3)–(6). In addition, our effort to talk about metaphysically paradigmatic duration is rendered problematic by the fact that we do not actually have any concepts or ranking scheme other than those that make *time* a paradigm of duration.

Stump and Kretzmann in effect grant that eternity is like a point rather than an extension when they state that "the occurrence of two of God's mental acts at different points in [eternal] duration . . . is . . . incompatible with the doctrine of eternity we presented . . . If . . . God's eternal existence were to include acts with different locations in (eternal) duration, it would not be a life possessed completely all at once."[35] If there is one crucial difference between any extension and a point, it is that an extension includes or covers many distinct points or positions (which is *not* to say that any extension has parts). Stump and Kretzmann claim that distinct positions in an eternal duration cannot be simultaneously occupied; this is part of their assertion that were God's mental acts at two positions within eternity, He could not live His life all at once. Perhaps they say this because they think that if positions in eternal duration are occupied simultaneously, they are not distinct but one single position. Regardless, Stump and Kretzmann also insist that there cannot be distinct nonsimultaneous positions in eternity, since if there were, eternity would contain relations of earlier and later. But if eternity cannot contain distinct simultaneous positions or distinct nonsimultaneous positions, eternity contains but one position. If it does, eternity is pointlike, not extensionlike.[36] So far, then, it seems that Stump and Kretzmann cannot maintain the Boethian claim that an eternal life is extended.

But perhaps they do not mean this claim quite as I have taken it.

34. I owe this point to Eleonore Stump.
35. Stump and Kretzmann, "AD," p. 215.
36. Stump and Kretzmann confirm their retreat toward a "point" view of eternity by reinterpreting the limitlessness of eternity. That eternity is limitless, they say, does not mean that it is a literal infinite length. Rather, it means that it is a present not limited by a past or a future ("AD," p. 218). This does not conflict with a "point" view of eternity, as the claim that eternity involves literal infinite extension does.

Stump and Kretzmann could be making use of something like the Thomistic theory of irreducibly analogous prediction.[37] On such a theory, eternity would be neither univocally or equivocally a duration.[38] Analogy rules out univocity. Thus if A and B are called Fs analogously, what it is for A to be F ≠ what it is for B to be F.[39] That is, if A and B are called Fs analogously, the character which "makes" A an F differs somehow from the character which "makes" B an F, and accordingly, "Fa" and "Fb" do not have precisely the same entailments. Analogy also rules out equivocity. If A and B are called Fs analogously, what it is for A to be F is not *wholly* discrete from what it is for B to be F.[40] Rather, A and B are both literally Fs, but either what it is for A to be F includes features also included in what it is for B to be F, or else what it is for A to be F and what it is for B to be F include no common features but are somehow alike.[41] Stump and Kretzmann warn that "in seeking . . . a list of all the features shared by temporal and atemporal duration . . . critics of the concept of eternity are seeking what cannot be found if . . . this . . . is a case of irreducibly analogical predication."[42] So if they are taking the analogy route, Stump and Kretzmann assert between what it is for time to be a duration and what it is for eternity to be a duration only likeness.

Stump and Kretzmann have said that the eternal present is a duration in that it "persists, encompasses time and is unbounded," and added that it "is a measure of existence, indicating some degree of permanence of some sort on the part of something that persists."[43] They claim, then, that these features "make" eternity a duration. But let us examine these. Whether eternity as they see it "really" persists is just what I am questioning, so Stump and Kretzmann cannot appeal to this in the present discussion. A time encompasses a time by lasting through it and/or by existing before and after it; presumably any more general sense of "encompassing" will be somehow allied to this. Eternity as Stump and Kretzmann see it does not last through or exist before or after time. It is prior to time causally only if an eternal being causes time to exist, and that this is so is not part of the concept of

---

37. Eleonore Stump and Norman Kretzmann, typescript of "Eternity Examined and Extended," a paper read at a UCLA conference on philosophical theology, March 31, 1990, Stump and Kretzmann make just this claim on p. 12. The paper is forthcoming in a volume in James Tomberlin's *Philosophical Perspectives* series.

38. Ibid., p. 11.
39. See Aquinas, *ST* Ia 13, 5.
40. Ibid.
41. This is Swinburne's line, *Coherence*, part 1, passim.
42. Stump and Kretzmann, "Eternity Examined," p. 12.
43. Ibid., pp. 7, 12.

either eternity or time in any obvious way. So it is not clear just what Stump and Kretzmann's claim that eternity "encompasses" time means, nor for that matter what a "measure of existence" is.

On the other hand, a time is unbounded (in one sense) if it has no time before or after it. Stump-Kretzmann eternity is unbounded in this sense by either time or eternity. A time is unbounded in a second sense if it has no first or last moment. Stump-Kretzmann eternity is unbounded in the second sense by temporal or eternal moments. These two sorts of unboundedness appear independent. A period of time can have time before and after it but have no first or last moment. For time is continuous, and for any distinct times t1 and t2, there is a period of time including neither t1 nor t2 but including every moment between t1 and t2. This period has times before and after it—minimally, t1 and t2. But this period has no first or last moment. For as time is continuous, between any two times there is a further time. So for every time t3 between t1 and t2, there is a time closer to t1 than t3 is and there is a time closer to t2 than t3 is. On the other hand, arguably a period of time can have a first or last moment but no time before or after it. For arguably time can have a first or last moment, and if it does, then the period of time including all times has a first and a last moment but no time before or after it.

An extent of time can be unbounded in both ways. Arguably a moment of time must be bounded in the first way, i.e., must have time before or after it. For arguably there cannot be such a thing as a single isolated moment of time. Such an entity would neither contain nor stand in any earlier-later relations. If it did not, it could not contain or be in a past or a future. It would be a "pure present," and would conform to one of our descriptions of eternity. Thus it is not clear what could make it a moment of *time*.

One can argue that a moment of time must be bounded in the second way. For a time has a first moment if some moment included in the time has before it no moment included in the time, and a time has a last moment if some moment included in the time has after it no moment included in the time. Necessarily, each moment includes a moment (itself) that satisfies both descriptions. Yet this argument is defective. For it is one thing to *have* a first or last moment and another to *be* a first or last moment. The argument shows that every moment *is* a first or last moment. But one can call bounded only something which *has* a first or last moment. I take it, then, that a moment of time is also unbounded in the second way.

Stump-Kretzmann eternity is unbounded in both of our senses. An extension of time can be unbounded in both ways. A moment of time must be bounded in the first way. So Stump-Kretzmann eternity is more extensionlike than pointlike with regard to unboundedness.

What then of permanence? We have already argued that a timeless entity "exists immutably," in Augustine's phrase, i.e., that such a being cannot begin or cease to exist. Does this entail that a timeless being is permanent? One wants to say that

> P1. x is permanent = df. x has no first or last moment of existence.

If (P1) is true, a timeless being counts as permanent. But as we have seen, there are finite periods of time that have no first or last moment of existence. A finite period of time does not exist permanently. So one might move from (P1) to

> P2. x is permanent = df. x has no first or last finite period of existence.

Any finite period of time fails this test. But (P2) will not do. We have already alluded to series of the order-type $\omega^* + \omega$, i.e., series which can be mapped 1:1 onto the series of positive and negative whole numbers,

$$\ldots -3, \; -2, \; -1, \; 0, \; 1, \; 2, \; 3, \; \ldots$$

and to the fact that such a series could be contained within a larger series, of order type $\omega^* + \omega^* + \omega + \omega$.[44] Consider then a series S of minutes of the order-type $\omega^* + \omega$ which is thus contained in a larger series of minutes. S has no first or last finite period of existence. Yet it does not seem apt to call S permanent.[45] There are minutes not contained in S. So there are times before and after which S does not exist, namely any minutes contained in the larger series but not contained in S. No temporal thing such that there are times before and after which it does not exist can qualify as permanent.

So one might replace (P2) with

> P3. x is permanent = df. x exists and does not begin or cease to exist.

44. See "Timeless Space" in chapter 3.
45. In this I dissent from Smith's "A New Typology" (see pp. 308, 314–317).

(P3) is distinct from (P2), for not beginning or ceasing to exist is not the same thing as having no first or last moment of existence. As we have seen, there are finite periods of time that have neither first nor last moments. So surely there could be an entity K which existed at all and only the moments contained in one such period. We would want to say that K begins and ceases to exist. It seems to us that K must, for there would be times before which and times after which K did not exist. Yet K would have neither first nor last moment of existence. Again, consider an instantaneous event E, which occurs at t. E has a first moment of existence, t, and a last moment of existence, t. But it is at least odd to say that E begins to exist at t, for beginning to exist at t usually connotes and arguably entails existing for some period of time after t. It is equally odd to say that E ceases to exist at t, for ceasing to exist at t usually connotes and arguably entails existing for some period of time before t.

As S is infinite, S "goes on forever" in either temporal direction. S neither begins nor ceases to exist. So S satisfies (P3). Paradoxically, there are times before and after S and yet S did not begin and will not cease. (This is why the last paragraph said only that it *seems* that K's having moments before and after its existence is reason to say that K begins and ceases.) Yet just because there *are* times before and after S, it does not seem apt to call S permanent. So (P3) is not an acceptable account of permanence.

One might replace (P3) with

> P4. x is permanent = df. there is no moment before which x does not exist and no moment after which x does not exist.

Any finite period of time fails (P4). On (P4), S comes out impermanent. Also, on (P4), a timeless being would count as permanent. But (P4) is not acceptable. Necessarily, there is no moment before time exists and no moment after time exists. Yet we can imagine circumstances in which it would surely seem odd to say that time existed permanently—for instance, suppose (as seems possible) that time had a beginning and will have an end, and the whole of time lasts exactly five minutes. Where *permanence* is in question, it seems, it is not enough that a thing last as long as anything ever does (as time must). Further, the intuition the five-minute-time example elicits does not depend on time's lasting a mere five minutes. We can stipulate that time last any finite length—say, a trillion years—and it will still seem odd to call time permanent as long as time *could* last longer or *does* have an end point.[46]

Perhaps, then,

> P5. x is permanent = df. x exists, x has no first or last moment of existence, and there are no moments before or after x exists.

Yet here too a problem arises. For it is possible that time has a finite extent and also has no first or last moment. In this case, time would have the structure of the interval of time which falsified (P1). Again, it does not seem that a finitely enduring span of time should count as permanent. So we must shift to

> P6. x is permanent = df. x exists, x has no first or last finite period of existence, and there are no moments before or after x exists.

(P6) seems adequate. On (P6), a timeless being qualifies as permanent.

It seems, then, that what it is for Stump-Kretzmann eternity to be a duration includes its being unbounded and being a way to exist permanently. But let us take a closer look at this. Stump-Kretzmann eternity qualifies as unbounded in both our senses because it has no first or last moment and has no time before or after it. Stump-Kretzmann eternity has no first or last moment precisely because it is relevantly more like a single moment, which *is* a first or last moment, than like an extension, which *has* a first or last moment. So what it is for Stump-Kretzmann eternity to be unbounded is for it to be pointlike.

In having no time before or after it, Stump-Kretzmann is related to time like a continuous temporal duration that includes all times. But this does not mean that Stump-Kretzmann eternity is a duration. It means only that it is related to time as a duration is. The basis of the relation differs drastically in the two cases. A continuous omnitemporal duration has no time before or after it because it *includes* all times. Stump-Kretzmann eternity has no time before or after it because it excludes all times. Again, Stump-Kretzmann eternity has no "moments of eternity" before or after it because it excludes all before-after

---

46. In "A New Typology," Smith offers as a general definition of permanence, "(D1) x is permanent = Df. There is no time t that is both later than x's existence and separated from x's existence by a finite number of nonoverlapping temporal intervals of equal length," (p. 308). Smith also appears to grant that it is possible that time begin and end (309). But if this is possible, then if my text's argument is correct, (D1) is false.

relations. A continuous omnitemporal duration has no moments of time before or after it because it *in*cludes all before-after relations. So while Stump-Kretzmann eternity and a continuous omnitemporal duration have the same relation to time, this hardly entails that they themselves, as the bases of the relations, are at all alike.

Finally, Stump-Kretzmann eternity not only is unbounded but also satisfies (P6) because in addition to having no first or last moment and having no time before or after it, it has no first or last finite period. But again, according to Stump and Kretzmann, eternity contains no first or last finite period because it contains no distinct positions. So what it is for Stump-Kretzmann eternity to satisfy (P6) is for it to be pointlike.

I have examined the features that Stump and Kretzmann claim "make" eternity (as they conceive it) a duration. If my reasoning is correct, these features amount to Stump-Kretzmann eternity's being a non-enduring, pointlike mode of being which is related to time as one sort of duration is. Thus it seems fair to say that Stump-Kretzmann eternity is really a duration *quoad nos* but not *in se*. Moreover, if my reasoning is correct, Stump-Kretzmann eternity *in se* is not even much like a duration. Stump-Kretzmann eternity seems more like a point.

Eternity must satisfy (3) or not be an extension, or even significantly extensionlike. As we have seen, Stump-Kretzmann eternity does not satisfy (3). One who wants to maintain with Boethius that eternal life is extended must therefore look elsewhere for aid. I will now argue that QTE can contain many distinct positions, thus fulfilling (3). I suggest that if QTE does contain distinct positions, an eternal being occupies all of these positions at once. I also contend that QTE is in fact more timelike than spacelike. If it is, then perhaps the discrete points along a QTE extension can at least be called earlier and later by analogy. So QTE may not wholly fail condition (6). But even if it does, QTE will still be distinct from and more defensibly a duration than Stump-Kretzmann eternity because it literally satisfies (3).

My case for the possibility of an extended QTE rests on an analogy with a space with a peculiar property, an analogy with an atom of time, and two other arguments. To give the analogies their point, I must note another facet of Boethius' concept of eternity.

Eternity and Divine Simplicity

Boethius thinks eternity to be the mode of duration proper to a simple God: "Imagine a set of revolving concentric circles. The inmost one comes closest to the simplicity of the center, [which is] God . . . the relationship between the ever-changing course of fate and the stable simplicity of providence is like that between that which is coming into being and that which is, between time and eternity, or between the moving circle and the still point in the middle."[47] Here Boethius suggests a parallel between two triples of concepts, that-which-is—coming-into-being/time/moving circle and that-which-is/eternity/still, simple point. It is a reasonable inference that in Boethius' eyes, just as duration through time is the mode of being proper to things that come to be, so eternal duration is the mode of being proper to the simple point, God.

Now this claim may seem to invite an objection. For Boethius, an eternal life is extended. But how can something simple or partless have an extended life? If a life is extended, and every extension contains parts, is not a being with an extended life a being with parts? So is not a pointlike instant a much better model for the "duration" of a pointlike, simple being? We can, I think, dismiss this objection. Boethius, Aquinas, and the whole orthodox medieval Christian theological tradition hold that a simple God cannot have spatial or material parts and so therefore spatial or material extension. But this does not commit them to denying a simple being temporal or durational parts, for there is an important disanalogy between spatial or material parts and parts of a duration, or temporal parts. An object is identical with that which is composed of its spatial parts; thus any object with spatial parts is composed of those parts and so not simple. But arguably, an object is not identical with that which is composed of its temporal parts. If I am a whole composed of temporal parts, then if I am wholly present, my whole temporal extent is present, just as if I am wholly present, my whole spatial extent is present. But my whole temporal extent does not exist at any point within my temporal extent. What is present at any moment is not the whole of my life, but a mere slice of my life. So if I am identical with a whole composed of temporal parts, I am not wholly present at any point during my life. Rather, what exists at each moment is only a slice of me. So if it is true that *I* am writing this paper, rather than that a temporal slice of me is writing this paper, I exist as a whole now and so am not identical with a whole composed of temporal parts.

A thing's temporal parts compose not the thing itself, but its duration or its life. Hence a thing with a temporal or atemporal duration is

47. "Nam ut orbium circa eundem cardinem sese vertentium qui est intimus ad simplicitatem medietatis . . . uti est . . . ad id quod est id quod gignitur, ad aeternitatem tempus, ad punctum medium circulus, ita est fati series mobilis ad providentiae stabilem simplicitatem." Boethius, *Philosophiae consolationis,* IV, chap. 6, in Stewart and Rand, *Boethius,* pp. 342–344, ll. 65–67, 78–82. Tr. of V. E. Watts.

not ipso facto composite or complex. The complexity or partedness of a duration is not identical with and does not obviously entail the complexity or partedness of the thing that has the duration. To this extent, then, God's having durational parts would not necessarily be incompatible with His being simple.

Although this is true, Boethius does not appeal to it in harmonizing simplicity and duration. Rather, Boethius denies that an eternal duration contains parts and so denies that every extension contains parts. To Boethius, the "parts" of a temporal duration are its past and its future, the present being a boundary point between them.[48] If for Boethius there is no earlier or later in eternity, as Stump and Kretzmann say, there cannot be past and future there, and so eternity is partless. As we have seen, if Boethian eternity is QTE, it cannot contain past and future parts either, though it does contain points ordered as earlier and later. Thus eternity, on Boethius' view, is a partless duration. For Boethius, being eternal thus would be compatible with being partless even if an eternal thing *were* identical with its duration. Of course, this raises a still knottier question: how can anything be a duration without having parts?

God's simplicity, which raised this question, will also answer it. Explaining God's simplicity in his *De Trinitate*, Boethius asserts that God is pure form and immaterial and therefore identical with His essence, incapable of bearing accidents, and wholly without parts.[49] Now in Boethius' view, members of the same species are made distinct from one another only by having distinct sets of accidental attributes.[50] So for Boethius, if a kind is such that its members cannot have accidents, this kind cannot have more than one member. Thus Boethius is committed to the claim that there cannot be more than one actual member of the kind "simple being." As we have seen, Boethius holds that only a simple being can be eternal. So by stipulating that eternity is proper only to simple beings, Boethius winds up committed to the claim that there can be at most one actual being with an eternal duration.

Now nothing said so far rules out the claim that in possible world W, A is the sole eternal being, and in possible world W*, B is the sole eternal being, and A ≠ B. But Boethius' conception of God's simplicity does rule this out as well. According to Boethius, all attributes

---

48. Cf. Aristotle, *Physics* IV, 11, 220a5–20; IV, 13, 222a10–12. A view of the present along these lines but educated by Dedekind might say that the present is a cut between past and future.

49. Boethius, *De Trinitate*, chap. 2.

50. Ibid., chap. 1.

of a simple being are really identical: for instance, since God is simple and just, to be God = to be just.[51] This entails that if there is an attribute of being identical with the individual who is God, this attribute = the attribute of simplicity. If there is no such attribute, at least there is a conjunction of attributes sufficient for identity with just this individual, and if God is simple, then each member of this conjunction = the attribute of simplicity. Thus for Boethius, it is not possible that there be a simple being not identical with God, nor therefore an eternal being not identical with God.[52]

On Behalf of a Partless Extension

These facts about Boethian eternity let me offer two analogies and two arguments on behalf of Boethius' claim that an indivisible, partless extension is possible. First, one analogy.

The original concept of a literal physical atom is the concept of an ultimate building block of matter, something of which all other material things are composed but which is not itself composed of any more basic building block. If there is such an ultimate particle, it is an extended but physically indivisible or partless entity. Yet if there is such an ultimate particle (henceforth "an atom"), it is not in all respects indivisible. Though without physical parts and physically indivisible, it occupies a divisible region of space and so is spatially divisible. When we call a region of space divisible, we mean at the very least that we can conceive distinct regions within it. But a space is divisible in a stronger sense than this. For a space can be really divided into regions really occupied by distinct spatial things—that is, if distinct things occupy distinct subregions of a spatial region, this seems to divide the space in some way that goes beyond mere conceptual division. Now consider this. Our belief that an atom's space is divisible likely rests on at least one of the following claims:

9. It is possible that the atom's space be occupied by another object, which can be divided in such a way as to divide the space.
10. It is possible that an object partly overlaps the atom's space.
11. It is possible that the atom's space be overlapped by two distinct objects, each of which occupies part of the atom's space.

51. Ibid., chap. 4.
52. It should be clear that this last argument in no way relies on Boethius' particular doctrine of individuation. Rather, it draws its force solely from the requirement that all of a simple being's attributes be identical.

12. Other spaces are divisible, and this atom's space is enough like these other spaces that it, too, likely is divisible.

13. Being a space entails being divisible.

Suppose that we came to know that in the case of one atom, (9)–(13) (as well as any other statements expressing reasons to call this space divisible) are all false. In this case, I submit, we would no longer have any reason to call this atom's space divisible. We might therefore conclude that its space is indivisible. Yet we could still perhaps have reason to call the atom extended, i.e., to say that the atom occupies more than one location at once and so that its space is extended. For one thing, we could at least conceive of dividing the space it occupies, even if this is in fact impossible. Moreover, our atom might have physical attributes that extensionless things cannot have. For instance, our atom might rotate. Only objects with circumferences can rotate, since an entity rotates only if points on its circumference are successively in different places. No extensionless entity has a circumference. Now if our atom's space is occupied by an extended thing, this space is genuinely extended even if it is indivisible.[53]

Now I want to suggest that if an atom's space were necessarily occupied only by that atom, and this atom were immutable, this would falsify (9)–(13). It clearly would falsify (9) and (11), for if this space is necessarily occupied only by this atom, then the space exists only if the atom fills it: it is not possible that another object fill or partially overlap this space. If an atom is immutable, this atom cannot grow, shrink, or move. So if necessarily, nothing other than one particular atom occupies a particular space, and this atom is immutable, (10) is false. Perhaps a space that must be occupied by just one immutable entity would for just this reason be enough unlike other spaces to render (12)

53. Nelson taxes Stump and Kretzmann this way: "to say that atemporal duration is infinitely extended entails that in it an infinite number of different positions can be designated. To say that this duration is atemporal is to say that none of these positions is past or future with respect to any other. Stump and Kretzmann claim further that none of these positions are earlier or later than any other, and that the content of none of these positions is different from that of any other. What . . . differentiates these infinite positions from one another? Not time. Not qualitative content . . . It is not eternity which separates or differentiates them, since Stump and Kretzmann take them all to be [eternally] simultaneous, *tota simul*" ("Time[s]," p. 16). I endorse Nelson's claim that extension requires distinct positions and agree that Stump and Kretzmann do not in the end provide these. But as will be seen, I do allow for an earlier-later distinction among eternal positions, *despite* their all being *tota simul*. Nothing else is needed for positions to be distinct; positions just are the kind of thing that can be nonidentical without being individualized by something else. (This is why space-time positions serve as ultimate individuators in so many contemporary ontologies.)

false. (It will be clear below that I do not need to insist on this.) Finally, given the falsity of (9)–(12), I suggest that this case would constitute a counterexample falsifying (13). Now if this case would indeed falsify (9)–(13), then in this case we would perhaps have grounds to call our atom's space an indivisible extension.

As Boethius conceives it, eternity is rather like a space necessarily occupied by only one atom. An eternal duration is necessarily occupied by an indivisible, partless object (cf. [9]). If some individual occupies an eternal duration, no second individual can do so, and so an eternal extension cannot be overlapped by two different objects (cf. [11]).[54] As to (10), if something can partly overlap an eternal duration, either (i) a second being can overlap the eternal duration of our first eternal being, or (ii) this eternal being can be of different duration than it actually is and so can overlap (in another possible world) its own actual duration. Let us consider (i) first. Only an eternal being can overlap an eternal duration, just as only a spatial being can overlap a spatial extension and only a temporal being can overlap a temporal duration. There cannot be a second being with an eternal duration. Thus no second being can overlap the eternal duration of our first eternal being. Let us therefore move to (ii). A duration is not as such an intrinsic attribute of a thing; I do not *have* a life seventy years long as I *have* the intrinsic attribute of humanity, for I am a human being, but I am not a life seventy years long. But if I have a life seventy years long, I have the intrinsic attribute of having a life seventy years long. Similarly, then, an eternal being has the intrinsic attribute of having an "eternally long" duration. Now on Boethius' view, whatever is eternal is simple. All intrinsic attributes of a simple being are identical. Thus an eternal being's intrinsic attribute of having a duration of the length it actually has is identical with its intrinsic attribute of identity with itself. If the latter is *de re* necessary to it, so then is the former.[55] So an eternal being's duration cannot be of a

54. Later I speak not just of an eternal duration, the extension of the life of an eternal being, but of an eternal frame of reference, something that is or is constituted by the obtaining of a set of simultaneity relations between eternal and temporal things. I claim that more than one entity can exist in an eternal reference frame. This claim will *not* contradict the claim that only one being can occupy (i.e., live through) an eternal duration, for it will emerge that existing in an eternal reference frame does not entail having an eternal duration.

55. This entails that an eternal being's intrinsic attributes are one and all *de re* necessary if any are. But this does not entail that an eternal or simple being cannot have contingent attributes. Instead, it could entail only that all contingent attributes of an eternal being are extrinsic (Aquinas defends a closely related claim in *ST* Ia, 13, 7) and may not even entail *this*. For a way to avoid the claim that an eternal being's intrinsic attributes are all *de re* necessary, see my "God and Abstract Entities," *Faith and Philosophy* 7, 193–217.

different length than it is. But then the eternal analogue of (10) turns out to be false; nothing can partly overlap eternity.

As to (12), to argue the divisibility of an eternal duration by analogy, we could compare it to time, to space, or to some other eternal duration. Eternity differs enough from both time and space (the other extensions with which we are acquainted) that their being divisible may be little reason to think that eternity is divisible. Nor is there eternal duration enjoyed by other beings with which to compare God's eternity, as there is space occupied by other beings with which to compare the space our atom occupies. Nor again is there unoccupied eternity to compare to God's eternity. Boethius defines eternity as a way life is possessed or lived. Thus the idea of unoccupied eternity makes as little sense as the idea of a life with nobody living it; talk of eternity as if it were some sort of independent continuum that things may or may not occupy is just a convenient façon de parler. Finally, there is little reason to think that being an eternity entails being divisible, given the foregoing (cf. [13]). If, then, supposing the falsity of (9)–(13) and their congeners might let us conceive of a spatial extension that we can have reason to call indivisible, perhaps the falsity of the eternal analogues of (9)–(13) might let us conceive an extended yet indivisible or partless eternity.[56]

Of course, if we concede that eternity is indivisible, then we will likely want to say that it is after all not extended. But perhaps some attributes we ascribe to an eternal God require that we think His way of possessing life to involve duration. This might be the case, for instance, if we want to say that our eternal God has experience, for perhaps we literally cannot conceive of a durationless experience. If we cannot, then perhaps we must conceive Boethian eternity to be extended. Alternately, perhaps the Boethian claim that God is eternal places us in a "two-model" situation, rather as certain quantum mechanical entities do. Perhaps we have no one image that will express all that we think true of an eternal God and can only oscillate between the conflicting yet equally necessary images of an indivisible extensionless point and an extended duration.

My first analogy compared eternity with a spatial atom. My second compares it with a *temporal* atom. The concept of a time-atom, or chronon, has a long history. Sorabji traces it back to Greek· atomist responses to Aristotle and forward to a minority party among contem-

---

56. If eternity is both extended and partless, both extensions and points can model it—in differing respects. This might account for the presence of both talk of infinite extension and talk of points and instants in classical and medieval treatments of eternity.

porary physicists.[57] It is basic to Whitehead's account of time.[58] In addition, certain versions of current antirealism may in fact be committed to chronons. For there may well be a minimum perceptible or measurable temporal duration, and this fact in conjunction with certain antirealist theses entails that there is a unit of time such that we cannot meaningfully claim there to be a smaller unit or (more strongly) that there is a unit of time than which there can be no smaller. A chronon is an indivisible minimum unit of temporal duration. It has been argued that a chronon lasts perhaps 10^{-24} seconds.[59] Whatever the precise number, the important point is that a chronon is *not* an instant but is conceived to have some very small duration. As a chronon endures, there are within it distinct temporal positions; otherwise it would not endure but would simply be an instant. Moreover, these distinct positions are ordered as earlier and later, else the chronon is not a unit of *temporal* duration (though if there is a succession of chronons, this succession could still constitute a time whose parts are ordered as earlier and later). But it is really impossible that a chronon be divided into smaller temporal parts, for if it could be divided into parts, it would not be an atom.[60] Moreover, despite its internal ordering, all the duration within that chronon which is now present is present, however long this chronon is. For if part of the chronon were past and part were future, this would constitute an objective division of the chronon into temporal parts, which the concept of a time-*atom* rules out ex hypothesi. Thus there is a sense in which within one chronon, earlier and later exist *at once*, i.e., in the same indivisible present. Now if a chronon has these traits, one may well wonder why it qualifies as an atom of *time*. One possible answer is that a chronon is an atom of time because it is by the succession of these that time exists. Another answer could combine time-atomism with a tensed theory of time, holding that chronons but not other kinds of atoms are subject to a radical difference in actuality depending on their location, so that chronons alone count as atoms of time. Finally, one could perhaps point out that each distinct point within a chronon can wholly contain a concrete spatially extended individual and that this is true only of points in time.

57. Sorabji, *TC&C*, chaps. 23–25, passim.
58. Alfred N. Whitehead, *Science and the Modern World* (New York: Macmillan, 1925), pp. 183–185; *Process and Reality* (New York: Macmillan, 1929), pp. 53, 105–107. I owe the Whitehead references to William Alston.
59. G. J. Whitrow, *The Natural Philosophy of Time* (London: Thomas Nelson and Sons, 1961), p. 156.
60. By this's being "really impossible" we may understand that in no possible world whose history is and physical laws are indiscernible from those of this possible world up to the present is any time-atom divided at any time later than now.

Now most scientists and philosophers do not believe that time is a succession of time-atoms rather than a continuum. But they object to the claim that the concept of a chronon applies to actual time, not the claim that this concept is coherent and possibly instantiated; some physicists are even prepared to claim that time really does consist of chronons.[61] So let us suppose that chronons are indeed possible. The features of the chronon mirror the most perplexing features of QTE—its being an indivisible, partless extension; its having earlier-later relations within a single present; and the existing at once of earlier and later within this present. If chronons are possible, then, this is reason to believe that QTE is.

QTE does differ from a temporal chronon in some respects. First, that QTE is not divided is absolutely rather than physically necessary. Second, eternity necessarily consists of only one unit of QTE, for if eternity consisted of a succession of QTE units, then part of it would be "passed away" and part "yet to come."[62] But there can be an infinity of chronons. Third, temporal chronons, if there were such things, would each last for only a very small portion of time's total duration. A "chronon" of QTE encompasses all of eternal duration. But these differences do not seem great enough to keep the possibility of time-atoms from counting in favor of the possibility of QTE.

Now to the first of the arguments mentioned at this section's outset. Formal logics of part and whole (mereologies) define the concept of proper part as follows: x is a proper part of y just in case y completely overlaps x and there is some z such that z completely overlaps x and does not completely overlap y.[63] From this it follows immediately that an extension is unable to have parts if and only if it is such that within it, nothing can overlap anything else. We have seen that this is precisely the case with eternity, because eternity is the characteristic duration of a simple being.[64] So it follows that eternity cannot have parts. Again, if

61. For references, see Sorabji, *TC&C*, p. 381 n. 57; Milic Capek, *The Philosophical Impact of Contemporary Physics* (Princeton, N.J.: Princeton University Press, 1961), pp. 230–231.

62. That there can be only one "chronon" of QTE renders QTE in a sense unlimited: QTE does not involve internal limits, i.e., boundaries of parts, and as there cannot be more than one chronon of QTE, QTE is not limited by the existence of further chronons of its own sort beyond its boundaries.

63. See, e.g., Nelson Goodman, *The Structure of Appearance*, 3d ed. (Dordrecht: Reidel, 1977), p. 35.

64. Goodman, *Structure*, allows that in a broader sense an entity that has an attribute distinct from itself is "overlapped" by that attribute. This makes sense only if one construes an attribute as a scattered spatiotemporal particular. If attributes of temporal things are temporal, then a nontemporal thing can have none of them, and so in this sense, too, an eternal being's duration cannot be overlapped. (Were this true, it would

this is so, one wants to ask why, then, eternity is extended at all. And again, the answer is perhaps that if eternity is a duration peculiar to God, and God has experience, it must be.

Eternity and the Experienced Present

Let us consider one more argument. It is a fact that we seem to experience a present with duration. To perceive in a single experience that spatial motion is occurring is to perceive, in a single experience, a moving object as first at one position, then another, then still another. If all of this occurs within the bounds of what seems to be a single present experience, then that experience seemingly must have some positive duration. Thus the concept of an extended "specious present" has been central to some accounts of the human experience of time and even of the nature of time itself—as it is in James and Whitehead.[65] Even if compelling philosophical arguments dictate that the real present is only an instant, this is not the way the experienced present *seems*. So we seem to experience a duration all of which is present. It can be argued, then, that eternity as Boethius describes it should make more sense to us than time, rather than less. For the eternal present is the one present that really does conform to the experiential character of the present we know best, actually having the duration the temporal present only seems to have.[66]

Moreover, there may be such a thing as a minimal human experienced present, an atomic length of human experiences such that no human experience can be shorter. If there is, then "specious presents" of this length are in one respect indivisible or partless: they cannot be broken into shorter segments that will still be specious presents. Perhaps we can conceive of an eternal specious present as a necessarily unique, atomic-length, sole eternally enduring thing that exhausts eternal duration. We consider a human minimal specious present temporally divisible. But if the reasons for this parallel (9)–(13), then

---

not reduce us to negative theology in talk about an eternal being. For we could talk positively about such a thing on the basis of resemblances not reducible to identities of attribute.)

65. For James's account of the experienced present, see his *Principles of Psychology* (New York: Dover, 1890), Vol. 1, chap. 15. This account becomes the basis of his metaphysical account of time in *Essays in Radical Empiricism and a Pluralistic Universe* (New York; Dutton, 1971). Whitehead's theory of time is broadly similar; for references, see n. 58.

66. Thus Stump and Kretzmann's claim that "it is only the discovery of eternity that enables us to make genuinely literal use of words for duration" ("Eternity," p. 445).

perhaps we could find reason to say that an eternal specious present, though of extended duration, is not durationally divisible.

Is Eternity Timelike or Spacelike?

This concludes such case as I can make for QTE's being a genuine extension. The claim that eternity is a duration, however, involves something further. To be a duration, eternity must be a *timelike* rather than spacelike extension. To explore whether eternity is a duration, then, we must find some significant disanalogies between time and space, at least as they are ordinarily conceived, and see which one eternity most resembles. The few differences I will speak of do not exhaust the considerable literature on the likeness and differences of space and time. I claim for the ones I mention only that they seem relevant to deciding our question about eternity.

I. Space is commonly thought to be three-dimensional, whereas time is commonly considered one-dimensional. There does not seem to be any analogue to three-dimensionality in eternity. If we conceive an eternal life as extended at all, we conceive it as extended along a single axis. In this way, then, eternity seems more like time as commonly conceived than like space as commonly conceived.

II. At least on some common views, temporal things that are absent from some temporal positions (those in our past or present) are for this reason not actual. There are no spatial positions such whatever is absent from these is not actual. Now for an eternal thing, being absent from any position in eternity would imply being nonactual. Since eternal duration is partless, any being occupying any of it occupies all of it. Any eternal thing is so by nature: it must be eternal if it exists.[67] Thus any eternal thing not located at any point in eternity does not exist. So eternity seems more timelike than spacelike in this respect.

III. As was argued above, if things' endurance through time constitutes a fourth dimension in which they are extended, for any x, x is wholly present at each point along its temporal extension. Things are otherwise with space; I am not wholly present at any individual point along my spatial extension. In at least one contemporary theory of time, this is one of the most important differences between spatial and temporal extension.[68] In this respect, eternity is more timelike than spacelike, for an eternal being is wholly present at all points in its

---

67. As whatever is eternal is simple, the attribute of being eternal is identical with an eternal being's attribute of being identical with itself. If the latter is *de re* necessary to it, so is the former.

68. See D. H. Mellor, *Real Time* (Cambridge: Cambridge University Press, 1981).

eternal duration. Still, though, eternity remains distinct from time. That a being in time is wholly present at one temporal location does not entail that it is present at all other temporal locations or present at once there. That an eternal being is wholly present at one eternal location entails that it is also wholly present at once at all other eternal locations.

IV. Fitzgerald's condition (6) above was that necessarily, any duration has an intrinsic order and direction among its parts. I have argued that QTE is a partless duration. Accordingly, QTE cannot be required to sustain an order or direction among parts; this does not count against its being a duration, if for other reasons it deserves the title. Moreover, QTE need not literally satisfy (6) to remain distinct from Stump-Kretzmann eternity. For QTE literally satisfies (3), and Stump-Kretzmann eternity does not. Further, as has already been noted, if there is a case to be made on other grounds that QTE is more timelike than spacelike, then if QTE literally satisfies (3), we can perhaps say that eternal locations are analogically earlier and later. For if QTE is an extension containing distinct points, then if QTE is a timelike extension, perhaps there is some timelike relation between QTE points.

But we can at least suggest a further move, which could give literal though not temporal sense to the claim that some points in eternity are earlier than others. Any defender of divine timelessness will say that even though none of God's mental acts precede others temporally, still some precede others *logically*. For instance, suppose that God timelessly hears Abraham's prayer and decides to spare Isaac. In this case He does not hear Abraham temporally before He decides to spare Isaac, or vice versa. But still He decides to spare Isaac *because* He hears Abraham, and not vice versa.[69] One can give an earlier-later sense to the relation between QTE points by holding that each point is or can be the primary locus of a discrete divine mental act, some of which presuppose others. Now all these mental acts are God's simultaneously; a being with QTE lives at once both earlier and later moments of its life. But nonetheless, this relation between QTE points seems to deserve the name earlier-later as well as any relation tenseless theories of time countenance.

Within relativity theory, causal relations provide an absolute ordering for time positions: if event A causes event B, A is temporally before B regardless of one's relativistic frame of reference. Causality provides no analogous ordering of spatial positions. If we allow an eternal order-

---

69. For fuller discussion, see William Alston, "Divine-Human Dialogue and the Nature of God," in *Divine Nature and Human Language* (Ithaca, N.Y.: Cornell University Press, 1989), pp. 144–161.

ing of divine mental events in QTE, then this ordering will be analogous to the absolute ordering causal relations establish in time and so
will constitute a further timelikeness of QTE.

Vale et Salve

I have argued that Stump and Kretzmann are correct in denying that
Boethian eternity is a frozen *nunc stans*. I have also argued that if it is a
duration, Boethian eternity is a more timelike sort of duration than
Stump and Kretzmann think. Nonetheless, Boethian eternity is not
just another temporal series, nor is Boethius' God internally temporal
though not temporally related to any temporal thing.[70] For time has
parts, and eternity has none; again, time is continuous and divisible,
but eternity is relevantly atomic. Temporal things can be different in
different parts of time; an eternal thing, though perhaps having many
different mental acts at earlier and later eternal locations, all the same
enjoys those mental acts in one and the same eternal now.

Eternity as I have depicted it is a mode of being midway between
temporality and the absolutely durationless existence of an instant (if
there are such things). This should perhaps not surprise us. One main
source of Boethius' concept of eternity may well have been Plotinus.[71]
In Plotinus' system, that which is eternal is Nous, which stands in the
hierarchy of being midway between temporal entities such as the world
soul and the absolute pointlike simplicity of the One. In Boethius'
combining of simplicity and eternity, then, we have one more step in
the process, begun before Augustine, of combining the attributes of
Nous and the One in a single conception of God.

70. See Nelson, "Time(s)," p. 17.
71. See Plotinus, *Enneads* III, 7.

The Roots
of Eternity

The previous chapter argued that one can understand Boethian eternity as a form of duration. This chapter argues that this is only part of the story and that one can also understand Boethian eternity on the model of an extensionless point. As we have already seen, eternality for Boethius is the mode of being appropriate to a simple being. I now argue that the concept of eternality in Boethius and those coming after him is also the concept of the kind of *life* a simple being could enjoy. That eternality is simple life provides intuitive motivation for both point and extension or line models of eternity. That eternality is the mode both of a simple being's life and of its existence should not give us pause. For as Aquinas liked to say, *viventibus vivere est esse:* for living things, to live is to be.

Points, Lines, and Eternity

Let us turn again to Boethius' definition of eternality, as "the complete possession all at once of illimitable life" (*interminabilis vitae tota simul et perfecta possessio*).[1] There are at least two distinct ways to picture the eternity Boethius describes. As we have seen, it could be a limitless timelike but timeless extension. Fitzgerald points out that one can also read Boethius' definition as modeling eternal life on a point.[2] For Boethius' claim that eternality is the possession of life "all at once" could mean that an eternal life occurs in a pointlike manner, without

1. Boethius, *Philosophiae consolationis* V, prose 6, in Stewart and Rand, *Boethius,* p. 400, ll. 10–11.
2. Fitzgerald, "SKTE."

being in any way "spread out" or extended over a duration, as lives in time are. That eternity is "complete possession" of life could reinforce this idea: temporal beings lose that of their life which is past and do not yet have that of their life which is future, but as eternal life is in no way extended, it is in no way out of the possession of or apart from its subject. One can also take the claim that eternality is possession of "illimitable" (*interminabilis*) life in accord with the point model. For what is not extended cannot be limited in its extent,[3] nor can one limit (set bounds to or "terminate") its extent internally by dividing its extension into parts.

Both extensional and "point" readings of Boethius' definition of eternity are prima facie plausible. Boethius' definition was a staple of medieval discussions of eternity. Thus it is perhaps not surprising that both extensional and "point" models of eternity figure in these discussions, often cheek by jowl. For instance, in the *Proslogion*, Anselm writes that "neither You nor the eternity which You are has any parts . . . but . . . Your eternity always exists as a whole,"[4] a fairly clear use of the point model. But then his next sentence adds, "through Your eternity, You were, You are, and You will be"[5]—that is, by being eternal, God endures. Anselm then goes on to qualify his duration model: "to be past is not to be future, and to be is not to be past or to be future. How then does Your eternity always exist as a whole? . . . Therefore it is not the case that You existed yesterday or will exist tomorrow; instead, yesterday, today, and tomorrow, You exist. Or better, You simply exist, beyond all time."[6] This qualification is motivated by the claim that God's eternity has no parts, and so by the point model. For Anselm fears that if we say that God's eternity existed in the past or will exist in the future, we divide His eternal existence into distinct temporal parts. Yet soon after making this qualification, Anselm once more applies the duration model, asserting that God's eternity "contains the ages of time . . . because of its endless immensity."[7] This text suggests that God's eternity is so great (or long) that all the ages of time "fit" within it and so treats God's eternity as a dura-

3. Stump and Kretzmann, "Eternity," p. 432.
4. "nec tu habes partes nec tua aeternitas quae tu es . . . sed . . . aeternitas tua tota est semper." Anselm, *Proslogion*, in Schmitt, *Opera*, vol. 1, chap. 18, p. 115.
5. "per aeternitatem tuam fuisti et es et eris." Ibid., chap. 19, p. 115.
6. "fuisse non est futurum esse, et esse non est fuisse vel futurum esse, quomodo aeternitas tua tota est semper? . . . Non ergo fuisti heri aut eris cras sed heri et hodie et cras es. Immo nec heri nec hodie nec cras es, sed simpliciter es extra omne tempus." Ibid., ll. 1–14.
7. "tua aeternitas continet etiam ipsa saecula temporum . . . saecula vero propter interminabilem immensitatem." Ibid., chap. 21, p. 116, ll. 7–9.

tion. Again, in *ST* Ia 10, 1 *ad* 1, Aquinas explicitly likens eternity to a point. Yet at once, in *ST* Ia 10, 1 *ad* 2, Thomas endorses the claim that eternity involves duration.

Stump and Kretzmann's "Eternity" considers the extension model the sole correct understanding of eternity. Fitzgerald thinks that only the point model will do. To opt for just one model of eternity commits one to calling the occurrence of the other model in medieval discussions at best a matter of loose, inappropriate usage. But perhaps the use of both models is deliberate or even necessary. The preceding chapter noted that the Boethian definition of eternity adopted by Anselm, Aquinas, and other mainstream medievals may involve a "two model" situation: just as one must use both particle and wave models in thinking about quanta, perhaps one must use both point and extension models in thinking about Boethian eternity. I now suggest that if this is so, it is because eternity is (inter alia) a kind of life that could be enjoyed by a metaphysically simple being. As eternity is a kind of life, it may require us to model it as a way of enduring, or a sort of duration. As eternity is the life of a simple being, it may require us to model it as lacking parts and so pointlike.[8] Moreover, even if eternity does not *require* both models, it invites both.

Boethius clearly holds that eternity is a mode of life of a simple being. For we have seen him define eternity as a kind of life, and in Chapter 6 we also saw him connect eternity and simplicity, suggesting that as time is the mode of being of things that come to be, so eternity is the mode of being of the simple point at the center of things, God. Aquinas makes the connections among simplicity, eternity, life, and our two models of eternity more explicit. Thomas argues that God's simplicity entails His immutability and His immutability entails His eternity.[9] To him, then, God's eternity is a direct consequence of God's simplicity. Again, Aquinas holds that necessarily, God alone is simple, and necessarily, God alone is truly eternal.[10] This commits him to the claim that necessarily, eternality is a mode of life proper only to a simple being. So it is hardly surprising that in *ST* Ia 10, 1, Thomas compares eternity to time as the simple to the composite, and that in expanding on this in *ST* Ia 10, 1 *ad* 1, he compares eternity with a

---

8. Plotinus could be an exception to this. In his system, that which is simple, the One, is "above" even being eternal, and that which is eternal is Nous, which is "below" the One. Hence perhaps in Plotinus, only the extensional model of eternity would apply. As has been mentioned, Augustine and later Christian writers in effect merged aspects of Plotinus' One and Nous in their description of God.

9. *ST* Ia 9, 1; 10, 2.

10. See *De Ente et Essentia*, chap. 4, and *ST* Ia 10,3.

point. Further, it is at least plausible that Thomas uses the point model precisely because of eternity's connection with God's simplicity. But Aquinas also uses the extension model. He connects this model of eternity with the life of an eternal being in *ST* Ia 10, 1 *ad* 2, writing, "that which is truly eternal not only exists but lives. Now living includes in a way activity . . . and flow of duration is more apparent in activity than in existence."[11] Thus Aquinas sees eternity as a sort of duration because it is a sort of life.

For Boethius as for Aquinas, eternity is the mode of life of a simple being. This may explain why both point and extension models provide viable interpretations of Boethius' definition of eternity. Given the roots of the concept of eternity in the doctrine of divine simplicity and the claim that God is alive, Boethius may well have had both point and extension models in view as he thought about eternity. So perhaps he deliberately gave a definition of eternity that could be explained in both ways, or perhaps both models at least at some level influenced his choice of expressions.

Most mainstream medievals would agree with Boethius and Aquinas on the connection of simplicity and eternity. For as was observed earlier, most medievals held that God is metaphysically simple, and despite differences in philosophical vocabulary, most meant the same thing by this claim. But if mainstream medievals had the doctrine of divine simplicity Aquinas and Boethius shared, any logical connections between simplicity and eternity unearthed in Aquinas and Boethius will be there in the positions of others, though these others' explicit awareness of these connections may in fact vary. We have seen that simplicity and eternity are connected. If we explore the doctrine of divine simplicity, we can see just *how* they are connected.

Eternity and Divine Simplicity

As we saw earlier, the doctrine of divine simplicity raises the question of whether God is an abstract entity. This doctrine makes God appear abstract because it identifies Him with an abstract entity. That simplicity entails complete immutability strengthens this appearance of abstractness, since the only examples of immutable things we possess are attributes and other abstracta. To the extent that the doctrine of divine simplicity makes God appear abstract, it makes Him appear

---

11. "illud quod est vere aeternum non solum est ens sed vivens. Et ipsum vivere se extendit quoddamodo operationem . . . Processio autem durationis videtur attendi secundum operationem magis quam secundum esse." Blackfriars text in McDermott, ed., *Summa*, vol. 2, p. 136. Tr. partly McDermott's.

impersonal and lifeless. Complete divine immutability compounds this problem. For it is hard to see how an immutable being can be alive, since life as we know it involves processes (growth, aging) and changes (e.g., the slowing of one's growth rate).

If a simple God cannot have a location in time, this adds still more force to the claim that a simple God must be abstract. Now if immutability entailed timelessness, as Aquinas thought,[12] then simplicity would entail timelessness in virtue of entailing immutability. But we saw above that events of beginning are both located in time and immutable. If so, immutability is compatible with being temporal and so does not entail timelessness (even if being TI does entail this). Stump and Kretzmann argue that "it is impossible that [a simple] God have any spatial or temporal parts . . . and so God cannot be a physical entity."[13] This argument may assume that necessarily, whatever is physical is spatially extended or a temporal continuant, and that

> T. if God is a temporal continuant (i.e., extends through time),
> God is composed of temporal parts.[14]

Suppose that (T) is true. As it is *de dicto* impossible that God exists at only one moment of time,

> T1. necessarily, if God exists in time, God is a temporal
> continuant.

Conjoined, (T) and (T1) entail that

> T2. if God exists in time, God is composed of temporal parts.

God's simplicity rules out God's being composed of any sort of parts, including temporal parts. So if (T2) is true, divine simplicity entails divine timelessness. But (T) is debatable, and so then is (T2). There are at least two alternate ways to view any divine temporal extension. Either falsifies (T).

First, one can maintain that any continuant (including God) has

---

12. *ST* Ia 10, 1.

13. Eleonore Stump and Norman Kretzmann, "Absolute Simplicity," *Faith and Philosophy* 2 (1985), 354.

14. One can also read Stump and Kretzmann as premising that necessarily, whatever is physical is both spatially and temporally extended. In this case the argument would not require (T) but could instead just claim that necessarily, whatever is physical is spatially extended, that every spatially extended thing has spatial parts, and that God cannot have spatial parts.

temporal extension but not temporal parts.[15] This view may sound paradoxical, but given that continuants have temporal extension, it follows from an intuitively plausible claim. It is plausible that what is reading this paper now is a person, not a temporal part or slice of a person. More generally, it is plausible that what exists at any point or during any interval along a person's temporal extension is a person, not a temporal part or slice of that person. But then what occupies any subregion of a temporal extension = what occupies the extension as a whole, and so persons have no proper temporal parts. Thus, viewed tenselessly, persons and other continuants are wholly present "at once" in many temporal loci.[16] On this view, God could have temporal extension without having temporal parts and so without violating His simplicity.

Second, one can deny that continuants have temporal extension at all and say instead that only their lifetimes or histories extend through time and that a person ≠ a history. On this account, if God is temporal, God's lifetime or history extends through time and has temporal parts, but God does not.[17] That a person ≠ a history seems clear. For one thing, histories are composed of events, but persons are not. For another, the identity-conditions for persons and histories differ. If one event in a given history is changed, we have a numerically different history, as (in the strict sense) making one change in the plot of a story gives us a new, distinct story. To suppose that Napoleon won at Waterloo, for example, is strictly speaking to suppose a complete alternate history for our world, not "the same history, with one change": histories are relevantly like ordered n-tuples of the events that make them up. But changing one event in which a person is involved does not entail that we have a different person. If it is possible that a person persist when a history does not survive, the person and the history must be distinct. Again, if a person = a history, only parts or slices of persons exist at any instant and so not a person but a person-slice is reading this page. So one could reject (T) by maintaining that though God has a history, since God ≠ His history, God has no temporal extension or temporal parts.

Anselm may have thought that God's simplicity closes off this second way to escape (T). For he argues in *Monologion* 16 that because God is simple, for every attribute F, if God is F, then God = Fness, and

---

15. Mellor, *Real Time*, chaps. 7, 8.

16. This might be the viable core of the old idealist claim that continuants are "concrete universals."

17. As in Dennis C. Holt, "Timelessness and the Metaphysics of Temporal Existence," *American Philosophical Quarterly* 18 (1981), 149–156.

infers from this that (as God is eternal) God = eternity. He then argues that "if [God] exists as a whole successively at different times . . . then His lifetime, which is His eternity . . . is extended by parts through the parts of time. Now His eternity is nothing other than Himself. Hence [God] would be divided by parts according to the distinctions of time . . . How would it remain stable . . . that [God] is in no way composite but supremely simple . . . if . . . God had parts distributed through differing times?"[18] Anselm seems to think, in short, that even if in general a person ≠ a lifetime or history, in God's unique case this is false, and so God and God's life must lack temporal extension. But if Anselm does think this, he may just be equivocating on two closely related uses of the term "eternity"—at least, he equivocates if he draws his claim that "its eternity is nothing other than itself" from *Monologion* 16.[19] "Eternity" can function as a name for a duration. It can also act as a name for the attribute of having such a duration, eternality. Anselm's argument in *Monologion* 16, strictly speaking, is that God = eternality. But what "would be extended by parts" in the quoted passage is God's lifetime or duration. A simple being must be identical with its attributes and with any other intrinsic metaphysical "components" (e.g., its "essence" or its "existence"). If a history, lifetime, or duration is not an attribute or some other sort of intrinsic "component," this does not entail that a simple being must be identical with its history and so must be complex or extended if its history is. That a simple being is its eternality does not entail that it is its history. And that a simple being's history is extended and complex does not entail that its attribute of having that history is. So (T) is not obviously available to show that simplicity entails timelessness. Can one show this in another way?

Another argument that a simple being must be timeless might run as follows. All attributes of a simple being are really identical. Now if a simple being exists at 12:00 and at 12:01, it has the attribute of existing at 12:00 and the attribute of existing at 12:01. These are distinct attributes, since in fact some things that have the first lack the second (e.g., those that cease to exist at 12:00 plus thirty seconds). Hence it seems that nothing with both these attributes could be simple. So either a simple God exists only at one moment of time or a simple God

18. "Si vero separatim et distincte tota est in singulis temporibus . . . Ergo eius aetas, quae nihil aliud est quam eius aeternitas . . . est partibus extensa per temporum partes. At eius aeternitas nihil aliud est quam ipsa. Summa igitur essentia erit divisa per partes secundum temporum distinctiones . . . Quomodo igitur stabit . . . quia illa summa natura nullo modo composita sed summe simplex est . . . si . . . per tempora distributas habet partes?" *Monologion*, chap. 21, in Schmitt, *Opera*, vol. 1, p. 37, ll. 19–24; p. 38, ll. 4–7.

19. I am not aware of any other candidate source for it.

is timeless. The first disjunct is, of course, *de dicto* necessarily false.

This argument assumes that such predicates as "____ exists at 12:00" express attributes. Some would argue that existence is not an attribute. If it is not, is existence at noon? Again, even if we allow that such predicates express attributes, that predicates are distinct does not entail that they express distinct attributes. The predicates "____ is a dog" and "____ is an animal" are distinct. All the same, it might be the case that Fido is an animal in virtue of exemplifying doghood rather than by having in addition to doghood a second distinct attribute, animality. In any event, if existing at any particular time is an attribute, it is not one acquiring or losing which entails going through some real change: as we have seen, many would allow that numbers undergo this change. This suggests that existing at a particular time would be not a real or intrinsic attribute of a simple being but a merely Cambridge attribute. But again, a simple being is identical only with its real or intrinsic attributes, for only having a distinct real, intrinsic attribute would entail involving real, intrinsic complexity. So this argument fails.

One also might argue from simplicity to timelessness by way of the fact that whatever endures through time has a history. My history in some sense helps to constitute me as myself. For it is at least a necessary condition of being me at a certain time that my history at that time is a continuation of a certain history with a certain unique beginning. Now plausibly a history segment S is a continuation of a history including a prior segment S* only if the subject of S emerges from the subject of S* by some sort of real development: my writing these words is a continuation of my history, starting at my birth, only if I am the person who grew out of my prior stages. If in such cases S continues S*'s history only if the subject of S is in some sort of process, then, it may be that a simple being cannot have a history. If so, a simple being cannot endure through time.

But I submit that if there is a simple being, it is false that for all S and S*, S continues S*'s history only if the subject of S is or has been in some sort of process. Clearly, S continues S* only if the subject of S = the subject of S*. But one can secure the claim that the subjects of two segments of simple-being history are identical just by showing (as I have) that there can be at most one possible simple being. If this is so, any two segments of histories of simple beings must be segments of the same history, whether or not a simple being goes through any process or real change. Thus the argument just given fails.

Another argument from simplicity to timelessness might be the following. Plausibly something more than and distinct from being a person who continues the history that up to now has been mine is involved in being me. This "more" must be distinct from being a continuation of the history that up until now has been mine, for something could continue and emerge from this history without being me, or at least without clearly being me (consider your favorite personal identity puzzle case). This requisite "more" must be real and intrinsic, since it determines my very identity. If this is plausible, then perhaps it suggests that anything with a history must be really constituted by at least two distinct intrinsic factors, being the continuation of a history and "something more." If so, nothing simple can have a history, since nothing simple can contain distinct intrinsic factors. So again, since whatever endures through time has a history, a simple being cannot endure through time.

Nonetheless, if this argument works, it shows only that anything that has a history and can fail to continue its history (being replaced instead by another individual) must be constituted of distinct intrinsic factors. A simple being cannot fail to continue its history. As we have seen, if possibly there is a simple being, this being exists necessarily. So (speaking loosely) if a simple being exists at some time in world W, it exists at all times in W. If so, the argument just completed fails.

So far, it has proven difficult to connect simplicity and timelessness. Nonetheless, I do believe that the former entails the latter. Let me briefly indicate one reason to believe this. Whatever extends through time or is located in time has a history. Even an instantaneous existent, something with location but no extension in time, would have a history, namely, all that happened to and with it in its instant of existence. It seems plausible that any such history could have been different in some particulars, however minute. It seems plausible, too, that if some facts or events of a history were different, the subject of that history would have been intrinsically different. For instance, had I had one more cornflake for breakfast today than I did in truth have, I would be very slightly heavier than I in fact am now. Let us say that a history composed only of this kind of fact and event is a being's *intrinsic history.*

Plausibly, there are facts and events in some histories which are such that if they had been different, the subject of that history would have been in no way intrinsically different. For instance, if there were one more resident of Mongolia today than there in fact is, this surely would not make me intrinsically different in any way. Let us call a history composed only of this kind of fact and event a being's *extrinsic history.* Let us say that something with an intrinsic history or both an intrinsic and an extrinsic history is intrinsically temporal and that something with only an extrinsic history is extrinsically temporal.[20]

All intrinsic attributes of a simple being are identical with its individual essence. An individual has its individual essence in all possible worlds in which it exists. Thus it is impossible that a simple being be intrinsically different in any way than it in fact is.[21] This being so, a simple being has no intrinsic history.

For let us say that in possible world W, S's intrinsic history is a conjunction C of facts about S or events involving S. Then by definition,

1. some conjunction other than C might instead have constituted S's intrinsic history, and
2. had C not constituted S's intrinsic history, S would have been intrinsically different.

Using a counterfactual operator of David Lewis, we can symbolize (2) as

3. C is not S's intrinsic history $\Box\!\!\rightarrow$ S is intrinsically different.

Now for any C, either (1) is true or (1) is false. If (1) is false, C does not constitute S's intrinsic history. Suppose, then, that (1) is true. If (1) is true, there is a possible world closest to W in which the antecedent of (3) is true. If S is simple, the consequent of (3) is necessarily false. So in the closest possible world in which (3)'s antecedent is true, (3)'s consequent is false, and so (3) is false. For no C can (1) and (3) be true together. Thus no C can constitute S's intrinsic history: a simple being has no intrinsic history.

A simple being, then, can have no intrinsic history and so must be intrinsically timeless; a simple being can be at most extrinsically temporal. I think it highly likely that this is what such men as Aquinas and Anselm meant to say by calling God timeless. Aquinas, for instance, held it to be compatible with God's timelessness that there be different propositions that we can affirm of Him at different times because of

20. For similar (but not identical) distinctions, see Wolterstorff, "God Everlasting," pp. 82–83, and Delmas Lewis, "Eternity Again," p. 76. Wolterstorff and Lewis argue that since God is extrinsically temporal, there is a real sense in which He is noneternal, but as far as I can see, this difference between their view and mine is just verbal.

21. This might seem to entail that all of a simple being's intrinsic attributes belong to it of necessity. I suggest a way to block this conclusion in "God and Abstract Entities," *Faith and Philosophy* 7, 193–217.

changes in temporal things that do not in any way change Him.[22] That
is, Aquinas allowed a simple, timeless being to have an extrinsic history
and so to be extrinsically temporal.

A second argument from simplicity to timelessness can build on
arguments given earlier. For we saw above that simplicity entails necessity of existence and that necessity of existence entails timelessness.
Hence simplicity entails timelessness. The claim that God is simple,
then, threatens to render God abstract because it entails not just that He
is identical with abstract entities and immutable but also that He is
timeless.

Eternity as an Answer to Abstractness

Because it makes God seem abstract, the claim that God is simple
forcefully raises the question of how God can be alive. So accepting
that God is simple makes it imperative to go on to say just what sort of
life a simple being can have, on pain of depriving God of any personal
characteristics. Thus I suggest that the doctrine of divine simplicity
gave a motive for the development of the concept of eternity. We have
seen that in Boethius' eyes, eternal life must be a simple life. I suggest
that Boethius' description of eternity as *interminabilis vitae tota simul et
perfecta possessio* serves him, Aquinas, and many other medievals committed to divine simplicity as (inter alia) a capsule description of a
simple being's life. Let us look briefly at how this perspective dictates
reading the Boethian formula.

Tota simul: Aquinas states at *ST* Ia 10, 4 that "even if time were to last
forever, it would be possible to mark both beginnings and ends in it by
dividing it into parts . . . this cannot occur in eternity . . . there still
remains the difference between eternity and time, as Boethius
says . . . that eternity is *tota simul,* while this is not appropriate to
time."[23] For Aquinas, that an eternal being has its life *tota simul* explains
the fact that its life cannot be divided into parts. To say that a life is had
all at once is to say that no point in the having—i.e., living—of this life
is earlier than any other. If the living of a life has no earlier or later
points, then either the life itself has no such points, or it has earlier and
later points that nonetheless are lived at once (i.e., it has QTE). Thus

22. See *ST* Ia 13, 7.
23. "etiam dato quod tempus semper duret tamen possibile est signare in ipso et
principium et finem, accipiendo aliquas partes ipsius . . . quod non contingit in aeternitate . . . adhuc remanebit differentia inter aeternitatem et tempus ut dicit Boethius . . .
quod aeternitas est tota simul quod tempori non convenit." Blackfriars text in McDermott, ed., *Summa,* vol. 2, p. 144.

the reason it is impossible to divide the living of an eternal life into parts, in Aquinas' eyes, is that such a life has no distinct points or that earlier and later points within this life are lived all at once. An eternal being, then, has its life *tota simul* because either its living or the life it lives has no earlier and later points: that is, because its living or its life is relevantly simple.

Interminabilis: in the text just quoted, Aquinas connects this term with God's simplicity. For Aquinas, eternal life or the living of an eternal life is "interminable" not merely because it lacks beginning and end of duration, but also because one cannot terminate parts of it and divide them from other parts of it. Thus again, eternal life or the living of an eternal life is partless, or simple.

Perfecta possessio vitae: is possessing life in the best possible way. As we have seen, Boethius calls it an imperfection of temporal lives to have a past that is lost and a future that has not yet come. A life possessed in the best possible way, then, will be a life all of which is present. Again, this requires that eternity or the living of eternity be simple or partless, as otherwise it would have past and future parts.

Can anything thus described be called a life, or is there just a contradiction between simplicity and life? One can make a case that simplicity and life are compatible, and I do so below. At present, though, let us note that if eternity is the mode of life of a simple being, both point and line models can be appropriate in thinking of it. For the point can represent this life's simplicity, and the line the duration that (we may think) goes with being alive. Moreover, if the previous chapter's reasoning was sound, an eternal life can literally *be* both pointlike and extensive. It can be pointlike insofar as it is without parts, i.e., without past and future, and extensive in the way a chronon of QTE is. QTE may be a duration, but it is a simple or partless duration.

[8]

Boethius: Foreknowledge, Eternity, and Simultaneity

The two previous chapters have given us a picture of what Boethius considers eternity to be. So we can now discuss the relations Boethius finds between time and eternity. It will be useful to approach these by discussing a project for which Boethius and his compatriots found the doctrine of divine timelessness important, that of showing that divine foreknowledge of our future is compatible with genuinely free human action.

One can base a claim that foreknowledge and freedom are *not* compatible on these premises:

1. There are truths about future human actions
2. Necessarily, God at all times believes all and only truths.[1]
3. What is past is beyond any human being's power to affect.

For suppose that one truth about future actions is that

P. on September 26, 1999, at 1:05 P.M., George feeds some ducks.

If God at all times believes all truths, then God believed P yesterday. If God is necessarily omniscient, it is not possible that God believed P and yet P is false; in any possible world in which God believes that on

---

1. In speaking of God as having beliefs, I follow current convention to simplify the discussion. Alston has thrown the claim that God really does have beliefs into question in "Does God Have Beliefs?" in his *Divine Nature*, pp. 178–193.

September 26, 1999, at 1:05 P.M., George feeds some ducks, George
does then feed some ducks. So George can avoid his fowl fate only if he
can effect it that yesterday God did not believe that P. But per (3), what
is past is beyond any human's power to affect. It follows, then, that
George cannot avoid feeding ducks. On a libertarian view of freedom,
one does an act freely only if it was in one's power to avoid doing it. So
on such a view of freedom, it seems, God's having foreknowledge
entails that George does not act freely; despite appearances, the ducks
are not getting a free lunch. Parallel arguments will work for any
human action of which it is at some time true that someone will do it.

   This argument seems valid; if it is, one can block it only by denying
one of (1)–(3). Recently, discussion has focused on the denial of (3);
some writers claim that human beings can affect some facts about the
past.[2] Boethius and his followers, though, block this argument by
denying that God is in time. If God is not in time, then while God
necessarily believes all and only truths, there is no time at which He
believes these things: (2) is false. If God is not in time, God's beliefs do
not occur at the same time as anything and so do not occur at any time
in our past. Thus freedom is saved.

   Well and good. But we want to know just how a timeless God
manages to have true beliefs about events in time. Boethius and the rest
explain this on the model of observation. Boethius states that an eternal
being is "always present to itself and [has] the infinity of mobile time
present to it."[3] Thus (in a famous image) an eternal God has all of time
spread before Him as a man atop a hill has all of a road before his gaze;
both have knowledge just by seeing what is there to be seen. Aquinas
writes on the same subject that "eternity . . . includes all time . . . all
things that exist in time are present to God from eternity . . . because
His intuition is carried from eternity over all things just as they are in
their presentiality."[4] Aquinas clearly is saying more than that God is
aware of temporal things. He is saying that God is aware of things that

   2. So, e.g., Marilyn Adams, "Is the Existence of God a 'Hard' Fact?" *Philosophical
Review* 76 (1967), 492–503; George Mavrodes, "Is the Past Unpreventable?" *Faith and
Philosophy* 2 (1983), 131–146; David Widerker and E. M. Zemach, "Facts, Freedom,
and Foreknowledge," *Religious Studies* 23 (1987), 19–28. For criticism of this strategy,
see, e.g., John M. Fischer, "Freedom and Foreknowledge," *Philosophical Review* 92
(1983), 67–79; Hasker, *God*, pp. 75–143.
   3. "necesse est et sui compos praesens sibi semper adsistere et infinitatem mobilis
temporis habere praesentem." Boethius, *Philosophiae consolationis* V, 6, in Stewart and
Rand, *Boethius*, p. 400, ll. 29–31. Tr. of Stump and Kretzmann, "Eternity," p. 430.
   4. "aeternitas . . . ambit totum tempus . . . omnia quae sunt in tempore sunt Deo
ab aeterno praesentia . . . quia eius intuitus fertur super omnia ab aeterno prout sunt in
sua praesentialitate." Aquinas, *ST* Ia, 14, 13.

are really present for Him to observe, even as you see this page that is really present for you to see.[5]

Now if a temporal thing is really present to God, it seems to follow that God and that thing exist simultaneously. We thus have what is at least a paradox. To solve the freedom-foreknowledge conundrum, Boethius et al. deny that God's existence is simultaneous with temporal events. Yet to explain how foreknowledge is possible, Boethius and company affirm that God's existence is simultaneous with temporal events. Charity dictates saying that Boethius and the rest are not just contradicting themselves and so have at least two sorts of simultaneity in mind. This raises two questions, though. First, is a second sort of simultaneity really needed, or have Boethius and friends just gratuitously made their lot harder? Second, if we grant a second sort of simultaneity, what kind of simultaneity relates a timeless God and temporal things? What do "this thing is present to God" or "God and this thing exist simultaneously" assert, if not "God and this thing exist at the same time"?

Addressing the first question, Stump and Kretzmann write that "unless its life consists in only one event or it is impossible to relate an event in its life to any temporal entity or event, we need to be able to consider an eternal entity or event as one of the relata in a simultaneity relationship."[6] Helm asks in response, "how could the life of a timeless being *not* consist of only one event . . . for it to consist of more than one event these events would have to be temporally ordered."[7] But Helm seems to have overlooked something. One can individuate actions on bases other than their times of occurrence. For instance, some philosophers would argue that by one and the same arm motion, I may perform two actions, raising my arm and opening a window. Arguably, every action is also an event, but in case this is questioned, one can offer another example of two events involving the same activity of the same entity at the same time: a top may be both spinning about its axis and moving slowly across a table. In like fashion, one could perhaps individuate actions of (or events involving) a timeless being by what they accomplish. Perhaps one and the same timeless activity accomplishes two distinct actions, the initial creation of the world and its sustaining throughout time.[8]

---

5. The final section of this chapter suggests that Aquinas saw matters differently earlier in his career, at the time of his disputed questions *De veritate*.

6. Stump and Kretzmann, "Eternity," p. 434.

7. Helm, *Eternal God*, p. 28.

8. If the activity of creating = the activity of sustaining, this is compatible with even the most rigorous doctrine of divine simplicity.

If this way of individuating divine actions is legitimate, though, it raises the question of what relation these actions have to one another. If one and the same timeless activity accomplishes both, it is strange to say that they simply are discrete, as distinct temporal series would be, and natural to say that they must be in some sense simultaneous: as natural as it is to say that this one timeless activity is somehow simultaneous with itself. So there is a case to be made for recognizing a relation of simultaneity between eternal entities.

Helm argues further that we need no simultaneity or other quasi-temporal relation between eternal and temporal beings, adducing "the distinction between author's time and character's time . . . The author is the author of the whole, but it does not make sense to . . . ask whether his writing the . . . novel is simultaneous with any of the events in the work. His writing, being in time, is simultaneous with what he writes, but the act of writing is not simultaneous with any of the events that occur in the work, not even if the author writes himself into the novel."[9] But there is a crucial difference between this and the case of Creation. The events of which a novelist writes do not occur during their writing, or for that matter at a different time than their writing, because they *do not really occur at all.* This is why we are content to let them be temporally disconnected from their writing. We will not suffer such disconnection if we consider the writing of a history rather than a novel. If asked whether the events of a history occur at the time of its writing, we will answer "of course not—they were over years before." That is, in this case there is no temptation to speak of a "time within the story" somehow discrete from real time. Instead, we feel that if real events are causally connected, as are historical events and the events involved in our writing about them, they must have *some* temporal or timelike relation. So our thoughts about causality impel us to grant some sort of timelike relation between time and eternity, given that we believe that an eternal being has caused the existence of temporal things. Our treatment of timeless existence as purely present, in the Augustine chapter, compels us to see this relation as one of present to present and so one of simultaneity.

Our second question above, as to what kind of simultaneity can connect the eternal and the temporal, may sound merely technical. I think that it is of broader import, for at least three reasons. First, if Boethius and friends cannot adequately explain their second sort of simultaneity and ground it in a plausible theory about the relations of eternity and time, their escape from contradiction will seem ad hoc and

9. Helm, *Eternal God*, pp. 30, 31.

unpersuasive. There is also a second way in which the question affects how we evaluate the Boethian treatment of foreknowledge and freedom. Boethius, Aquinas, and the rest picture the *whole* of time spread before a timeless God's gaze. Thus they see all times, including both our future and our past, as related to God's vision in the same way. So for Boethius et al., if a timeless God's believings are simultaneous with our future, they are also simultaneous with our past. If they are simultaneous with our past, though, we may have the freedom-foreknowledge problem all over again. For if God's believings are simultaneous with our past, then perhaps they are after all *in* our past or are *as if* past in a relevant way. If the freedom-foreknowledge problem does not arise anew, we want to be told why. To tell us why, Boethius and company must explain their second sort of simultaneity. Only if this sort of simultaneity does not underwrite the claim that God's believings are in our past or as if so is the Boethian resolution of the freedom-foreknowledge problem finally viable.

Let me try to clarify this "as if past" status. Plantinga argues this way:

> Suppose in fact Paul will mow his lawn in 1995. Then the proposition "God (eternally) knows that Paul mows in 1995" is now true. That proposition, furthermore, was true eighty years ago . . . Since what is past is necessary, it is now necessary that this proposition was true eighty years ago. But it is logically necessary that if this proposition was true eighty years ago, then Paul mows in 1995. Hence his mowing then is necessary in just the way the past is. But then it neither now nor in future will be within Paul's power to refrain from mowing.[10]

The key premises of Plantinga's argument are that

4. "God (eternally) knows that Paul mows in 1995" is now true, and

5. If "God (eternally) knows that Paul mows in 1995" is now true, it was true eighty years ago.

According to Boethius and his allies, God is related in the same way to all times. This supports (5): if God's relation to time is such as to permit the truth of (4), it would equally have let "God (eternally) knows that Paul mows in 1995" be true eighty years ago. If (4) is true, then, a timeless God is as if in our past, because even though He is not

10. Alvin Plantinga, "On Ockham's Way Out," *Faith and Philosophy* 3 (1986), 239. Helm offers a similar argument in "Timelessness and Foreknowledge," pp. 526–527, and *Eternal God*, pp. 95–108.

literally in our past, truths about Him have for us the necessity of the past. For according to Plantinga, truths about a timeless being were true *at* times eighty years ago. So per the distinctions of my third proposal in Chapter 4, these truths do literally have the necessity of the past, for they existed and bore the attribute of truth eighty years ago. To fully vindicate the Boethian response, then, one must show how a Boethian can plausibly deny (4). I suggest later than on one construal of Boethius' second sort of simultaneity, a Boethian can do this.

A third reason to explore Boethius' second sort of simultaneity is that if God and temporal things cannot in any sense exist simultaneously, one must withdraw or seriously qualify either the claim that God is timeless or the claim that God and temporal creatures are present to one another. The first claim is one of the main contributions of later Greek philosophical thought to orthodox Christian theology. The second seems basic to the biblical picture of God as aware of and interacting with temporal creatures. Thus at this rather dry, abstract juncture, we have a test of whether one heirloom of Greek metaphysics really can cohere with the heritage of Hebrew monotheism in a single conception of God.

In their "Eternity," Stump and Kretzmann offer as an exegesis of Boethius a creative, sophisticated attempt to shed light on timeless-temporal simultaneity.[11] They base their account of eternal-temporal (ET-) simultaneity on a metaphysical picture of the relation of time and eternity. This picture has two chief components: the claim that eternity is infinite life without succession and the Einsteinian claim that simultaneity is relative to reference frames. I have already discussed Stump and Kretzmann's claim that eternity is infinite life without succession. Those who agree that Stump and Kretzmann's conception of eternity is problematic can substitute QTE for it. Those who find any conception of an extended present troubling can simply view eternity as a "frozen instant," something pointlike. The time-eternity relations I describe would obtain equally with eternity so construed. Let me therefore discuss the relativity of simultaneity and the picture of time and eternity which Stump and Kretzmann develop.

Stump and Kretzmann on Time and Eternity

I turn first to the Stump-Kretzmann picture of time-eternity relations. Let us make the common assumption that only that of time which is present is actual. We can then picture time and Stump-

11. Stump and Kretzmann, "Eternity," pp. 434–444.

Kretzmann eternity as "two infinite parallel horizontal lines, the upper one of which, representing eternity, is entirely and uniformly a strip of light (where light represents . . . an indivisible present . . .), while the lower one, representing time, is dark everywhere except for a dot of light moving steadily along it."[12] As the moving dot of light glances on each portion of the lower strip, that portion of the strip is simultaneous with the upper strip or, more precisely, with the *whole* of the upper strip: as the upper strip is ex hypothesi a single indivisible duration, if any of it is simultaneous with the dot, all of it is. Were the lower dot simultaneous with only part of the upper strip, part of the upper strip would be earlier than the dot-simultaneous part and part would be later, and so the upper strip would contain relations of earlier and later. Because each dot location is simultaneous with the whole upper strip, each is simultaneous with precisely the same portion of eternal duration, namely, all of it. Yet the dot locations are not temporally simultaneous with each other. They remain discrete, one after another, on the lower line. Nor are they simultaneous as the upper line and the lower dot are, since this latter relation, ET-simultaneity, links an eternal and a temporal term, not two temporal relata. In this metaphysical picture, then, the relation of being-somehow-simultaneous is not transitive. That dot locations are ET-simultaneous with the same upper line does not entail that they are in any sense simultaneous with one another.

This view of the relation between time and eternity raises a great many questions. One worth discussing (because its answer introduces ideas I use later) is this: how can dot locations be simultaneous with the same portion of the upper strip and yet be in no way simultaneous with one another?

The Relativity of Simultaneity

To answer this question, Stump and Kretzmann invoke the Einsteinian thesis of the *relativity of simultaneity*.[13] According to the special theory of relativity (henceforth STR), the question of whether two events occur at the same time does not have only one answer. Rather, its answer depends on one's state of motion. Stump and Kretzmann invite us to consider this standard example: a train passes by an observer standing still relative to the ground. The train is struck at both ends by lightning, just when (the observer would say that) the train's

12. Stump and Kretzmann, "AD," p. 219.
13. Stump and Kretzmann, "Eternity," pp. 437–440.

midpoint is directly in front of this observer. Light from the front and rear lightning strikes travels the same distance (half the length of the train) at the same speed (light speed) to reach the observer. Thus the light of the front strike reaches the ground observer just when the light of the rear strike does; this observer sees the strikes at once. In this person's experience, then, the strikes are simultaneous.

There is another observer sitting down within the train. The train is at rest relative to this observer, since he is moving exactly as it is. Relative to the ground observer, the train is traveling at three-fifths the speed of light. The train observer, then, is moving toward the front lightning strike and away from the rear one at three-fifths light speed (as the ground observer sees it). So light from the front strike reaches the observer on the train sometime before light from the rear strike does. If the train observer sees both strikes, then, he sees the front one some time before he sees the rear one. In this person's experience, the two events are not simultaneous.

For the ground observer, the two lightning strikes occur at once. For the train observer, they do not occur at once. According to STR, neither observer sees things distortedly or makes a mistaken judgment of simultaneity. Both are right. The events are truly simultaneous relative to the ground observer and truly nonsimultaneous relative to an observer who is in motion relative to the ground observer. Given STR, there is no such relation as absolute simultaneity, or simultaneity regardless of point of view. There is only simultaneity relative to different observers in motion relative to one another or, more generally, to different objects in relative motion. Let me now introduce a term that will prove useful: an *inertial frame of reference* is a system of objects at rest relative to one another. Thus the ground and the ground observer constitute one inertial reference frame, and the train and the train observer constitute another. What the example shows is that there is no absolute simultaneity, but only simultaneity relative to different frames of reference.

Given STR, the relation of being-somehow-simultaneous (i.e., being simultaneous relative to some reference frame) is intransitive. For all x, y, and z, if x is somehow simultaneous with y and y is somehow simultaneous with z, we cannot infer that x is somehow simultaneous with z. For it could be that x is simultaneous with y in one reference frame, y is simultaneous with z in another, and there is no third frame of reference in which x and z are simultaneous. If being-somehow-simultaneous is intransitive, then there is just no problem in the claim that dot locations ET-simultaneous with the same portion of the upper strip are in no way simultaneous with one another. There only appeared to be a problem because the question was posed in the outmoded terms of absolute simultaneity and transitive somehow-simultaneity.

The Stump-Kretzmann Definition

Stump and Kretzmann try to capture their picture of time and eternity in their definition of ET-simultaneity. Taking eternity to be *like* a frame of reference in addition to any temporal reference frames, they define ET-simultaneity thus:

> For every x and for every y, x and y are ET-simultaneous iff
> (i) either x is eternal and y is temporal, or vice versa; and
> (ii) for some observer, A, in the unique eternal reference frame, x and y are both present—i.e., either x is eternally present and y is observed as temporally present, or vice versa; and
> (iii) for some observer, B, in one of the infinitely many temporal reference frames, x and y are both present, i.e., either x is observed as eternally present and y is temporally present, or vice versa.[14]

This definition directly reflects Stump and Kretzmann's picture of time and eternity; it expresses, or tries to express, what it is for the top strip of light in Stump and Kretzmann's image to be together with the lower light dot. Clause (ii) speaks of a *unique* eternal reference frame. The rationale for this, I suspect, is as follows. Distinct temporal reference frames exist iff the same temporal events bear incompatible temporal relations to one another: that is, iff some temporal events A and B, as wholes, are both simultaneous and nonsimultaneous. Part of what distinguishes eternity from time, to Stump and Kretzmann, is that eternity lacks earlier and later "parts." If this is so, eternal entities or events cannot be earlier or later than one another; all eternal entities or events must exist or occur simultaneously. So eternal entities or events cannot bear incompatible eternal relations to one another, and therefore the basis for distinguishing multiple eternal reference frames necessarily is lacking.

Can Events Be Temporally Present in Relation to Eternity?

Herbert Nelson has objected to (ii) that if an eternal God is not temporally simultaneous with temporal things, we can attach no sense

14. Ibid., p. 439.

to the claim that such a God observes events *as temporally present*.[15] Nelson reasons that "just as nothing in [a time series A] can know anything in (another discrete temporal series, B) *as temporally present* . . . so . . . God cannot know anything in (time) *as temporally present*. For . . . nothing in (time) stands in any temporal relationship to . . . God."[16] Nothing in series B is present in A. For if anything were, B would not be discrete from A. Nor can anyone in A know anything in B as present in B. For to know this would mean knowing that something in B is *now* present in B. One can know this only if the present in A in which one knows this = the present in B at which this is true, i.e., only if some time is "now" in both A and B. But again, if this is so, A and B are not discrete. So Nelson is correct that in one sense, to know something as temporally present, one must be with it in the same temporal framework. He concludes from this that if God is not in time, nothing is temporally simultaneous with Him and there-fore nothing is temporally present for Him.[17] But given the simile of the two lines, we can see that Nelson has missed something. Stump and Kretzmann are not saying that God knows the temporally present the way temporally present things know it. They mean, rather, that it is only qua temporally present that things or events are simultaneous with an eternal being. What the eternal being coexists with, on their view, is not the past or the future of any given moment, but that moment itself. This is true for all moments, and so in a sense, on their account, from an eternal being's viewpoint all moments and their con-tents occur at once. I discuss this implication at length in Chapter 10.

Questions of Interpretation

Clauses (ii) and (iii) may seem to say that x and y are ET-simultaneous because x and y are simultaneous both in the eternal and in a temporal reference frame. But on this reading, eternal x would exist in time and temporal y would exist in eternity. Stump and Kretzmann deny that this occurs: "Nixon is temporal, not eternal, and so are his life and death. [That Nixon is both alive and dead in the eternal present] then cannot be taken to mean that the temporal entity Nixon exists in eternity, where he is simultaneously alive and dead, but rather (that) one and the same eternal present is ET-simultaneous with Nixon's being alive and . . . with Nixon's dying, although Nixon's life and Nixon's death

15. Nelson, "Time(s)," p. 8, cf. pp. 4–5.
16. Ibid., p. 8.
17. Thus in a sense (as argued below), an eternal God cannot know "what is happen-ing now."

are themselves neither eternal nor simultaneous."[18] To Stump and Kretzmann, for an eternal thing to occur in time would make it temporal, and for a temporal thing to exist in eternity would make it eternal.[19] Thus temporal things cannot exist in eternity, nor eternal ones in time. Nor (say Stump and Kretzmann) is there a third overarching framework, in addition to time and eternity, in which both eternal and temporal things can exist or occur.[20] This given, it seems that in (ii), x is eternally present with an eternal event of observing a temporal y, and in (iii), y is temporally present with a temporal event of observing an eternal x. Thus (ii) and (iii) seem to suggest that it is because eternal and temporal beings can observe one another that they can exist simultaneously without existing in single overarching framework.

Were this the meaning of (ii) and (iii), ET-simultaneity could not do the job that Boethius and Aquinas ask of it. These writers claim that God and temporal things exist at once to help to explain how a timeless God can perceive temporal things. Now we humans can observe only events, states, etc., in our immediate pasts. This is because we depend for our experience on causal signals from these events, and such signals take some time (however little) to reach our organs of perception. Boethius, Aquinas et al. probably did not know that perception thus involves a time lag. When they claimed that God perceives events that are strictly simultaneous with His own existing, they probably thought that the events we perceive occur just when our perceivings of them occur and that they were modeling God's perception exactly on human perception. In fact, however, were God's perception strictly modeled on our own as we now understand it, temporal things would have to be in God's immediate past to be observed. But though Boethius and company may have had some incorrect reasons to make it, the claim that God perceives events that are somehow simultaneous with His existence is correct. As a timeless being can have no past (or future), a timeless being cannot perceive events in its past (or future); all that a timeless God perceives is in His timeless present. Moreover, God's knowledge is traditionally called immediate. One implication of this is that His knowledge does not depend on time-taking causal signals, however observationlike it might be otherwise. So one can argue that even if He exists in time, still because God's knowledge does not depend on a time-taking signal, there is no temporal gap between an event's occurring and God's knowing that it has occurred. If this is so,

18. Stump and Kretzmann, "Eternity," p. 443.
19. Ibid., p. 436.
20. Ibid.

God's knowing is still (temporally) simultaneous with the event known.

Boethius et al., for whatever reason, recognize that events' being simultaneous with God's existence is part of what explains God's "observational" knowledge of them. So Boethians cannot in turn explain how God and temporal things exist at once by asserting (inter alia) that God observes temporal things, for this would render the first explanation vacuous. Stump and Kretzmann are in a like position. Early in their discussion of ET-simultaneity, they write that "we need . . . a simultaneity relationship between two relata of which one is eternal and the other temporal. We have to be able to characterize such a relationship coherently if we are to be able to claim that there is any connection between an eternal and a temporal entity or event."[21] If eternal and temporal things observe one another, there certainly is a "connection" between them. So like Aquinas and Boethius, Stump and Kretzmann need to characterize ET-simultaneity without appealing to eternal-temporal observation.

There are at least three further reasons for Stump and Kretzmann not to appeal to ET-observation in defining ET-simultaneity. First, as they stand, (ii) and (iii) seem to entail that two things or events are not ET-simultaneous unless two observers note that this is so. But surely relations of simultaneity exist even if there are no observers, provided that if there were observers, they *could* note the appropriate relations. Second, one might wonder whether any possible observer *could* observe what (iii) requires: is "eternal presence" an observable quality?

Third, (ii) requires an eternal being to observe something, and the fact that whatever is eternal is simple renders this theologically inappropriate. Let me explain. Suppose that a simple deity observes the universe. Now it is plausible that for all x and y, x observes y only if y causally contributes to x's having a certain experience and so only if y causally contributes to the existence of x's observational knowledge. A simple God = His knowledge.[22] Hence if a simple deity observes the universe, the universe causally contributes to God's existence: that is, the universe is a logically and causally necessary condition of God's existence. Theists will not accept this and so cannot grant that a simple God has literal observational knowledge.

One can derive a conclusion even more repugnant to theists as follows: x's observing y requires that y causally contribute to x's experience rather than that y cause (simpliciter) x's experience, because in

21. Ibid., p. 435.
22. See Aquinas, SCG I, 21, 45.

ordinary human cases, the causal contribution of y is necessary but not sufficient for the existence of observational knowledge. My observation of you, for instance, is caused not only by you but by the light that you reflect and the operation of my nerves, and it also requires the operation of the relevant natural laws. But virtually all theists will grant that God's knowledge does not depend on physical intermediaries or the operation of natural laws. In these and some other relevant senses, God's knowledge is immediate. If so, perhaps it is the case that the contribution of y would be necessary *and* sufficient for the existence of divine observational knowledge: that y would not just causally contribute to but cause that knowledge's existence. Were this the case, then if a simple deity observed the universe, the universe would cause God to exist. Again, as no theist would accept this, no theist could ascribe literal observational knowledge to a simple God.

This leads to a more general point. If anything on which a simple God causally depends for knowledge causally contributes to His existence, He can causally depend for knowledge on nothing He creates. For if He did, then given the transitivity of the relation "causally contributes to," it would follow that He causally contributes to His own existence. Now one can at some time t contribute causally to one's existence at t + 1. We do so each time we take a breath. But a simple God exists only at the "time" of eternity. Hence for a simple God causally to contribute to His own existence, His existence at t (= eternity) would have to causally contribute to His existence at t (= eternity). This is surely impossible. Hence no created thing can causally contribute to a simple God's knowledge. A simple God cannot in any sense receive knowledge from created things.23

We must ask, then, just how vital Stump and Kretzmann's talk of ET-observation is. This talk looms large in (ii) and (iii), and so in discussing (ii) and (iii), Delmas Lewis, Paul Fitzgerald, Steven Davis, Richard Creel, Paul Helm, and William Hasker have taken ET-observation as integral to Stump and Kretzmann's meaning.24 But Stump and Kretzmann state in a footnote that their talk of observation is dispensable. "It is important to understand that by 'observer,' we mean only that thing, animate or inanimate, with respect to which the reference frame is picked out."25 Thus Stump and Kretzmann circumvent

23. Of course, this raises a large question: how, then, does a simple God know what is the case in Creation? I offer a suggestion on this later.
24. See Delmas Lewis, "Eternity Again"; Fitzgerald, "SKTE"; Davis, *Logic and the Nature of God*, pp. 20–21; Richard Creel, *Divine Impassibility* (New York: Cambridge University Press, 1986), pp. 92–95; Helm, *Eternal God*, pp. 32–33; Hasker, *God*, pp. 164–166.
25. Stump and Kretzmann, "Eternity," p. 438 n. 15.

the problems just raised. Observers need not exist for reference frames to exist. The temporal "observer" need not observe eternal presence, because it need not even be sentient. The eternal knowledge in question need not be observational.

Clauses (ii) and (iii) refer to observers because a standard relativistic definition of distant simultaneity does so: two events at a distance are said to be simultaneous in a frame of reference just in case within that frame, light signals from those events reach an observer at the midpoint between those two events simultaneously.[26] This definition's reference to an observer is inessential. One can rephrase the definition as follows: two events E and E1 are distantly simultaneous in a frame of reference just in case within that frame, event E2 (E's light signal reaching midpoint P) caused by E and event E3 (E1's light signal reaching midpoint P) caused by E1 are locally simultaneous. Reference to an observer is added to this definition for at least two reasons. First, local simultaneity is understood to be directly observed or observable simultaneity, and being clear on what is and is not observable can be important in discussing the epistemic status of certain claims of special relativity. Second, if E2 is not in either of E3's light cones and E3 is not in either of E2's light cones (i.e., if it is not physically possible that E2 and E3 be causally connected), then if E2 and E3 lie at any spatial distance from one another, however small, they are distantly simultaneous. If local simultaneity is not to be just one more case of distant simultaneity, local simultaneity must involve occurring at the same *place and* time. One way to ensure this is to have E2 and E3 be distinguishable parts or aspects of a single event E4 that is an observer's observing E and E1.

So perhaps for Stump and Kretzmann's purposes, the only important thing in the relativistic definition of distant simultaneity is that the light signals it involves would coincide temporally at the midpoint. To use this facet of the definition, Stump and Kretzmann must invoke an eternal event caused by a temporal event and a temporal event caused by an eternal event. They can then say that events E and E1 are ET-simultaneous iff

(i) E is eternal and E1 is temporal, and
(iv) at point A, in the unique eternal reference frame, E and E1 are both present—i.e., either E is eternally present at A or an

<hr />

26. For discussion of this definition's basis, problems, and implications, see Wesley Salmon, *Space, Time, and Motion,* 2d ed. (Minneapolis: University of Minnesota Press, 1980), chaps. 3, 4, esp. p. 73, and Lawrence Sklar, *Space, Time, and Spacetime* (Berkeley: University of California Press, 1976), pp. 276–294, esp. p. 277.

event E2 caused by E is eternally present at A, and E1 is causally related as temporally present, in that an eternal event E3 caused by E1 occurs at A, and

(v) at point B, in one of the infinitely many temporal reference frames, E and E1 are both present, i.e., either E1 is present at B or an event E4 caused by E1 is present at B, and E is causally related as eternally present, i.e., a temporal event E5 caused by E is present at B.

But here we hit a problem of circularity. For Stump and Kretzmann suggest that to make sense of how an eternal God can have effects in time, or temporal beings have effects in eternity, we must first work out a simultaneity relation between the atemporal and the temporal: "we need . . . a simultaneity relationship between two relata of which one is eternal and the other temporal. We have to be able to characterize such a relation coherently if we are to be able to claim that there is any connection between an eternal and a temporal entity or event . . . ET-simultaneity is a sufficient condition of the possibility of a causal connection . . . between an eternal and a temporal entity or event."[27] According to Stump and Kretzmann, if one term of a causal relation is timeless and the other is temporal, cause and effect must exist simultaneously.[28] Further, as Stump and Kretzmann see it, to explain how ET-causal relations are possible, we must invoke ET-simultaneity. But then any definition of ET-simultaneity which invokes any form of ET-causality (or ET-observation, or other causally implicated ET-knowledge) is implicitly circular. For to fully explain how ET-causation can occur, we must bring in the concept of ET-simultaneity. If we do, we cannot then define ET-simultaneity by invoking ET-causation, for then the concept to be defined in effect recurs in the definition.

Given this problem with ET-causality, one might want to recur to Stump and Kretzmann's (i)–(iii) and stipulate that the eternal state of knowledge involved in no way involves causal connection with temporal things. But this move would face three problems. First, it is hard to see how a timeless God could know temporal creatures in a way involving *no sort* of causal connection if a timeless God is these creatures' Creator. For if a timeless God is their Creator, then His beliefs about them are among the causal conditions of their existence: He causes them to exist because He believes that they should be. Second, it

27. Stump and Kretzmann, "Eternity," pp. 435, 451, 435.
28. "An eternal entity or event cannot be earlier . . . than . . . any temporal entity or event . . . any relationship between what is eternal and what is temporal . . . must be some species of simultaneity," ibid., p. 435.

is hard to see how knowledge not involving causal connection would be at all relevant to the question of simultaneity. Finally, even if one stipulated a form of knowing that involved no causal connection of knower and known at all, still one would surely have to say that the existing of some entity A is part of what explains its being the case that God knows that A exists. (For instance, one can say that God knows that A exists because He believes that A should be and therefore effects it that A exists, and knows that He does so.) But then some relation in virtue of which A explains (part of) the content of God's belief-state must itself cross the line between time and eternity and so arguably will also have ET-simultaneity as a condition of its possibility.

If we delete all mention of causality and of knowledge, then x and y are ET-simultaneous just in case

(i)   either x is eternal and y is temporal, or vice versa; and
(vi) in the unique eternal reference frame, x and y are both present—i.e., either x is eternally present and y is temporally present, or vice versa; and
(vii) in one of the infinitely many temporal reference frames, x and y are both present, i.e., either x is eternally present and y is temporally present, or vice versa.

But how can an eternal thing be eternally present in a temporal frame or a temporal thing temporally present in an eternal frame? According to Stump and Kretzmann, this cannot involve a temporal thing's literally being in eternity or an eternal thing's literally being in time, or a third overarching framework. Yet if our ET-relation is to be any kind of simultaneity-relation, the two things must somehow be copresent, and to avoid circularity, this copresence must be explicable without recourse to ET-simultaneity. We seem to have reached an impasse.

We can move beyond the impasse only if we alter the definition yet again, to say that for every x and y, x and y are ET-simultaneous iff

(i)   x is eternal and y is temporal, and
(viii) in the unique eternal reference frame, x is eternally present and y is present with respect to x (though not located within x's frame of reference), and
(ix)   in one of the infinitely many temporal reference frames, y is temporally present and x is present with respect to y (though not located within y's frame of reference).

In commenting on an earlier version of this chapter, Stump explained "present with respect to" in (viii) and (ix) as simply meaning "neither past nor future with respect to." As Stump and Kretzmann deny that there are such relations as eternal or ET-pastness and -futurity, (viii) and (ix) so taken can only deny to x and y temporal pastness and futurity with respect to each other.[29] Now temporal pastness and futurity indeed can link only pairs of temporal entities, not a temporal and an eternal being. But why does this fact entail that eternal and temporal beings are in any sense copresent? They or their durations could have at least two other relations: they could be discrete or they could be incommensurable.

Discrete Times and Eternity

I stated earlier that if one moment is earlier or later than or simultaneous with a second, the two moments are temporally connected, that two discrete temporal series would be two series of moments, A and B, such that every moment in A is temporally connected with every moment in A, every moment in B temporally connected with every moment in B, yet no moment in A is temporally connected with any moment in B, and that possibly there are two such series. If discrete time series are possible, perhaps eternity and time are related as such series would be. On what grounds might one reject this suggestion? The only ground that occurs to me is this. Events in discrete time series would be causally insulated from one another. Theists who believe that God is eternal believe that God's intentions have had effects in time and so maintain that there are causal relations between eternity and time. If there are such relations, then eternity and time are not causally insulated and so not discrete. But even if this is an adequate response, Stump and Kretzmann cannot give it. For they hold that one must first make sense of ET-simultaneity before one can appeal to ET-causal relations.

Incommensurable Times and Eternity

Even if discrete temporal series are not possible, that times and eternity cannot be earlier or later than one another is compatible with their being just incommensurable. Events A and B are temporally incommensurable (TI*) under a certain description just in case under that description one cannot have reason to affirm or deny that A and B

29. N. 28 quoted Stump and Kretzmann's denial that ET-pastness and -futurity exist. Stump and Kretzmann hold that "because an eternal entity is atemporal, there is no past or future, no earlier or later, within its life . . . no eternal entity has existed or will exist: it *only* exists" (p. 434). This entails that a relation of pastness or futurity between eternal entities would be unexemplifiable—which seems a good reason to say that no such relation exists.

are temporally connected. For instance, let A be an event locally simultaneous with my clock's striking two in framework of reference R, and let B be an event causally independent of A and locally simultaneous with my clock's striking two in frame of reference R*.[30] Under these descriptions, A and B are TI*. Within one reference frame, we can say whether A and B occur at once. Again, if A causes B or vice versa, this establishes a temporal priority between them which holds in all frames of reference and so holds even when A and B are considered under the descriptions given. But there is no "super-reference frame" with respect to which we can say whether causally independent events described as in distinct reference frames are simultaneous *under that description*. So again, as so described, A and B are TI*. If events can be TI* under a description, that events are neither past nor future with respect to one another under a description does not entail that they are present with one another under this description. I am careful to relativize my conclusion to events as *described* in certain ways in order to render this second case independent of the first. If discrete times are impossible, then if events are not in one another's past or future, it follows that they occur at once. So events can *in fact* be TI* only if discrete times are possible. But even if, given all the facts, two events must occur at once, it can still be the case that given only that these events fall under certain descriptions, we cannot validly infer that they occur at once. That events are TI* is at least an epistemic possibility (as long as we do not *know* that discrete times are impossible) if not in fact a metaphysical possibility. But if this is in *any* sense possible, I can suggest that the incommensurability of time and eternity is a metaphysical possibility.

Let us say that events A and B are *durationally* incommensurable if A is temporal, B is eternal, and we cannot have reason to affirm or deny that A and B are simultaneous. To Stump and Kretzmann, eternity is like another temporal reference frame. Stump and Kretzmann deny that the same event can occur both in eternity and in time. Further, by their own stipulation, they cannot appeal to causal relations between eternal and temporal events to explain the simultaneity of the eternal and the temporal. Thus it seems that for Stump and Kretzmann, if A occurs in eternity and B at some time, no description is available under which they occur at once or do not occur at once within a single reference frame, and we cannot appeal to causal relations between them

---

30. I specify local simultaneity to avoid problems that arise for ascriptions of distant simultaneity within relativity theory. For a discussion of these problems, see Wesley Salmon, *Space, Time*, pp. 73, 93–127.

to establish their durational order: their relations are just like those of A and B described as occurring in distinct frames of reference. So arguably, A and B are durationally incommensurable.

In sum, if x is temporally present (in some reference frame) and y is eternally present, it just does not follow that x and y are in some sense simultaneous. They could instead be discrete or incommensurable. If so, then for eternally present and temporally present beings to exist simultaneously, some further condition must be satisfied. It is not clear what that further condition might be or could be. If we cannot come up with one, this may reveal an underlying flaw in the Stump-Kretzmann picture of time and eternity.

Another Approach

To save the concept of ET-simultaneity, then, one must either explain it without appealing to ET-causation or to an eternal God's knowledge or will of temporal things, or not explain it at all, taking it instead as somehow primitive and not further to be analyzed, or jettison the assumption that ET-simultaneity is conceptually prior to and helps to explain ET-causation or the possibility of ET-causation. I suggest that the third is the most promising strategy. If one adopts this strategy, the conceptually most economical moves would be to take ET-causation as at least relatively primitive and explain ET-simultaneity in terms of it, or else to explain both in terms of some third relatively primitive concept. I do not know what this third concept could be, though, and so taking ET-causality as relatively primitive and as the basis of ET-simultaneity seems the more appealing alternative.

Taking ET-causality as the basis of ET-simultaneity may initially seem counterintuitive. But it accords well with the fact that if God is eternal, there are temporal relata for ET-relations only because an eternal God creates them. For if this is the way ET-causality and ET-simultaneity are really related, it makes sense to use the former to explain the latter. The view that one must use ET-simultaneity to explain ET-causation (or the possibility of ET-causation) parallels the widespread belief that temporal concepts are more primitive than causal, i.e., that one must use temporal concepts in explaining causal relations (or their possibility) and so cannot in turn explain these temporal concepts causally. But some philosophers deny this claim about time and causality. Advocates of causal theories of time claim to base temporal relations on causal relations. So a causal theory of ET-relations would not be wholly without parallel. Further, giving a causal-theoretic explanation of temporal order, in particular, would require one to produce an analysis of causal order which does not invoke temporal order. If this could be done, perhaps it would also be possible to analyze causal relations between eternal and temporal entities without invoking ET-simultaneity. If we could provide such an analysis of ET-causal relations, three benefits would follow:

1. we would be able to include causal relations in a definition of ET-simultaneity without circularity,
2. we could use the existence of causal relations between the eternal and the temporal to distinguish time and eternity's being simultaneous from their being discrete, and
3. we could appeal to causal relations between the eternal and the temporal to establish a durational order between them, thus blocking the claim that they are durationally incommensurable.

It may be, then, that something along the lines of (i), (iv), and (v) can serve to define simultaneity between the eternal and the temporal; at least nothing said here rules this out. Of course, for anything like (i), (iv), and (v) to be viable, one must spell out fully the relevant causal relations. As I do not know whether or just how this could be done, I do not know whether the concept of ET-simultaneity can be saved.[31]

Other Problems

Even if one could successfully produce a causal theory of ET-simultaneity, two other qualms about the Stump-Kretzmann view of ET-simultaneity would deserve mention. First, Stump and Kretzmann

31. In their latest work, Stump and Kretzmann appear to accept the need for a causal condition in an adequate account of ET-simultaneity. For in "Eternity Examined and Extended" (p. 28), they give as necessary and sufficient conditions for any x and y to be ET-simultaneous that

   i. x is eternal and y is temporal,
   x. x is in the eternal present with respect to some A in the unique eternal reference frame,
  xi. y is in the temporal present with respect to some B in one of the infinitely many temporal reference frames, and
  xii. both A and B can enter into direct, immediate causal relations with both x and y, and (if capable of awareness) can be directly aware of each.

Given a causal theory of ET-simultaneity, which Stump and Kretzmann do not appear to adopt, these may well constitute necessary and sufficient conditions for x's and y's standing in a relation of ET-simultaneity. But again, I do not know whether a viable causal theory of ET-simultaneity can be constructed.

posit four distinct simultaneity relations: ET-simultaneity, ordinary temporal simultaneity, eternal simultaneity (linking two eternal relata existing in the same eternal present)[32], and the generic simultaneity relation "existence or occurrence . . . together," of which the other three relations are species.[33] One would prefer to have fewer.

Second, the Stump-Kretzmann theory of ET-simultaneity does not rid us of (4) and could almost be tailor-made for affirming it. That a timeless being's knowing what He knows is simultaneous with the present moment seems a good reason to say that "God (eternally) knows that Paul mows in 1995" is now true, or true *at* the present moment. No denial of (4) can be plausible if the now at which God knows when Paul mows is simultaneous with the present moment. Stump has objected to this claim. She argues that the inference that "if the eternal present is ET-simultaneous with the temporal present, then . . . what is true in the eternal present is also true in the temporal present . . . is invalid, taken generally. In the eternal present, it is now true that Antichrist is active, since the eternal present is ET-simultaneous with every instant of time as that instant is present. But it does not follow that in the temporal present it is now true that Antichrist is active. (This result is not surprising, since ET-simultaneity is not transitive.)"[34] This response, however, has a problem. The statement "in the eternal present, it is now true that Antichrist is active" admits of three readings, One one, it asserts that

> 6. it is now true in the eternal present that Antichrist is now (i.e., at the "now" of the eternal present) active.

On Stump and Kretzmann's terms, (6) is false, for as a temporal being, Antichrist neither exists nor acts in the "now" of the eternal present. Of course, "God now knows that P" entails "P is now true." But it is not the case that an eternal God now (at the "now" of eternity) knows that Antichrist *is* active. For the present-tense "is" of "Antichrist *is* active" picks up the present of the *knower,* and again, Antichrist is not active in eternity.

What is true in the eternal present is that at a certain point t in time, it is *then* (i.e., at t) true that Antichrist is active. What God knows in the eternal present is that latter claim. Knowing at one "now," t, that P is the case at another "now," t1, does not in general entail that P is the case at t. If I now know that tomorrow I will shower, it does not follow

32. Stump and Kretzmann, "Eternity," p. 435.
33. Ibid.
34. In a personal communication.

that I am now showering. Eternity is a "now" distinct from any temporal "now" even if simultaneous with them all. So God's knowing in eternity that Antichrist is active at t does not render it now true (at the "now" of eternity) that Antichrist is active. In consequence, it is not the case that my original argument entails (6). As it does not, the fact that we cannot also say that Antichrist is active at the temporal present does not invalidate my inference from truth in eternity to truth at the present time.

On a second reading, "in the eternal present, it is now true that Antichrist is active" asserts that

    7. in the eternal present, it is now (in eternity) true that it is then (i.e., at the appropriate time[s]) true that Antichrist is active.

(7) is harmless, for again, "it is true at t that P at t1" does not entail "it is true at t that P," and so my inference again is not invalidated. On a third reading, "in the eternal present, it is now true that Antichrist is active" asserts that

    8. in the eternal present, it is now (in eternity) true that it is true at some time that Antichrist is active.

(8) is harmless for the same reason (7) is.

On the Stump-Kretzmann theory, ET-simultaneous with the temporal present, God knows that at t, Antichrist is active. This does not entail that Antichrist's activity is in any way simultaneous with the temporal present. It does, however, entail that God's knowing is simultaneous with the present and that for every P God knows, "God knows P" is true simultaneous with the present. I suggest that

    9. whatever the sort of simultaneity in question, what is true simultaneous with t is true *at* t.

(9) is compatible with the Stump-Kretzmann claim that ET-simultaneity is not transitive. For (9) makes no claims about what simultaneity relations do or do not obtain; (9) only asserts that the obtaining of whatever simultaneity relations do obtain has a consequence for truth at t. Accordingly, I do not see that Stump has an argument against (9), and intuition favors (9)'s truth. But if (9) is true, then on the Stump-Kretzmann theory of ET-simultaneity, it is not just the case that "God knows that P" is true and is enunciated now. Rather, this claim is true now. If so, (4) is true, and the Boethian attempt to reconcile freedom and foreknowledge fails.

A Historical Footnote

Stump and Kretzmann offer an extremely sophisticated position on Boethius' behalf. There is room to question whether it is a position Boethius actually held. Boethius and Stump and Kretzmann hold that an eternal God sees all events happen at once.[35] But the statement "an eternal God sees all events happen at once" is ambiguous. It might assert that God's *seeings* of each individual event happen at once. This is how Stump and Kretzmann (and William Hasker) take it.[36] In the Stump-Kretzmann picture of time and eternity, each new dot location on the lower line is ET-simultaneous with the same portion of the upper line, while this upper portion is eternally-simultaneous with itself: so this portion as seeing one dot location is eternally-simultaneous with this portion as seeing another. But the most natural reading of Boethius' image of an eternal God as a man on a hill seeing the whole expanse of a road is that all of the road is really there at once to be seen. Again, Boethius asserts that an eternal God is related to time as the center point of a circle is related to the circle. Were Boethius thinking in Stump and Kretzmann's terms, we would have to read this image as suggesting that the center's relations to the various points exist all at once, but no two points of the circle coexist with one another. But this is not the most natural reading of the image. All points of a circle coexist at once with its center. So the circle image suggests the claim that God perceives all temporal events simultaneously because all temporal events somehow are really simultaneous.

At the least, then, it seems that Boethius does not unambiguously opt for one rather than the other reading of his claim that God sees all events happen at once. All the same, there is a historical precedent for Stump and Kretzmann's view: a text in Aquinas' early disputed questions *De veritate* suggests a theory like Stump and Kretzmann's. For Aquinas explains God's timeless knowledge of the whole of time with this analogy:

> Were someone to see many travelers along a road successively, over a certain period of time, in each part of that time he would see some passersby as present, so that over the whole time of his vision he would see every traveler as present. He would not see all as present at once because the time of his seeing is not all-at-once. If his seeing were able to exist all at once, he would see at once all as present, although they do not

35. Stump and Kretzmann, "Eternity," p. 457.
36. Stump and Kretzmann, "Eternity"; William Hasker, "Concerning the Intelligibility of 'God Is Timeless,'" *New Scholasticism* 57 (1983), 190–192.

all pass by as present at once. Whence because the vision of God's knowledge is measured by eternity, which is all at once and yet includes all of time . . . God sees what happens in time not as future but as present.[37]

This is precisely how Stump and Kretzmann explicate the claim that God sees all of time at once.[38]

Whatever the historical pedigree of Stump and Kretzmann's view, I advance below another theory of time-eternity relations which dispenses with the concept of ET-simultaneity. This theory is preferable to Stump and Kretzmann's on three grounds. It does not require us to produce problematic causal definitions. It involves fewer species of simultaneity. And it salvages the Boethian approach to freedom and foreknowledge.

---

37. "Si aliquis videret multos transeuntes per unam viam successive, et hoc per aliquod tempus, in singulis partibus temporis videret praesentialiter aliquos transeuntes, ita quod in toto tempore suae visionis omnes transeuntes praesentialiter videret; nec tamen simul omnes praesentialiter quia tempus suae visionis non est totum simul. Si autem sua visio tota simul posset existere, simul praesentialiter omnes videret, quamvis non omnes simul praesentialiter transirent; unde cum visio divinae scientiae aeternitate mensuretur, quae est tota simul, et tamen totum tempus includit . . . sequitur ut quidquid in tempore geritur, non ut futurum sed ut praesens videat." Aquinas, *QD de veritate* 2, 12, in R. Spiazzi, ed., *Quaestiones Disputatae* (Turin: Marietti, 1948), vol. 1, p. 24.

38. Still, other passages in Aquinas suggest the other explication. Thomas adopts Boethius' images of a man on a hill (*ST* Ia, 14, 13) and an eternal God as the center point of a circle (*SCG*, 66 [7]). Were it the case that Boethius himself clearly used his images to suggest a theory of ET-simultaneity, Aquinas' adopting Boethius' images would have to count as evidence for a lifelong adherence to a view like Stump and Kretzmann's. But it seems clear that Boethius' own thinking about time and eternity is not developed well enough to let one say with confidence that he did or did not opt for ET-simultaneity. Arguably, then, Aquinas used these images as more naturally construed, to suggest that somehow all of time really does exist at once. If so, then he shifted later in life from Stump and Kretzmann's "Boethian" theory to what I call an Anselmian theory of time and eternity.

[9]
Anselm: Eternity and Dimensionality

If the work of Stump and Kretzmann adequately represents Boethius' view of time-eternity relations, then, that view is open to objections. Anselm of Canterbury inherited the work of Augustine and Boethius on time and eternity. For Anselm as for Boethius, God is eternal because He is simple and alive. Also as in Boethius, God as eternal is somehow present with all moments of time equally: Anselm explicitly derives this thesis from God's simplicity and role as the creator of time. Anselm develops Boethius' suggestion that God has all of time present to Him into a doctrine of God's temporal omnipresence. For Anselm, God is simultaneously present at discrete, nonsimultaneous times, *without* wiping out their temporal distinction. Anselm claims, in so many words, that God is present at different times *at once*.[1]

Anselm also developed a view of how this is possible. By the time he wrote his late *De concordia,* he had come to see eternity as like a supertemporal dimension, "containing" time and temporal entities rather as time "contains" space and spatial entities. *De concordia* asserts that "eternity has its own simultaneity, in which all things exist which exist at the same time and place and which are diverse in times or places."[2] Thus Anselm claims that in the dimension of eternity, God and temporal things exist at once, i.e., occupy the same coordinate. If this is so,

---

1. E.g., Anselm, *Monologion,* chap. 21.
2. "Habet enim aeternitas suum simul, in quo sunt omnia quae simul sunt loco vel tempore et quae sunt diversis in locis vel temporibus." Anselm, *De concordia* I, 5, in Schmitt, *Opera,* vol. 2, p. 254, ll. 13–15.

God, temporal things and times are literally at the same location, and so simultaneous, but are not at the same *temporal* location, so that times remain *temporally* discrete. Thus Anselm provides a simultaneity relation linking time and eternity without positing a relation of ET-simultaneity. His work, then, represents an alternative to Stump and Kretzmann's theory which is worth exploring.

Anselm on Time and Eternity

Anselm holds a tensed theory of time. He affirms the flow of time in such claims as that "it is never possible for a past thing to become not-past, as a present thing is able to become not-present" and that what temporal things "are in the fleeting, most brief present hardly exists."[3] Anselm adopts this tensed theory as part of his adherence to an Augustinian metaphysics, according to which (as we have seen) "true" or "unqualified" existence is immutable eternal existence, and changeable, temporal things by contrast "hardly exist."

Yet Anselm holds in addition that flowing temporal beings and flowing time itself also exist frozen and immutable in eternity: "I do not say that something never exists in time which always exists in eternity. For I do not say that my action of tomorrow at no time exists. I only deny that it exists today, though nevertheless it always exists in eternity."[4] " . . . something is called mutable in time before it exists, which in eternity remains immutably . . . that which in eternity cannot be changed, is changeable by free will at some time before it exists."[5] Because he holds that all times and temporal beings are with God in the simultaneity of eternity, Anselm holds that God is present at once to all times, while they yet remain temporally discrete and nonsimultaneous. Let us see how Anselm arrives at these views and whether they are tenable.

---

3. "Numquam enim fieri potest, ut res quae praeterita est fiat non praeterita; sicut res quaedam quae praesens est potest fieri non praesens." Ibid., I, 2. " . . . hoc quod in labili brevissimoque et vix existente praesenti sunt vix est." Anselm, *Monologion,* chap. 28, in Schmitt, *Opera,* vol. 1, p. 46, ll. 12–13.

4. "non dico aliquid numquam esse in tempore quod semper est in aeternitate, sed tantum in aliquo tempore non esse. Non enim dico actionem meam crastinem nullo tempore esse, sed hodie tantum nego eam esse quae tamen semper est in aeternitate." Anselm, *De concordia* I, 5, in Schmitt, *Opera,* vol. 2, p. 255, ll. 15–18.

5. "dicitur aliquid esse mutabile in tempore, antequam sit, quod in aeternitate manet immutabiliter . . . ita quod in aeternitate mutari nequit, in tempore aliquando per liberam voluntatem, antequam sit, esse mutabile probatur." Anselm, *De concordia* I, 5, in Schmitt, *Opera,* vol. 2, p. 255, ll. 22–24; p. 254, ll. 4–6.

Eternity in the *Monologion*

Monologion 20–24 treat God's relation to time and space in parallel, as far as Anselm thinks the matter allows. I will deal only with Anselm's discussion of God and time, save when the parallel discussion of God and space helps in interpreting the former. *Monologion* 20–24 first argue that God exists in every time, then argue that God exists in no time, then try to reconcile the two claims: Anselm brings in his account of God's eternity to make sense of God's being temporally omnipresent and omniabsent at once. Let us first see how Anselm moves to the conclusion that God is temporally omnipresent.

Anselm's argument for this claim leans on the thesis that

(N) when God does not exist, nothing exists.[6]

In *Monologion* 20, Anselm first notes that God must exist at no time, at only some times, or at every time, then denies on the basis of (N) that God exists at no times or only at some times. If (N) is true, Anselm reasons, then there cannot be such a thing as an existent time from which God is absent. So to speak, if God does not exist at some time, there can be no time there at all. So if there are times at all, Anselm concludes, God is there. Anselm's argument that God exists at every time is essentially this: Without the presence of God's power, no time could exist: thus there could not be a time at which God's power was not present. But as He is simple, God = God's power. Hence God is Himself present with His effects. This argument amounts to an explication of (N).

The claim that God cannot exist in only some times, supported by (N), also figures in Anselm's counterargument that God exists at no time (chap. 21). In harmonizing the claims that God is temporally omnipresent and exists at no time, Anselm never withdraws (N). Nor does he withdraw the claims directly based on it, that God cannot exist at no time or at only some times. Again, when seeking support in chap. 22 for the claim that God is *able* to be present at once at all times, Anselm finds it in the claim that God is Creator and as such must be beyond and exempt from the created laws which might prevent this. So once more, it is a fact about God's power which explains His presence

6. "ubi ipsa non est, nihil sit." Anselm, *Monologion*, chap. 14, in Schmitt, *Opera*, vol. 1, p. 27, l. 19. Anselm's discussion is phrased in terms of the presence of "summa natura" and like expressions. Since there is no real doubt Whom he means, I will refer to this being as God.

to time. Finally, in summing up his position in chap. 22, Anselm says
that one can say that God is in every time because every other existing
thing is sustained in existence only by His presence.[7] (N), it seems, is
the core of Anselm's treatment of temporal omnipresence. To understand this treatment, then, we must try to understand (N).

Anselm's *Monologion* 20 explication of (N) reasons that in general,

    1. the power of a cause is present to its effect, with it and when it
       is,

but since

    2. the power of God = God,

it follows that

    3. if a cause is God, it is present to its effect, with it and when it
       is.

Given that every time and every temporal thing are God's effects,[8] and
that God also exists when God exists, (3) entails that

    4. when something exists, God exists,

and thus that

    N. when God does not exist, nothing exists.

Given our preanalytic notion of a cause as exerting some force or
power on its effects, (1) can appear plausible or even perhaps necessarily
true. For arguably, to say that the power of a cause is with its effect or
where its effect is is to say that the cause's power is *effective* in that place.
So to speak, if a power makes itself felt at a location, it is not unreasonable to say that in some sense it is there to be felt. Anselm's backing for
(2) is his doctrine of divine simplicity. Assessing this doctrine's merits
calls for a book of its own, and so I will not try to do this here. (4) and
(N), then, follow from the conjunction of the doctrine of divine simplicity and the claim that God is cause of all that is other than Himself,
given the necessary truth of (1) and the claim that God exists when God

7. Anselm, *Monologion*, chap. 22, in Schmitt, *Opera*, vol. 1, p. 41, ll. 6–7.
8. Ibid., p. 39, l. 26–p. 40, l. 5.

exists. Read in light of this, Anselm's doctrine of temporal omnipresence would say that God is present where and when His creatures are, in something like the way a field of force is present in an area in which the effects of that field are perceptible.

If one wishes to avoid the doctrine of divine simplicity, there is a second route to Anselm's doctrine of temporal omnipresence. When he introduces a spatial analogue of (N) in *Monologion* 14, Anselm gives as his reason for holding it *Monologion* 13's argument that

> 5. God is constantly sustaining His creation.

So Anselm believes that (5) entails (N)'s spatial analogue. I suggest that he also thinks (5) to entail (N). For as we noted above, Anselm treats the issues of spatial and temporal omnipresence in parallel save where forced to do otherwise, and nothing seems to force him to deny that (5) entails (N). In fact, through its mention of constancy, (5)'s connection with (N) is clearer than its connection with (N)'s spatial analogue. But (5) entails (N) only in conjunction with the claims that God as sustaining creation is a direct cause of its existence and that

> 6. a direct cause is present to its effect, with it and when it exists/occurs.

So (N) may covertly rest on (6), or on something like (6). Still, whether (N) rests on (6) or on (1) and (2), it is the case via (N)'s role in *Monologion* 20–22 that the presence of cause to effect is central to Anselm's argument for and explication of God's temporal omnipresence. At the very least, it can be said that for Anselm, we know that God is temporally omnipresent because we know that He is the sustaining cause of all time and that a cause (or a simple cause) is somehow present with its effect.

Causal Presence

We thus need some defensible account of a cause's presence to or with its effect, if Anselm's views are to seem cogent. (6) appears to be a denial of action at a spatiotemporal distance, and (1) and (2) deny this in the case of God. The most influential physical theories of antiquity rejected the possibility of action at a distance.[9] Aristotle, for instance,

---

9. Mary Hesse, "Action at a Distance and Field Theories," in Paul Edwards, ed., *The Encyclopedia of Philosophy*, vol. 1 (New York: Macmillan, 1967), pp. 9–15.

held that "any two things, of which one acts and the other suffers action in the proper sense of the terms . . . must be capable of reciprocal contact . . . [though] if anything imparts motion without itself being moved, it may touch the moved and yet itself be touched by nothing."[10] The mention of things that impart motion without being moved reveals how strongly Aristotle takes his denial of distant action. For Aristotle, unmoved movers must be immaterial things. For Aristotle, only material things have places.[11] Thus immaterial beings have no literal place, for Aristotle, and so cannot literally be next to anything. Nor can they literally touch anything, since touching is a contact between the surfaces of material things. Yet Aristotle is sure that action at a distance is a conceptual impossibility—after all, if the claim that action at a distance does not occur is to be part of an Aristotelian science of physics, it must be a necessary truth. For this reason, Aristotle infers that there must be *some* sense in which an immaterial thing is directly with and in contact with any material thing it acts on. Thus when he writes that "that which is the first movent of a thing . . . is always together with that which is moved by it . . . there is nothing intermediate between them,"[12] his phrasing is carefully chosen. Material movers are in direct literal contact with the things they move, and so there is nothing between these agents and their patients. Immaterial agents, though not literally touching their material patients, still are in direct causal contact with them: they do not act through intermediary agents, and so in this sense "there is nothing intermediate between them." This is true in a second sense as well: as immaterial movers have no proper location in space, there is no space between them and their material patients. Thus Aristotle can maintain that immaterial causes satisfy the same direct-presence condition material causes satisfy.

Through Aristotle's influence, the majority of late-medieval philosophers of nature also denied action at a distance, and Aquinas explicitly uses this denial from Aristotle's physics to explain his own doctrine of spatial omnipresence.[13] Now it is highly unlikely that Anselm had direct access to Aristotle's *Physics* or the late-classical literature it spawned. But he could well have had contact with Aristotle's ideas through the reports, rejections, or simple absorptions of authors he

10. Aristotle, *De gen. et. corr.* I, 6, 322b28–29, 323a33–34.
11. See Aristotle, *Physics* IV, 4, 212a5–7.
12. Aristotle, *Physics* VII, 2, 243a4–5.
13. For a historical survey of the issue of action at a distance in the later Middle Ages, see Francis Kovach, "The Enduring Question of Action at a Distance in St. Albert the Great," *Southwestern Journal of Philosophy* 10 (1979), 161–235. For Aquinas' use of Aristotle's physical principle, see *ST* Ia 8, 1c.

had available, such as Augustine, Boethius, and Cicero. If we assume that Anselm's general model of causality is Aristotelian enough to reject action at a distance, we can read (6) precisely as such a denial or (1) and (2) as such a denial in God's case. We can then take Anselm to be doing basically what Aristotle did before him—taking (6) as some sort of necessary truth (or else using [1] and [2] to the same end), inferring that there must be *some* sense in which *any* direct cause (or a simple direct cause) is directly with its effect, and applying this result to an immaterial being's case via (N).

Were this reading of Anselm to be correct, philosophical evaluation of his position might hinge on what we make of the idea of action at a distance, on whether, if true, (6) or the conjunction of (1) and (2) is also necessarily true, and on whether, if either is necessarily true, the phrase "direct cause" retains when applied to God enough of its ordinary meaning to warrant extending (6) or (1) to God's case. I make only two points here. First, as Mary Hesse has put it,

> there are empirical considerations to be taken into account in discussing the possibility of action at a distance, but these can never ultimately be decisive because it is open to a field theorist, at any stage, to hold that apparent action at a distance must be reducible to action in a still-hidden medium, and it is open to an action-at-a-distance theorist to hold that any field theory is compatible with action at a distance between still-hidden, subtle particles. Thus a metaphysical question may remain after all empirical considerations have been taken into account.[14]

In other words, whether (6) is true is ultimately a conceptual issue, and so (6) very likely is necessarily true if true at all. We have already seen that (1) is arguably necessarily true. (2) follows from the doctrine of divine simplicity, which can be shown to be true necessarily if at all. For nothing can be contingently simple. If A is simple in one possible world, in that world the attribute of being A = the attribute of simplicity. But attribute-identities are necessary. Hence in all worlds, the attribute of being A = the attribute of simplicity, and so nothing can be A unless it is simple. In short, (6), (1), and (2) all have the modal status the present strategy requires.

Second, my argument below suggests that at least insofar as God's timelessness affects matters, we can apply a great many terms to God in pretty much their ordinary senses, among them "agent." To this extent, then, there will be reason to say that "direct cause" applies to God univocally. But it could be that Anselm would not accept a defense of

14. Hesse, "Action," p. 13.

his position which premises this. For Anselm became convinced in the *Monologion* and remained convinced in the *Proslogion* that only the merest scraps of terms' ordinary meanings can apply to God.[15] So insofar as deriving (N) via (6) requires us to make many positive claims about God which we also and in much the same sense make about creatures, there is room for doubt that this is *Anselm's* intent, even if the strategy is viable. Moreover, the issue of action at a distance lies beyond my present purview, and so we will not settle the question of whether this approach to temporal omnipresence is correct.

(N)'s spatial analogue plus either (6) or (1) and (2) could provide Anselm premises for arguing God's spatial omnipresence. They could perhaps even provide a model for conceiving God's presence *with* if not literally *in* places. For Aristotle as for common sense, if two entities touch, they are directly contiguous: the one is not literally in the other's place, but the two have nothing between their places. If God is non-spatial, He cannot be spatially next to or literally touch anything. But suppose that we instead define spatial contiguity along these lines:

SC. For all x and y, x and y are spatially contiguous just in case there is no space between x and the place of y.

(SC) or any relevantly similar definition will apply to all cases of spatial entities' being next to each other, yet it does not require that the relation of spatial contiguity have two spatial terms. If God is nonspatial, there is no space between Himself and any place. But just for this reason, given (SC) or any relevantly similar definition, God counts as spatially contiguous with every spatial thing—literally *with* it, though not in its place. Thus given (SC) or any relevantly similar definition, God's omnipresence can be considered the presence of an entity spatially next to all spatial things, and one can say that only a nonspatial entity can be so.

The import of (6) or (1) and (2) for God's temporal omnipresence is similar. Read as concerning time rather than space, (6) could require that a cause's action be simultaneous with its effect's occurrence or (read more loosely) that there be no temporal gap between the action of the cause and the inception of its effect. But once more, if God is not in time, there can be no time between God's action and His temporal effects' occurrence, and so it would seem that He qualifies as temporally contiguous with His effects, per (6). One can reach a like result via (1) and (2). One can support the claim that this was what Anselm

15. Anselm, *Monologion*, chap. 65, and *Proslogion*, chap. 15.

meant to say. For in summarizing his results, Anselm says that "if the common mode of speech permitted it, it would appear more appropriate to say that [God] is *with* a place or a time than to say that [He] is *in* a place or a time."[16] This summary seems to fit the line of argument I have sketched. If this is Anselm's line of argument, it is one worth pondering. For if it works, it provides a strong and literal sense for God's temporal omnipresence while yet preserving His timelessness: God is *with* times, not *in* times, and so remains timeless.

Whichever strategy Anselm would have endorsed, it seems that he can in fact develop a reasonably cogent defense of his claim that God as cause is somehow present with His effects, if he can defend his doctrine of divine simplicity. He can even defend his claim without this doctrine *or* a general denial of action at a distance. For action at a spatiotemporal distance is impossible for an agent beyond space or time. If the reasoning of the last paragraphs is sound, it follows that the very denial that God is in time or space entails that if He is a cause, He is a cause somehow immediately present to all of His spatiotemporal effects. Moreover, we can bypass Anselm's entire argument by way of God's causality if reasoning such as that involving (SC) is cogent. For if it is, the mere facts that space and time exist and God exists outside them entail that God is spatially and temporally omnipresent. So far, then, Anselm's account of temporal omnipresence seems to stand on fairly firm ground.

Why Temporal Omnipresence?

As we have seen, Anselm holds that God is temporally omnipresent. In Anselm's eyes, God is present with or at all times because God must exercise a *constant* sustaining causality for temporal things and times themselves to exist. For Anselm, that is, God does not just create time and temporal things and then send them on their way, but rather actively holds them in existence for so long as they exist. Anselm asserts this without argument.[17] But there is in fact a good argument to be made that if God creates time and the temporal, God must sustain time and the temporal.

Suppose that we adopt a tenseless view of time and say that what really exist are things extended in four dimensions, composed of spatiotemporal parts. If what we think of as continuants and continuing

---

16. "si usus loquendi admitteret, convenientius dici videretur esse cum loco vel tempore quam in loco vel tempore." Anselm, *Monologion*, chap. 22, in Schmitt, *Opera*, vol. I, p. 41, ll. 1–2.

17. Anselm, *Monologion*, chap. 13, in Schmitt, *Opera*, vol. I, p. 27, ll. 5–7.

time are really objects composed of spatiotemporal parts, then it can be true that God has created the whole of each thing (as all theists want to maintain) only if He has created the whole extension of each thing in the temporal dimension. For God has created the whole of a thing only if He has created all of its parts. To create all of a thing's (or time's) spatiotemporal parts is just to do what appears within a tensed view of time as creating and constantly sustaining the whole of time or the temporal.

Suppose, on the other hand, that we adopt a tenseless theory of time but deny that temporal objects have temporal parts. As we have seen, we could do this by holding that while temporal objects are extended in time as well as space, they are wholly present at each point within their temporal extensions. Still, on such a theory, time and temporal things do have temporal extensions. Thus to have created all of time and all of temporal things, God must have created all of their temporal extent, as above. So again, if God creates the whole of time and of each temporal thing, He does what is equivalent within a tensed theory of time to His creating and constantly sustaining the whole of time and all temporal things. That is, on these two approaches to time and the temporal, God creates time and the temporal only if He also constantly sustains them.[18]

Suppose that we adopt a tensed view of time and say that what really exist are things and events that do not in any sense exist save when they are present. If time is thus transient, then each moment of time God creates exists only at that moment.[19] A moment is not the sort of thing that persists, so there is no question of God's first creating a moment

18. A third tenseless approach to time, mentioned earlier, would hold that only the lives of things and not things themselves are extended through time. The argument I develop to deal with God's relation to tensed time applies also to this view, with appropriate changes made.

19. One can consistently view time as an extended continuum made up of extensionless moments; contemporary measure theory permits this. See Adolph Grünbaum, "The Resolution of Zeno's Metrical Paradox of Extension for the Mathematical Continua of Space and Time," in his *Philosophical Problems of Space and Time,* 2d ed. (Dordrecht: Reidel, 1973), pp. 158–176.

This picture of God and time might seem to lead to occasionalism, since it may seem to say that what acts is not a temporal creature that, acting at t, has effects at t + 1, but rather God, who creates the creature as acting at t, then creates its effect at t + 1. But this is not where the picture leads. Any current analysis of causal relations will allow as terms of these relations being conserved as this picture demands. See Philip Quinn, "Divine Conservation, Secondary Causality, and Occasionalism," in Thomas Morris, ed., *Divine and Human Action* (Ithaca, N.Y.: Cornell University Press, 1989), pp. 50–73. For a rather different argument that if God creates time and temporal things, God must constantly sustain both, see Jonathan Kvanvig and Hugh McCann, "Divine Conservation and the Persistence of the World," in the same volume, pp. 13–49.

and then letting it go its merry way. Rather, time persists only if ever-new moments appear, succeeding old ones. Let us suppose that nothing exists save God and time and that God created all moments of time up to and including some time t, and then ask whether after t it could be the case that God is not creatively responsible for any moment's existence. It is clear that a moment cannot somehow cause the existence of some further moment: a moment is not the sort of thing that can be a cause. Now in some cases, the existence of a moment may *entail* the existence of other moments. For as we have seen, it may be absolutely impossible that just one moment of time exists. After all, it is plausible that time exists only if there are relations of earlier and later; what would make a single isolated moment a moment of *time*? If this is impossible, then if one moment exists, it follows that other moments have existed or will exist. But it does not follow that these moments are *future* moments.[20] The one moment in question could even be the last moment of time. Moreover, to say that one moment entails other moments does not entail that the first moment in any sense produces or accounts for the existence of the others. Intuitively, this does not seem possible. So if God creates all of time up to t, then if there are moments after t, only God can account for their existence: which is to say that either they exist wholly without explanation or God creates them.

A theist, at least, will find no reason to adopt the former option and so will hold that if God creates any moments of tensed time, God creates each new moment when it exists. In this case, God's creating each moment in its turn will constitute His creating the whole of time as it continues and so will constitute His constant sustaining of time. For convenience I have spoken of moments, but the argument would work as well without mentioning them. The point is that if time is a transient continuum and is God's creation, God must be constantly creating the new extension of that continuum if in fact that continuum continues to continue.[21] But of course, temporal things exist only if time does. So in virtue of His constant creation of ever-new time, it follows that God is constantly sustaining temporal things, if only by constantly providing a necessary condition of their persistence.[22]

The argument just completed in effect treated time as an absolute, independent thing. Suppose, however, that moments are not indepen-

---

20. This would follow only if the moment in question were necessarily the first moment of time. I cannot see reason to say this of any moment.

21. For simplicity's sake, I have spoken as though God were temporal. Just how to qualify this statement so as to preserve the point and yet remain strictly within the constraints of the claim that God is timeless becomes clear in subsequent chapters.

22. I do not rule out His also sustaining them in some meatier sense.

dent things but instead are sets or functions of the events that do or can occur at them. In this case God can create and sustain time as it continues only by creating and sustaining the objects and events that exist and occur at times, and nondivine entities could account for the existence of subsequent moments if they could account for their own existence at those subsequent moments. Now it is clear that an object's existing or an event's occurring at t does not entail its existence or occurrence at t + 1. This is so even though there are "soft" events or processes, i.e., events or processes that can occur at t only if they continue to occur at some later time.[23] One such process is a game of poker: anything that can count as a game of poker must last for some time after its first moment. But even though if anything is a game of poker, it lasts for some time after its first moment, it is not necessary that any event or process that begins at t must wind up counting as a game of poker. A process could begin at t that would count as a game of poker were it to continue long enough, but be cut off before enough time passes.

Hence the occurrence of a moment as we are now understanding moments does not entail the occurrence of future moments. Nor does the existence or activity at t of any agent other than a Creator causally necessitate the existence of some entity (and so some moment) later than t. Nondivine causes do not account for the existence of things. They instead merely cause alterations of things. Scientific laws governing created causality deal only with things' changes of state. These laws assume and do not account for the existence of the things whose changes they describe.[24] So again, on this understanding of moments, if God creates any moments, God must create each new moment as it occurs, by constantly creating/sustaining the entities of whose changes moments are sets (or functions, or whatever). Nothing else can account for the appearance of new moments. Thus again, if God creates time and the temporal, God must also sustain them.

Omnipresence and Omniabsence

Because of God's creative responsibility for all times, *Monologion* 20 concludes that

OP. God is present in all times.

23. The term "soft" derives from contemporary discussions of "hard" and "soft" facts. For explication of the hard fact/soft fact distinction, see, e.g., Alfred Freddoso, "Accidental Necessity and Logical Determinism," *Journal of Philosophy* 80 (1983), 257–278, or Joshua Hoffman and Gary Rosenkrantz, "Hard and Soft Facts," *Philosophical Review* 93 (1984), 419–434.
24. See Kvanvig and McCann, "Conservation," pp. 31–33.

I have taken some steps toward defending (OP) by arguing that Anselm can build a case for his claim that a cause (or a simple cause) is somehow present with its effect and his claim that God sustains the whole of time. Yet *Monologion* 21 takes as premises (OP) and the claim (argued in in chap. 17) that God has no parts, and works its way to the conclusion that

NP. God is present in no time.

The argument for (NP) runs this way:

9. God is present in all times.
10. Necessarily, whatever is present in all times is so because part of it is in all times and part beyond all times, or because parts of it are in the various times and no parts of it are beyond all times, or because it is wholly present in all times.
11. Necessarily, God is not part in, part beyond time.
12. Necessarily, God does not occupy time by His parts' occupying parts of time.
13. So necessarily, God is wholly present in all times (from 10–12).
14. Necessarily, if God is present in all times, He is so either at once or successively.
15. Necessarily, God is not present in all times at once.
16. Necessarily, God is not present in all times successively.
17. So necessarily, it is not the case that God is present in all times (from 14–16).
18. Necessarily, God is present in all times, some times, or no times.
19. God is not present in only some times (from [N]).
20. So God is present in no time (from 17–19).

The argument is plainly valid; we must ask, then, what reasons we have to consider its premises true. (9) is the hypothesis for reductio. (10) is intended to be true in virtue of exhausting all the possible alternatives. Now one can imagine further alternatives that might have been included in (10), e.g., that God be part in and part outside of time and that the part of Him which is in time occupy times part by part. But if (10)'s first two contained disjuncts are false, further disjuncts specifying these further alternatives would also be false. So although (10) does not, strictly speaking, exhaust all the alternatives, we could replace it with a premise that did and that would serve Anselm as well.

If God cannot have parts, or temporal parts, (11) and (12) are true, for only if He has parts can He be partly within time and partly without, and only if He has temporal parts can He occupy time by having one temporal part of Himself in one location, another part in another. We saw above that in fact, something is simple only if it necessarily simple; thus Anselm's God not only does not but cannot have parts. Moreover, we have seen that whatever is timeless is necessarily so. So if a timeless God can have neither temporal nor spatial parts, and if these are the only sorts of part one recognizes, one can hold that divine timelessness itself suffices to yield (11) and (12). (14) is true in virtue of exhausting all the possible alternatives, as is (18). We have seen that (N) and (19) are defensible. So if Anselm has good arguments for (15) and (16), he has good reason to consider this argument sound.

Anselm has two arguments for (16). The first is that ∼(16) is incompatible with the claim that God has no parts. As Anselm sees it, were God present at all times successively, God's lifetime would have temporal parts. But God, Anselm thinks, is identical with His lifetime, and hence it would follow that God Himself has parts. Hence ∼(16) is true only if possibly God is not simple. But Anselm has already argued that God is simple, and we have seen that whatever is simple is necessarily so.[25] Now Anselm is correct that the life of whatever is present successively at different times has temporal parts. For at the very least, each such life is partly past and partly still to come (save at its first and last moments, at which it is partly past *or* partly still to come). But one has to wonder how he can support the bizarre premise that God = God's lifetime.

The only justification the *Monologion* offers appears in *Monologion* 16. Anselm there argues that God = justice, intending this to illustrate a general truth, that for every attribute F, if God is F, then God = Fness.[26] Anselm infers from this specifically that as God is eternal, God = eternity.[27] But Anselm really means by this that God = *eternality,* the attribute of having an eternal duration. In the argument for (16), Anselm claims that God = eternity as a duration of a lifetime. The claim that God = eternality does not at all support the claim that God = God's eternal duration. As there seems no good reason to hold so strange a thesis, and as Anselm gives us none, we can simply reject it, and with it Anselm's first argument for (16).[28]

25. Anselm, *Monologion,* chap. 21, in Schmitt, *Opera,* vol. 1, p. 37, l. 16–p. 38, l. 7.
26. Ibid., chap. 16, p. 30, ll. 7–9, 12–16.
27. Ibid., l. 7.
28. Dennis Holt objects also to Anselm's claim that if God exists at different times, then God has a lifetime, which is extended and composite (Holt, "Timelessness," pp.

Anselm's second argument is that if part of God's duration were past, part future, then God would undergo change, which is not compatible with the claim, argued in chap. 16, that God is identical with each of His real attributes.[29] Anselm is correct that such identity is incompatible with undergoing real change. For nothing can be identical with an attribute with respect to which it can change. If a thing A can change with respect to an attribute F, it possibly does not have that attribute: "Fa" is contingent. But if a thing is identical with an attribute, then it has (or is) that attribute in every possible world in which it exists: "Fa" is necessary. As no proposition can be both necessary and contingent, identity with an attribute one can fail to have is impossible.

Anselm is correct that if God = each of his real attributes, God cannot change. But it is arguable that simply persisting through time, so that successive parts of one's life are first future, then present, then past, is not a real change. Mere persistence is a paradigm case of what we ordinarily mean by an object's *not* changing.[30] Still, one can perhaps reason this way: if God persists through time, then God's awareness of what happens at moment t is first precognitive, then (perhaps) some sort of direct awareness, then memory. Whether or not persistence is a real change, the difference between an act of precognition, an act of direct awareness, and an act of memory is a real difference. If so, changing from one to the others is a real change. Thus if God exists in time and is conscious of temporal events as they flow by, God undergoes real change. So Anselm can perhaps warrant (16). But he does not argue at all for (15).[31] In fact, he eventually rejects it, in the interest of retaining (OP).

So far, then, the argument for (OP) has made a case that if God is creator of all times, He is ipso facto present in all times, and the argument for (NP) has made a case that if God is simple, He cannot be in any way present in any time. It thus appears, at the end of *Mono-*

151–152). Holt observes that we need not be committed to any such entity as a lifetime, since we can always paraphrase such statements as that "God's lifetime is infinitely long" by saying, e.g., that God lives forever. Although this is true, I do not see that it creates a problem for Anselm. Even if there is no such entity as a lifetime, still if God is a temporal being, He lives only one moment at a time, as the rest of us do—a condition that is inferior to enjoying all of His life at once, as Anselm suggests that He does. Holt also notes, as I did in chapter 2, that strictly speaking we should not talk of things being located at times, because what is located at time t is not John but (say) John's existence (ibid., passim). Again, I cannot see that this creates much difficulty for Anselm. It does not seem to require more than a small rephrasing of his arguments.

29. Anselm, *Monologion*, chap. 21, in Schmitt, *Opera*, vol. 1, p. 37, l. 16–p. 38, l. 7.

30. See Lawrence Lombard, *Events* (London: Routledge and Kegan Paul, 1986), pp. 84–85.

31. Anselm, *Monologion*, chap. 21, in Schmitt, *Opera*, vol. 1, p. 37, ll. 17–19.

logion 21, that nothing can be both creator of all spatiotemporal things and simple. Perhaps this is why Plotinus segregated the two attributes, holding the One to be wholly simple but the Creator only of Nous, and Nous nonsimple and the creator of all save itself and the One. As a monotheist, Anselm does not have this option. He seeks rather to explain how both (OP) and (NP) can appear true of one and the same being and just how both are or are not in fact true.

Anselm's attitude to (OP) and (NP) does not appear symmetric. Anselm does not seem to want to qualify the two to precisely the same degree. He resolves the apparent contradiction of (OP) and (NP) by maintaining that God "can be said to be in every time in His own way, because whatever is other than He is sustained by His presence. He is in every time because He is absent from none, and He is in no time because He has no time, nor receives into Himself such distinctions of time as now or then or sometime. Still, these can in a way be said of God, as He is present to all limited and changeable things as if He were changed during the same times as they. So it is clear how God always exists and exists at no time."[32] This summation retains (OP); God truly does exist in every time, just as if He were so completely in it as to be changeable, as truly temporal things are.[33] (NP) seems reduced to a mere qualification, specifying the *way* (OP) is true. So it appears that to render the two conclusions compatible, Anselm qualifies (OP) but strictly speaking *denies* (NP), retaining only an allied but distinct thesis, that God is not in any time in the way *other* particular things are, in such a way as to "receive . . . distinctions of time" (of which more anon).

Though Anselm denies (NP), the opening of *Monologion* 22 suggests that he believes that the arguments for both (NP) and (OP) are valid. For he asks there "how then will these two theses [(OP) and (NP)], so necessary by their proof, be reconciled?"[34] One deals with a valid argument for a conclusion one rejects by denying a premise of the argument. The next sentence of chapter 22 clues us in to what Anselm will deny: "Perhaps God is in time in some way which allows Him to exist at once as a whole in distinct times, and yet His life is not divided

32. "in omni . . . tempore suo quodam modo dici potest esse, quoniam quidquid aliud est ne in nihilum cadat ab ea praesente sustinetur. In omni . . . tempore est, quia nulli abest, et in nullo est, quia nullum . . . tempus habet. Nec in se recipit distinctiones . . . temporum, ut . . . nunc vel tunc vel aliquando . . . et tamen haec de ea quodammodo dici possunt, quoniam sic est praesens omnibus circumscriptis and mutabilibus, ac si illa eisdem . . . mutetur temporibus. Patet itaque . . . qualiter summa omnium essentia . . . semper et nusquam . . . sit." Ibid., chap. 22, p. 41, ll. 4–17.

33. See also *Proslogion*, chap. 13.

34. "Quomodo ergo convenient haec . . . tam necessaria secundum probationem?" Anselm, *Monologion*, in Schmitt, *Opera*, vol. 1, chap. 22, p. 39, ll. 3–4.

into a past, a present, and a future."[35] Anselm wants to deny (15), for which (as we saw) he offered no argument. He argues that (15) is false and possibly God is present as a whole in all times at once, and that He is possibly so because though He is present in time, God is not temporal.[36]

God's Presence in Time

As he begins to explore God's presence in time, Anselm states that God "goes beyond" the times He is in, then adds that (15) is false in the case of things that "go beyond" or transcend time.[37] So apparently, God's transcending time explains His ability to be wholly present at different times at once. Let us ask, then, what it is to transcend time. Anselm asserts that "something has a place only if the place contains its quantity by circumscribing it and circumscribes it by containing it. Something has a time only if the time somehow terminates that thing's duration by measuring it and measures it by terminating it. So if no limit of place limits a thing's size, no place is truly said to be its place, and if no limit of time limits a thing's duration, no time is truly said to be its time."[38] Anselm's treatment of place explains his treatment of time. Anselm claims that a thing has a place only if the boundaries of the place are its spatial boundaries—if it is "enclosed" or "bounded" by that place's limits.[39] If a thing is in a place but not bounded by that place's boundaries, in a straightforward sense it goes beyond that place. In the same way, then, something goes beyond or transcends a time if it exists during that time but that time's limits are not boundaries of its duration. Anselm expresses God's relation to a time He transcends by saying that God is present at or with that time, but not contained in it.[40] The phraseology may be rooted in Augustine,[41] but it is also quite

35. "Fortasse quodam modo est summa natura in . . . tempore, quo non prohibetur sic esse simul tota in singulis . . . temporibus, ut tamen . . . eius aetas . . . non sit distributum in praeteritum, praesens et futurum." Ibid., chap. 22, p. 39, ll. 4–8.
36. Anselm, *Monologion*, chap. 22.
37. Ibid., p. 39, ll. 8–13. Cf. I. 10, "temporis diuturnitatem . . . excedant."
38. "tantum eius rei sit aliquis locus, cuius quantitatem locus circumscribendo continet et continendo circumscribit; et . . . eius solum rei sit aliquod tempus, cuius diuturnitatem tempus metiendo aliquomodo terminat et terminando metitur. Quapropter cuius amplitudini aut diuturnitati nulla meta vel a loco vel a tempore opponitur, illi nullum esse locum vel tempus vere proponitur." Ibid., p. 39, ll. 14–19.
39. "eorum metis clauditur." Ibid., p. 40, l. 7.
40. Ibid., p. 41, ll. 1–2.
41. "The temple of God . . . is called the place of God, not because he is contained in it, but because he is present there." Augustine, *Eighty-three Different Questions*, tr. David Mosher (Washington, D.C.: Catholic University of America Press, 1977), q. 20, pp. 47–48. The terminology also harks back to Aristotle's *Physics* IV account of place.

natural. What is contained in a time is presumably not elsewhere. For if
it were, that time would not (wholly) contain it; it would go beyond or
transcend that time.

Now if at t God were to exist only in t, all of God that then existed
would exist in t; t would contain God, and God would not transcend t.
So if God is to be literally in t and yet transcend t, God must be in t and
simultaneously exist at other times. If God is to be in t and yet transcend all times, God must be at t and yet simultaneously at all other
times and simultaneously beyond time. Only if this is so is it the case
that no time constitutes a limit of God's duration, a point beyond
which that duration does not extend, and yet all times are locations of
God's duration. So in fact, if God transcends time, then God somehow
exists at and beyond all times at once. But as yet we have no clue as to
why God might be said to transcend time. Only when we have found
the feature that explains God's transcendence of time will we know
why God is able to be simultaneously at and beyond all times.

Before we explore this, though, let us clarify Anselm's claim that
God is timeless but also has limitless temporal duration. In *Proslogion*
20, Anselm lists a variety of senses in which God's duration extends
"beyond" even omnitemporal beings' duration. So Anselm claims that
there is a distinction between even omnitemporality and genuinely
unlimited temporal duration and asserts that the only genuinely unlimited temporal duration is that of a being that is intrinsically timeless.
Let us see what Anselm considers the difference between omnitemporality and genuinely unlimited temporal duration to be. As we have
seen, for Anselm, something "has a time only if the time somehow
terminates that thing's duration by measuring it."[42] What terminates a
thing's duration is an endpoint. Anselm adds that "if God had a beginning or an end, He would not be true eternity."[43] So for Anselm, it
seems, if a thing has a beginning or an end, it is temporal, and if it has
neither, it is eternal. We can confirm this by noting that Anselm held
that God is the creator of time, and as an orthodox medieval Christian
he also held that God created time with a first moment. This commits
him to the claim that every temporal thing has a beginning. If so, every
temporal thing has a beginning or an end, and so Anselm indeed holds
that being temporal is equivalent to having a beginning or an end.

Thus for Anselm, the existence of an omnitemporally existing being
would have at least one endpoint. By contrast, if God is timeless, God's

42. Anselm, *Monologion*, chap. 22, in Schmitt, *Opera*, vol. 1, p. 39, ll. 15–17; Latin
given in n. 38.
43. "Si summa illa natura principium vel finem habet, non est vera aeternitas." Ibid.,
chap. 18, p. 33, ll. 9–10.

existence never ends and did not begin with the first moment of time—
at least in the sense that had time not begun, God would still have
existed. Perhaps we could put this as follows. A God who would have
existed had time not begun has a first moment of temporal existence
and has no phase of His existence before that moment (since there is no
"before" the first moment of time). But the first moment of His existence is not a *limit* on His existence, since He would have existed had it
not occurred, and so in this sense it is not strictly speaking a beginning
of His existence. In a similar way, a last moment of time would not
limit His existence either. An omnitemporal duration, by contrast,
must have begun with the first moment of time, in that it could not
have existed had that first moment not occurred. An existence could
also be omnitemporal if time had a last moment, provided that it lasted
through all moments of time including the last. But the last moment of
time would be a true limit of this being's existence. So for Anselm, the
only being that is in any sense located in time and has a duration not
limited in either direction is timeless.

Is this an adequate account of a distinction between omnitemporality
and the limitless temporal duration of an eternal being? Aquinas, for
one, could not accept it. Aquinas explicitly insists that time could be
without a first or last moment.[44] Suppose that it is. Then if some being
exists at all moments of time, that being is fully temporal and yet has
neither beginning nor end. Thus on Anselm's account, this being has
an eternal mode of being and so is at once eternal and temporal. But
this is impossible and also fails to distinguish omnitemporal existence
from eternal existence in time.[45] Hence if time can be without endpoints and an omnitemporal being can exist, Anselm's account of this
distinction is inadequate.

Aquinas himself *modalizes* his account of temporality and eternality.
At *ST* Ia 10, 4, Aquinas notes that even if it actually has no beginning
or end, a temporal duration *possibly* begins and ends at any number of
points; a period of time has parts, into which one can divide it at least
conceptually. Eternal duration, Aquinas states, *cannot* begin or end or
contain beginnings and endings; it cannot be divided into parts. So on
Aquinas's account, the distinction between eternality and unlimited
temporal duration is at root modal. Boethius may have intended this.

44. *ST* Ia 46, 1.
45. Being located both in eternity and in time is *not* the same thing as being at once
temporal and eternal, as will emerge. If the two attributes are not identical, whether
being located in time entails being temporal is at least an open question. So perhaps
Anselm can allow that possibly an eternal being is located in time while yet not allowing
that possibly one being has both the eternal and the temporal mode of being.

At any rate, his claim that eternal duration is *illimitable* may ascribe to it the modal property Aquinas ascribes. For one can understand by "limiting" a duration beginning it or ending it or inserting any boundaries between its parts, as boundaries between temporal parts are beginnings and endings of those parts. Hence on this reading, a duration is illimitable iff it cannot begin or end or contain beginnings or endings.

Anselm's sufficient condition for eternality and account of the distinction between omnitemporality and limitless duration are adequate only if time's duration is necessarily bounded in one direction. As this is a doubtful proposition, we must ask how Anselm might rectify matters. He could, of course, just endorse Aquinas' account. But the *Proslogion* hints a different modalization. Anselm there asks God, "How are you beyond those things which will not have an end? Is it because . . . these can be thought to have an end, and you cannot at all be thought truly to have an end?"[46] Even a necessarily omnitemporal being would be able to have a beginning or an end if time can and so would possibly have a beginning or end of existence. So if time can have an endpoint, then one can contrast eternal and omnitemporal beings by saying that only an eternal being necessarily has no beginning or end of existence. Even if an eternal being is somehow present in time, then, it remains intrinsically eternal, because it retains this modal property. It also retains the modal property of being able to exist even if time does not exist, a property that again no truly temporal being can have.

Anselm, then, offers an account of eternity according to which eternity, though not a temporal mode of existence, is not incompatible with location in time—unless location in time entails possibly having a beginning or an ending.[47] This may explain one further difference between Anselm's and Aquinas' accounts of eternity. Aquinas denies that there can be a beginning or an end *of* God's duration and also denies that there can be beginnings and ends *in* that duration.[48] For Anselm, that God's duration is limitless means that there cannot be a beginning or an ending *of* that duration. If we confine ourselves to what he explicitly says, Anselm does not rule out beginnings or endings *within* that duration. Anselm's not making this further denial *could* be a

<hr/>

46. "Qualiter enim es ultra ea quae finem non habebunt? An quia . . . illa cogitari possunt habere finem, tu vero nequaquam?" Anselm, *Proslogion*, chap. 20, in Schmitt, *Opera*, vol. 1, p. 115, ll. 20–21, 23–24.

47. One need not say this to maintain that being temporal entails possibly having a beginning or an ending. For one can consistently maintain that all temporal beings can have beginnings or ends of existence and that all temporal beings are located in time but not *only* temporal beings are so.

48. *ST* Ia 10, 4.

way to maintain that God is literally present in some way in time. (Clearly, a concept of eternity that allows an eternal being to be located in time would be useful to a Christian theologian concerned to maintain both that God is eternal and that God was incarnate in Christ.) It lets us say, for instance, that though the boundaries of the minute between 12:00 and 12:01 of September 26, 1988, do not *contain* God's duration, that duration is literally there within those boundaries. For a duration is within those boundaries only if one can (so to speak) mark those boundaries on that duration, and if God's duration can contain beginnings and endings, marking these boundaries on it is not conceptually excluded.

Thus it could be that Anselm's God is able to be both eternal and present in time. If He is present in time, though, Anselm will insist that he is not temporally present there. God is present in time in that He literally exists within its boundaries; God exists from 12:00 to 12:01. But God's presence there is not temporal because that of His life which exists then is not succeeded by that of His life which exists later. Rather, He enjoys His whole duration all at once and so is wholly present at all points in His duration at once. As we have seen, this entails that time does not exist unless Anselm also makes some further move, but we will shortly see that Anselm does do this. Finally, to recur to the point with which this section began: if this view of time and eternity is possibly true, Anselm can deny (15) of the argument for (NP) and maintain (OP).

Simplicity and Temporal Omnipresence

We have now seen what Anselm means by calling God's duration time-transcendent and in just what way Anselm thinks an eternal God to be in time. Whatever feature explains God's transcending time explains His ability to be wholly present at different times at once. We now must ask what feature does explain this.

In arguing that God's duration has no limits, Anselm asks rhetorically, "which . . . rational reflection does not preclude . . . that any spatial or temporal restraint encloses the creative and supreme substance, which necessarily differs from and is free of the nature and the law of all things which it created from nothing."[49] On the face of it, this argument is not very strong. Why should a creator not exist under the

49. "Quaenam . . . rationalis consideratio . . . non excludat, ut creatricem summamque omnium substantiam, quam necesse est alienam esse et liberam a natura et iure omnium quae ipsa de nihilo fecit, ulla loci cohibitio vel temporis includat?" Anselm, *Monologion,* chap. 22, in Schmitt, *Opera,* vol. 1, p. 39, ll. 26–29.

conditions of Its creation once the latter has been created? One wants to
know more than this. To learn more, we must detour through Anselm's doctrine of divine simplicity. This, I suggest, provides a model
of how something can be wholly present at once in many distinct
points in time and space and a reason to believe that God's nature is
relevantly like the nature of the model; it also explains God's being
time-transcendent. In *Monologion* 16, Anselm presents this argument:

21. Whatever is just is just through justice.
22. So God is just through justice.
23. God is just through Himself.
24. So God = justice.

Anselm draws the moral that "as God is not properly said to have
justice but to exist as justice, when God is called just, it is proper to
understand 'existing as justice,' not 'having justice' . . . when 'existing
as justice' is said, one says what He is . . . it is the same thing to say of
God that He is just, and that He is existing as justice."[50]

If God "exists as justice," God = justice. Having argued that such
identity statements as "God = justice" are true, Anselm goes on to
privilege such statements over against such predications as "God is
just." Anselm seems to think that when we say "God is just," "God is
justice" would *better* represent what we are trying to say. The identity
statement is more proper than the predication, Anselm thinks, because
having an attribute predicated of one entails participating in it, or
"having" an attribute from beyond oneself, whereas God is absolutely
a se.

Anselm could easily endorse these counterintuitive identity statements without privileging them or claiming that they are somehow
more perspicuous metaphysically than predications. Again, he could
easily have said that if God = justice, this means that justice exists as
God, not vice versa. Or he could have taken the view Aquinas was later
to take. Though endorsing such claims as that God = justice for much
the reasons Anselm did, Aquinas states, "All names we impose to
signify something complete and subsisting signify as concrete terms,
as is appropriate to composite things. Names imposed to signify simple forms signify something as that by which something exists . . .

50. "Quoniam summa natura non proprie dicitur quia habet iustitiam, sed existit
iustitia: cum dicitur iusta, proprie intelligitur existens iustitia, non autem habens
iustitiam . . . cum dicitur existens iustitia . . . dicitur . . . quid est . . . de illa suprema
essentia idem est dicere: quia est iusta, et: quia est existens iustitia." Ibid., chap. 16, p.
30, ll. 22–28.

Because . . . God is both simple and subsistent, we ascribe abstract names to him to signify His simplicity and concrete names to signify His subsistence. Still, both sorts of name fall short of his mode of being, just as in this life, our intellect does not know Him as He is."[51] Aquinas refuses to privilege either statements using abstract nouns (like the identity statement "God is justice") or statements using concrete nouns (like the predication "God is just"). For him, each sort has a valid use, and each can mislead; neither gives special insight into the way God is.

Anselm's stated reason to make the counterintuitive move of taking abstract terms like "justice" better to reveal the divine nature than concrete terms like "just" is that this more accurately reflects the complete independence of God.[52] But he may also make this move to ground the ascription to God of certain abstract-entity features: or at least this does in fact ground this ascription. For to identify God with an abstract entity, justice, and assert that the identity renders God more like justice than like a just thing entails that God has some significant abstract-entity features.

A universal, nature, or abstract what-have-you is precisely the sort of thing that can be wholly present at once at many discrete spatial locations.[53] The universal attribute of *being water* is wholly present in every molecule of water at once. This is so just because each molecule is fully a molecule of water; none requires other molecules' presence in order to be itself a molecule of water. The universal *being water* is also present as a whole, not a part, in each of its temporal locations; every water molecule now in Lake Superior is wholly water now, and any of these molecules that still exist and are in Lake Superior tomorrow will be wholly water then. *Monologion* 22 ascribes four features to entities that transcend space and time: they do not have spatial dimensions or temporal limits, they do not have spatial or temporal parts, they do not

---

51. "Omnia nomina a nobis imposita ad significandum aliquid completum subsistens significant in concretione, prout competit compositis. Quae autem imponuntur ad significandas formas simplices significant aliquid . . . ut quo aliquid est . . . Quia . . . Deus simplex est et subsistens est, attribuimus ei nomina abstracta ad significandem simplicitatem eius et nomina concreta ad significandem subsistentiam . . . ipsius; quamvis utraque nomina deficiant a modo ipsius, sicut intellectus noster non cognoscit eum ut est secundum hanc vitam." Aquinas, *ST* Ia 13, 1 *ad* 2. In Blackfriars' *Summa*, vol. 3, p. 50.

52. Anselm, *Monologion*, chap. 16.

53. There are important differences among universals, common natures, and other abstract entities. I speak this way not to gloss over them, but because the differences are not in respects that matter for my argument and because it is quite hard to nail down what precise theory of universals (or whatever) Anselm held. See Jasper Hopkins, *Anselm of Canterbury*, vol. 4 (Toronto: Edwin Mellen Press, 1976), pp. 57–96.

undergo spatial or temporal growth or diminution, and they are able to be wholly present at many distinct spatial or temporal loci at once.[54] Universals or natures have all four features.

A universal such as justice or whiteness is not the kind of thing that can have spatial dimensions. White patches may be three inches wide and just persons may be six feet tall, but the claims that whiteness is three inches wide and justice six feet tall sound nonsensical.[55] Nor can a nature such as justice or whiteness have temporal limits. Just institutions and persons may cease to exist, but justice cannot. In fact, if justice is an independently existing abstract entity, it is plausible that justice would exist even if time and temporal things did not. Whiteness and justice do not undergo spatial or temporal growth or diminution. Justice does not grow old, though just people do. Whiteness does not shrink, though white patches shrink; perhaps this is because spatial growth and diminution involve change of spatial dimensions, so that only things with spatial dimensions can grow or shrink. Whiteness and justice do not have spatial parts, though white and just things do. Nor have they temporal parts. As we have seen, perhaps not even white *things* have temporal parts. But suppose that white and just things are composed of (inter alia) temporal parts. Even so, there is no more reason to say that whiteness or justice have temporal parts than to say that they have spatial parts. The logic of the situation is the same: what has the part is the extended surface or concrete subject that the attribute qualifies, not the attribute itself.

Further, the histories or careers in time of abstract entities are not composed of (inter alia) temporal parts. As we saw in chapter 7, this is so if an entity has a history but is wholly present at every temporal location that history encompasses. Abstract entities are wholly present wherever they are present in space or time. Perhaps the histories of concrete objects also lack temporal parts, for perhaps they, too, are wholly present at every time at which they exist. But even if this is so, there is still a difference between the histories of abstract and of concrete objects. If a concrete object is wholly present at t and wholly present at t + 1, the object's presence at t is earlier in its career than its presence at t + 1: stages of its history are nonsimultaneous. If an abstract object is wholly present at t and at t + 1, its presence at t is *not* earlier in its career than its presence at t + 1.

54. Anselm, *Monologion*, chap. 22, in Schmitt, *Opera*, vol. 1, p. 39, ll. 17–19; p. 40, ll. 2–13.
55. If this is not so, then whiteness and justice are not universals or other sorts of abstract objects but scattered concrete particulars, as is contemplated in various writings of Goodman and Quine.

If an abstract entity—say, justice—were present at t + 1 *later* than it was present at t, its history would have reached a later stage at t + 1 than it had reached at t. Just for this reason, justice would be older at t + 1 than it was at t. But it is intuitively odd to say that justice ages. The argument of chapter 3 supported this intuition. For chapter 3 argued that the truthmakers of absolutely necessary truths are intrinsically timeless. Justice is a truthmaker of at least one such truth, for it is absolutely necessary that justice is a virtue in social institutions. Accordingly, if justice is present at t and at t + 1, its presence at t + 1 is not later in its career than its presence at t, for otherwise it would not be a timeless entity. This is not as strange as it looks. Standard extensional mereologies routinely countenance the existence of spatially scattered objects, e.g., the object consisting of all the noses in the world.[56] Spatially scattered objects occupy scattered places. Their places are single places in just the same way the objects are single objects. To say that an abstract entity's presence at t + 1 is not later in its career than its presence at t amounts to saying that the career of an abstract entity is a *temporally* scattered object, and that just as the scattered places of the Great Sum-Nose constitute one place, the scattered times at which justice occurs constitute a single time.

I have argued that stages of an abstract entity's career do not stand in the later-than relation. This suggests further that if an abstract entity is present at t and at t + 1, its presence at t + 1 is at the same "stage" of its career as its presence at t—that all "phases" of its career are simultaneous. The alternative to this is to claim that all "phases" of an abstract entity's career are either discrete or incommensurable. The stages are discrete if they definitely have no temporal relations at all. They are incommensurable if there is no definite answer to the question of whether they have temporal relations. But if these stages were discrete or incommensurable, the entity would not *have* a career or a history, for the members of a set of temporal events and states composes a career only if they are temporally connected. It seems plausible that an abstract entity can have a career of a sort in time. If so, then, we must say that all "stages" of this career occur at once.

So if we can speak at all of abstract entities as having temporal presences and careers, we ought to say that all phases of their existence are simultaneous. Thus even if a white wall existed yesterday, then was destroyed, and today a white building was put up in the same place, the existence of whiteness in the wall is in a sense simultaneous with the

56. For details, see Peter Simons, *Parts* (New York: Oxford University Press, 1987), part 1, passim.

existence of whiteness in the building. [57] *An abstract entity is just the kind of
thing that can be wholly present in many temporal locations "at once."*

An abstract entity such as whiteness or justice, then, has qua abstract
a mode of being that transcends space and time. Even if it is wholly
present in a place or time (by being instanced), that place or time does
not contain it, strictly speaking, because the dimensions of that place or
time are not its dimensions. "No place is truly said to be its place,"[58]
even though some places are places where it is, and similarly no time is
its time. Anselm mentions all these features in application to God. But
we can see that they constitute respects of likeness between a common
nature's presence in space and time and God's: both are wholly present
at once at some nonsimultaneous times and nonidentical places. Anselm nowhere explicitly asserts this likeness. Nonetheless, it is as if he
is guided by it, once he has identified God with certain abstracta.

Given this identity and these likenesses, we can perhaps expand and
strengthen as follows Anselm's argument from God's creatorhood to
God's transcendence of space and time. Because God is the absolute
creator of all things other than Himself, He is utterly *a se;* any other
being from which He could derive anything at all exists only subsequent to His creative act. Being *a se,* God = justice, goodness, and
whatever other attributes He might have. For this reason, God is relevantly like an abstract entity and so is present to time and space as
abstract entities are, i.e., has certain features that we consider to be
abstract-entity features. Abstract entities are present in many discrete
temporal loci at once, without abolishing the nonsimultaneity of these
distinct times. So too, then, is God. God's abstract-entity features
explain His ability to be present in this way, roughly as scientific laws
explain particular phenomena. To subsume a phenomenon under a
scientific law in order to explain it is (in some cases) to say, "This event
had property P because it is an event of kind K, and events of kind K
typically are Ps." To explain the mode of God's presence through time
by His abstract-entity features is to say that He is this way because He is
abstract-entity-like, and all similarly abstract-entity-like beings are like
this. In the present instance, we can even explain why abstract-entity-
like beings are like this: they are not able to have spatial parts, and yet
they do in fact coexist in space with things that do, and their careers are
not able to have earlier or later points, and yet these careers intersect
with careers that do. Anselm marks the distinction between the way

57. This has the interesting result that the wall's presently being white is not the same
SOA as white's being present in the wall. For the latter is and the former is not
simultaneous with white's being present in the building.

58. Anselm, *Monologion,* chap. 22, in Schmitt, *Opera,* vol. 1, p. 39, ll. 18–19. For the
Latin, see n. 38.

abstracta are in space and time and the way concreta are there by the contrast of being present in and being contained by a time or a place.

Anselm's *Monologion*, then, is an ambitious attempt to have it all—to show that God is timeless and yet in some sense literally *in* time, and so present with His creatures in this strongest sense. Whether one accepts this reconciliation of divine immanence and divine transcendence depends finally on whether one is willing to accept definitions of temporality and eternality as modal properties having to do with beginning and ending. Other accounts of these attributes might say, for instance, that whatever has a location in time is ipso facto a temporal being. On such accounts, an eternal God could also be present in time only if it is possible to be present at a time and yet not located at that time. But this sounds flatly contradictory.

If one finds alternate definitions of temporality and eternality persuasive, one must hold that Anselm's attempt to have it all fails. One must say that even if God is present *with* times, He is not temporally present in any greater degree, and say that in the end, Anselm forfeits (OP) as well as (NP). But note this. If neither (OP) nor (NP) is true, Anselm can use this fact to emphasize God's timelessness. For if neither (OP) nor (NP) is true, Anselm can argue that "God is timeless" is not merely a negation but a category-negation. He can claim that it says not merely that God is not in time, but that God is so far from being in time that He is not even the kind of thing that one can simply deny to be temporal.

Intrinsic Eternity

Anselm closes *Monologion*'s treatment of eternity by moving his attention from God's temporal omnipresence to His intrinsic nature. God, he writes, "has been established not to have a past, a future, or a temporal (i.e., fleeting) present such as we have, for His lifetime, or eternity . . . is immutable and partless. So if 'always' is said of God, does it not more truly signify eternity . . . than the variety of times? . . . Thus if God is said always to exist . . . nothing better is understood than to exist or live eternally, i.e., to have at once and perfectly the whole of an illimitable life."[59] God may be temporally omnipresent, but for Anselm, His intrinsic nature accords with

59. "Eandem quoque summam substantiam constat . . . nec habere praeteritum aut futurum nec temporale, hoc est labile praesens quo nos utimur; quoniam aetas sive aeternitas eius . . . immutabilis et sine partibus est. Nonne ergo "semper" . . . multo verius si de illa dicitur, intelligitur significare aeternitatem . . . quam temporum varietatem . . . Quare si dicitur semper esse . . . nihil melius intelligitur quam aeterne esse vel vivere, id est interminabilem vitam perfecte simul totam obtinere." Anselm, *Monologion*, chap. 24, in Schmitt, *Opera*, vol. 1, p. 42, ll. 10–20.

Boethius' conception of eternity. If God is immutable, His present cannot change or pass away. If God's life has no parts, He cannot live only part of it at once. So He lives all of it at once, in a present that is completely whole, i.e., embraces the whole extent of His life.

Eternity in the *Proslogion*

In the *Monologion*, Anselm had labored to preserve (OP) and with it the claim that God is somehow present in time. For instance, Anselm had allowed us to say that God "was or is or will be,"[60] insisting only that it is incorrect to think that this means that "something of His eternity vanishes from the temporal present with the past . . . or passes with the present, which scarcely exists, or is going to come with the future."[61] Yet in *Proslogion* 19 we read that

> since neither you nor your eternity (which you are) have parts . . . your eternity always exists as a whole. But if through your eternity you were and are and will be, and to have existed is not to be future, and to be present is not to have existed or to be future, how does your eternity always exist as a whole? Is nothing of your eternity past, so as not to exist now, or future, as if it did not yet exist? Then it is not the case that you existed yesterday or will exist tomorrow, but yesterday, today, and tomorrow, you exist. Or not even this, but rather, you simply exist, beyond every time.[62]

This is a flat denial that we can make with truth such tensed statements as that God "was or is or will be." It abandons (OP) in favor of a claim that God is in all ways beyond all time.

A second change from the *Monologion* is more a matter of emphasis than of doctrine. To say that God is temporally omnipresent makes it sound as if creation is a receptacle that contains and so transcends its creator. Anselm wants to avoid this implication. In the *Monologion* he writes that God is "in all things which exist, not as what is contained

---

60. "fuit aut est aut erit." Ibid., chap. 22, p. 40, l. 21.
61. "aeternitatis eius aliquid vanuit a praesenti tempore cum praeterito . . . aut transit cum praesenti quod vix est, aut venturum est cum futuro." Ibid., chap. 24, p. 42, ll. 21–23.
62. "Quoniam ergo nec tu habes partes nec tua aeternitas quae tu es . . . aeternitas tua tota est semper. Sed si per aeternitatem tuam fuisti et es et eris, et fuisse non est futurum esse, et esse non est fuisse vel futurum esse, quomodo aeternitas tua tota est semper? An de aeternitate tua nihil praeterit ut iam non sit, nec aliquid futurum est quasi nondum sit? Non ergo fuisti heri aut eris cras, sed heri et hodie et cras es. Immo nec heri nec hodie nec cras es, sed simpliciter es extra omne tempus." Anselm, *Proslogion*, chaps. 18–19, in Schmitt, *Opera*, vol. 1, p. 115, ll. 1–14.

but as what contains all by penetrating all."[63] In this Anselm follows Augustine, who wrote that "God is not anywhere. For what is some-where is contained in a place . . . since [God] is and yet is not in a place, all things are in him rather than he himself being anywhere."[64] Aquinas makes a similar Augustinian move when he writes that "spir-itual things contain that in which they exist, as the soul contains the body."[65] For Aquinas, the soul is a form that actualizes the body's matter. So we can infer from this statement that a form, an entity itself abstract, contains that which instances it. In the *Proslogion,* Anselm announces that he will henceforth make the reverse-containment thesis his proximate explanation of God's omnipresence: "You are not in space or time, but all things are in you. For nothing contains you, but rather you contain everything. *Therefore* you fill and complete all things."[66] But Aquinas' remark on soul and body suggests that one can take reverse-containment as a consequence of God's abstract-entity features. If one can, then even if he offers a new proximate explanation, Anselm may still be offering the same ultimate explanation of divine omnipresence.

The *Proslogion*'s most significant development, though, is a parallel to the reverse-containment thesis, an assertion that eternity literally contains time: "Your eternity contains the ages of time. It is an age because of its indivisible unity, but it is many ages because of its interminable immensity."[67] This text states that eternity somehow in-cludes all of time and yet is itself without the sort of parts and distinc-tions characteristic of time. We can perhaps gloss the text this way. In itself, eternity is one "age." Its "*immensitas*" is its property of not being "measured" by any further "ages," i.e., not contained as time is. Eter-nity, then, "is" many ages in virtue of its "*immensitas*" in the sense that its being the outermost, uncontained "age" entails its containing all other "ages." Thus the *Proslogion* treats eternity as something like the outermost dimension of a many-dimensional reality, a dimension that contains other dimensions but is not itself contained by any. The con-

---

63. "in omnibus quae sunt, non velut quae contineatur, sed quae penetrando cuncta contineat." Anselm, *Monologion,* chap. 23, in Schmitt, *Opera,* vol. 1, p. 41, ll. 21–23.
64. Augustine, *Eighty-Three Different Questions,* tr. David Mosher, q. 20, pp. 47–48.
65. "spiritualia continet ea in quibus sunt, sicut anima continet corpus." *ST* Ia 8, 1 *ad* 2. Blackfriars text, in McDermott, ed., *Summa,* vol. 2, p. 112.
66. "non es tamen in loco aut tempore, sed omnia sunt in te. Nihil enim te continet, sed tu contines omnia. Tu ergo imples et complecteris omnia." Anselm, *Proslogion,* chaps. 19–20, in Schmitt, *Opera,* vol. 1, p. 115, ll. 14–18. My emphasis.
67. "tua aeternitas continet etiam ipsa saecula temporum. Quae saeculum quidem est propter indivisibilem unitatem, saecula vero propter interminabilem immensitatem." Ibid., chap. 21, p. 116, ll. 7–9.

cept of dimension, at best adumbrated in the *Proslogion*, proved to be Anselm's key to a new strategy for relating time and eternity.

Anselm's Later Work on Time and Eternity

Anselm's fullest treatment of eternity's containing of time is in his late *De concordia*. There his central claim is that "in eternity there is only a present, which is not a temporal present like ours, but an eternal present, in which all of time is contained. As the present time contains every place and the things which are in any place, so the eternal present contains at once the whole of time and whatever exists at any time . . . Eternity has its own simultaneity, in which exist all things which exist at the same place or time and all things which are diverse in place or time."[68] Delmas Lewis has recently set out some implications of the time/space//eternity/time analogy:[69]

25. As space and spatial things are literally in time, time and temporal things literally do exist in eternity.

26. As spatially distant things exist in one and the same temporal present at once, so temporally distant things exist in one and the same eternal present at once.

27. As spatial objects remain spatial even though they exist in time, so temporal objects remain temporal even though they exist in eternity.

28. As existing at the same time does not wipe out spatial differences of here and there, so existing in the same eternity does not wipe out temporal differences of here and there, i.e., of present versus past or future.

29. As the temporal present contains all space without being in any way spatial, so the eternal present contains all of time without being temporal.

30. "X exists in space" entails "x exists in time," but not vice versa. In the same way, "x exists in time" entails "x exists in eternity," but not vice versa. (An eternal God does not necessarily exist also in time.)

68. "Quamvis autem nihil ibi sit nisi praesens, non est tamen illud praesens temporale sicut nostrum, sed aeternum, in quo tempora cuncta continetur. Si quidem quemadmodum praesens tempus continet omnem locum et quae in quolibet loco sunt: ita aeterno praesenti simul clauditur omne tempus et quae sunt in quolibet tempore . . . Habet enim aeternitas suum simul, in quo sunt omnia quae simul sunt loco vel tempore et quae sunt diversis in locis vel temporibus." Anselm, *De concordia* I, 5, in Schmitt, *Opera*, vol. 2, p. 254, 11. 6-10, 13-15.

69. Delmas Lewis, "Eternity, Time, and Tenselessness," *Faith and Philosophy* 5 (1988), 77-78.

31. As a nonspatial object (e.g., an angel) can exist with all spatial objects in one temporal present, so a nontemporal object (God) can exist with all temporal objects in one eternal present.

Anselm's overall point is plainly this. Objects viewed in terms of a coordinate system of n axes may seem to have entirely discrete locations. But the same objects, set within a coordinate system of n + 1 axes, can in fact have the same coordinate along the n + 1th axis, while remaining wholly separate on all n other axes.[70] Thus things that are spatially distant can all have the same time coordinate, i.e., exist or occur at once. Thus further, Anselm suggests, things that are temporally distant can have the same eternal coordinate, i.e., exist in the one eternal present. Now an axis of a coordinate system can represent a distinct dimension of a geometry. Anselm's claim that eternity contains time, then, amounts to the claim that time is embedded in a further dimension, location in which has at least some timelike qualities. Location in this dimension can be regarded as a perfected, paradigmatic version of temporal location. To borrow an image from Plato's *Timaeus* (which Anselm knew at least through Boethius' *Consolation*), it is what temporal location tries and fails to be. God's presence to all times equally, which is a function of His eternity, thus becomes a matter of His occupying with all times the same coordinate in this further dimension. God is present to all times because God and time are copresent at eternity.

The analogy of a coordinate system breaks down at (30) and (31). That an object is located on the fourth dimensional axis of a 4D geometry entails that it is also located in the three dimensions that the fourth encompasses. This is why some writers argue from the truth of the Minkowskian/relativistic treatment of space and time to the falsity of the thesis that mental events have locations in time but not in space.[71] But (30) and (31) allow that an object located in the dimension of eternity, God, has no location in the other dimensions eternity encompasses. Still, another analogy, with STR, may also help in expressing Anselm's conception. According to the standard Minkowskian treatment of STR, what we ordinarily take as discrete, independent space and time does not really exist as such. What there is is a four- (or

70. This way of putting the matter is inspired by a remark of Eleonore Stump in conversation.

71. See, e.g., Robert Weingard, "Relativity and the Spatiality of Mental Events," *Philosophical Studies* 31 (1977), 279–284; John Cox, "Must Mental Events Have Spatial Location?" *Pacific Philosophical Quarterly* 63 (1982), 270–274; Michael Lockwood, "Einstein and the Identity Theory," *Analysis* 44 (1984), 22–25.

perhaps more) dimensional continuum, space-time, which we interpret in terms of three spatial dimensions plus perdurance through time. Ordinary spatiality and temporality are the perspective-relative, varying projections on our perspective-relative, varying coordinate systems of a single, absolute, and invariant reality of space-time extension and relations. Eternity, on Anselm's view, is somewhat like a relativistic invariant. We coordinatize the world in terms of three spatial dimensions plus time. The world's eternal dimension is not represented as such in our schemes, any more than its 4D space-time character is. The invariant facts of space-time "show up" within our coordinate systems as various spatial and temporal facts. The fact that God and things share the same eternal coordinate "shows up" within our coordinate systems as the fact that God is wholly present with each time, in some sense at once, and yet these times are not temporally simultaneous. It is not that God is present with time by somehow sharing temporal coordinates, as Anselm argued in the *Monologion*. Rather, He is present with each time in that He shares the same supertemporal coordinate with each moment of time. That God is wholly present with all times at once sounds paradoxical. But an account of an object's relations in a third spatial dimension would sound equally paradoxical to a dweller in two-dimensional Flatland. On Anselm's view, our awareness of eternity is like the awareness of the third dimension which someone in our universe would have who thought and perceived himself to live in Flatland.

A further implication of the dimension model is worth noting. What has no extension in a lower dimension can prove extended in a higher. A point picked out in a two-dimensional plane can be the intersection with that plane of a line perpendicular to it, in the third dimension. On Anselm's model, the same can hold of eternity and time. That God has no temporal extension need not entail that He has no extended duration of any sort.

Anselm's surprising claim that eternity is a supertemporal dimension can resolve at least one conceptual difficulty for him. The difficulty is posed by his Aristotelian treatment of conditionals. For Anselm as for any adherent of Aristotle's syllogistic, universal conditionals have existential import. If so, and if "God is temporally omnipresent" entails "for all x, if x is a time, God is at x," God can be temporally omnipresent only if times exist. Now Anselm, like any other orthodox Christian of his day, held that anything other than God exists only because of God's free choice. Hence it is a contingent matter that God is temporally omnipresent, if that requires that there be created time for Him to occupy in His own way. But God's omnipresence is usually considered an essential attribute. Moreover, if God is temporally omnipresent only if created times exist, God depends for His attribute of temporal omnipresence on creatures, contradicting Anselm's belief that He is utterly *a se,* and God is changed in some manner by becoming the Creator (i.e., by actually creating), counter to Anselm's doctrine that He is absolutely immutable. Anselm's positing of a supertemporal dimension proper to God addresses these difficulties. For given this supertime, God is temporally omnipresent even if no ordinary time exists for Him to be present to: even without ordinary time, He still exists in eternity's "supertime."

Since we do not share Anselm's view of conditionals, this consequence will not recommend his view of eternity and time to us. But one could argue directly for Anselm's thesis that eternity is a supertemporal dimension containing time, as follows. As we saw in chapter 4, eternity is a date, logically speaking. So one would expect that eternity can have some qualities or stand in some relations that only dates can bear. I have said that eternity stands in relations of temporal contiguity, and that it is the unique date which is temporally contiguous with every date. I want now to make a further claim, that eternity stands in relations of temporal distance, and the temporal distance from eternity to any other date is zero. If it is not ill-formed or nonsensical to say that date 1 is contiguous with date 2, it is not ill-formed or nonsensical to say that date 1 has a distance-relation with date 2. For contiguity *is* a relationship of distance. It is the relation points or particulars p1 and p2 bear if there is no distance between p1 and p2. To say that there is no distance between p1 and p2 is to make a claim about their distance-relation. It is thus to grant that talk of the distance between the two is well-formed and meaningful.

I suggest, then, that we can speak meaningfully of the temporal distance between eternity and a given time, and that if eternity is temporally contiguous with every date, eternity lies at a zero temporal distance from any date. If so, then eternity lies at the same temporal distance from every date. This does not entail that eternity lies in a temporal *direction* from any date. Earlier and later are the only temporal directions. What lies at zero temporal distance from a date is neither earlier nor later than that date. Thus in particular no time lies in any temporal direction from eternity; eternity is neither earlier nor later than any time. Thus all times are in the same direction from eternity, namely, the null temporal direction. But if locations 1 and 2 are equidistant from location 3 in the same direction, locations 1 and 2 are at the same place. Distinct times are not at the same time. So there must be a higher dimension that encompasses time, within which locations 1 and 2 do have the same coordinate.

This argument concludes to the literal existence of a higher, eternal dimension. But we need not commit ourselves to this. For even if we do not, it remains the case that a timeless God's relation to temporal creatures has the logic of copresence with them in a higher dimension. Since this logic is coherent, so is the claim that an eternal God is immediately present to all times at once, though these times nonetheless remain temporally discrete.

We have uncovered more than one view of time and eternity in Anselm. We have seen a line of thought drawing on a temporal analogue to (SC) and concluding that God is *with* all times. We have seen the *Monologion*'s elaborate dialectic struggle for a way to say that an eternal God is somehow present *in* and located *at* all times, though not contained by any. Finally we have seen Anselm argue that eternity is like a supertemporal dimension containing time: that God and temporal creatures share the same supertemporal coordinate, and this allows God to be *with* all times and temporal creatures at once while all these remain temporally discrete. We earlier examined Stump and Kretzmann's Boethian theory of ET-simultaneity and found it lacking. Anselm's view that eternity is a supertemporal dimension lets one affirm the time-eternity relations Stump and Kretzmann sought without having to define a concept of ET-simultaneity. Anselm's theory does without ET-simultaneity because on Anselm's view, both eternal and temporal entities exist, at once, in eternity. The next chapter explores and defends this paradoxical claim.

10

A Theory of Time
and Eternity

According to Stump and Kretzmann, a relation of ET-simultaneity links events in time and entities in eternity. We have seen that the concept of ET-simultaneity is problematic. According to Anselm, a relation of *eternal* simultaneity links temporal events in eternity and eternal entities in eternity. At first glance, Anselm's view is at best incredible and at worst incoherent. But this chapter tries to recommend Anselm's picture of time and eternity on its merits. I show that this alternate view removes the need to define a relation of ET-simultaneity and makes do with fewer distinct sorts of simultaneity than the Stump-Kretzmann view. I also argue directly in favor of Anselm's position and block some serious objections to it. The next chapter argues that Anselm's view lets one defend the Boethian resolution of the foreknowledge-freedom problem.

An Anselmian Advantage

The claim that God is timeless entails that God "sees" all at once all temporal events that He ever sees. For if He did not, there would have to be real succession in His experience. He would first see one set of events and then see another, and so His life would have past and future phases and would be temporal. So if God is timeless and omniscient, then

ST. God "sees" all temporal events happen at once.

I now argue that if (ST) is true, Anselm's theory that temporal events are present in eternity is in some respects the best available view of the relations between time and eternity.

(ST) hides an important ambiguity. One can read (ST) as claiming that (ST1) *what God sees* is all temporal events occurring at once. But one can also read (ST) as asserting that (ST2) *God's seeings* of temporal events all occur at once. Anyone who holds that God is timeless and omniscient must affirm (ST2). For if God's "seeings" are not simultaneous, then since seeings of the same person cannot be discrete or incommensurable (per our earlier discussion of Ward), God's seeings exist at different times, and so God is temporal. Our question, then, must be whether a doctrine of God's timelessness should also include (ST1).

A defender of divine timelessness should not affirm (ST1) unless he or she is also prepared to affirm that events *really do* happen at once. For if what God "sees" is all events occurring at once, and they do not really do so (i.e., are not really simultaneous in any reference frame), then God "sees" things inaccurately. We need not then conclude that God believes that things are as He sees them, and errs. An omniscient God does not err. So if God is omniscient, (ST1) is true, and events do not really occur all at once, then God does not believe that events are as He sees them. But even if He does not, if (ST1) is true and events do not really occur all at once, one must say that the way God sees things is not the way or even a way they really are. This sits ill with the claim that God is cognitively perfect.

But suppose that one affirms (ST1) and then adds that events really do happen at once. One could infer from this that no event is later than any other event. But this has unacceptable consequences. For one of the following claims surely is true:

1. Time exists iff some events stand in earlier-later relations.
2. Time exists iff some events stand in earlier-later or temporal simultaneity relations.
3. Time is "absolute," or exists whether or not any events stand in temporal relations.

If no event is later than any other and (1) is true, time does not exist. If no event is later than any other and (2) is true, then just one moment of time exists. If no event is later than any other and (3) is true, all events occur at the same moment or over the same stretch of time. All of these consequences are false. So let us see what else one might infer if (ST1) is true and events do occur all at once.

There is no temporal reference frame in which all events occur at once. Actual causal relations place constraints on simultaneity which all temporal frames of reference respect. If event A causes event B, A and B occur at once in no temporal reference frame, and so no temporal reference frame contains a simultaneity relation linking A and B. So if there is a simultaneity relation linking all actual events, and causal relations link some of them, we might infer that this simultaneity relation exists in an atemporal reference frame: if all events really occur at once, they occur at once in an atemporal reference frame. On this alternative, then, temporal events occur all at once in eternity, in addition to occurring at various points in time. So on this view, eternal simultaneity is not the relation in which two *eternal* events stand if they occur at the same "eternal present," as Stump and Kretzmann say. It is instead the relation in which *any* events stand if they occur at the same "eternal present." On this Anselmian view, all temporal events occur at once for God and really do occur at once, in eternity. Events' being related to a timeless God places them in a new relation of simultaneity in which they would not stand if there were no timeless being. I suggest, in short, that a doctrine of divine timelessness should include (ST1) just in case it should include an Anselmian view of time and eternity.

Let us ask, then, whether a doctrine of divine timelessness gains anything by supplementing (ST2) with (ST1). (ST2)'s talk of divine "seeing" demands interpretation. One could take this talk fairly literally, as modeling one mode of divine knowledge on human vision or sense perception. In this case one could conjoin (ST2) with an indirect or a direct realist theory of divine perception or with a theistic version of phenomenalism. Or one could take (ST2)'s talk of divine "sight" as mere metaphor for a mode of divine knowing which is intuitive but nonperceptual, i.e., noninferential and perhaps nonpropositional but not founded on the object of knowledge's having a direct or indirect causal impact on the knower. This last maneuver is Aquinas'. Although Thomas frequently talks of divine "intuition" or "intuitive cognition," he explicitly denies that God's knowledge is much like sense perception.[1]

Theistic phenomenalism will likely find few takers; many will find it too close to a Berkeleyan denial of the reality of matter. Again, there are difficulties in working out an account of a divine intuitive but nonperceptual knowing; we meet some of them in the next chapter. Thus the positions that accept (ST2) and model God's "seeing" on

---

1. See *ST* Ia 14, passim; *Quaestiones de Potentia Dei* 3, 15 ad 4.

direct or indirect realist perception seem most promising. Suppose, then, that one holds that

(ST2a) God's seeings of temporal events all occur at once and involve indirect realist perception of temporal events.

(ST2a) affirms that all events occur at once in God's timeless experience (even if *only* in God's experience) because the direct objects of God's awareness are not events themselves, but timeless representative entities.[2] On this reading, events occurring all at once are not the object but the medium of God's "vision." There is no hint that God judges that things really occur all at once. Still, (ST2a) complicates our ontology by introducing eternal divine equivalents of sense data. Arguably, it lessens the perfection of God's mode of knowing by making it indirect rather than direct. It also forces us, again, to say that the way things are presented to God is not the way or a way they really are.

One might therefore affirm that

(ST2b) God's seeings of temporal events all occur at once and involve direct realist perception of temporal events,

as Alston does. On Alston's view, events occur sequentially in time and also all at once for God, though they do not really occur at once and though there are no divine sense data. For Alston, God eternally is directly aware of temporal events precisely as temporal and successive. Yet as Alston explicates (ST2b), God's awareness does not vary, because the whole span of time is included in God's *specious present*. As Alston puts it,

> In using the concept of the specious present to think about human perception, one thinks of a human being as perceiving some temporally extended stretch of a process in one temporally indivisible act. If my specious present lasts for e.g. one-twentieth of a second, then I perceive a full one-twentieth of a second of e.g. the flight of a bee "all at once." I

2. According to Hasker, this is an element of Aquinas' view ("Yes, God Has Beliefs!" *Religious Studies* 24 [1988], 385–394). For Hasker, the representative entity would be God's own nature (see *ST* Ia 14, 5), and in Hasker's eyes it follows that for Aquinas, God's knowledge is not immediate. But even if this is Aquinas' view, Hasker's conclusion does not follow. To Aquinas, God's nature = God (*ST* Ia 3, 3), God's nature = God's act of knowing (*SCG* I, 45), and God's nature = the medium through which He knows (*SCG* I, 46). I suggest, therefore, that though Aquinas couches his views in the language of a representative theory of perception, he does not hold that God's knowledge is nonimmediate. For on Aquinas' view, no entity not identical with God and His act of knowing stands between that act and the entities it knows.

don't *first* perceive the first half of that stretch of the flight, *and then* perceive the second. My perception, though not its object, is without temporal succession. It does not unfold successively. It is a single unified act. Now just expand the specious present to cover all of time, and you have a model for God's awareness of the world . . . a being with an infinite specious present would not, so far as his awareness is concerned, be subject to temporal succession at all . . . *Everything* would be grasped in one temporally unextended awareness.[3]

Still, by modeling God's knowledge on human sense perception, (ST2b) commits itself to a causal relation between temporal and eternal events and so inherits Stump and Kretzmann's problems in defining ET-simultaneity. (ST2b) also inherits the difficulties of the concept of the specious present.[4] Finally, of itself, (ST2b) affords no resources for saving the Boethian reconciliation of foreknowledge and freedom.[5]

But suppose that one couples (ST2b) and (ST1). The resulting Anselmian position remedies the defects of (ST2a): there is no need for divine sense data if the objects of God's knowledge really are given all at once in eternity. There likewise is no need to invoke the specious present or define a concept of ET-simultaneity. We will see, too, that an Anselmian view can save the Boethian reconciliation of foreknowledge and freedom. For these reasons, arguably, an Anselmian view gives one the best account of time and eternity if (ST) is true.

I speak of *an* Anselmian view rather than *the* Anselmian view because more than one Anselmian theory of time and eternity is possible. We have just seen that one such theory could include (ST2b). But medieval

3. William Alston, "Hartshorne and Aquinas: A *Via Media*," in Alston, *Divine Nature*, pp. 121–143. See also Milic Capek, "Time and Eternity in Royce and Bergson," in Eugene Long and Bowman Clarke, eds., *God and Temporality* (New York: Paragon House, 1984), pp. 133–154; Jantzen, *God's World, God's Body*, pp. 59–66; James Harris, "An Empirical Understanding of Eternality," *International Journal for Philosophy of Religion* 22 (1987), 165–183. Though Capek, Jantzen, and Harris deny that God is timeless, they use the concept of the specious present much as Alston does.

4. For discussion of these, see J. D. Mabbott, "Our Direct Experience of Time," in Richard Gale, ed., *The Philosophy of Time* (N.J.: Humanities Press, 1968), pp. 304–321; C. W. K. Mundle, "How Specious Is the Specious Present?" *Mind* 63 (1954), 26–48; J. D. Mabbott, "The Specious Present," *Mind* 64 (1955), 376–383; C. W. K. Mundle, "Consciousness of Time," in Paul Edwards, ed., *The Encyclopedia of Philosophy*, vol. 8 (New York: Macmillan, 1967), pp. 134–138; R. M. Gale, "Has the Present Any Duration?" *Nous* 5 (1971), 39–47; Gilbert Plumer, "The Myth of the Specious Present," *Mind* 94 (1985), 19–35.

5. Hasker ("Concerning the Intelligibility") adopts this view and does (I think) save the Boethian argument by *combining* this view with a rejection of ET-simultaneity and an insistence that though an eternal being's knowledge exists, it exists *at no time*. But it will be clear, I think, that it is the latter two commitments rather than the former which solve the Boethian argument's problems.

Anselmians typically did not accept (ST2b). As we have found, these writers held not just that God is timeless but also that God is simple, and the doctrine of divine simplicity rules out (ST2b) by ruling out the creature-God causal connections needed to model God's knowing on human perception. So medieval Anselmians conjoined (ST1) with an intuitive but nonperceptual model of God's knowing. Whether such a view is preferable to the conjunction of (ST1) and (ST2b) depends on whether the doctrine of divine simplicity brings advantage enough with it to offset the loss of the appealing direct realist model of God's knowledge. We cannot judge that matter here. So my treatment of Anselmian views of time and eternity is neutral between these options; with this understood, I return to speaking of *the* Anselmian view.

I try shortly to explain and defend the Anselmian alternative. Before I do, though, I argue directly for the most paradoxical part of this position, the claim that temporal things exist both in time and in eternity.

From God's Spacelessness to Creatures' Timelessness

Traditional theists affirm that God has no spatial location. Now there can be distance only between discrete locations in space or objects at such locations. So if God is not located in space, there can be no spatial distance between Himself and spatial creatures. If there can be no distance, there is none. That is, we may infer from this what I call the Zero Thesis: the distance between God and every spatial creature is zero. This zero distance is always between the *whole* of God and every creature. If God has no spatial location, He has no spatial parts, and if He has no spatial parts, it cannot be that one part of Him is at one distance from a spatial thing and another part is at another.

Many philosophers may object to my derivation of the Zero Thesis. Let us therefore examine the matter more closely. I have asserted that

D1. there is no distance between God and any spatial entity.

I want to read (D1) as

D2. there is a distance-relation between God and any spatial entity, and the distance between them is zero.

Let "Dx,y" symbolize "x has a distance from y," "Sx" symbolize "x is spatial," and "val(Dx,y) = ϕ" symbolize "the distance between x and y is ϕ." Then in symbols, (D2) asserts that

D2*. (y)(Sy ⊃ ((Dgod, y)·(val(Dgod, y) = 0))).

Many philosophers would reject reading (D1) as (D2). They would argue that (D1) really claims that

D3. it is not the case that there is a distance-relation between God and any spatial entity,

or, in symbols, that

D3*. (y)(Sy ⊃ ~ (Dgod, y)).

The question, then, is whether any good arguments favor (D3) over (D2).

Russellians might argue that for any y, "Dgod, y" is not well-formed, or not meaningful. A Russellian might claim that the distance relation takes only points or regions of space and their occupants as terms. The Russellian might conclude that (D2) violates a type restriction on that relation, and so is ill-formed or meaningless. This conclusion is questionable; if the Zero Thesis and (D2) are ill-formed nonsense, how can we understand them well enough to grasp their connection? But more importantly, this conclusion is too strong to recommend (D3) over (D2). For (D3*) = (D3). (D3*) contains a negation of "Dgod, y." The negation of an ill-formed formula is itself ill-formed; so is any formula that contains it. Again, some philosophers might argue that talk of distance between items presupposes that the items are in space. They might infer that by including "Dgod, y," (D2) violates the rules for significant talk about distances, and so just does not make a statement. But again, this line of attack rejects (D3) with (D2). (D3) contains the negation of "Dgod, y." The negation of a claim that makes no statement itself makes no statement. Neither does any claim that contains it. A Strawsonian might claim that "Dgod, y" presupposes that God is in space, and so lacks a truth-value, like any claim with a false presupposition. But if "Dgod, y" lacks a truth-value, so does its negation. Now consider this instance of (D3*),

D3**. Sa ⊃ ~ (Dgod, a).

If (D3**)'s consequent is truth-valueless, so is (D3**). So (D3*), which quantifies (D3**), is truth-valueless or false.

So a would-be friend of (D3) must take (D2) to be straightforwardly false. Someone who objects to (D2) says that if God has no spatial location, God has no spatial relations. This objection does not draw on any particular facet of the concept of God. So presumably it reflects an endorsement of some such claim as that for all x, if x has spatial relations, x has a spatial location. But this claim is false. "Is not located in" expresses a spatial relation. But it is not problematic that God or a set has this spatial relation to every space. Perhaps, then, the objector means to say that for all x, if x has *positive* spatial relations, x has a spatial location. But "is external to" expresses an apparently positive spatial relation equivalent to "is not located in." To disqualify "is external to," the objector must tell us what a positive spatial relation is. It will not do to answer the question by enumerating a set of positive spatial relations and saying that to be a positive spatial relation is to be a member of this set. For if the set of positive spatial relations does not include externality, the objection will fail, and if the set does include externality, the objection will beg the question. The objector to (D2), then, must give us a suitable non-question-begging account of what makes a spatial relation positive. This task looks difficult.

One could circumvent it if one could argue a relational theory of space. One would argue, then, that to be located in space = to bear some spatial relation other than externality. If this is true, no spaceless being can bear spatial relations other than externality, and so (D2) is false. Now to establish such a theory of space would be a tall order. But let us grant this theory. We have seen that even if bearing *some* spatial relations entails being in space, it does not follow that bearing *any* spatial relation at all entails being in space: externality does not entail this. If bearing certain spatial relations entails being in space, then perhaps anything which stands at any positive distance from something is in space. But it does not follow that anything which stands at *zero* distance from something is in space, and we need not grant this if (as the case of externality shows) it is not the case that, necessarily, all spatial relations link only entities in space. If x is at zero distance from y, x and y are spatially contiguous. The Zero Thesis asserts in effect that God is spatially contiguous with every spatial entity.

In chapter 9, we suggested the following definition of spatial contiguity:

SC. For all x and y, x and y are spatially contiguous just in case there is no space between x and the place of y.

This definition is not quite right as it stands. For sometimes regions of space are contiguous. (SC) does not let us say that they are, for spatial regions do not have places: they *are* places. So a better definition would be

> SC1. For all x and y, x and y are spatially contiguous just in case x has or is a location in space and there is no space between x and y.

(SC1) is clear, intuitively plausible, and eminently defensible. It requires that one term of a spatial contiguity relation be spatial, and so does not generate such odd claims as that the number 9 is contiguous with the color purple. But (SC1) does not require that both terms of a spatial contiguity relation be spatial. So if (SC1) or something relevantly like it defines spatial contiguity, then a relational theory of space is compatible with (D2).

To make a case against (D2), then, the relationalist will have to find some non-question-begging way to show that (SC1) is illegitimate, and should be replaced by, say,

> SC2. For all x and y, x and y are spatially contiguous just in case x and y have or are locations in space and there is no space between x and y.

This would, again, be a tall order.

The Zero Thesis's foes might try to attack it with ridicule. They might press their case this way: "you say that as there is no space between God and spatial things, they are spatially contiguous. By the same token, there is no space between the color yellow and spatial things. Are we to conclude that these too are spatially contiguous? Surely it is preferable to say that there just are things with no spatial relations of any sort. But then surely God is one of these." But I think anyone who inclines to the Zero Thesis can simply accept that yellow, the number 3, and any other entity without a spatial location are spatially contiguous with all spatial things. The Zero Thesis may just tell us a surprising truth about what it is not to be in space, one parallel to our earlier result that a time not located in a second time is temporally contiguous with every time in that second time.

It seems so far that the Zero Thesis, though shocking, is defensible. But should the Zero Thesis really be shocking? Opposition to it may rest on a misunderstanding. I suggest that the Zero Thesis is problematic only if a zero distance is a positive distance. But a distance of zero is just an absence of positive distance. To say that the distance between God and any spatial thing is zero is not to say that God is located where some thing is. We saw earlier that there is more than one way to be temporally contiguous with a time. So too, there is more than one way to be spatially contiguous with a place. One can overlap it. One can "just abut" it—(SC) is a first step toward a precise definition of this. And, I submit, one can also exist without location in space.

We can assert a zero distance in a positive form involving a distance-relation just because we use the word "distance" in denying distance. So the difference between the jarring (D2) and the innocuous (D3) may be smaller than it appears. To read (D1) as (D2) and not (D3) is just to acknowledge that when one says that there is no distance between God and spatial things, one talks about the distance between them. One does not say that there is no such relation. Rather, one says that the relation between them is such that they are not at a distance from one another. This is a claim about their distance-relation. So the Zero Thesis is not just defensible. It arguably is defensible as a reading of (D1). If it is, then I can claim to have argued the Zero Thesis at this section's outset in deriving (D1).

That argument, again, was this. It is true and intelligible that necessarily, there is no positive (i.e., non-zero) distance between God and any spatial thing. If a proposition is true and intelligible, so is whatever it entails. But as what is necessarily true is actually true, that necessarily there is no positive distance between God and any spatial thing entails that actually there is no positive distance between God and any spatial thing. The Zero Thesis merely rephrases this claim. So to avoid the Zero Thesis, we must deny the modal rule that $\Box$P entails P; the rule that if a proposition is true and intelligible, so is whatever it entails; or the claim that our premise is a necessary truth. An opponent of (D2) will not deny the third claim. But the first two seem beyond reproach. So we are stuck with the Zero Thesis.

The Zero Thesis has a startling consequence. A moves (changes place) relative to B just in case first the distance between A and B (in a particular frame of reference) is D and then, though A and B still exist, it is not D. But the distance between God and any creature is always the same: every part of God is always at zero spatial distance from any creature, in any reference frame. Thus if God is spaceless, there is no motion relative to God. This does not, however, deny the reality of motion *tout court*. Recall that according to STR, motion is relative to a frame of reference, i.e., to a system of other entities. That there is no motion relative to God does not entail that there is no motion relative to *other* things. There is nothing problematic in the thought that an object at rest in one frame of reference (e.g., God's) is in motion in other reference frames.

Now I consider the following thesis eminently defensible:

M. There is no change of any sort involving spatial, material entities unless there is also a change of place, i.e., a motion involving some material entity.

(M) entails, for instance, that there are no thoughts in human beings unless there are (say) changes in the brain which involve motion of microparticles, and that there is no change of color without (say) rearrangement of microparticles somewhere in the color-perceiving situation, and that there is no rotation of ultimate microparticles (if there are any) without their distinguishable though inseparable parts' changing places, etc. (M) is not a reductive thesis. Rather, it asserts only that other changes supervene on changes of place. Nor does (M) impose any restriction on what entities are involved in these changes of place. If (M) is true, though, then no spatial thing can change in any way in relation to God.

There may be no nonspatial things apart from God. Or it may be that there exist apart from God only nonspatial things that obviously cannot change, e.g., various sorts of abstract entity. If either is so, then we have already ruled out all change in relation to God, and no more argument is required. Partisans of changeable angels or discarnate souls and so on might contend that these things may exist. But even if such things exist in some possible world, they do not exist in the possible world that is actual, at least if there is any truth in contemporary physics. For as we have already seen, according to contemporary physics, only spatial things are temporal. Now whatever changes first has a property F, then has a property that entails having not-F (as when a face first is pale, then blushes). Nothing can have contradictory properties at the same time. Hence change requires that the subject of change be located in time: *only temporal things can change.* So given the space and time of the actual world, only spatial things can change. Note that I am not claiming that these conclusions hold in all possible worlds. Perhaps there is a possible world in which time is *not* a fourth dimension of a physical geometry, and in this world perhaps there are spaceless, temporal, and changeful things.

My argument, then, is that given the Zero Thesis, (M), and one very general property of time (its being a fourth dimension of an extensive continuum), it follows that in the actual world there is no motion or change relative to God. So if a frame of reference is a system of objects at rest relative to one another, then it appears that God and all spatial objects share a frame of reference, one in which nothing changes. Now if an event occurs in one frame of reference, it occurs in all, albeit in some cases at the same time as very different events. So all events that occur in other reference frames occur in the frame at rest relative to God. But how can this be, if nothing changes there? The answer, I think, is that relative to God, the whole span of temporal events is actually there all at once. Thus in God's frame of reference, the correct judgment of local simultaneity is that all events are simultaneous. But all events are simultaneous in no temporal reference frame. Therefore the reference frame God shares with all events is atemporal.

Now this argument may seem wild. But I submit that if the Zero Thesis is true, the argument is quite reasonable. For to define motion relative to an object, all one needs is time coordinates and a relation of relative distance, and if one can define relative motion between two objects, one can speak of the two as sharing or not sharing an inertial reference frame. Perhaps this argument will seem to some to be a reductio of the Zero Thesis; one person's *modus ponens* is another's *modus tollens*. But let me pose a question on behalf of the Zero Thesis. Theists hold that though He is spaceless, God is omnipresent. The Zero Thesis lets one give literal meaning to the claim that a spaceless God is omnipresent. If one denies the Zero Thesis, is literal omnipresence at all possible for a spaceless God?

A Medieval Objection

The fourteenth-century philosopher John Duns Scotus took Aquinas to hold what we have called Anselm's theory, that temporal events are all simultaneously present to God in eternity. Scotus launched against Aquinas what became a well-known comeback to this claim.[6] According to Scotus, if an event occurs only at t, only at t can God be copresent with it. The event just is not there to be with God at other times. If this is so, then given a tensed theory of time, which Anselm and Aquinas appear to accept, God is not yet present to the future, because the future does not yet exist, in any sense.[7] So, Scotus concludes, it is false that all events are simultaneously present to God. Scotus' key assumption is that temporal events occur only at the temporal location of their occurrence. With the aid of this claim, Delmas Lewis constructs another objection, turning Anselm's time-containing-space analogy against Anselm.[8] Let us say that x and y presently coexist in space just in case there is some space, however large, in

6. This response became a standard move in later Scholastic debate. See, e.g., *De concordia*, tr. Alfred Freddoso, pp. 125–126.
7. See Duns Scotus, *Ordinatio* I, d. 39, q. 5.
8. Delmas Lewis, "God and Time" (Ph.D. diss., University of Wisconsin, 1984; Ann Arbor, Mich.: University Microfilms, 1985), pp. 38–39.

which both presently are located. Equivalently, we can say that x and y presently coexist in space just in case x presently lies at some positive distance in some non-null direction from y. Lewis suggests that just as (i) if x and y do not presently coexist in space, they do not presently coexist in time, so (ii) if x and y do not presently coexist in time, they do not presently coexist in eternity. But for all events E and E* such that E is in one of E*'s light cones, E and E* do not presently coexist in time. Hence, all such E and E* do not presently coexist in eternity. So again, it appears false that all events occur at once in eternity.[9] Scotus' assumption is there, unremarked, in the claim that just as (i)'s antecedent implies (i)'s consequent, (ii)'s implies (ii)'s. For (ii)'s does so only if temporal events occur only at the temporal location of their occurrence. If this is false, if events that occur at a temporal location can also occur at some non-temporal sort of location, then perhaps events that do not occur at the same temporal location can co-occur at this other sort of location.

Lewis's objection incorporates a tensed theory of time. But one can formulate the objection in terms of a tenseless theory as well. Let us now say that x and y coexist in space just in case there is some space, however large, in which both were or are or will be located. Equivalently, we can say that x and y coexist in space just in case x did or does or will lie at some positive distance in some non-null direction from y. Then if x and y do not coexist in space, they do not coexist in time: there is no temporal system in which both were or are or will be located. Given this much, one can press the argument as before.

Though Scotus also assumes tensed time, one who holds a tenseless theory of time can also press a Scotist objection. A tenseless theorist can insist that if a temporal event is not located in time save at t, God cannot be present with it at times other than t. Lewis summarizes Scotus' argument when he writes that "God cannot be metaphysically present with future things because these things do not yet exist, [i.e.] do not exist at all in the only way they ever exist—namely, at the time of their occurring or existing."[10] A de-tensed version of this would simply be that for all events E, if $\{t \ldots t_n\}$ are the sole locations in time at which E occurs, E's existence is located only at $\{t \ldots t_n\}$, and so God can be copresent with E only at $\{t \ldots t_n\}$. So these tensed-theory objections to Anselm's claim that all events really occur at once in

9. Lewis does not make use of the concept of a light cone. Nor does he use the locution "presently coexists." I have introduced the latter to explicitly incorporate Lewis' assumption of tensed time and distinguish his version of the argument from the tenseless version.

10. Lewis, "God," p. 40.

eternity do not really turn on a tensed theory of time. Their nub, again, is the claim that temporal events occur only at the temporal location of their occurrence. This assumption yields the conclusion that God can be copresent with E only at $\{t \ldots t_n\}$. Given this conclusion, even a tenseless theorist can argue not just against Anselm's view of time and eternity but against the very claim that God is timeless. For a tenseless theorist of time, there is an important distinction between the "duration" of a timeless being and a temporal duration: the latter has parts and the former does not. Suppose, then, that E occurs only at t. If God is timeless, God's "duration" has no parts, and so that of it which is present with E at t = that of it which is present at t + 1. If this is so, then it is false that God is present with t only at t. Rather, the very phase of divine "duration" which is at t is also at t + 1. This is reason to say that God-at-t + 1 is present with t and so that God is present with t at t + 1. Thus even on a tenseless theory of time, it cannot be the case both that God is timeless and that God is co-present with events only at their temporal times of occurrence. (This argument, like all else in this chapter, is compatible with the claim that eternity is a duration and with the negation of that claim.)

As becomes clearer below, the Anselmian theory denies the Scotist argument's nub, the claim that events occur only at the temporal location of their occurrence. It holds instead that events also occur at the "time" of eternity.[11] But this does not carry unacceptable consequences. Suppose that t lies in our future. On Anselm's view, God is eternally present with t and with what occurs at t *in eternity*. Since what occurs at t in eternity is identical with what occurs at t in time, it can now be said with truth (though not with *present* truth, per Chapter 4) that God is present to a future event t. Yet as will emerge, it remains the case that in time, t is not yet actual—or in the tenseless version, that t is not located at (say) t − 1. Further, that in time, t arrives and events that occur at t occur in no way entails a change in God or in His presence to creatures. For events' occurrings at t exist as well in eternity. It is these to which God is eternally present.

An Objection: Does Occurring in Eternity Entail Tenseless Time?

Scotus argued that if events are not yet present in time, they are not yet present to God in eternity. William Lane Craig, Bowman Clarke, Richard Creel, and Delmas Lewis have in effect revived Scotus' argu-

---

11. In the terminology to be introduced below, it denies, that is, that B-located events must B-occur if they A-occur.

ment.[12] They contend that if it is now true to say that events exist in eternity, it is also now true to say that these events exist in time, reasoning this way: If all temporal events occur at once in eternity, then all temporal events occur at once. If they do, it is false that some exist now, others no longer exist and still others do not exist yet. Rather, since all events exist at once, past and future events are as fully actual as present events. Thus the claim that all temporal events occur simultaneous with a timeless entity and with one another wipes out the ontological distinction between present, past and future, enforcing instead a tenseless theory of time. Creel, Clarke, and Lewis take this reasoning as decisive against the claim that God is timeless, as each thinks he has good reason to consider tenseless theories of time false. Lewis adds this twist:

> In the eternal present in which God beholds all of temporal reality, there is no contrast between past, present and future with respect to existence . . . Since God is unaware of an objective nonrelational difference between the existence of things present and the existence of things past and future, there is no such difference as there appears to be from our perspective in time. Otherwise God does not apprehend temporal things and events as they truly are . . . God's view of things must be the correct view . . . Hence if God is eternal, then the present does not differ with respect to existence from the past and the future.[13]

Perhaps it is partly to avoid such arguments that Stump and Kretzmann give the account they do of ET-simultaneity, avoiding the claim that temporal events are eternally simultaneous.

Now I am not going to enter the lists for or against tenseless theories of time. Rather, whatever the merits or demerits of a tenseless view, I hope to show now that the existence of a timeless being and of the eternal simultaneity relation I suggest is compatible with a tensed theory of time, i.e., with the claim that only present (and perhaps past) events exist in time, so that there is a genuine and radical ontological distinction between present (and perhaps past) events and future events. Craig, Lewis, and the others seem to suppose that if an event occurs in eternity, then it occurs simpliciter and so does not remain to be brought into existence with the passage of time. I think this conditional is false. I think that a defender of God's timelessness can assert

12. William Craig, "Was Aquinas a B-Theorist of Time?" *New Scholasticism* 59 (1985), 475–483; Bowman Clarke, *Language and Natural Theology* (The Hague: Mouton, 1966), p. 113; Creel, *Impassibility*, pp. 95–97; Delmas Lewis, "Eternity, Time," pp. 72–86.
13. Lewis, "Eternity, Time," pp. 82–83.

that (in a strictly limited sense) one and the same event is present and actual in eternity though it is not yet or no longer present or actual in time. That is, it can be true at a time t that an event dated at t + 1 has not yet occurred in time, and yet also correct at t to say that that very event exists in eternity. That all events occur at once in eternity, I submit, does not entail that they all occur at once in time.

We can see how this can be so by applying anew the relativity of simultaneity. If simultaneity and presentness are relative to reference frames, then if present events are actual in some way in which future events are not, this sort of actuality is itself relative to reference frames. Thus there is a (strictly limited) sense in which the relativity of simultaneity entails a relativity of actuality, if one restricts full actuality to present events. Consider three events: Harpo, Chico, and Groucho. Let us say that in reference frame R, Harpo and Chico occur at once and occur before Groucho, and that in reference frame R*, Harpo occurs before Chico and Groucho, which are simultaneous:

Frame R		/	Frame R*	
Harpo	Groucho	/	Harpo	Groucho
Chico		/		Chico
past →→→→→→→→→ future		/	past →→→→→→→→→ future	

It seems to me that in this case, Chico is actual in R before Chico is actual in R*. By saying that Chico is actual or occurs in R "before" it is actual in R*, I do not imply that there is some single temporal "superframe" overlapping R and R*, relative to which we can construct a single time series on which to order events occurring in the two frames, and relative to which Chico's-occurrence-in-R is before Chico's-occurrence-in-R*. Nor do I mean to suggest that Chico in R is in any way really distinct from Chico in R*, or that Chico's occurrence in R is in any way really distinct from Chico's occurrence in R*. I mean only to point to this fact: in both R and R*, Harpo is before Groucho, and in R, Chico occurs with Harpo, whereas in R*, Chico occurs with Groucho.

Let me put this more precisely, subscripting temporal terms like "now" to indicate the reference frame with respect to which I am speaking (e.g., "now_R"). To help make my point, let me also introduce a nontemporal relation P of causal priority. This relation will generate causal series defined without reference to temporal position or modality. P-series will be constituted of just those causal relations that are absolute and invariant within all temporal reference frames. In the example given, for instance, Harpo is P-prior to Groucho, and Chico is not a member of this segment of this P-series, though unless Chico has neither causes nor effects, Chico occurs somewhere in some P-series. Now let us suppose that a further event, Zeppo, is in fact a member of no P-series whatsoever. Even if Zeppo is so, if Zeppo is simultaneous$_R$ with an event in a P-series, we can still place Zeppo in a P-series *in R*. For we can say that Zeppo occurs in R at the P-series location of the P-series event with which it is simultaneous$_R$.

With these devices, let me describe the situation diagrammed above. In this situation, relative to the P-series, Chico occurs (is actual) in R before Chico occurs (is actual) in R*; the P-point at which Chico occurs in R is P-prior to the P-point at which Chico occurs in R*. Also, in this situation, if in R it is now$_R$ the P-point at which Harpo occurs, that Chico is now$_R$ actual in R does not entail that Chico is now$_{R*}$ actual in R* (though it does follow that Chico is$_{R*}$, was$_{R*}$, or will be$_{R*}$ actual in R*). The relativity of simultaneity to reference frames brings with it a relativity of presentness and so a relativity of actuality. The claim that Chico is actual with Harpo in R is compatible with the claim that Chico is actual with Groucho in R*. Each is a true description of the single physical reality as it exists within a particular real reference frame.

One might think to use this relativity of actuality to argue that the apparent difference in ontological status between the present and the future is merely illusory.[14] The argument would trade on the claim that

SO. for all events E and E*, if E is actually occurring and E*'s occurrence is simultaneous with E's, E* is actually occurring.

In R, Harpo and Chico occur at once. In R*, Chico and Groucho occur at once. Both frameworks' facts of simultaneity are genuine. Hence Harpo and Groucho occur at once: though Groucho is in the future according to R, via (SO) Groucho is actually occurring (thanks to R*)—and so a future event is already occurring. Tensed theories of time entail that no future events are already occurring. Hence tensed theories of time are false, and there is no ontological difference between present and at least some future events. The slip in this argument, a defender of tensed time can say, is that it overlooks the framework-

---

14. See, e.g., Hilary Putnam, "Time and Physical Geometry," in Hilary Putnam, *Mathematics, Matter, and Method* (New York: Cambridge University Press, 1979), pp. 198–205, and Robert Weingard, "Relativity and the Reality of Past and Future Events," *British Journal of the Philosophy of Science* 23 (1972), 119–121. For discussion of related issues, see Lawrence Sklar, "Time, Reality, and Relativity," in Richard Healey, ed., *Reduction, Time, and Reality* (Cambridge: Cambridge University Press, 1982), pp. 129–142, and William Godfrey-Smith, "Special Relativity and the Present," *Philosophical Studies* 36 (1979), 233–244.

relativity of simultaneity. As we have seen, given STR, the relation of being-somehow-simultaneous is not transitive. That Harpo and Chico occur at once and Chico and Groucho occur at once does not render Harpo and Groucho in any way simultaneous. Hence we cannot apply (SO) between Harpo and Groucho to conclude that Groucho is actually occurring "when" Harpo is.

At a deeper level, the argument presumes that there is just one actuality, actuality-simpliciter, and that things simply either have this or do not. A tensed theory of time can deny this and hold instead that a distinction between present (and perhaps past) events and future events is real but framework-relative. If present actuality is ontologically special, then as there is no absolute simultaneity and so no absolute, framework-independent now, there is no absolute present actuality. There is merely present actuality in this framework and that; things are not just actual-simpliciter or not, but are actual-in-R, actual-in-R*, and so on. There is only one Chico and one occurrence of Chico, but this one occurrence is actual in many different frameworks and so has many different actualities. If events in the future in reference frame R "already" are present or past in some other reference frame, still they are not already actual in R. Only this latter would constitute an actual future of the sort tensed theories of time must deny.

That an event is present and actual at t in a frame R does not entail that it is present and actual at any particular time in another frame R*. We can take eternity as one more frame of reference, distinct from any temporal frame of reference. The argument from the Zero Thesis presents one reason to do so, but not the only reason. Another arises from our claim that eternity is logically a date. If eternity is the date of God's existence, God's existence is the sort of thing that can be dated, and so it makes sense to speak of God's existence as simultaneous with God's existence. This simultaneity relation is not the simultaneity of any temporal frame of reference. For God's existence is not located in any temporal frame of reference, and a relation does not obtain if its terms are not given. Different relations of simultaneity entail the existence of a different frame of reference. So if eternity is the date of God's existence, there is an eternal frame of reference. If we take eternity as one more frame of reference, then, we thus can say that a temporal event's being present and actual in eternity does not entail that it is present and actual at any particular time in any temporal reference frame (though it does follow that this event is, was, or will be actual in all temporal reference frames). Again, an event occurs in eternity simultaneously with all other events, but this does not entail that the event occurs at the same time as all other events in any other reference frame. Rather, in eternity, all events occur at once, and they occur in sequence in temporal reference frames. Events are present and actual all at once in eternity, but present and actual in sequence in other reference frames. An eternal frame of reference, I submit, just is one in which all events occur at once, even though they occur sequentially in any temporal frame of reference. *If Chico can occur with Groucho in R*, and this does not wipe out the ontological asymmetry between the present (and past) and the future, Chico can occur with all events in eternity without destroying the ontological asymmetry between present and past or future.*

Thus on the implications of eternity for time, I partly agree and partly disagree with Lewis et al. With them and counter to Stump and Kretzmann, I hold that if there is an eternal being, all temporal events are really simultaneous. Unlike Lewis et al., though, I hold that these events are simultaneous not in time but in eternity. Counter to Lewis and the others, I maintain that temporal events' occurring at once *in eternity* does not entail that they do so in time or that tensed theories of time are false. Also counter to Lewis, I suggest that there is no fact of present occurrence of which God is unaware. For the occurrence of things in eternity with God, which He "perceives" there, is the very occurrence by which they occur in time, though there occurrences are successive rather than all at once.

That in God's frame of reference all events occur at once does not entail that God does not know all the facts about simultaneity which obtain in temporal reference frames. God's being located in just the eternal frame of reference does not put a limit on what He knows. From any reference frame, one can extrapolate what judgments of simultaneity would be correct in other reference frames. Presumably, then, an eternal God can have this knowledge in His own way. So (as Stump and Kretzmann observe)[15] for every temporal now, God knows what is happening now (i.e., simultaneous with that now), and for every eternal now, God knows what is happening now (namely, everything). Stump and Kretzmann suggest that this constitutes an adequate response to the question of whether a timeless God can know what is happening now—that is, can know what is expressed by propositions involving ineliminable temporal indexicals. I discuss this matter in chapter 14.

An Objection: Must Whatever Occurs in Eternity Be Eternal?

My proposal naturally prompts a question: if events exist in eternity, then are they not eternal beings? Aquinas plainly does not think so. For

15. Stump and Kretzmann, "Eternity," p. 457.

him, time and eternity are "measures," of beings that can change and
beings that cannot, respectively.[16] To be a temporal being, then, is to
be a changeable being, one measurable by time—but not necessarily to
be a changing being.[17] That a being exists in a reference frame within
which it cannot change does not change the fact that the very same
being, as existing in other reference frames, can and does change.
While it is *de dicto* necessarily true that for any x, if x is in eternity, x
does not change, still if a changeable particular A is in eternity, it
remains *de re* necessarily true that A is changeable, i.e., able to change
in some reference frame or other, though not in eternity. Moreover,
even if we countenance immutable temporal beings, we can preserve
their temporality in eternity by taking temporality modally. Suppose
that a durationless temporal event occurs in eternity. Even so, it remains *possible* that this event occur in time; even if an event in eternity is
not actually later than any other event, this event *could* be later than
some other event. Thus even as existing in eternity, a temporal being
remains temporal. Let us distinguish eternity, a frame of reference,
from eternality, the quality of being an eternal being, i.e., one that can
exist only in eternity. If we do, there seems no clear reason to say that
occurring in eternity entails having eternality. Rather, some beings that
exist in eternity can also exist in time, and some cannot. Only the latter
are eternal; the others are temporal, even though they exist in eternity.

One response to the present objection, then, will take being temporal and being eternal as mutually exclusive modal properties. It will
say that an entity is temporal if it is the kind of thing that *can* be located
in a series of earlier and later events, states, processes, etc., and that an
entity is eternal if it *cannot* be so located. If being temporal is a modal
property, then even if an entity is located in an eternal frame of reference, it remains fully temporal, because it retains its modal properties.
One can also answer the objection by noting that in fact and perhaps
necessarily, any temporal event located in eternity is *also* located in
time. This remains true even if the event *is* in eternity, and this is again
an adequate basis for distinguishing temporal from eternal entities.

Stump and Kretzmann deny that eternal and temporal entities can
"exist or occur together" in eternity or time, because they think this
would make temporal things eternal and eternal things temporal. In
accepting this consequence, they implicitly accept a different view of
what it is to be temporal and what it is to be eternal. On their account,
to be temporal is to be located in time, and to be eternal is to be located

16. Aquinas, *ST* Ia 10, 4 and 5.
17. See Aquinas, *In IV Physica,* I. 20, ##606–610.

in eternity.[18] So on the Stump-Kretzmann view, my second suggestion amounts to claiming that all temporal things are also eternal things.

But there is a clear sense in which a temporal thing located in eternity would *not* be an eternal thing. A temporal being in temporal reference frames has its duration by successively enjoying parts of it. Thus within eternity

a. its fourth-dimensional extension or duration would have parts.

b. not all parts of its duration would occur at the same temporal present (i.e., at the same point in the tenseless extension that represents temporal relations. Of this more anon). This would entail at least that if this is a conscious thing, it could at any point in its duration be aware of some other points in its duration only by memory or perhaps precognition.

c. its duration's parts would be ordered as earlier and later.

d. in most cases, its duration would have a beginning and an end.

e. if it had no duration, still it would stand in a sequence representing the earlier-later relations obtaining between it and other events. (We saw earlier that a single durationless event not earlier or later than any other event would not count as a temporal event, regardless of whether we viewed it as located in eternity. But any event that stands in earlier-later relations in time stands in some other appropriate sequence in eternity.)

There thus is a distinction to be made between being located in eternity and being eternal. Even if we ignore modal definitions of eternality and temporality, to be eternal is to have a partless duration in a single present, which may or may not be viewed as in some way infinitely extended, and to stand in (or be) no sequence representing earlier-later relations. (If we held that a timeless being had QTE, we could not say that a timeless being's duration did not involve earlier-later relations. But a timeless duration would still differ from a temporal being's duration in being partless and from the "duration" of an instantaneous temporal event in being extended.) Thus even if temporal events occur in eternity, they differ significantly from truly eternal beings. All of this seems quite conceivable, and so appears possible. If this *is* possible, being located in eternity does not entail being eternal. As the present account of temporality and eternality respects the fact that this entail-

18. Stump and Kretzmann, "Eternity," p. 436.

238]   Time and Eternity

ment fails and the Stump-Kretzmann account does not, the present
account is preferable.

Earlier I suggested that the problems with Stump and Kretzmann's
definition of ET-simultaneity may manifest an underlying problem in
their picture of time and eternity. The problem *may* lie here. Because
Stump and Kretzmann take temporality and eternality to be locational
rather than modal attributes, they cannot allow temporal and eternal
beings to be located together in a single frame of reference. Thus they
are forced to try to define a sort of simultaneity (ET-simultaneity) that
is not within but between reference frames. They could not say more
about this (and it is not clear that one *can* say more about this) than that
iff temporal entities are temporally present and eternal entities are eternally present, they are copresent. We saw above that this definition
does not succeed.

Time and Eternity

All of the foregoing has led up to some proposals about the natures
of time, eternity, temporal beings, and eternal beings which I now
develop. I first state these proposals informally, then develop some
technical terms, then use these technical terms to state the proposals
more precisely.

I suggest defining a temporal entity as one that can exist earlier than
or temporally simultaneous with some entity. That is, I suggest that a
temporal entity is one the existence of which can be part of what
McTaggart calls a B-series, a sequence of events and/or SOAs linked
by the relations of temporal precedence and simultaneity. I suggest that
an eternal entity is (inter alia) one that cannot bear these relations. As I
have argued, this definition allows a temporal entity to remain temporal even if it is present in eternity. That an eternal being cannot be
located in a B-series entails that an eternal entity is necessarily eternal.

If temporal events occur within an eternal reference frame, they must
occur all at once, even though within temporal reference frames the
occasions of their actuality are ordered sequentially. If they did not occur
all at once, there would be change within eternity, first one event and
then another being actual. But as we have seen, where there is no time,
there can be no change. Now a four-dimensional timeless solid can
harbor "change" in the sense that at one point along its temporal
dimension it is F, and at another such point it is not F. But this is not the
sense of "change" or of existing at two points in time which I mean to
exclude. The 4D solid A always (tenselessly) involves two facts about A
and F, that A is F at t and that A is not F at t + 1. Where there is change in

the meatier, "purely temporal" sense, first A is F, and there is no other relevant fact linking A and F, and then A is not F, and there is no other relevant fact linking A and F. It is in this sense of change that what exists in eternity cannot change. In eternity, events are in effect frozen in an array of positions corresponding to their ordering in various B-series.[19] Yet these same events really do occur in the meatier, purely temporal sense within all temporal reference frames, as do changes of the kind eternity precludes.

As eternity does not allow change, we can define an eternal reference frame as a frame such that all events that occur within it must occur simultaneously, even if they may occur nonsimultaneously in other reference frames, and a temporal reference frame as one in which events can fail to occur simultaneously. If we do this, again, we define an eternal reference frame in terms that allow that events may occur in eternity which also occur in time.

Let us now develop the machinery to say all this more precisely. First, let us so understand "now" that occurring now does not entail having a position in a B-series of earlier and later events. That is, let us in effect take "now" and "occurring now" as primitive terms univocally applicable to temporal and eternal or timeless things. Anyone who does not want to render the phrases "eternal now" or "eternal present" flat-out contradictions or equivocations must do this.[20] This move does not create a "third mode of existing" embracing the timeless and the temporal; timeless-temporal remains an ultimate and exclusive disjunction. Nor does this move entail that occurring-now is absolute rather than framework-relative. A semantic point can hardly dictate a physical conclusion. And even if it could, how could stipulating that occurring now does not entail location in any B-series entail that all located nows must have the same location in all B-series?

Second, let us define two locutions, A- and B-occurs. Let us say that an event E A-occurs iff E occurs now. Let us also say that event E B-occurs iff E's location in a B-series of earlier and later events is t, and it is now t. Obviously, whatever B-occurs occurs now, or A-occurs. But I reject the reverse inference. If whatever occurred now B-occurred, occurring now would entail having a location in a B-series.

Let us now define two relations, A- and B-simultaneity. Two events

19. Every temporal frame of reference generates its own unique B-series. This is a consequence of the relativity of simultaneity to reference frames. Thus it is oversimple to say that God, in eternity, sees all events spread out in their temporal order. Events have many temporal orderings. If God is omniscient, He must be aware of all of them.

20. I take it, with Scotus and Swinburne, that so-called analogy theories of God-talk reduce to forms of univocity (or equivocity) theory in the end.

are B-simultaneous iff they have the same location in a B-series in the same reference frame. Intuitively, A-simultaneity is a relation of occurring at the same now. Two events are A-simultaneous if they are B-simultaneous and they B-occur. Also, all A-occurring events not located in a B-series but located at the same atemporal now are A-simultaneous.

An event A-occurs and does not B-occur if it is not located in a B-series or else if it A-occurs and is located in a B-series but does not A-occur at its B-series location. If such an event occurs and does not occur at a B-series location, it occurs in some atemporal now. This is what we have when a temporal event occurs in an eternal frame of reference. Of course, there is a sense in which an event that occurs in eternity occurs in its place in its B-series. For presumably, it has a location in a timeless array of events which represents atemporally the temporal sequence of the B-series, and in temporal reference frames the event B-occurs at this location.

Note that these definitions do not involve special temporal or eternal kinds of simultaneity, though in fact nothing timeless can B-occur or be B-simultaneous with something else. These definitions do permit us to speak of simultaneity among temporal, timeless, and both timeless and temporal things; temporal things can be A- and B-simultaneous, and timeless things can be A-simultaneous with one another and with temporal things. More important, these definitions do not make eternal-temporal simultaneity into something sui generis. On the Stump-Kretzmann account, while ET-simultaneity is an instance of generic simultaneity, it is still a unique kind of simultaneity that can obtain only between an eternal and a temporal being. It thus seems somewhat ad hoc and suspicious. On the present account, the A-simultaneity that obtains between a timeless God and temporal entities is univocal with the A-simultaneity that obtains between temporal entities. Finally, while Stump and Kretzmann's theory of simultaneity involves four distinct simultaneity relations, the present theory involves only two, or perhaps three if one contends that it tacitly includes generic simultaneity. This is a gain in simplicity.

With this background, let me offer these tentative definitions:

R is an *eternal reference frame* iff R is such that necessarily, all events that A-occur in R A-occur A-simultaneously-in-R. Alternately, R is an eternal reference frame iff within R, the relations "earlier" and "later" can hold only between locations in the atemporal analogue of a B-series and not between B-occurrences.

R is a *temporal reference frame* iff it is not the case that R is such that necessarily, all events that A-occur in R A-occur simultaneously. Alternately, R is a temporal reference frame iff within R, the relations "earlier" and "later" can apply not only between locations in a B-series but also between A- and B-occurrences.

K is a *timeless entity* iff K can A-occur/exist but cannot B-occur/exist: that is, iff K can exist now but cannot be located in a B-series. Alternately, K is eternal iff K can be A-simultaneous but cannot be B-simultaneous with other entities.

K is a *temporal entity* iff K can B-occur/exist: that is, iff K can have a location in a B-series.

If these definitions hide no nasty surprises, they let us say that a temporal thing can occur within an atemporal reference frame without compromising the absolute distinction between temporal and timeless things or reference frames. They let us say that an eternal frame of reference includes an A-simultaneous array of events located sequentially in temporal B-series. They also let us say that events A-occur in both eternity and time, but B-occur only in time. Yet temporal events that A-occur in eternity also B-occur in time, and so occur in eternity as ordered in timeless analogues of their B-relations.

Eternity and Tense

Having set out this view of time and eternity, let me offer an additional argument for its truth, based on considerations of tense. Let us ask this question: if a timeless God were mentally to token some proposition "P" about a temporal event, in what tense would P's main verb be? We have seen that the system of tenses relates times or timelike loci to sentences' times of utterance. Our answer to our question about God's tense, then, will depend on the relation of what God talks about to His eternal present.

The nature of timelessness requires that God use some sort of present tense. For as we have seen, nothing can be past or future to a timeless being. But I submit that God could not use a discrete-present tense. Earlier we saw reason to say that where cause and effect are temporal, cause and effect are temporally connected. By analogy, there is reason to suppose that where cause is timeless and effect is temporal, the two are somehow *durationally* connected—i.e., that they are not discrete. Hence as the tense God uses will depend on His creatures' relation to His present, it will not be a discrete-present tense. Accordingly, God's tense will be a present tense that is used to speak of events with which His existence is simultaneous.

Say, then, that God knows that there is snow in Nome, Alaska, and that God mentally tokens "there is snow in Nome." The "is" of this proposition picks up God's own present, the timeless present. In the same way, if I say "there is snow outside," the "is" picks up my present. So if God mentally tokens "there is snow in Nome," He mentally speaks of what is true during His present. He is not (or at least not obviously) speaking of what is true during a temporal present not included in but ET-simultaneous with His present. To speak of what is true during a temporal present distinct from though ET-simultaneous with His eternal present, God would have to say not "there is snow in Nome" but something like "there is snow *then* (i.e., at that present) in Nome."

So God's present-tensed "there is snow in Nome" (henceforth "P") is true during His present. Its truthmaker cannot be durationally discrete from His present, since God has created the snow in Nome. If its truthmaker is ET-simultaneous with God's present, then though P is in effect straightforwardly present-tensed, the "time" at which God knows P is not a time at which its truthmaker makes it true (though it is ET-simultaneous with such a time). But God's tense appears to be an eternal analogue of an ordinary present, and this creates some presumption that the time at which He knows P = the time at which P's truthmaker makes P true. Again, were God speaking of an SOA which obtains during a temporal present distinct from though ET-simultaneous with His eternal present, it would seem more apt for Him to say not "there is snow in Nome" but something like "there is snow *then* (i.e., at that present) in Nome."

So it seems that God's token of P concerns an SOA obtaining in eternity. It seems that like an ordinary present-tensed claim, God's token of P is true during His present because during that present, the entities to which the claim's referring devices refer occur or exist and satisfy the claim's predicates. So it seems that it is because temporal entities exist and events occur also in eternity that the truths God knows about them are true during eternity.

Suppose on the other hand that God tokens a tenseless claim, "at t, in Nome, it snows." A tenseless truth is true during all times. So if eternity is a time, then perhaps tenseless truths are true during eternity, whence we can argue that tenseless facts obtain in eternity. A less debatable point relies on tense logic. According to a law of tense logic, "at t, in Nome, it snows" is true only if it is true that Pr(at t, in Nome, it snows).[21] In God's case, the present the latter claim involves is again God's timeless present. So it seems that corresponding to a tenseless

---

21. More precisely it is true only if Pr(at t, in Nome, it snows) or discrete-Pr(at t, in Nome, it snows), and because we are dealing with a timeless God who creates all temporal things, in this case it cannot be true that discrete-Pr(at t, in Nome, it snows).

truth there is a truth true during God's timeless present, one which arguably involves tenseless facts' obtaining in eternity.

If these arguments work at all, they will go through even if God's knowledge is not knowledge of propositionally formulated truths, but is instead some sort of direct intuition of facts.[22] For even if God's knowledge is thus intuitive, one can still ask whether God could in principle express it by tokening a present-tense proposition, and then the rest of the argument will proceed as before. Now there is no obvious reason to deny that God can know truths (or facts that can be expressed in truths) of the form "there is snow in Nome" or "Pr(at t, in Nome, it snows)." But if He can, this seems to be reason to affirm a presence of temporal entities and events in eternity. Thus it seems that if one holds that God is timeless and omniscient, one has reason to say that the objects of God's knowledge, including all temporal creatures, exist with Him in eternity.

Now this argument does not assert that a timeless, omniscient God logically depends on the existence of creatures for His character of omniscience. My claim is only that if a timeless God's omniscience includes knowledge of temporal creatures, these creatures also exist in eternity. Whether God's omniscience is to do so, and what temporal creatures there are, is entirely up to God. Moreover, nothing said here in any way supports the claim that God depends causally on creatures for knowledge. So I do not think that this logical dependence of God on creatures contradicts the claim that God is *a se*.

An Objection: Is Eternal Presence Otiose?

This explanation of the tie between an eternal presence of temporal beings and divine knowledge lets us turn back an otherwise impressive objection to the Anselmian theory. The objection is this. Boethius and Aquinas use the image of the man atop a height to explain how God knows temporal beings and especially how He foreknows events that to us are future. Saying that God knows the future because He, as it were, surveys it from a height, they suggest that just as we would see a road from a hill because the road is there to be seen, so God sees a future that is there to be seen. Now if we saw a road from a hill, the road would be among the causal conditions of our seeing. The road's real presence would explain our knowledge only by causally conditioning it. So, then, the future's real presence will explain God's knowledge

22. As is argued in Alston, "Does God Have Beliefs?" in Alston, *Divine Nature*, pp. 178–193.

only if it causally conditions God's knowledge. But given God's aseity, the literal presence of creatures in eternity has no causal-explanatory value, for it cannot be that future events causally condition God's experience.[23] If eternally present creatures cannot causally explain God's knowledge, there seems no gain in positing them. Further, if perchance God's knowledge did really depend on creatures, what would be gained by positing eternally present creatures as objects of His knowledge? Why should we not simply say that God immutably knows what will be the case in the future, based solely on the purely temporal fact that it will in fact be, or the fact that at that now-future time, it obtains?[24]

Our response, clearly, is that this argument misconstrues the way timelessly existing creatures help to explain God's timeless knowledge. Creatures' contribution to God's timeless knowledge is semantic, not causal; the timeless real presence of creatures with God provides a semantics of timeless omniscience. God cannot know that P unless P is true. Hence any condition that explains the truth of P makes a contribution to the explanation of God's knowledge. If God is timeless, the timeless existence of temporal creatures is a semantic presupposition of His knowing truths about them. Thus creatures' timeless existence helps to explain God's knowledge without causally explaining it.

Applications

The notion that we are always present with God in eternity may have interesting religious implications. It is sobering to reflect that any action we take is eternally not just in God's foresight or memory but a living presence "before His eyes." There is no possibility that distance may ease the grief our sins cause God; they are literally ever with Him. Again, there is a strand in Western spirituality that holds that temporal things, being of lesser reality than the timeless, are of little worth. We now can suggest that even if eternal beings have higher reality than temporal, still even a temporal being's smallest thoughts and deeds have in fact the lastingness of eternity. The mark we make on the world does not vanish; we are never threatened that all of reality will one day be as if we have never been. Christians may find the Anselmian view of time and eternity still more sobering. For if it is true, then the Crucifix-

23. In texts cited earlier, Aquinas speaks of God as "intuiting" the whole of time. But just because there can be no explanation of God's state of knowledge in terms of creatures' causal activity, Aquinas rules out literally calling God's knowledge a sort of sensing. Cf. *QD de Potentia Dei* 3, 15 *ad* 4.

24. See J. Loinaz, *Praelectiones*, pp. 271, 272–274.

ion is not an episode God went through once and now relives only in memory. Rather, God's love for the world is so great that He is willing to be eternally crucified for its sake, and all of His dealings with the world are commingled with His present undergoing of that pain. Yet it is also the case that God eternally lives His triumphant union with believers at the far end of history and that this joy is great enough to transfigure even the pain of crucifixion even as He undergoes it. These consequences (and others like them) are not, however, peculiar to Anselm's theory. Any version of the doctrine of divine timelessness must live with them. For since there is no past or future in eternity or for an eternal being, at no point in God's eternal existence is His creation of the world yet to come. Given that God is eternal and has created, He has eternally had the world, our sins, and our other doings for company, is eternally crucified and is eternally glorified.

The notion that we are always present with God in eternity may also be of philosophical use. Some philosophers have puzzled over how an eternal entity can act on and perceive events in time. If the definitions above are viable, we may be able to dissolve this puzzle. For perhaps we can argue that an eternal entity acts on those temporal entities that are present with it in eternity, and these actions have consequences for temporal entities as they exist in time. (We could say that actions in eternity are prior to consequences in time not temporally but "by nature.") Perhaps, that is, a timeless deity need not act on temporal things in time to act on temporal things. Again, perhaps a timeless thing need only be eternally copresent with a temporal thing to observe it, or to know it in whatever way serves it in place of observation. Of course, these moves leave us the task of explaining causal relations between timeless and temporal entities in eternity. But perhaps we can make headway on this via counterfactuals expressing dependence. I try to do so below.

A more important application of the theory of time and eternity developed here is to vindicate Boethius' response to the freedom-foreknowledge problem. I try to do so in the next chapter. Here let me instead recall finally that several chapters ago I raised a question: can the timelessness of God be reconciled with the biblical picture of God and creatures as present to one another? Some philosophers have in effect argued that if God is present with us, He must be present with us in time. I have tried to suggest that God may be present with us because we are present with Him in eternity—and yet are fully temporal. On these assumptions, timelessness and the biblical picture can indeed be reconciled.

11

Timelessness, Freedom, and Foreknowledge

I have claimed that the theory of time and eternity developed here will vindicate Boethius' response to the freedom-foreknowledge problem. I now try to make that claim good. The freedom-foreknowledge problem, we recall, arose from a libertarian definition of freedom (that an agent S is free with regard to an action A in circumstances C at time t iff it is within that agent's power in C at t both to do A and not to do A) in conjunction with the claims that

1. there are truths about all future human free actions, that
2. necessarily, God at all times believes all and only truths, and that
3. what is past is beyond any agent's power to affect.

For given (1) and (2),

B1. if S does A in C at t, then God believes before t that S does A in C at t, and
B2. if S does not do A in C at t, God believes before t that S does not do A in C at t.

All verbs in (B1) and (B2) are tenseless. Now seemingly,

PP. for all propositions P and Q, if P ⊃ Q, then S can at t effect it that P is true only if either Q is already true at t, or S can at t effect it that Q is true, or some other agent can at t effect it that Q is true.[1]

Given (PP), we can infer from (B2) that

B3. if S can in C at t effect it that S does not do A at t, then either God believes before t that S does not do A in C at t, or S can at t effect it that God believes before t that S does not do A in C at t, or some other agent can at t effect it that God believes before t that S does not do A in C at t.

Suppose, then, that (it is tenselessly true that) S does A in C at t. If so, then by (2) it is not the case that God believes before t that S does not do A in C at t, and by (3) it is not the case that S or any other agent can at t effect it that God believes before t that S does not do A in C at t. But then by (B3) it is not the case that S can in C at t effect it that S does not do A at t. As this argument can apply to all S, A, and t, it appears that (1)–(3) eliminate human libertarian freedom.

This argument to S's unfreedom is valid. Hence the theist who wishes to preserve human freedom must deny one of its premises. Molina and his contemporary followers might object that (B3) over-looks something.[2] For Molinists, even if S has no power at all over the past, there may still be a noncausal relation of counterfactual dependence between S's actions and God's belief: though S cannot now effect it that God did not believe that S does A in C at t, S now can perform an action such that if S *were* going to perform it, God would not have believed that S does A in C at t—to wit, S now can refrain from doing A in C at t.[3] Molinists deploy their theory of "middle knowledge" to explain this noncausal connection.[4] According to this theory, God knew before creating the world just what free agents would freely choose to do if placed in certain situations, and He created in light of this knowledge. Suppose, for instance, that God wants to create a world in which Peter will freely deny Christ. By His "middle knowledge," God knows in just what situations Peter would in fact do that. So God can so create and order the world as to bring Peter into one such situation. Thus God knows in advance what Peter will freely do.

1. (PP) is a member of a family of claims Hasker calls "power-entailment principles" (*God*, pp. 104–115).
2. Molina, *De concordia*, tr. Freddoso, pp. 53–62.
3. Ibid., p. 60.
4. For exposition of this theory, see Molina, *De concordia*, tr. Freddoso, passim.

Further, even though Peter has no power over God's past states of knowledge, had Peter been going to remain faithful to Christ, God would have known that instead. For it would have been the case that God wanted to create a world in which Peter freely remained faithful, had done so, and knew that he had done so.

Given the theory of middle knowledge, then, Molinists might argue that what is true is not (B3) but

> B4. if S can in C at t effect it that S does not do A at t, then either God believes before t that S does not do A in C at t, or S can at t effect it that God believes before t that S does not do A in C at t, or some other agent can at t effect it that God believes before t that S does not do A in C at t, or had S been going not to do A at t, God would not have believed before t that S would do A in C at t.

(B4) does not warrant the conclusion that humans lack libertarian freedom, Molinists believe, for it allows S the power to refrain from A in C at t. The Molinist might add that the argument to (B3) went awry because it contained a false premise, (PP); what is true, the Molinist might say, is not (PP) but

> PP1. for all propositions P and Q, if P ⊃ Q, then S has at t the power to effect it that P is true only if either Q is already true at t, or S has at t the power to effect it that Q is true, or some other agent can at t effect it that Q is true, *or* Q is false but it is the case that were S going to effect it that P, Q would have been true.

The Molinist position is sophisticated and impressive. But I think that (PP1) is false and moreover irrelevant to the issue of human freedom. (PP1) entails that

> PP2. for all propositions P and Q, if P ⊃ Q, then if Q is false but it is the case that were S going to effect it that P, Q would have been true, then S has at t the power to effect it that P is true.

The sense of (PP2), given the Molinist case for accepting (PP1) rather than (PP), is that we can ascribe to S a power to effect it that P even if S cannot remove an obstacle (Q's falsity) to S's effecting it that P, provided that were S going to effect it that P, the obstacle would not have been there. But if this is so, what S has can be called a power to effect it that P only in a Pickwickian sense: for the connection between S and Q's truth *is expressly noncausal,* i.e., is not based on any power of S. It is compatible with its being the case that P ⊃ Q, Q is false, and were S going to effect it that P, Q would have been true, that S have no power at all to render Q true. But if this is the case, then even if S *would have* had the power to effect it that P *had* Q been true, S does not *actually* have the power to effect it that P, for Q's falsity prevents this. If its being the case that P ⊃ Q, Q is false, and were S going to effect it that P, Q would have been true does not entail that S actually has the power to effect it that P, (PP2) is false. So, then, is (PP1).

A Molinist might object to this argument. After all, couldn't we just as easily say that S has the power to effect it that P, but on this occasion is prevented from exercising it? But the definition of libertarian freedom rules out this reply by requiring that S be able to do A *in S's then-actual circumstances.* For S's actual circumstances include conditions that block S from doing A. So we can conclude, then, that (PP2) and (PP1) are false. Further, only actual powers possessed in actual circumstances (which in the case at hand include Q's falsity) matter for the libertarian definition of freedom. So given that (PP1) does not truly ascribe to S an actual power in actual circumstances, (PP1) is irrelevant to libertarian freedom.

It seems, then, that one cannot escape the argument by denying or tinkering with (B3). So theists who wish to preserve human freedom can escape the argument only by denying one of (1)–(3). Some theists are willing to deny (1).[5] But most theists hold that God has some sort of knowledge of our future and so want to maintain (1). Other theists, who call themselves Ockhamists, are willing to qualify (3) and allow various sorts of power over the past.[6] These theists contend that some facts about the past are "soft," i.e., not determinate until some later time, and so within the power of later agents to determine. A sample "soft" fact would be Aquinas' having written a hymn exactly 730 years before the moment this book's first copy was bound. Let us suppose that we are not living in a physically deterministic universe (for if we are, no theological move can save human libertarian freedom, because that freedom is eliminated before the theological discussion begins). On this assumption, it is plausible that when Aquinas wrote his hymn, it both could and could fail to turn out that he wrote his hymn exactly

<hr/>

5. So Swinburne, *Coherence of Theism.* Hasker, in *God,* argues that God knows about the future only how probable various future events are. But probability-judgments are not really knowledge about the future at all; the statement that a certain event has a probability of .5 states how probable it is *now* that that event come about later.
6. See the notes to Chapter 8.

730 years before the moment this book's first copy was bound. There arguably was no fact about this past matter until 730 years later, when the actions of editors, copysetters, etc., determined whether it was the case 730 years ago that Aquinas wrote his hymn exactly 730 years before the binding of this book's first copy. Now intuitively, if God has foreknowledge at all, what God's beliefs were is not a soft fact.[7] If God believed before t that S would do A at t, then God was then in a certain concrete cognitive state. God could have given before t a perfectly determinate answer if asked whether S would do A at t; He would not have told His questioner that He as yet had no determinate belief at all on that subject. Ockhamism, then, does not look like a promising out for the theistic libertarian.

The only remaining ways out involve (2): the theistic libertarian might deny that God knows all truths, or that He does so at all times, or that He does so necessarily. The Boethian strategy denies (2) while preserving the claim that God is necessarily omniscient. For it affirms that God is necessarily omniscient and yet rejects (2) because no time is a time at which God knows what He knows.

Let me flesh out how the Boethian strategy works. Consider a set of claims including (1), (3), and in place of (2),

2a. necessarily, God believes all and only truths.

This set of claims does not raise problems for human freedom. God's knowledge creates a problem for human freedom only if its existence somehow closes off options we would otherwise have or limits the extent of our power. The mere claim that God knows or necessarily knows that S does A at t does not have this effect. For this claim is compatible with the claim that God knows this by "watching" S do it, and God's "watching" is, of course, compatible with S's doing A freely.

This suggests that what matters for human freedom is not that God has knowledge of our future, but the vantage from which He has it. The key question is whether this vantage determines that God's knowledge curtails human power. For again, if God's knowledge is past or (as in Plantinga's argument cited earlier) as if past, it rules out human libertarian freedom, but if God knows that S does A after S does A, or knows that S does A while S does A by "watching" S (i.e., from a causally posterior vantage) rather than by willing that S does A (i.e.,

---

7. For similar arguments, see Fischer, "Freedom and Foreknowledge," and Hasker, *God*, pp. 79–80. An interesting counterargument is Widerker and Zemach, "Facts," pp. 19–28.

from a causally prior vantage), this in no way limits S's power or closes off S's options. As we are temporal agents, our options are closed off only if they are closed off (temporally or causally) *before* we have the chance to choose among them. If an option is not closed off before we choose, then it still exists when we choose, and so we still have that option.

If God is timeless, God's knowledge is not in the temporal past, present, *or* future of S's action, and so (2) is false. If God's knowledge is wholly outside time, it cannot have the sort of temporal relation to our actions which would let it determine them. If we say that God timelessly knows that S does A, our assertion that God knows that S does A is without temporal modifiers at all.[8] Our assertion is then relevantly like (2a), and so its truth would not entail that human freedom is restricted. If God knows timelessly that S will do A, then in fact S will do A, and will not choose not to do A. But it does not follow that S had no option to not do A, for it does not follow that God knew this (temporally or causally) *before* S chose to do A, nor therefore that there was in reality beforehand something that determined that S would do A. Of course, all this is the case only in temporal reference frames. But in eternity, God's knowledge is simultaneous with the free creaturely acts God knows about, and (as will emerge below) one can hold that God's knowledge is not causally prior to them, and so again, God's knowledge does not determine their occurrence.

Thus by rejecting (2), the Boethian blocks the argument from (1)–(3). Now blocking the argument from (1)–(3) does not dispose of all questions about God and human freedom. Some theists claim that God not only "foreknows" but "forewills" our future—i.e., that God's willing that S do A at t is necessary and sufficient for S's doing A at t.[9] Arguably, the Boethian strategy does not address at all the problems this further claim poses for preserving human freedom. Further, rejecting (2) does not even dispose of all questions about the relation between God's *knowledge* and human freedom. For all the falsity of (2) shows is that God's *having* knowledge of our future actions does not preclude human freedom. The argument from (1)–(3) does not broach the issue of what explains God's having that knowledge. Even if the bare exis-

8. If this is so, then in a sense, we cannot call God's knowledge that S does A *fore*knowledge, for God does not know this *before* S does A. Of course, as many have noted, it can be called foreknowledge *quoad nos,* insofar as God has knowledge of matters that *for us* are future.

9. This follows, e.g., if God must cause the existence of every entity other than Himself and human actions are entities not identical with God. For discussion, see William E. Mann, "God's Freedom, Human Freedom, and God's Responsibility for Sin," in Morris, ed., *Divine and Human Action,* pp. 182–210.

tence of foreknowledge is compatible with human freedom, it could be
that what explains God's having that knowledge generates further
threats to human libertarian freedom. It could even be that what threatens freedom is an explanation of how God comes by His knowledge of
our future which a defender of divine timelessness is forced to give. If
this is so, then in the end, the Boethian's denial of (2) is unavailing:
even if it blocks the argument from (1)–(3), it does not actually preserve human freedom.

Still, blocking the argument from (1)–(3) is at least a first step toward reconciling divine knowledge of what to us is future and human
freedom. The Anselmian view of time and eternity does let one block
this argument. Like Stump and Kretzmann's, the Anselmian view of
time and eternity explains why an eternal God's simultaneity with the
events of our past does not locate Him in time in our past. The Stump-
Kretzmann explanation is that ET-simultaneity just is not the sort of
simultaneity that has this consequence. The Anselmian explanation is
that God's believings are simultaneous with events of our past only in a
nontemporal reference frame: that is, in a frame where *nothing* is past
(though things' temporal order is respected in another way). Thus in
any frame in which there is a past, it is false that God's believings are in
the past, for in such a frame, God's believings are simultaneous with no
creaturely event.

Another challenge to Boethius arose from the claim that an eternal
God's believings are *as if* in our past and the claim that

4. "God eternally knows that Paul mows in 1995" is now true.

(4) might seem to follow from

5. God eternally knows that Paul mows in 1995

by a rule of tense logic, that (letting "Pr[]" symbolize the tense-logical
operator "it is now the case that") for any formula P, regardless of its
tense, P entails Pr(P). But it does not; instead it follows by this rule
only from

5a. "God eternally knows that Paul mows in 1995" is true.

I now argue that (4) and (5a) are false.

Let us begin by asking about the tense of "knows" in (5). The
Boethian wishes to reject (4). If (4) is false, then there is a time at which
(5) is not true. If a proposition is tenselessly true (in a given time

series), it is true at all times (in that series). So it follows that in (5), "knows" is not tenseless. If (4) is false, further, "knows" in (5) is not in the ordinary present tense. For if it were, (5) clearly *would* entail (4). Thus without recognizing a discrete- or an eternal-present tense, a Boethian cannot explain the tense status of the verb in (5). If one grants that there is an eternal- or a discrete-present tense, then a Boethian can plausibly say that the verb in (5) is in one of these tenses.

For present purposes we need not decide between these two alternatives.[10] For if (5) is in the eternal-present tense, (5) is true, but not true at any time before, during, or after the present: (5) is relevantly like a claim in the discrete-present, about a temporal series discrete from ours. We saw in Chapter 4 that if "B" names such a series, such claims as that

4a. "God (in B) knows that Paul mows in 1995" is true now

are false.[11] If (4a) is false, then since (4a) is quite like (4), (4) too is false. So too, then, is (5a), since the tense of "is true" is the ordinary present. So if (5) is in the eternal- or discrete-present tense, (4) is false, and the Boethian treatment of freedom and foreknowledge stands. Further, even if there is no eternal- or discrete-present tense, and the tense status

10. I suggest that (5) involves a distinctive eternal-present tense. For if a claim uses the discrete-present, we cannot say whether the claim is in true in the past, present, or future of its own "time series." (Strictly, then, one should call it a discrete-*time* tense rather than a discrete-present). To see this, let "now" denote the now of our time series, and "now$_d$" the now of a second, discrete time series, and note this: if a claim *is* true in the past of its "series," the now$_d$ that series now has is now$_d$ past the time at which that claim is true. That is, the use of our present tense ("a claim *is* true") brings in a reference to our now. But this claim entails that there is a now$_d$ which that second series now has—i.e., that some now and some now$_d$ are simultaneous, contrary to the hypothesis that the series are discrete.

(5) deals with a timeless being. We have seen that in eternity there is no past or future: a timeless being must have its knowledge in the eternal present. Thus we know that (5) is true in the present of its "series" (and we know it without having to relate that present temporally to ours). Thus there must be not just a discrete- but an eternal-present tense, and (5) involves the latter.

11. Of course, per Chapter 4, even if (4a) is false, it can still be that "God (in B) knows that Paul mows in 1995" is true and is uttered now.

I argued in Chapter 4 that if such claims as (4a) are true, the temporal series involved are not discrete, because they are causally linked. It could seem, therefore, that my argument will not apply to the case of a timeless God and time, since God and time are causally linked. But this is not the case. I am claiming that a timeless God is *temporally* related to time as a second time series would be, not that such a God is *causally* or in any other nontemporal respect related to time as a second time series would be. That is, my claim is that *whatever* the precise reason a second time series would so relate to ours as to disqualify such claims as (4a), a timeless God is temporally related to time just as a second time series would be and so in a way that falsifies (4).

of (5) is just unclear, (4) is still false provided that (as is true on the present account but not on the theory of ET-simultaneity) in time, eternity is in no sense simultaneous with any time and so is relevantly like a discrete time series.

Now even if all this is true, we can still say, e.g., that God now knows that Paul mows in 1995. But we can say this with strict truth only because we, too, stand in the eternal now and so can use "now" to refer to the eternal now rather than any temporal now. We can use "now" this way because "now" has a sense something like "simultaneous with this utterance," for this utterance is simultaneous in the eternal reference frame with the eternal now.

The present theory allows that if a proposition P is true at t, "P at t" is true at eternity. So on the present view, truths corresponding to truths about future human free actions are also true in eternity. But these are not true in eternity before we perform the actions in eternity, for nothing in eternity is before anything else. Nor are they true in eternity at times before our free actions; eternity is not in our past or as if in our past. Of course, that a proposition about a human action is true in eternity at a particular point in an eternal B-series array lets us infer just when the action occurs in some reference frame's time (as from a proposition's truth at 2:00 in R plus appropriate further information one can determine just when it is true in another reference frame). But what we can infer is just that the proposition is true when our action makes it true, not that it was true before. For a Boethian can consistently deny that a proposition about a future human free act is true or false before the act. That a proposition has a truth-value in eternity does not entail that it has a truth-value at any particular point in time (other than the time at which we make it true), because in time, eternity is in no way simultaneous with any time. Nor does the fact that such a claim as "S freely does A" is true eternally just at point t in a B-series infringe human freedom. This entails at most that S *does* A at t, not that S could not have avoided doing A at t, because "S freely does A" is not true at that B-series point *before* it is true in time.

That "S does A at t" is true eternally entails that S does A at t. If the truth of "S does A" at t entailed that "S does A" was true before t and thence led to fatalism, this would be so for reasons independent of the doctrine of divine timelessness or the existence of God. But nothing said here requires us to endorse the omnitemporality of truth or therefore the fatalist inference. Again, if God is immutable, His cognitive state cannot be changed. Hence I cannot change His cognitive state, and so, if God is essentially omniscient and holds that I do A at t, it follows that I do A at t: for if I did something else at t, it would change

God's cognitive state, or else God would not be omniscient. But that I *will* do A at t entails not that I could not have done otherwise, but just that I will not. For God's unchangeable knowledge does not have the relation to my action at t which would render it a determining condition of that act: it does not exist *before* I act. I submit, then, that the present theory of time and eternity lets one reject (2) and to this extent rescues the Boethian approach to freedom and foreknowledge.

Whether the doctrine of divine timelessness offers an overall adequate response to the freedom-foreknowledge problem depends on two larger matters: first, its ability to provide an explanation of why God *has* foreknowledge that does not threaten human freedom, and second, its relation to the issue of divine "forewilling." On both subjects, it is important to distinguish between what we can say of a timeless being and what we can say of an eternal being, for the fact that an eternal being must also be simple complicates matters somewhat. If we can make sense of causal relations within eternity—a question I address below to some extent—then we can consistently say that a timeless being's knowledge of what to us is future is a causal consequence of the events foreknown and so account for this knowledge in a way compatible with human freedom. But as we have seen, a simple God's knowledge cannot be a causal consequence of anything created. Again, nothing in the doctrine of divine timelessness forces us to endorse the claim that God forewills all human actions. It is open to a defender of timelessness to reject this claim, and one who does so is spared having to grapple with this further issue.[12] But it can be argued that the doctrine of divine simplicity does commit one to the forewilling claim.[13]

Still, perhaps the doctrine of divine simplicity does not pose insuperable problems. Let me briefly sketch an account of divine knowledge of free creaturely acts which is compatible with divine simplicity, avoids forewilling, and explains this knowledge in a way that safeguards created freedom. For an Anselmian, God's knowledge of actions that are future to us is not foreknowledge. It is rather knowledge of something that is going on at the "time" God knows that it is going on, namely, eternity. If God is simple, He knows what is going on "without looking," i.e., without being affected by causal signals from the free acts. Nonetheless, what He knows about are the free acts themselves. So our first step to clarifying God's knowing is to say something about the actions God knows.

12. Alston rejects it in "Divine-Human Dialogue and the Nature of God," in *Divine Nature*, pp. 144–161.
13. As in Mann, "God's Freedom."

We are responsible for what we freely do. An agent is responsible for an act only if the agent produces the act. But if we act with libertarian freedom, then though our earlier inner states (beliefs, desires, etc.) may influence what we do, they do not fully explain our acts. We act freely only if at the time we act, it is absolutely and causally possible that we refrain from that act. So if we act freely, our prior inner states do not entail or cause our acting. Thus prior inner states of a free agent can never make a free action more than probable. If so, our prior beliefs, desires, etc., fully explain only our having been likely to perform that action. If the action was free, our doing it did not follow logically or causally from the prior presence of those beliefs and desires. Rather, the action took place only because we made it happen. Perhaps the minimal contribution one can make to one's action is to consent to acting on an involuntary strongest present desire. Let us therefore call the agent's distinctive contribution to a free action a consent. If an action was free, its agent's consent was spontaneous, or not causally determined by any preceding factor, including any prior inner state of the agent.

We must now ask why the agent consents to what he or she does, rather than something else. If not even the agent's own prior beliefs and desires can causally determine the agent's consent, the explanation of an agent's consent must lie within the agent himself, the entity (whatever it is) that *has* those beliefs and desires and does the consenting. If there is no explanation there, all free action contains an ultimately unexplained component, and the agent's consent happens for no reason at all. But this cannot be so if agents are morally or even causally responsible for what we call their free actions (if it is correct to speak of agents as causing their acts). For an agent is responsible for his or her action only if the agent is responsible for his or her consent. A person is responsible for a consent only if that person is in some way the source of that consent. But if that person is the source of the consent, some aspect or activity of the person explains the consent's occurring. If nothing in the agent explains the occurrence or direction of the consent, what reason is there to treat the consent as an act of the agent rather than a random occurrence *within* the agent? I suggest, then, that if anyone performs an act with libertarian freedom, an explanation of that person's consent lies somehow within that person.

I suggest that not just beliefs and desires but persons contribute to the explanation of actions. Suppose that Fred wants an ice-cream cone more than he wants anything else, believes that he can get one at a particular store, and then does go to the store for some ice cream. If we ask why Fred consented to his desire for ice cream, we will accept the answer that Fred did so because he is a rational agent, and it is characteristic of rational agents to consent to their strongest desires when no other considerations intervene. We are willing to explain what Fred did by what Fred is—a rational agent, or person. Suppose now that Fred has a choice between eating his ice-cream cone or giving it to a hungry-looking beggar, and Fred in fact gives away his cone. If we ask why Fred did it, we will accept the answer that Fred has strong feelings of sympathy and charitable impulses, and he just is the sort of person who often consents to these. We are willing to explain Fred's consents by appealing to what Fred is—what *kind* of person he is.

This strategy may seem ineffective. For seemingly, "what kind of person Fred is" is a matter of Fred's character traits. But if Fred's consent is free, one wants to say, Fred's character traits cannot absolutely or causally necessitate it and so cannot fully explain it either. Yet our ordinary mode of speech incorporates a response to this problem. If we appeal to an aspect of Fred's character to explain his consent, we can avoid treating this aspect as something that can causally influence Fred's consent. We may instead treat this trait as internal to and constituting Fred. Causes must be entities distinct from their effects. To ensure Fred's spontaneity, we in effect deny that the nature to which we appeal is distinct from Fred. We say instead that Fred *is* the underlying character or nature that explains Fred's consent. We speak of the kind of person Fred *is* rather than the kind of character Fred *has*. We do not treat persons as "bare particulars" to which all personal traits are superadded. We instead treat persons as intrinsically charactered and intrinsically such as freely to consent to some acts rather than others. (It should be clear that a person's character or "nature," in the present sense, need not be an essential attribute of that person. Traits may come or cease to be part of this nature, and one may mold one's own nature for good or ill.)

I will now argue that it may be that a person's intrinsic character explains why that person consents to a particular action. A person in a certain situation *might* consent to many different acts. But it may be that because of the kind of person the agent is, in that situation, there is just one act to which that agent *would* consent. It may be, in other words, that

> 6. for all agents S and acts A, even if S does A freely, any agent qualitatively identical with S would do A in a situation qualitatively identical with S's.

I will argue this by considering what it would take to produce a duplicate of a person. But first I must field an objection. One might think that if one *would* freely do just one action in a certain situation, it is false that in that situation one *might* do otherwise.[14] But I do not think that one need draw this conclusion. Tomorrow I will walk through my front door. I may then turn right and I may then turn left. But though I might do either, there is just one that I *will* do—say, turn left. Suppose now that a slightly different future were going to come about instead, one in which I do not leave the house at all tomorrow. It would then be the case that had the world been slightly different and had I been going to go out tomorrow, I might have turned right and I might have turned left, and in fact would turned left. This seems to make sense. If it does, the fact that I would have done one particular thing does not deprive me of alternatives. If I were in fact not going to leave the house tomorrow, then had I left the house and turned left, I would have done so freely, having it in my power to go right instead.

Let us return to the main line of argument. Suppose that we want to duplicate perfectly a free agent—say, W. V. O. Quine. To simplify matters, let us assume that Quine's brain produces Quine's thought and behavior. Then suppose that we clone Quine, temporarily accelerate the clone's aging process to produce a body with Quine's current degree of wear and tear, and then etch onto the clone's brain precise duplicates of the memory traces and so on that currently enable Quine's brain to generate Quine's thoughts and actions. Have we duplicated Quine? Rather than try to answer this question, let us consider one way to argue that we have not. Suppose we know that in a certain situation S, Quine would do A. Suppose, then, that we take the Quine clone straight from the lab into S (so that experience differing from Quine's would have only a very small chance to produce behavioral dispositions other than Quine's), and that when put into S, the Quine clone does not do A. I suggest that this result would make us wonder whether the Quine clone perfectly duplicates Quine. For even if Quine has libertarian freedom, it is to some degree plausible that

14. As does David Lewis. See "Counterfactuals and Comparative Possibility," *Philosophical Papers*, vol. 2 (New York: Oxford University Press, 1986), pp. 8–10. Lewis (along with many others) maintains that the counterfactual operators "might" ($\Diamond\rightarrow$) and "would" ($\Box\rightarrow$) are interdefinable, claiming that $\phi \Diamond\rightarrow \Psi = $ df. $\sim (\phi \Box\rightarrow \sim \Psi)$ and that $\phi \Box\rightarrow \Psi = $ df. $\sim (\phi \Diamond\rightarrow \sim \Psi)$ (David Lewis, *Counterfactuals* (Cambridge, Mass.: Harvard University Press, 1973). This assumption lies at the base of his (and others') counterfactual logic. So in holding that it can be the case both that I would do act A and that I might do $\sim$ A, I am setting myself squarely against this aspect of standard counterfactual logics. All I can say is that the example the text sketches seems coherent, and that if it is, the standard logics' assumption is wrong. This would not be the first time impressive systems of thought have lost contact with their intuitive data by searching too hard for systematic neatness.

7. if we have perfectly duplicated Quine, the Quine clone does in every situation just what Quine would do.

The reason (7) is somewhat plausible may be that though the connection between prior inner states and action is not logical or causal, it is still fairly tight. For if this connection is tight, then if the Quine clone contains precise replicas of Quine's prior inner states, it is highly likely that the Quine clone will do in every situation just what Quine would do. Thus if the clone does not do what Quine would do, we will begin to wonder whether the duplication was imperfect—whether in some physical or mental respect, the Quine clone differs from Quine.

If we wonder about this, we do so because we take failure to duplicate behavior as evidence that the replication was not perfect. David Lewis, Ernest Adams, and Frank Jackson have argued that we determine how probable we find an indicative conditional "if A, then B" by assessing the probability of the conditional's consequent given the conditional's antecedent: that is, the more probable we think it that B will occur given that A occurs, the more probable we find it that if A, then B.[15] In general, then, we treat the probability of "if A, then B" as equal to the probability of B given that A occurs. Now we do take it as some evidence of imperfect replication that the Quine clone does not do what Quine would do. If we do this, we in effect say that if we have perfectly duplicated Quine, there is some positive probability that the Quine clone does in every situation just what Quine would do. For unless we took perfect replication to raise the probability of behavior duplication, we could not rationally take failure to duplicate behavior as evidence against perfect replication.

But if we assign some positive probability to B given A, we are committed to assigning some positive probability to "if A, then B." Accordingly, the fact that we treat failure to duplicate behavior as *some* evidence against perfect replication commits us to grant that (7) is at least somewhat plausible. Given some uncontroversial assumptions, (7) is equivalent to an instance of (6). So it appears that (6), too, is at least somewhat plausible. If (6) has some plausibility, there is some reason to say that because of the kind of person one is, there is just one action one would freely do in a certain possible situation.

Now if this is so, then perhaps by comprehending a person's nature, one can learn what that person would do in a certain situation. Suppose

15. Ernest Adams, "The Logic of Conditionals," *Inquiry* 8 (1965), 166–197; David Lewis, "Probabilities of Conditionals and Conditional Probabilities," *Philosophical Papers*, vol. 2, pp. 133–152; Frank Jackson, "On Assertion and Indicative Conditionals," *Philosophical Review* 88 (1979), 565–589.

that I know a man extremely well, but have been with him in only a very limited range of situations. Suddenly he and I find ourselves in a situation radically unlike anything we have experienced before: perhaps we die and find ourselves in an unexpected and utterly outlandish afterlife. The situation we face may be so unlike anything we have seen before as to render my friend's past actions a poor basis for induction: he has never had to choose between options remotely like these, and so his actual past choices may not be strong evidence about his upcoming choices. All the same, I may have acquired through my experience of the man a general sense of or feel for what sort of person he is. This sense may dictate a firm belief that he will opt for one particular course of action. A belief formed on the basis of this "feel" is justified by the whole history of my acquaintance with that person. If it turns out to be true, then, perhaps my belief has the right sort of justification to count as knowledge. I suggest, then, that through sufficient understanding of the kind of person a person is, one might in some cases know "without looking" what a person would do or is doing in a certain situation.

One can call my belief about my friend's character "intuitive," in a broad sense: for it is acquired neither by perception nor by explicit inference from actual past behavior. Perhaps, then, God's knowledge of free creaturely actions is not "intuitive" in the sense of perceptual, but "intuitive" in this sense. My intuitive beliefs about others' behavior can err, because I do not have full insight into the character and situation of the persons I know. Arguably, God's intuitive beliefs would be founded on absolutely full knowledge of what He creates. If this is so, then arguably, God's beliefs would not err.

One can explicate the claim that God's knowledge of what He creates is absolutely full by saying this. God has in mind "before" creating a precise, maximally detailed image of every creature He wishes to create and every situation in which He wishes to place them.[16] This image includes both mental and physical properties of creatures. God completely grasps the content of this image. Thus He has an absolutely full understanding of the SOAs He wills to obtain. God wills that Creation perfectly duplicate what He has in mind. God's will that a possible SOA obtain cannot be impeded. So Creation does duplicate what God has in mind. For a large class of SOAs, then, God knows that those SOAs obtain because He knows that He wills them to obtain and that if He wills them to obtain, they do obtain. (My later chapters suggest that this class includes every SOA whose causal antecedents do not

16. Such images might be what Aquinas calls divine Ideas. See *ST* Ia 15, 1; for the origin of the tradition in which Aquinas stands, see Augustine, *Eighty-three Different Questions*, q. 46.

possibly include an action of a free nondivine agent.) In this timeless act of will, God also makes an initial contribution to the natures of all free agents who exist throughout history. Thus God also knows about this component of their natures. Note that on this scenario, God knows that all these SOAs obtain, but His knowledge does not depend causally on their obtaining. Still, His knowledge is not causally unrelated to the SOAs' obtaining. His cognitive state is not a cosmic coincidence and so can count as knowledge.

This first willing in effect sets up initial conditions within which the libertarian free will of creatures will have effect. Our question, then, is just how God knows what actions free agents perform. Let us make the case a bit easier by assuming that all nondivine free agents have been human and (as all of the Western monotheisms hold) that there was a first human being. On these assumptions, the entire content of the nature this first human brings to the first nondivine free action is determined by God's creative volition: God knows what Adam's nature is because He knows what He has willed it to be. God fully comprehends what He has willed to exist. One can therefore suggest that God knows Adam's nature well enough to know how Adam will freely react to the situation he confronts. By knowing this and knowing what the situation is, God knows what Adam does, without causally depending on Adam's actual action for this knowledge. Knowing what Adam does, God also knows its consequences, because He knows how this action *would* affect the world. Thus God knows how these consequences change Adam and the situation Adam faces. Knowing these things, God knows what circumstances Adam faces next and what nature he brings to them, and so God can thus know the next free act Adam does, and the next, and so on. If Adam's actions eventually lead to the presence of other free agents, God knows the natures of these agents, by knowing what He has contributed to the overall situation and knowing the consequences of prior nondivine free actions. Thus God can in this way know the actions of all nondivine free agents.

If this scenario is possible, it represents one way a simple God could know about the free actions of created agents without causally depending on their actions for His knowledge. This account of God's intuitive knowledge may strike one as implausible. But the bottom line is that however implausible this story may seem, it is not obviously impossible. For we have seen that (6) is at least somewhat credible, and given (6), the rest of the story is acceptable. If we do not know that (6) is false, this scenario is an at least epistemic possibility. If it is, then the doctrine of divine simplicity appears compatible with an explanation of divine foreknowledge which does not imperil human freedom. Further, if this scenario is epistemically possible, then even if the doctrine of divine simplicity entails that God "forewills" all free actions, this does not create a difficulty for human freedom. For on the present scenario, one can say that some of these "forewillings" are *logically* posterior to human action and God's knowledge of human action. It allows, that is, that some of these willings are endorsements rather than causes.

The theory I have sketched resembles the Molinist theory of middle knowledge. In both views, God knows what actually occurs, His knowledge does not depend causally on what actually occurs, and God knows what He does in virtue of willing the actual state of Creation. It might seem that on this or the Molinist view, God in effect determines what free agents will do by determining what their circumstances will be. But it does not seem improper to say that agents do freely what their natures dictate that they do in these circumstances—at least if one accepts my suggestion about the relation of person and nature. For given this suggestion, to say that a person's nature determines what he or she will do in certain circumstances just is to say that there is in fact something that he or she will freely do, because of the kind of person he or she is.

Like Molinism, the present view holds that God knows creaturely free actions because of His grasp of creatures' characters or natures.[17] But the present view differs from Molinism in one key way. Unlike Molinism, the present theory does not affirm that there are any truths about how creatures might or would act antecedent to God's action. So the present view need not try to explain what makes such truths true, thus circumventing some major objections to Molinism.[18] Again, unlike Molinism, the present view preserves human freedom. For this view allows, as Molinism does not, that at the time of doing A, it is in the agent's power not to do A. On this view, God's knowledge does not stand as an obstacle on whose removal the agent's power depends.

I submit, then, that this "quasi-Molinism" represents one way in which a simple, timeless God might have knowledge of free actions that to us are future. I would also like to sketch briefly a second possibility. According to quasi-Molinism, once God has established (or helped to establish) the natures of free agents, these natures ground truths about what those free agents would do in various situations. My second option dispenses with the claim that there are truths about what free agents would do in varied situations. If there are none, God does

17. See Molina, *De concordia*, tr. Freddoso, pp. 51–53, 78–81.
18. For discussion of these, see, e.g., Molina, *De concordia*, tr. Freddoso, pp. 62–81, and Hasker, *God*, pp. 19–52.

not know any and so does not know what free agents in fact do by knowing them.

Let us say, then, that in God's logically first creative willing, where the actions of agents with libertarian freedom are concerned, God does not will that any free creature perform any particular act or will that any free agent face circumstances in which there is just one thing he or she would do. Instead, let us say that at each juncture in history where a free act may occur, God wills a disjunctive SOA.[19] God wills, say, not that Peter deny Christ in Jerusalem at t, but that Peter do that *or* deny Christ in Jerusalem at t + 1 *or* deny Christ in Joppa at t − 2 *or* affirm loyalty to Christ in Jerusalem at t. God could will this disjunction directly or could will it by setting up a set of definitely obtaining conditions that so determine events as to limit their outcomes to items that are parts of this disjunction. Now this disjunction will be true just in case at least one of its disjuncts is true. But on the view I am now sketching, God does not at first will one of the disjuncts to be true— that is, God does not do so at the first conceptually but not temporally distinct "moment" of His inner life. Rather, God leaves the settling of this matter to agents other than Himself.

Let us suppose that some other agent does settle this, i.e., does perform just one of the actions in the disjunction. How, then, might God know which action an agent performs? Consider an author writing a novel. At a crucial plot juncture, the author has to choose between having the hero do A and not do A. There *is* no truth about whether the hero does A until the author decides what the truth should be. Nor is there any truth about what the hero *would* do until the author decides *that*. All the same, the author's hand at this juncture may not be wholly free. Certain actions by the hero will "fit" the hero's character, the overall story, and the overall style of the novel as so far developed. Others will not. Authors sometimes speak of having their characters run away with a story or develop a life of their own. Authors mean by this that they began to write with a certain plot outline in mind but found as they developed their characters that the previously envisioned plot just did not seem plausible: once the author fleshed the characters out, it did not appear that those characters would do those things. So while there is no truth about what the characters will or would do until the author creates it, all the same the prior content of the story, in conjunction with the author's aesthetic sense, narrative skill, etc., may favor certain continuations of the tale over others.

---

19. I owe the device of disjunctive divine volitions to Peter van Inwagen, "The Place of Chance in a World Sustained by God" in Morris, ed., *Divine and Human Action*, pp. 211–235.

Let us view history as a novel God is writing. God's authorial contributions include the existence and order of nature, the initial conditions free agents face, and much of the contents of these agents' characters. (Conjoined, these set up the action disjunctions mentioned above.) Through these and other means, God "writes into the plot" of history His broad ideas about its direction and outcome and His "aesthetic sense" of how it should move toward its goal, what patterns it should exhibit, what lessons it should teach, and so on. On a more subtle level, as a novel may bear the distinctive stamp of an author's personality, the whole character of history bears the mark of God's character. Though He alone can fully appreciate this, it is through and through the kind of thing He would expect from Himself (so to speak). In this sense, even if He never appears as a character, God has thoroughly written Himself into the story.

God's characters have libertarian free will and so "run away with" His story as no other characters can. Now a human author's characters may "run away with" a story in a direction the author did not anticipate. This may happen because a human author may have imperfect understanding of just what he or she is building into those characters, or just what sort of story he or she is turning the book into, or most basically just what sort of person he or she is and how this has distinctively marked his or her product. (A perceptive reader can at times pick up on this last, even if perhaps the author cannot.) God suffers no such lack of insight. His understanding of Himself and of what He has put into His story is complete. If this is so, then perhaps it is not utterly implausible that even though there is no definite truth about what God's characters will or would do until they act, God can "predict" what truths they will establish. God knows Himself, He knows what to expect from Himself, and so He knows what products with His distinctive mark on them can be expected to do. The beliefs God thus forms would be "intuitive" in the sense of resting on and expressing an "insight" into God Himself and the characters God creates. If these beliefs could qualify as knowledge, they would do so because God's grasp of Himself and of what He has created provides some justification for them.

Whether one finds this second view acceptable will depend on how plausible it seems that an absolutely perfect comprehension of free agents' natures and circumstances, of His own nature, and of the way the former reflect the latter would permit God to "predict" just what free agents will freely choose to do. Perhaps it is just barely possible that God would get all of His "predictions" right and not do so by chance or lucky guess. If so, this second theory about His knowledge is just barely possible. But again, all I need at present is a possible theory, however implausible, that offers a way a simple God could have knowledge of the free actions of His creatures without depending causally on those actions for His knowledge. For all I am suggesting is that it may not be utterly impossible to adopt the doctrine of divine simplicity and still preserve the overall success of the Boethian response to the freedom-foreknowledge problem—i.e., that some possibly true story, however implausible, will allow us to conjoin divine simplicity and the Boethian response. If this second view were possible, it would in some respects be preferable to quasi-Molinism. One cannot help suspecting that on the quasi-Molinist picture, God really would determine which SOAs of the above Petrine disjunction are actualized. For in quasi-Molinism, God knowingly determines what Peter's nature and circumstances will be. But on the present view, God has no responsibility for which SOA of the disjunction is actualized. Rather, God wills circumstances within which Peter can deny or affirm Christ, and then it is just up to Peter. The present view does not place God's knowing that in C, Peter would do A and willing that Peter be in C among the causal conditions of Peter's doing A in C. This renders it more clearly nondeterminist that Molinism or quasi-Molinism.

I suggest, therefore, that whether or not one conjoins it with a doctrine of divine simplicity, an Anselmian theory of time and eternity permits one to rescue Boethius' approach to freedom and foreknowledge. It does so by avoiding the claim that in some temporal reference frame, the existence of an eternal God's knowledge is somehow simultaneous with the existence of temporal things. This latter claim does respond to a real pressure on the doctrine of divine timelessness. For if a timeless God is the creator of temporal things, then arguably, we must say that His acting and existence are somehow simultaneous with the existing of the things He creates: cause and effect cannot be discrete or incommensurable, and nothing can be earlier or later than the action of a timeless cause. But on pain of forfeiting Boethius' reconciliation of human freedom and divine foreknowledge, we cannot say that God's acting and existence are somehow simultaneous with temporal things' existences *in time*. So the Anselmian view accommodates this pressure by allowing that God and temporal things exist at once *in eternity* and not in time. The Anselmian view thus provides what the Boethian approach to freedom and foreknowledge requires and yet gives full scope to the intuition that (in the case of a timeless God) causality requires simultaneity. Of course, this comes at a price. For suppose that there are two temporal entities A and B whose existences do not overlap at all in time and that a timeless God

has created both. If timeless causality requires simultaneity, God's acting and existing are somehow simultaneous with A's and with B's
existing. If the Boethian approach is to succeed, this simultaneity cannot obtain in time. Hence in a nontemporal frame of reference, God's
existence is simultaneous with the existence of x and with the existence
of y. Simultaneity is transitive within a single frame of reference. So it
follows that within this other frame of reference, eternity, x and y exist
at once, although they do not do so in time. I have tried to show that
this conclusion is not the scandal it seems. If I have been persuasive,
then perhaps this conclusion does not seem too high a price to pay for
the benefits of the Anselmian view.

It is integral to the Stump–Kretzmann view to claim that in some
temporal reference frame, the existence of an eternal God's knowledge
is somehow simultaneous with the existence of temporal things. Thus
if my arguments are sound, the Anselmian view of time and eternity
rescues Boethius and the Stump–Kretzmann view cannot—a strong
advantage for the Anselmian view. If the Anselmian view rescues
Boethius and (as I have tried very sketchily to suggest) no non-
Boethian reconciliation of freedom and foreknowledge is available, this
constitutes a strong reason to adopt the doctrine of divine timelessness
and the Anselmian view of time and eternity.

[12]

A Case for God's
Timelessness

At this point I can outline the position I wish to defend. I hold that God is timeless. I take it that the relations between God and temporal beings are as Chapter 10 sets forth and that God is temporally omnipresent and omnicontiguous, as if eternity were a higher dimension in which He and temporal things coexist. I do not, however, assert that God has QTE. I regard the latter as a defensible claim, and I believe that it could be useful in constructing an overarching theistic metaphysics. [1] But for the present it is a needless complication.

Why, then, ought one to think that God is timeless? One can give quite a few good arguments for this conclusion. I begin, however, with one that is questionable.

Timelessness and Infinite Time

Helm contends that if God exists in time, "the idea that God exists in an infinitely backward extending time . . . requires that an infinite number of events must have elapsed before the present moment could arrive. And since it is impossible for an infinite number of events to have elapsed, and yet the present moment has arrived, the series of events cannot be infinite. Therefore either there was a time when God

---

1. For one thing, it could provide underpinning for the Augustinian/Boethian claim that temporal things exist only insofar as they resemble eternal things, by allowing duration to be a positive respect of resemblance between the temporal and the eternal.

began to exist, which is impossible, or God exists timelessly."[2] Helm's
argument runs this way:

1. Either time extends backward infinitely or time had a first
   moment.
2. If God exists in time and time had a first moment, God's
   existence had a first moment.
3. If time extends backward infinitely, an infinite series of events
   has occurred prior to the present moment.
4. It is impossible that an infinite series of events has occurred.
5. Hence there has not been an infinite backward extent of time.
6. Hence time had a first moment.
7. It is impossible that God's existence had a first moment.
8. Hence it is not the case that God exists in time.

Several points are in order here.

First, (3) is false. If time extends backward infinitely, all that follows
is that an infinite series of events has occurred or at least one event of
infinite duration has occurred or an infinite extent of empty time existed prior to some first event. Ruling out the third possibility would
require an elaborate metaphysical argument. It is hard to see what sort
of argument could rule out the claim that an infinitely long event has
occurred. A theist who holds that God is in time and that time had no
first moment could contend that there have been many of these, e.g.,
God's occurrently knowing that He is God and God's occurrently
approving all that is morally good. Helm himself grants that "it is
possible that there should be a sempiternal being that had a belief that it
never acquired, that is a being such that it had existed for all time and
there was no time at which it failed to have the belief."[3] I cannot
imagine how Helm could argue that this belief must be dispositional
rather than occurrent. I suggest therefore that it need not be. But then
let us suppose that God's believing is occurrent. A believing that is not
dispositional is not a mere state of belief; it is something actually going
on. Yet this going-on is not a process. A process typically involves
stages and development. Nothing of the sort is involved in God's
having a belief. But then it seems reasonable to construe an occurrent
believing as an act that is also an event. If it is, then unless Helm can
argue that the sempiternal belief in question must be dispositional,
Helm seems to have granted the possibility of an infinitely enduring
event.

2. Helm, *Eternal God,* pp. 37–38.
3. Ibid., p. 50.

Second, (4) is highly contentious. Though I cannot here delve into its pros and cons, I stand with a large majority of contemporary philosophers in denying it. Finally, if we take (2) in the sense needed for (2), (6), and (7) to entail (8), there is no reason to grant (2). (7) is true only if having a first moment of existence includes having a limit of existence or having come into existence; divine perfection clearly rules out only the latter two things. But we saw in our discussion of Anselm and Aquinas that having a first moment of existence does not entail these things. If God existed in time once time existed and time had a first moment, then God would have a first moment of existence: there would be a moment before which He did not exist, because there *was* no "before" that moment.[4] For that matter, arguably, God could have a first moment of existence even if God did not exist in time once time existed. Helm insists that the question, "What does God (timelessly) know now?" is equivalent to "What does God (timelessly) know at the time this utterance is being made?" and insists that one can properly answer that God now timelessly knows every truth.[5] If Helm allows this, he must similarly allow that God now timelessly exists, in the sense that at the time of this utterance, God timelessly exists. But then if there was a first moment of time, there was a first moment at which God timelessly existed—which seems in a relevant sense to be a first moment of God's existence.[6] Yet even if He in one of these ways had a first moment of existence, one could still call God's existence unlimited were it understood that He would have existed even if time did not. For as long as this is true, we cannot infer from God's having had a first moment of existence that God *came into* existence or would not have existed save if time did. For these reasons, then, we should really read (2) and (7) as

> 2a. If God exists in time and time had a first moment, God's existence had a first moment and God has a limited existence, or would not have existed had time not existed, or came into existence at His first moment of existence, and
>
> 7a. It is impossible that God's existence had a first moment and God either has a limited existence, or would not have existed

---

4. Some may find this an additional reason to deny that God exists in time once time exists.

5. Helm, *Eternal God,* pp. 103, 105. Helm takes this argument seriously enough to infer from it that God's knowledge is as if past for temporal beings and that therefore human beings lack libertarian freedom; see ibid., pp. 105–106.

6. Modeling God's relation to time on that of a discrete temporal series rules out just this sort of move. For as we have seen, if there is a second temporal series, though it is true that such a series exists, it is not true *now* that it exists.

had time not existed, or came into existence at His first moment of existence.

But given the alternate possibilities we have sketched, there is no reason to believe (2a). For the reasons given, then, Helm's argument fails.

Timelessness and Infinity

The thoughts about limitation we have just alluded to lead to a better argument for divine timelessness. God is thought to be a supremely perfect being. That we think Him so gives rise to a rule for determining what predicates apply to God: if we are considering which of two mutually exclusive predicates F and G to apply to God, and both are compatible with the rest of what we wish to say about God, then if whatever satisfies F is qua F in a relevant respect greater or more perfect than whatever satisfies G is qua G, we must call God F rather than G. Now we consider the fact that we exist for a limited duration regrettable. However much life we have, we generally wish we had more. To feel this way is to feel that limited duration is an imperfection, and that other things being equal, greater duration is better than lesser. If these things are so, unlimited duration is a perfection, and so we ought to ascribe to God the least limited duration compatible with the rest of His attributes. Now omnitemporal, everlasting duration would be the least limited temporal duration. But we have already seen (in Chapter 9) a significant sense in which an intrinsically timeless being would have a still less limited duration. Accordingly, we ought to say that God is timeless.

Timelessness and Necessary Existence

We saw in the third chapter that whatever exists necessarily is intrinsically timeless. There are strong reasons to say that the concept of God is such that if God exists, God exists necessarily. To give just one (with an obvious debt to *Proslogion* 3), God is thought to be a supremely perfect being. This entails that if God's having some attribute F would render God more perfect than He would otherwise be, and God's having F would not conflict with His having any other perfection, it follows that God has F. But necessary existence is just such a perfection. For to be immune to so much as the possibility of nonexistence is to exist with the maximum degree of security, to be maximally rooted in reality. We consider our liability not to exist an imperfection, a quality of our existence we regret. We think that other things being equal, it is better to have more security of existence than to have less. These things being so, we have reason to consider freedom from the liability not to exist a perfection. Nor (prima facie) does necessary existence conflict with the possession of any of the standard range of divine perfections. Further, if it did, it could be argued forcefully that some other perfection(s) ought to give ground.[7] Hence if God exists, God exists necessarily. So if God exists, God is intrinsically timeless.

One could rejoin that as necessary existence entails timelessness, if timelessness conflicts with other traditional perfections, so does necessity. But this response would be beside the point. My present claim is rather that necessary existence taken purely *in itself* may conflict with nothing, in which case it at least has a strong prima facie claim to inclusion in the concept of a maximally perfect being. If this is so, the independent warrant of the claim that God exists necessarily generates prima facie warrant for the claim that God is timeless, whether or not God's being timeless turns out to conflict with His having other perfections. If, then, we are able to defuse arguments that such conflicts exist, we will have good reason to say that God is timeless.

Timelessness and Spatiality

We saw in Chapter 2 that something has a location in time if and only if it has a location in space. But leaving aside the Christian doctrine of the Incarnation, theists universally reject the claim that God has a location in space. They have good reason: it sounds absurd to say that one could get closer to God by walking. Now such absurdities count against the claim that God has a particular limited location in space. But if God were literally located at every point in space, He would be located in space and yet one could not get closer to Him by walking.[8] Hence we need another argument to rule out this latter possibility. Perhaps it is enough, though, to note that if God is literally at every point in space, I walk through God whenever I walk,[9] and pour coffee

---

7. Theodore Guleserian has argued that nothing can be necessarily existent, omniscient, omnipotent, and good; see his "God and Possible Worlds: The Modal Problem of Evil," *Noûs* 17 (1983), 221–238. But even if this is true, there seems no strong reason that necessary existence should be the perfection we reject. Guleserian himself rejects necessary goodness.

8. The Zero Thesis argument in the previous chapter concluded not that God is at every or at any point in space, but instead that He is directly contiguous with every point in space—which is possible only if He occupies none of them.

9. Paul's claim that "in Him we live and move and have our being" (Acts 17:28) is surely not meant quite this literally!

272]   Time and Eternity

through Him whenever I have myself a cup. Hence theists should
affirm that God is without location in time.

Now as we saw earlier, theists who hold that God exists in time
might respond to this by distinguishing relativistic time, location in
which implies location in space, from the time in which God exists.[10]
Hasker has put the temporalist argument this way: God is not in space.
So God is not in a time that is a fourth dimension of an extensive
continuum. But God is in time. So the time in which God is is not a
fourth dimension of an extensive continuum.[11] Now there appear to be
two ways to take this position. The temporalist could be saying that
God exists in a time series discrete from our own or that God exists in
the very time we inhabit, which is not *really* relativistic or the fourth
dimension of a continuum.

The first option is not promising. Holding that God exists in a
discrete time series forfeits one of the main advantages of temporalism,
the ability to say *when* God acts, e.g., to say that God responds to our
prayers *after* we pray. Further, we have seen good reason to doubt that a
being in one temporal series can create or act in a second temporal
series. Hence the second reading of the temporalist move is best: the
temporalist who makes this move should be interpreted as denying that
STR tells us the literal truth about the nature of time. Hasker puts it
this way: "What forces us, in our Einsteinian universe, to regard time
as a fourth dimension is the relativity of simultaneity. And this in turn,
of course, is the result of the finite speed of light . . . God does *not*
become aware of temporal events through the transmission of physical
signals. Whenever something happens, God is *immediately* aware of it.
And what this means is . . . that God knows which events are absolutely simultaneous even though we do not."[12] Here two points need
making. First, that the finite speed of light *reveals to us* that simultaneity
is relative does not entail that simultaneity is relative only for beings
who depend on physical signals for their knowledge. One can say
instead that the finite speed of light shows us that space and time have a
certain structure, that this structure accounts for the relativity of simultaneity, and that if space and time do have this structure, they have it
objectively and so regardless of anyone's means of knowledge. Second,
that the temporalist is driven to deny the literal truth of STR confirms
the validity of my argument's inference: if STR is true, as I am assuming, then a spaceless God is also timeless.

10. So Alan Padgett, "God and Time: Toward a New Doctrine of Divine Timeless
Eternity," *Religious Studies* 25 (1989), 209–215.
   11. William Hasker, personal correspondence, June 27, 1989.
   12. Ibid.

Timelessness and Omnipotence

We have seen that alternate temporal series are possible and that a temporal God could not create an alternate temporal series. We have also seen that temporal series must exist contingently. Hence if God is temporal, possibly there is a contingent entity He cannot create and a contingent state of affairs He cannot actualize. Nor is there any plausible restriction on the power of an omnipotent being which would generate these inabilities.[13] Accordingly, if God is temporal, He is not omnipotent. Hence if God is omnipotent, He is timeless.

Timelessness and the Modal Status of Time

We have already argued that nothing can be merely contingently temporal. So if God is temporal, God is necessarily temporal. If God is necessarily temporal, time is an absolutely necessary precondition of God's own existence. Thus if God exists necessarily (as was argued above), so does time, for He cannot exist unless it does. But time exists contingently. Hence either God exists contingently or God is timeless. Hence again, as God exists necessarily, God is timeless.

Timelessness and the Creation of Time

If God is temporal, God is necessarily temporal. If God is necessarily temporal, time is an absolutely necessary precondition of God's own existence. So if God is essentially temporal, then God's creating time would involve His making His own existence possible. If it is absurd to talk of something making itself actual, it is even more so to speak of a thing making itself possible. So if God is essentially temporal, He cannot create time, and He cannot destroy it unless He can commit suicide. It could be replied to this objection that God could (say) act at t to ensure the existence of time at t + 1, act at t + 2 to ensure the existence of time at t + 3, and so on—so that every moment of time is created by God in a prior moment of time, and so God is responsible for the existence of time moment by moment. But this scenario would amount to God's everlastingly preserving time rather then His creating time. To create time is to account for the fact that the set of times has

13. A restriction on an omnipotent being's power is plausible if, and perhaps only if, it can be shown to be not "really" but only verbally a restriction, as is the case, e.g., with the "inability" to create the logically impossible. For discussion of some such plausible restrictions, see Thomas Flint and Alfred Freddoso, "Maximal Power," in Thomas Morris, ed., *The Concept of God* (New York: Oxford University Press, 1987), pp. 134–167.

members. If God acts from within time, at (say) t, to create t + 1, then when God acts, it is already true prior to His action that the set of times has members, and so it is false that God accounts for its having members. Thus again, if God is essentially temporal, He cannot be time's creator. In fact, this last result holds even if God is (per impossible) not essentially temporal. So long as God acts only *at* a moment of time, then it does not matter if He *could* have acted from outside time: the fact remains that God cannot account for the set of times' having members. For suppose that God acts only at times—i.e., that for every divine action, there is a time t at which God performs it—and consider God's action at some t.

At t, God cannot create times prior to t, if (as I assume) He has no causal power over the past. Nor can God create t at t. For if God acts and exists at t, and God's action presupposes God's existence, then God's action at t presupposes His existence at t, and hence presupposes the existence of t. Suppose that God *could have* acted from beyond time. If He had, His creation of t from beyond time would not presuppose His existing at t. But even so, God's actually existing at t is among the actual conditions of God's actual action. That the action could have taken place had a different condition (God's existing timelessly) taken this condition's place does not alter that fact. No action can account for the obtaining of its own actual conditions. For if the condition's obtaining at t helps to explain the action's taking place, and the action explains the condition's obtaining at t, the condition helps at t to explain its own obtaining at t. But nothing can contribute at t to explaining its own obtaining at t.

It seems, then, that at t God can at most create times later than t. Hence for every time t, there is a time which God cannot have created: no action of God located at any time can account for the existence of all times. If this is so, at every time, the set of times has members independent of God's action. That is, at no time is it the case that there would have been no times save for an action of God at that time. So at every time it is false that God's action at that time accounts for the fact that the set of times has members. Therefore no action of God located at any time can create time.

The concept of God includes the note that God is the source of all that is other than Himself. The concept of God is such that if theists can find a way to trace some reality back to God, they feel impelled to do so. God can be the creator of time only if He is timeless. If (as I would argue) only His being temporal could be an impediment to the claim that God creates time, then theists will be impelled to affirm that God is the creator of time and therefore timeless, provided that the claim that God is timeless should prove tenable.

Timelessness and the Creation of the Universe

If only a timeless God can create time, then only an atemporal God can create the entire universe of temporal things. Just what is involved creating the entire universe of temporal things depends on what "the entire universe" includes. On a substantialist account of space-time, in addition to all material spatiotemporal things there is also a further particular, space-time. On this view, the universe consists of all material things plus space-time itself as one more "spatiotemporal thing," and so God creates the entire universe of temporal things only if He creates space-time. On a relational account of space-time, the existing of space and time is consequent on the existence of spatiotemporal things, as it consists in relations among these things which obtain if and only if the things themselves exist. So once more, if God creates the entire universe, God creates space-time, for He creates things as standing in the appropriate relations. For God to create the whole universe of temporal things, then, He must also create time. But then per our earlier argument, a temporal God *cannot* create the entire universe of temporal things. So if God *can* create the entire universe of temporal things, God is timeless.

Timelessness and the Beginning of Time

Theists would like to trace to God not only the existence of time but also its large-scale features. But if God is temporal, there is at least one large-scale feature of time for which He cannot be responsible: it cannot be up to God whether time had a beginning. For if God is temporal, then if (as I would claim) there is no causal power over the past, there cannot be a time at which God makes a choice that is responsible for there having been infinite time, i.e., for time's having had no beginning.

Suppose that t is such a time. Then there was an infinite period of time before t, or there was a finite period of time before t, or t is time's first moment. On the first alternative, infinite time has already existed, and so its existence is not up to God unless we credit Him with the power not to undo but to effect the past, and say that there has always been a universe because at t God chose for there to have been one. But this sort of power over the past does not seem possible.[14] On the

14. Quentin Smith suggests that a series of finite intervals of time could have order-type $\omega + \omega$, i.e., stand in 1:1 correspondence with the series of natural numbers 0, 2, 4 . . . 1, 3, 5 . . . (Smith, "A New Typology," pp. 314–319). In this case, one infinite period of time comes after another, and so it would seem possible that during the first infinite period of time, God wills that the second infinite period of time exist. But this would not affect the text's argument. In such a case, there would be an infinite period of

second alternative, time has had a beginning, and so God can effect it that time has been beginningless only if He is able to wipe out the past and replace it with a new one. But there is little reason to believe that this sort of power over the past is possible either. Let us consider the third alternative. God could effect it that time is beginningless by annihilating t. For if time is a series of moments with a first moment t, then between t and every other moment there is some other moment—that is, for every moment t* such that t* ≠ t, there is a moment closer to t than t* is. Thus if t were annihilated, the series of moments left behind would be one that approached ever closer to its previously existent limit, t, without ever reaching t. Such a series would have no first moment. God could also effect it that t is not time's beginning by effecting it that there are moments prior to t. Let us consider whether God could annihilate t. God cannot act at t to effect it that t does not exist: if God annihilates t, then it must be false that God acted at t to do so. For if God acts at t, t exists and so is not annihilated. If t was time's first moment, there was no time before t, and so a temporal God could not have prevented t's existence. But then God can annihilate t only from some temporal location later than t, by an exercise of power not just to alter but to eliminate the past—which seems impossible. Hence God could effect it that t is not time's first moment only if He could act at t to make it the case that before t there were other times. But this would be power to effect the past. We have already rejected this sort of power.

So if we deny power over the past, then no divine choice at any time could effect it that time had no beginning. If time had no beginning and God is temporal and God lacks the relevant sorts of power over the past, then, God is not responsible for time's having had no beginning. This is so even if every time t has existed because God willed prior to t that t exist. That God can beginninglessly be responsible for time's existing does not entail that God can be responsible for time's existing beginninglessly. Even if God is causally responsible for the existence of all of infinite time, it does not follow that he is responsible for its infinity: though He acts to create it, He may not be in control of its existence.

Whether a proposition P is true is up to an agent A only if A has libertarian freedom with respect to P. That is, P's truth is up to A only

---

time that God could not have chosen to have—call it ℵ01—and another, ℵ02, that God had chosen to have. But then the totality of time, ℵ01 + ℵ02, would not be a period God had chosen. The text deals solely with the question of whether the existence of the totality of time is up to God.

if it is in A's power both to render P true and to render P false. Thus if it is not up to an agent whether it is true that P, it is not up to that agent whether it is true that ~P. Accordingly, if God is temporal, then if time had a beginning, its having had one was not up to Him. No divine choice at any time could be responsible for time's having had a beginning if it had one. We can reach this conclusion in a second way. For if we rule out power over the past, then the only moment at which God could effect it that time has a first moment is time's first moment: any moment thereafter would be too late. But if God is temporal, God exists and chooses only at times: His existence presupposes time's existence. Hence time's first moment must exist in order for God to choose that it exist. (If on the contrary that moment's existence presupposes God's existence, then God exists "logically before" that moment does. If so, God in effect makes "outside" time His choice that that moment exist—in which case He is intrinsically timeless.) Even if God's choice occurs at that moment, it presupposes that moment's existence and so cannot account for that moment's existence.

No divine choice at any time can be responsible for time's having or lacking a beginning. If God is temporal, all of His choices are choices at times. So if God is temporal, God is not in control of this large-scale feature of time, even if His activity causally accounts for it. On the other hand, if God is timeless, God can control whether time had a beginning, for then it is not the case that His choice about the shape of time takes place at some time. Accordingly, if the shape of time is up to God, God is timeless. More generally, a timeless God would have a greater control over time than a temporal God. So if it is a perfection to have a greater control over the large-scale features of creation, a timeless God would be more perfect in this respect than a temporal God. Thus if God is maximally perfect, then God is timeless unless His being so is somehow incompatible with other perfections we believe Him to have (and these other perfections are more central to the concept of God, and so take precedence over timelessness in this concept). In other words, if God is maximally perfect, then if it is possible that God is timeless, then God is timeless.

Timelessness, Creation, and Providence

If time is an absolute entity on its own, in addition to temporal things, then if time exists contingently and God is temporal, there is a contingent entity that God cannot have created. Thus it is false that God is the creator of all contingent things and false that God can create all possible contingent entities. Suppose, on the other hand, that time is

not an absolute entity on its own. In this case, the existing of time =
the obtaining of a set of temporal relations between temporal things.
Given this identity, to create time would be to account directly or
indirectly for the obtaining of all these temporal relations. As we have
seen, if God is temporal, God is not time's creator. But if time is not
absolute, then if God accounted directly or indirectly for the obtaining
of all temporal relations, God would be time's creator. So if time is not
absolute and God is temporal, there obtains at least one temporal
relation for the obtaining of which God is in no way responsible, either
directly (by causing) or indirectly (by permitting). But then God is not
in provident control of the whole of history, contrary to primary
religious discourse. So if, as theists insist, God is the creator of all
contingent things, can create all possible contingent things, and is in
provident control of history, God is timeless.

Timelessness as Metaphysically
Superior to Temporality

We have seen Augustine argue that timeless beings have a higher
degree of existence than temporal beings, and we have seen reason to
say that his way of speaking is coherent and his conclusion is true.
Accordingly, it would most befit the claim that God is a perfect being
for God to be timeless.

Timeless Life and Time's Tooth

As Boethius notes, whatever has a location in time is ipso facto
unable to enjoy what is past or future for it: its past is gone, and its
future has not yet come. Let us focus on the pain of pastness. Even
perfect memory of one's past is a far different thing than actually living
it; the past itself is *lost,* and no memory, however complete, can take its
place—for confirmation, ask a widower if his grief would be abated
were his memory of his wife enhanced in vividness and detail. Further,
whatever has unique, irreplaceable qualities is lost through time's passage, even if other things of value in turn arrive. As L. J. Tomkinson
notes, if a parent can mourn the loss of a stage of a child's life, a fortiori
an omniscient temporal God would mourn the loss of His beloved
creatures as they are no more.[15]

Robert Cook, concurring with Swinburne, replies that "an omnipotent deity could recreate qualitatively similar events whenever he

15. L. J. Tomkinson, "Divine Sempiternity and Atemporality," *Religious Studies* 18
(1982), 177–189.

chose."[16] But Cook is constrained to admit that even this might be impossible where free creatures are involved: perhaps no creature could ever freely recreate the uniqueness of another person. Suppose, moreover, that a grieving widower were offered, on the day of his wife's death, a mate qualitatively indistinguishable from his dead wife. I think that if he accepted this offer and ceased to grieve, we would think him at best deluded and at worst crass. For though his new mate would be just like his wife, *it would not be her.* So if the widower took his new mate to be his wife revived, he would be deluded. If he knew it not to be her and just did not care, he would be crass. He would lack respect both for his wife's individual personhood and for the irreplaceable history he shared with her. God cannot be deluded. If He is morally perfect, God will not fail to value His creatures as they should be valued. Hence God would not replace His beloved creatures with qualitatively indistinguishable counterparts even if He could.

On the other hand, if God is timeless, He lives all His life at once—there is no part of His life, including those parts He shares with beloved creatures, which He ever ceases to live. So the joy of a timeless God would suffer no tinge of loss. Accordingly, if God's joy is the most perfect sort, God is timeless. Hasker has suggested that any argument that it is better for God to experience the world timelessly than temporally will draw at some level on some sort of general metaphysical preference for changelessness over change.[17] Now we have already seen that this preference can be supported. But in any event, such a preference does not seem to figure in the present argument. The argument draws only on a very concrete and very intuitive claim, that it is better to be with those one loves than to remember them.

Timelessness and Perfect Knowledge of the Past

God is said to be a perfect knower. A perfect knower has the best possible justification for His beliefs. But where these concern events in time, the best justification is to be there yourself and be in direct cognitive contact with them as they occur. If God is temporal, God knows what is past for Him not by direct cognitive contact but by memory. If God is timeless, nothing is past for Him, and God can know what is past (for us) by direct cognitive contact. Accordingly, if God is temporal, then if possibly God is timeless, God's mode of knowledge of the past is less perfect than it could be. I argue that God is

16. Cook, "God, Time, and Freedom," p. 86. Cf. Swinburne, *Coherence*, p. 220.
17. Hasker, *God*, pp. 179–183.

possibly timeless. Hence if God is a maximally perfect knower, God is timeless.[18]

Timelessness, Freedom, and Foreknowledge

We have seen that the claim that God is timeless does reconcile human freedom and what is usually called divine foreknowledge of our future free acts.[19] At the very least, this provides some support for the claim that God is timeless: every advantage this claim purchases is another reason to adopt it. If it is the case (as I have briefly argued) that no other adequate resolution of the freedom-foreknowledge problem is possible, theists must either embrace divine timelessness or reject either divine foreknowledge or human freedom.

Timelessness, Omniscience, and Divine Dialogue

As Alston has pointed out, there is a problem with the claim that an omniscient being can engage in genuine dialogue with others. For an omniscient being will foreknow all the contributions to dialogue its interlocutors will make and will have all its responses worked out in advance: it will even foreknow its own responses. But if God knows in advance all that will transpire, the exchange between God and human beings is not in the meatiest sense a dialogue, for the truest, meatiest sort of dialogue is one in which each participant works out his or her own contribution *as* the other makes his or hers, each providing occasion for the other newly to mint a fresh response, on the spot.

---

18. If God is timeless and also simple, this argument *may* lose its force, *if* the only acceptable models for a simple being's knowledge involve no direct cognitive contact with creatures. But contact-involving models of a simple being's knowledge are available. For instance, one could argue that a simple being knows all created SOAs, including those involving free creaturely actions, by effectively willing the obtaining of all SOAs. (For an argument that this is compatible with creaturely freedom, see Mann, "God's Freedom.") This would involve a sort of direct cognitive contact. For if God is simple, God's will = God's knowledge, and God's will is in "direct contact" with its objects. So perhaps this argument can retain its force even if God is not just timeless but simple. Further, even if the claim that God knows the actions of free creatures by effectively willing them is false (because if God effectively wills creatures' actions, they are not free), one can maintain that God knows in this way the histories of non-free creatures (insofar as these do not depend on the actions of free creatures). But then at least *some* of a timeless, simple God's knowledge involves direct cognitive contact with entities and events that to us are past. Given this, the text's argument goes through.

19. Again, if God is timeless, then on the Anselmian view of time and eternity, the term "foreknowledge" is not appropriate. For on this view, God knows in eternity events with which He is timelessly copresent, while within temporal frames of reference one cannot locate God's knowledge in the past, present, or future.

Alston notes that if God is timeless, then though He is omniscient, He does not know His partner's action *in advance*. Instead, on our Anselmian theory, within time, God's part in the dialogue cannot strictly be called past, present, or future, whereas within eternity it is copresent with His partners' parts and may *logically* presuppose or be presupposed by them, as the case requires. (I have more to say about this later.) Thus timelessness reconciles strict omniscience and genuine dialogue. So if God is both strictly omniscient and in the fullest sense a partner in dialogue with human beings, God is timeless.[20]

Timelessness and God's Foreknowledge of His Own Acts

Some philosophers have contended that if God has foreknowledge of all future actions, He foreknows His own actions, and that if God foreknows His own future choices, He cannot make them freely.[21] These writers premise that

    i.   any agent A can choose freely to do only what appears to A to be one alternative among a field of open alternatives,

    ii.   an alternative cannot appear open to A unless it appears open relative to what A believes,

    iii.   an alternative appears open relative to what A believes only if A does not already believe that he or she will do it or refrain from doing it, and

    iv.   if God is omniscient, then for any action and time t, God knows prior to t whether He will or will not do that action at t.

I am not sure that these premises are true. Premise (i) suggests that a choice is free only if the chooser believes (or would if made aware of the options believe) that the choice is free or believes (or would believe) claims that in fact entail that it is free. This thesis is questionable. Again, in (i) and (iii), the term "open" can mean "not yet chosen" or "choosable." Taking "open" the first way, (iii) is trivially true but (i) begs the question at issue. Taking "open" the second way, (i) is trivially true but (iii) is flatly false: one can know that an alternative is choosable while also knowing that one will not choose it.

20. This entire argument derives from Alston, "Divine-Human Dialogue and the Nature of God," in *Divine Nature*.

21. For what follows, see Tomis Kapitan, "Agency and Omniscience," read to the Society of Christian Philosophers at Wofford College, April 1988. Carl Ginet and Richard LaCroix have offered related arguments.

These criticisms may or may not be decisive. But if some argument along the lines (i)–(iv) suggest is otherwise acceptable, God's being timeless will enable one to deal with it. For such an argument contends that God's *fore*knowing of His choices renders them unfree via (i). If God is timeless, God does not *fore*know His choices; His knowing what He does is not really prior to His doing it. Thus God's knowledge logically cannot constrain His choice in the manner the argument envisions.

The Road Ahead

I take it, then, that there is a strong prima facie case for the claim that God is timeless. But even if God must be timeless, the question still stands: *can* he be so? For if God must be timeless and cannot, what follows is not that God is nonetheless timeless but that the concept of God is inconsistent. By arguing that God must be timeless, then, I put myself at risk of being forced to grant that God necessarily does not exist. I must therefore pass to the defensive and argue, against the available objections, that God *can* be timeless.

Timelessness
and Personhood

Many objections to the claim that God is timeless center on the claim that a timeless being cannot have the personal attributes central to the Western theistic concept of God. It is argued that a timeless being cannot live, be conscious, be an agent, be free, have knowledge, or (more specifically) deliberate, plan, or remember. Let us turn to these objections.

Mind and Time

J. R. Lucas argues that conscious states or events must occur in temporal sequence with other conscious states or events, in God as in us: "God is ; . . a conscious personal being, and time is an inevitable concomitant of consciousness . . . I cannot conceive of a mind being conscious of something about whom the question 'when' does not arise . . . I cannot enjoy any state of consciousness at all without having some idea of its being before or after some other states of consciousness, and being something of which it must always be intelligible to ask when I had it."[1] Now it is a fact that all human mental events and states occur at some particular time and in some temporal sequence. But that all *human* mental events and states *do* so hardly entails that *all* mental events and states *must* do so. One could, however, argue that all mental events or states must occur at a time in this way. If we are to apply mental-event or -state terms to something, the mind in question must manifest itself in changes within our environment. Causing

---

1. J. R. Lucas, *A Treatise on Time and Space* (London: Methuen, 1973), pp. 30, 7.

changes requires that the mind itself change and so change at a time. Thus causing events in time requires that the agent him- or herself be in time.[2] In this way, one could conclude that anything that we could ever have reason to call a mental state or event must occur at a time.

I argue below that a timeless being *can* be causally responsible for changes that occur in time. If one can, a timeless mind could manifest itself in environmental changes. But even if my argument is wholly unsuccessful, and everything we could have reason to call mental must be temporal, this does *not* entail that everything that *is* mental is temporal. I find nothing odd in allowing to be a mind a thing that we could not even in principle have reason to call a mind; why assume that the reasons we can have to say this exhaust the reasons there can be to say this? (For that matter, as part of an unfashionable realism, I would be prepared to claim that something could be a mind which no other being could even in principle have reason to call a mind.) Finally, even if God's being or having a mind must make the question "when did God think so-and-so" appropriate, as eternity is logically speaking a time, "at eternity" is a sufficient answer to it.

The claim that a mental state or event must be conceived as involved in a temporal series of mental events or states can be traced back at least to Hume.[3] The best way to counter it will be to describe a mental event or state that need not be seen as involved in such a sequence. Lucas himself may be committed to one. For he claims that God is temporal, he seems to claim that God's present experience is or can be of infinite duration,[4] and he also holds that God need not have created entities other than Himself.[5] If all three claims are true, then perhaps God could have a single experience (of Himself and the infinity of an empty time) that would endure infinitely, without beginning or end and without being preceded or succeeded by any other experience. But perhaps Lucas could reply that he is claiming only that every mental event or state is *possibly* before or after other mental events or states and that even the single divine experience just described satisfies this condition. I will therefore now try to describe a mental "event"[6] that is not

2. See Pike, *God*, pp. 125–127, chap. 6, passim.

3. David Hume, *Dialogues on Natural Religion*, pt. 4, in *The Empiricists* (Garden City, N.Y.: Doubleday, 1974), pp. 458–459.

4. Some authors have claimed that God's experienced or "specious" present could involve the whole duration of infinite time. See, e.g., Josiah Royce, *The World and the Individual* (New York: Macmillan, 1901), vol. 2, chap. 3, passim; Jantzen, *God's World*. But I am not wholly sure Lucas means to claim this. His language is elegant and allusive but therefore elusive.

5. Lucas, *Treatise*, pp. 300–301, 306.

6. The term "event" is scare-quoted because we often use this term to indicate mental happenings that do not persist (as versus states, which do persist). The per-

possibly part of a temporal series of mental events. I contend that a
timeless being could be involved in a sort of event that figures in our
understanding of sentences.[7]

Understanding and Time

To understand a sentence is to know something—namely, what the
sentence says. I will now argue that a timeless being could have this
sort of knowledge. The first step of this argument will be to show that
understanding a sentence does not take time. The second step will be
to argue that such an understanding need not be located in time.

Understanding can be a process or what Ryle called an achievement.
Understanding a philosophical argument is a process. Understanding
what a sentence says need not be. It can instead be an achievement.
Consider your understanding of the sentence "this is a book." As you
read, you recognize the shapes on the page as words. You become
ready to assign them a meaning once you have seen their entire senten-
tial context. Once you have read the entire sentence, you "just see"
what it says: comprehension is there all at once. This does not involve
any process of coming to see. Rather, first you do not yet understand
the sentence, and then all at once you do understand it. To "just see" in
this way what the sentence says is to achieve its understanding. Now
our ways to become acquainted with sentences may involve processes.
We may say words to ourselves or visually scan pages or attend to
speech. But these are not processes of coming to understand. They are
rather processes by which we become acquainted with what we understand. Saying the sentence to oneself in different ways, etc., is not part
of "seeing" what it says (as distinct from jogging one's memory for
words' meaning, etc.). Nor is any such process of becoming acquainted
necessarily part of understanding a sentence. It seems possible that God
create someone who has at the first instant of his or her existence an
apparent memory of having read the sentence "I am God's creation"
and so understands what this sentence says at his or her first moment.

---

sistent/nonpersistent distinction may not apply to a timeless being, if a persistent entity
is one that exists at more than one moment of time, and a nonpersistent entity is one
that exists at just one moment of time. For a state of a timeless being exists at no
moment in time. Thus (I suppose) if the persistent/nonpersistent distinction is as
described, one could as easily call what I describe a state.

7. In this argument I use the term "proposition" repeatedly. I mean by this only
whatever it is that accounts by its commonality for sentences' expressing the same
claim. That is, I use the term "proposition" as a placemarker indicating the phenomena
theories about propositions try to explain, not to assume or offer any such theory.

"Just seeing" what the sentence "this is a book" says is not a process. It does not pass through stages during which partial understandings accumulate. Rather, you see it at all only if you have seen it as a whole, and you see it as a whole only all at once. To be seeing it is to have seen it, i.e., to have completed the seeing of it; the first instant of seeing it at all is also the first instant of having fully seen it. In the same way, to be achieving this is to have achieved it, and to be understanding in this way is to have understood. So this sort of achieving of understanding does not take time: achieving understanding is instantaneous. Nor does having "just seen" what a sentence says entail having gone through a process of understanding. It is not a result of any such process. Nor does having "just seen" what a sentence says presuppose a process of becoming acquainted with what one understands.

As achieving understanding is a durationless event, we do not experience it independently. All of our experiences are experiences of the contents of some stretch of time. To achieve understanding of a word or sentence is (normally) to begin to have the disposition of understanding that word or sentence. So we usually experience the enduring state of understanding that an achieving of understanding inaugurates. We also often experience understanding after not having understood. We experience a transition from not understanding to understanding. In so doing, we have an experience that includes beginning to understand or achieving understanding. So our experience includes this and also includes something else, and even if the achievement is (in some sense) *in* our experience, it goes by too quickly (so to speak) for us to note it as a distinct event. But whether or not they in some sense appear in our experience, we have reason to believe that achievings of understanding occur. For we have argued that there are events of beginning, and achievings of understanding are often beginnings.

Even if they are not beginnings, achievings are still instantaneous. To win a race is normally to begin to have won it; the moment of winning is always the first moment of having won. But it seems conceivable that the last moment of time be the very moment at which the first runner in a certain race hits the finish line. If this occurred, the runner would win and would have won. Arguably the runner would not begin to have won, precisely because no state of having won would follow that first moment. But even if the runner would not begin to have won, the winning would still be an instantaneous event.

This event would be so by virtue of being an achieving. It is not even possible that it take time to win a race (in the achievement sense, as distinct from taking time to run the race and thereby win). To win a race is to change from not having won to having won. If this took any time, it would have to pass through intermediate stages, and there would have to be a time when it was no longer true that the runner had not won and not yet true that the runner had won. But this is not possible. In a race, there is no third state: either one has won or one has not. In the same way, it cannot take time to pass from not understanding a sentence to understanding it, as we typically do in achieving understanding.

To achieve understanding is to know something occurrently—namely, what a sentence says. Achieving understanding is a durationless event. Hence it is also a durationless sort of knowing. Apparently, then, to know something occurrently does not require duration of any sort.

That an achieving of understanding is a durationless event does not entail that it, or any other durationless event, can occur independent of a continuing process or disposition of which it constitutes a boundary. One can doubt that this is in fact possible. Achievings are "point events," events with location but no duration. We generally view points solely as (involved in) the boundaries of extensions. Moreover, we generally refer to them via the extensions whose boundaries they are, or via a system of coordinates that (if Strawson is right) requires a system of spatially or temporally extended objects for its mooring.

I want to suggest, nonetheless, that an achieving of understanding could occur even if no continuing processes or states occurred. To begin with, if achievings of understanding do not result from prior processes of coming to understand, it is hard to see why an achieving of understanding would have to supervene on any prior process in order to exist. It seems possible, again, that God create a being that understands a proposition from the first moment of its existence. Such a being's understanding would not require the prior existence of *any* processes. (Note, incidentally, that per earlier argument, this being's achieving of understanding would not be a change in it. As we saw earlier, an event at a time t is a change in a thing only if the thing existed before t and was in a different state before t. If a being understands a proposition at its first moment of existence, it was not in any state before this moment, and so this understanding is not a change in it, though it is an occurrence.)

So I suggest that an achieving of understanding can occur without any prior process. If such an event can occur independent of concurrent and subsequent processes as well, then such an event can be wholly independent of processes. What of concurrent processes? Only living things can understand, and human or biological life exists only if various organic processes go on. But we cannot let this count as an argument that there cannot be an achieving of understanding the existence of which logically requires no concurrent processes. For perhaps human or biological organisms are not the only sorts of thing that can be alive. If on other counts we can make sense of the claim that an achieving of understanding involves no processes, this will just be reason to conclude that life itself does not necessarily involve processes. So perhaps there can be an achieving of understanding presupposing the existence of no concurrent processes.

Let us now ask about subsequent processes. It does not seem impossible that an achieving of understanding be, say, the last event in a universe, i.e., that an achieving of understanding occur at the last moment at which a universe exists. Just as the last moment of a universe's existence might be the very moment a runner reaches a race's finish line, the last moment of a universe's existence might be the very moment a reader "sees" what a sentence says. But if an achieving of understanding requires the subsequent existence of a disposition of understanding, this is in fact not possible. So it seems that an achieving of understanding can occur even if no subsequent state of understanding exists. If this is not required, it is hard to see why any other subsequent continuing state or process would be.

I suggest further that an achieving of understanding could be the first *and* last event in some universe. If an achieving of understanding could be the first event, this is because of what it is to achieve understanding. If it is, then it holds of every achieving of understanding that as such it could be first. Again, if an achieving of understanding could be the last event, this is because of what it is to achieve understanding. So it holds of every achieving of understanding that as such it could be last. If these claims hold of every achieving of understanding, then it is possible that there be an achieving of understanding which is both a first and a last event.

If there can be a universe whose first and last event is an achieving of understanding, then achievings of understanding need not occur during processes. For any process takes time. If so, then any universe in which a process occurs cannot have one and the same instantaneous event as both its first and its last event. Rather, there must be time between the first and last events in such a universe. So a universe whose first and last event is a single achieving of understanding is ipso facto a universe in which no processes go on while this event occurs. Perhaps, then, achievings of understanding can occur even if no processes take place. Perhaps too, then—since understanding entails being alive—it is not the case that being alive requires processes of living.

If there can be a universe in which an achieving of understanding is both the first and the last event, then surely there can be a universe in which an achieving of understanding is the only event that ever occurs. For there just seems no necessity that there be something else going on while such an event occurs. Further, it seems possible that this achieving of understanding not be a change from a prior state of this universe, for as we have seen, achievings of understandings are not necessarily changes. So it seems possible that there be a one-state universe, a universe such that some being's achieving understanding constitutes the only state this universe is ever in.

It is also surely conceivable that in this one-state universe a relational theory of time is true—that is, there is time only if there are events ordered as earlier and later. But if a relational theory holds in this one-state universe, then in it an event of understanding occurs, yet there is literally no time at which it occurs: nor need there be, as this event is not a change. If it is possible at all that there be a one-state universe, is there anything incoherent or absurd about there being no time at which this universe's one state occurs? If there is not, then apparently we have conceived of a timeless event of achieving understanding.

There is a good case to be made that possibly some understanding being exists outside *our* time series. For we have seen that possibly there are other time series, and there seems no reason to say that it is impossible that beings rather like ourselves dwell there. As we have seen, an alternate time series has to our time series the same relation a timeless being would have. Hence it seems possible that a being with the relation to our time of a timeless being think and achieve understanding. So it is not possible that there be a timeless event of achieving understanding or that a timeless being achieve understanding only if something about the nature of thinking or understanding requires being located in some time series or other.

But why think that this is required, if achievings of understanding are not necessarily changes? I can think of one way to argue that this is required. Even if it is otherwise conceivable that there exist an achieving of understanding that is independent of temporal processes, etc., perhaps there cannot be such an event. For a being that achieves understanding has understanding. Arguably a being that *has* understanding must be able to possess and manifest its knowledge. Again, arguably manifesting its knowledge would take time or else locate it in time. This is essentially Nelson Pike's argument against the claim that a timeless being can have knowledge.[8] But we will see that a timeless being can be responsible for temporal effects if a timeless being can

8. See Pike, *God*, pp. 125–127, chap. 6, passim.

create the universe. If one can do so, a timeless being can manifest its knowledge while remaining timeless, and there remains no obstacle to claiming that a knowing or thinking being can exist timelessly: if we can conceive of kinds of thinking or understanding that do not extend over time and need not be located in time, we can conceive of kinds of thinking or understanding that a timeless being could perform. Moreover, as we have seen that whatever is timeless is necessarily so, to conceive of a timeless act of thinking or understanding is to conceive of an act that is not possibly part of a temporal sequence. Finally, whatever thinks or understands is alive.[9] So apparently we can conceive a timeless being to be alive—if, that is, we can maintain that a timeless being can create the universe. So we now turn to the issue of creation.

Creation and Timelessness

One hoary objection to the claim that a timeless God creates is that at least within the Western religions, to create a world entails *beginning* a world and so entails beginning to create, after first not creating. Augustine formulates this objection in his *Confessions:* "What was God doing before he made heaven and earth? If . . . he did nothing, why was this not so from then on and always? . . . If any new change or new will were to arise in God, in order to establish a creature he had never established before, how then would there be true eternity?"[10] We can dissolve this argument merely by bearing in mind the implications of God's being timeless.

If God is timeless, there is no before and after in His life.[11] No phase of His life is earlier or later than any other phase, for only temporal durations and their phases stand in these relations. As it lacks earlier and later parts, a timeless life *has* no phases, even if it is somehow extended. So if God is timeless and a world or time exists, there is no phase of His life during which He is without a world or time or has not yet decided to create them, even if the world or time had a beginning.

9. This strategy of argument goes back at least as far as Aquinas, *SCG* I. For argument that nothing can be both timeless and alive, see William Kneale, "Time and Eternity," 99, 107.

10. "quid faciebat Deus, antequam faceret caelum et terram? Si enim . . . non operabatur aliquid, cur non sic semper et deinceps . . . si enim ullus motus in deo novus extitit et voluntas nova, ut creaturam conderet quam numquam ante condiderat, quomodo iam vera aeternitas . . . ?" Augustine, *Ouevres*, vol. 14, pp. 290–292, 272, ll. 9–15.

11. If God has QTE, there are earlier and later points in His life, but He lives these all at once rather than living one before He lives another. But I am not maintaining that God has QTE and so ignore this complication.

For a life without phases cannot have one phase that is without the world or time and another phase that is with it. The whole of God's life is identical with the "phase" of it during which the world or time exists and during which God has decided to create them.

Further, whether or not the world or time had a first moment, there is no sense in which God from His own perspective exists "before" the world or time. As there is no before or after in a timeless being's life, a timeless God cannot exist "eternally before" the world or time. As the concept of temporal priority does not apply to a being not located in time, a timeless God cannot be temporally before the world or time. Whether or not time has a first moment, then, there is no moment of time when God does not exist with time, and there is no "phase" of eternity that exists "before" time exists. So a timeless God's relation to time is precisely the same whether or not time has a first moment. Moreover, even if there was "empty time" before the material universe began, God from His own perspective was in no sense ever without the material universe. For though time existed temporally before a universe existed, the phase of God's life during which time alone exists = the phase of God's life during which the world and time exist.

God need not *begin* to do anything, then, in order to create a world with a beginning. That action that from temporal perspectives is God's beginning time and the universe is in eternity just the timeless obtaining of a causal dependence or sustaining relation between God and a world whose time has a first moment. If we can make sense of timeless causal dependence, then, creation will pose no further problem.

Sustaining and Timelessness

Pike doubts that such sense can be made. He argues that any intelligible account of a sustaining relation must have the consequence that the sustaining action occurs (and so the sustaining agent exists) at the same time the sustained SOA obtains.[12] But on the present account, one can simply grant Pike his point. In the reference frame of eternity, the time at which the action occurs = the time at which the SOA is sustained = eternity. In other reference frames this is not so. Rather, in these, the time at which the SOA is sustained is some particular point in time, and the action nonetheless occurs at eternity. But we can accept this with equanimity. STR allows that events or states simultaneous in one frame of reference may be nonsimultaneous in others.

One could urge in response that STR also insists that there are the

12. Pike, *God*, pp. 113–117.

same temporal relations between causes in all frames of reference. But the foundation of this relativistic demand is the finite velocity of causal signals (i.e., that no causal impulse can travel faster than light). As divine causality is not physical and does not work by the transmission of a physical signal, it escapes this requirement, though we can nonetheless apply in its case a *conceptual* move (the relativity of simultaneity) that special relativity shows to be legitimate.

Again, one could argue that the event of God's sustaining the world includes the event of the world's being sustained and then question whether it makes sense to have components of the same event "scattered" over time and eternity. I deal with this at greater length in Chapter 16. For now, I can note that there is nothing unusual in a single event's having a scattered location. Suppose that I shoot Al Capone and he dies an hour later, and let us ask when the event of Leftow's killing Capone occurred. It did not occur at the time I shot him, for he did not die then. Nor did it occur when he died, for I was not then doing anything to him. Nor does it seem reasonable to say that the event took an hour, even if my shooting him caused a one-hour process of Capone's dying, for I was not doing anything to him for an hour. One reasonable response might be that the event has two temporally discrete components—that part of it took place when I shot him and the rest took place an hour later, or perhaps that the event does not divide into parts, but instead simply does take place in a temporally scattered locale. If this is reasonable, it might also be reasonable to say that the event of God's sustaining the world is "scattered" over time and eternity. I discuss objections based not on scattered location as such but on scattering over time and eternity in Chapter 16. For now, I can suggest that if logically, eternity is a "time," and if temporally scattered events are possible, these objections may not be viable.

I wonder, though, whether Pike's claim that sustaining involves temporal simultaneity is strictly true. Suppose that we adopt some counterfactual account of sustaining relations: suppose, that is, that we say, e.g., that

> S. A sustains B = df. (i) A and B occur contingently, (ii) B occurs continuously over more than one temporal position, (iii) A does not occur later than B does, (iv) A and B do not occur in and are not discrete temporal series, (v) in every nonactual world W such that no world is more like the actual world than W, A occurs only if B occurs continuously over more than one temporal position,[13] and (vi) were A not to

---

13. Clause (v) serves to block certain counterexamples to which some counterfactual analyses of causal dependence relations are prey. See, e.g., John Pollock, *The Foundations*

occur, then if B's continuance is not overdetermined or redundantly caused, B would not do so.[14]

We might need to add further conditions to (vi) to render (S) truly adequate. For if B's continuance is not overdetermined (i.e., if there are not two events that are each causally sufficient to sustain B) and B's occurrence is not redundantly caused (i.e., if it is not the case that A sustains B, but had A not occurred, some other event C would have sustained B), there may still be other situations that could complicate this account of why B occurs.[15] But the form of (vi) is such that inserting these further conditions will only add to the plausibility of (S). The crucial point about these further conditions is this. Nothing in (S) forces us to say that A has a temporal location or a temporal relation to B, for a timeless being does not exist later than any temporal thing. It is plausible that no further conditions will require us to render A temporal either.

(S) certainly appears intelligible, despite Pike. (S) can apply to a timeless being if a timeless being can have a contingent act of will, for then this timeless act of will could sustain a contingent being in accordance with (S). Nothing we have said rules out the claim that a timeless being can have a contingent act of will. So to this extent at least, (S) seems able to let a timeless being sustain something contingent.[16] One might ask whether (S) expresses a genuine relation of causal dependence. In response we can note that (S) is deliberately modeled on Davis Lewis' counterfactual account of causal dependence,

CD. *e* is causally dependent on *c* = df. were *c* to occur, *e* would occur (in symbols, $c \:\square\!\!\rightarrow e$), and were *c* to not occur, *e* would not occur,[17]

---

of *Philosophical Semantics* (Princeton, N.J.: Princeton University Press, 1984), pp. 148–149. Clause (i)'s stipulation that A and B occur contingently is similarly motivated. Despite this stipulation, I believe that (S) will apply to the case of a simple timeless being, but I defer consideration of whether it does to this volume's sequel, *Divine Simplicity*.

14. This definition takes states as occurrents. A's existing is a state of A; hence this definition allows B to depend on A's existing.

15. An interesting discussion of various cases that might suggest further conditions is David Lewis' "Postscript" to his "Causation," in Lewis, *Philosophical Papers*, vol. 2, pp. 173–213.

16. I have argued elsewhere that a necessary being can sustain the existence of other necessary beings ("God and Abstract Entities" *Faith and Philosophy* 7, 193–217). (S) can be modified to apply to this case by deleting (i)'s stipulation of contingency and deleting (iv) and (v), which in this instance become redundant.

17. David Lewis, "Causation," in Lewis, *Papers*, vol. 2, pp. 166–167.

but has been complicated to avoid certain counterexamples to (CD). I submit therefore that if one can develop (CD) into an adequate definition of a causal dependence-relation, (S) either can develop into or is such a definition.

Lewis uses (CD) to define a relation of causality (as distinct from causal dependence). Lewis asks us to "let c, d, e . . . be a finite sequence of actual particular events such that d depends causally on c, e depends causally on d and so on. Then this sequence is a causal chain. Finally, one event is a cause of another iff there exists a causal chain leading from the first to the second."[18] For Lewis, then, one event is a cause of a second just in case a chain of causal dependence relations extends from the first to the second. Now it is a controversial matter whether Lewis' or any other counterfactual account of causality succeeds. But we can at least note that (S) also permits one to give an account of timeless-temporal causation. Consider this claim:

> S*. A timelessly sustains B = df. (i) A and B occur contingently, (ii) A occurs timelessly, (iii) B occurs continuously over more than one temporal position, (iv) in every nonactual world W such that no world is more like the actual world than W, A occurs only if B occurs continuously over more than one temporal position, and (v) were A not to occur, then if B's continuance is not overdetermined or redundantly caused, B would not do so.

I suggest that if some counterfactual analysis of causation can be adequate, then (S*) either is or can with further complications develop into a viable analysis of a timeless being's sustaining causation of a temporal being's existence. (S*) does, for instance, handle two problems that crop up for Lewis' account of causation.

First, consider a causal chain with only two members, c and e. It may be the case that $(c \,\square\!\!\rightarrow\, e)$ and $(\sim c \,\square\!\!\rightarrow\, \sim e)$. But one can easily imagine its also being the case that $(e \,\square\!\!\rightarrow\, c)$ and $(\sim e \,\square\!\!\rightarrow\, \sim c)$. For instance, c and e could be emissions of photons in an isolated region of space, such that e could have been caused only by c and (through an absence of possible interfering factors) c would have to lead to e if c occurred. Yet we would not want to say both that c caused e and that e caused c.[19] Clauses (ii) and (iii) of (S*) rule out all such cases of reverse dependence. It cannot be the case that a temporal being timelessly sustains a timeless being.

18. Ibid., p. 167.
19. Ibid., p. 170.

A second difficulty is raised by John Pollock.[20] Pollock notes that if c and e both occur and $(\sim c \,\square\!\!\rightarrow \sim e)$, then c and e satisfy Lewis' condition, since $(c\cdot e)$ entails $(c \,\square\!\!\rightarrow e)$. But then if c and e both occur and d is sufficiently independent of c and e, it can also be the case that $((\sim c \cdot \sim d)$ $\square\!\!\rightarrow \sim e)$. It follows that $\sim(c \vee d) \,\square\!\!\rightarrow \sim e$. But then if a switch's being closed caused a light's being on, it is also the case that the switch's being closed or Hitler's having been a German caused the light's being on. This seems absurd. Clause (iv) of (S*) blocks this argument by blocking the inference from "c and e both occur and $(\sim c \,\square\!\!\rightarrow \sim e)$" to "$c$ causes e." The thought behind (iv) is that if there is no genuine causal connection between c and e, then it is possible that the world be just as it is, save that c occurs and e does not.

These are two relatively simple problems; there is a large literature that raises vastly more complex issues for counterfactual theories of causation. But my point, again, is a limited one. I am suggesting only that *if* any counterfactual analysis of causation can deal successfully with the challenges such analyses face, then (S*) or some descendant of (S*) can successfully analyze a timeless being's sustaining of temporal entities.

(S*) *is* open to Pike's charge that if one strips down divine sustaining sufficiently to make it compatible with God's timelessness, it does not appear that God is active or *does* anything.[21] We can deal with Pike's pique by just specifying that in the case of God sustaining the world in existence, A is a timeless act of divine willing. But then we run head on into the plaint of Sorabji and others that the notion of an atemporal action or willing is somehow incoherent.[22]

Intentional Action and Timelessness

If atemporal intentional action is impossible, though, this is either because

i. there can be no action without duration, or because
ii. there can be no action without temporal location, or because
iii. there can be no intention without duration, or because
iv. there can be no intention without temporal location, or because
v. there can be no action without change, and whatever changes is in time.[23]

20. Pollock, *Foundations*, p. 149.
21. Pike, *God*, p. 115.
22. Sorabji, *TC&C*, p. 257.
23. So Stewart Sutherland, *God, Jesus, and Belief* (Oxford: Blackwell, 1984), p. 56, and Lucas, *Treatise*, p. 302.

One can grant (i) and argue (as we have seen) that eternal life involves its own sort of duration. But one can also reject (i). A deliberate thought (a thought one in some sense is responsible for having) is a sort of action. When one grasps the conclusion of a line of argument, one is *doing* something. Yet there can be durationless, instantaneous acts of thought, and perhaps grasping a conclusion is one of them. Hence perhaps grasping a conclusion is a durationless action. Again, one can suggest that if counting is a (prolonged) action, so is beginning to count. The two are distinct, for possibly time had no first moment, and possibly some being has existed throughout all of past time and has been counting at every instant: in which case this being has always been counting but never began to count. But beginning to count is another durationless action.

This last argument will also tell against (iii), since one can intentionally begin to count. Against (ii) one can press the point that logically, eternity *is* a "time"—that is, that eternity has whatever characteristics forge any conceptual connection between action and temporal location. Thus, for instance, if someone insists with Swinburne that "if we say that P brings about x, we can always sensibly ask *when* does he bring it about,"[24] one can reply that "at eternity" is "when" enough.[25] Swinburne also notes that God is said to act, forgive, and warn, and that "if P at t brings about x, then necessarily x comes into existence simultaneously with or subsequently to P's action. If P at t forgives Q for having done x, then Q did x prior to t. If P at t warns Q not to do x . . . there must be a time subsequent to t at which Q has this opportunity."[26] Here one can note that the "t" at which God acts to bring about x, forgives, or issues His warning is eternity and that there is a logical, not a temporal, priority between an eternal act and its temporal consequence, or between a temporal act requiring forgiveness and an eternal act of forgiving, or between an eternal warning and a temporal opportunity.

Sorabji presses (iv) when he reasons that "any purposive agent must have a rudimentary idea of the difference between the future desired state of affairs and the present actual state; in other words, he must have some crude awareness of time."[27] William Kneale expresses the same

24. Swinburne, *Coherence*, p. 221.
25. One can give a like reply to E. J. Khamara's insistence that "knowledge is datable . . . if A knows that p, then it always makes sense to say that A knows that p *now* . . . or . . . *then*" (see E. J. Khamara, "Eternity and Omniscience," *Philosophical Quarterly* 24 [1974], 211).
26. Swinburne, *Coherence*, p. 221.
27. Sorabji, *TC&C*, p. 7.

thought when he writes that "to act purposefully is to act with thought
of what will come about after the beginning of the action."[28] Richard
Gale adds a related argument: "An agent performs intentional actions
so as to bring about some goal or end. But to have a goal or end, the
agent must have desires . . . only a temporally incomplete being can
have a desire or intention, since one cannot desire or intend what one
already has. The rich man does desire and intend to be rich, but what
he desires is the continuation of his richness into the future."[29] The
claim of Kneale and Sorabji may be that to intend an action is to treat it
as *not yet* performed or not yet completed; they and Gale seem to think
that to intend an act, one must treat its goal as not yet attained. But
none of these claims is true. It is true that anyone who deliberates over
and chooses an action, and so intends one in *that* sense, must do so
temporally before the action. But one can intend an action while one is
performing it, in the sense that one is responsible for performing it. In
this sense of intention, the possibility of a durationless deliberate
thought would suffice to show that a timeless being can intend. Moreover, there are actions that by their nature are complete and attain their
goals at every moment at which they are performed. Seeing (as distinct
from coming to see or working to see) can be something one does for a
period. If one does it intentionally, then at every moment during that
period one is intending to achieve what one is in fact achieving.

One can deal with (v) by distinguishing the time of an action from
the time of its effect.[30] If eternity is logically a time, then that an act
occurs in eternity while its effect occurs at some time is no more
peculiar than an act's occurring at one time and its effect's occurring at
another. And this is not at all peculiar. My action of throwing a ball at a
wall may occur at 2 P.M., whereas its effect, the ball's striking the wall,
does not occur until 2 P.M. plus five seconds. But given the time of
act/time of effect distinction, one can hold that all the change an act
involves occurs as part of its temporal effect, and the act itself exists
changelessly in eternity.

Passage, Power, and Timelessness

It could be argued that the passage of time deprives God of power,
that this is a real change in God, and that accordingly He cannot be
timeless. For before February 9, 1999, God has the power to effect it

28. William Kneale, "Time and Eternity," p. 99.
29. Richard M. Gale, "Omniscience-Immutability Arguments," *American Philosophical Quarterly* 23 (1986), 333.
30. See Stump and Kretzmann, "Eternity," pp. 447–453.

that the moon turn to green cheese on February 9, 1999. After this date
He no longer has the power to turn the moon into green cheese on
February 9, 1999, though He is still able to do this on all subsequent
dates. For if He had this power, He in effect would be able to alter the
past, i.e., to act on February 10 to make the moon to have been green
cheese on February 9, and this is impossible.

This argument can be answered in at least three ways. First, some
writers might be prepared to argue that power over the past is not
impossible. Second, it is unclear that there is any such thing as a
distinct power to turn the moon to green cheese on February 9, 1999.
Our practices of individuating powers make it far more plausible to say
that God has a general power to change moons to green cheese, which
He has various opportunities to exercise on various dates. That God
loses an opportunity to exercise this power would not entail that God
Himself loses any power or therefore suffers any intrinsic change.
Third, the objection presupposes that God can act on February 9 or
February 10. If God is timeless, this is false; the only "time" at which
God acts is eternity. God eternally brings about both effects that are
now in our past and effects that are now in our future—but all this
action is in His eternal present and so involves no power over any past
or future relative to God. Again, as time does not pass in eternity, God
cannot change or lose any power He has.

Some Other Mental Concepts

There can doubtless be more and more sophisticated objections
along the lines set forth above. The responses they call forth can corre-
spondingly be ever more complex; of the making of many books there
is no end, as the Preacher has it. Still, I submit that these suggestions
are promising—that they can in fact provide lines along which to
respond to ever more complex objections. It seems, then, that we can
make sense of a timeless being's being a person, i.e., having knowledge
and being able to act intentionally.

This is not to say, of course, that a timeless being will be your
common or garden-variety person. A timeless being cannot remember, since one can only remember what is in one's past. Helm
disputes this, suggesting that one can be said to remember P if one
knows P and has not forgotten P and that a timeless individual remembers P if he or she knows P and cannot forget that P.[31] But one knows
that P and has not forgotten that P at the first moment that one knows
P. Moreover, an essentially omniscient temporal God could know that

31. Helm, *Eternal God*, p. 59.

P and be unable to forget that P at His first moment of knowing P. If a timeless individual in this state remembers P, why should we not say that a temporal God in this state remembers P? But it would be absurd to say that anyone's first instant of knowing P is a remembering of P. So it seems that what Helm calls a sufficient condition for remembering is not really one.

Again, a timeless being cannot anticipate, since one can only anticipate what is in one's future. Nor can a timeless being deliberate, since one can deliberate only over an action that one has not yet performed. If choosing presupposes a temporally earlier state of indecision, then in a sense a timeless being cannot choose, even if such a being can will or intend. Again, if a timeless God wills, His willing is *simultaneous* with His doing what He wills—though perhaps there is between His willing and His action some asymmetrical relation in virtue of which the former explains the latter and not vice versa, or some other nontemporal relation if one ascribes to God the distinct-mental-act-location version of QTE. But a being that has knowledge and will is person enough for philosophical and theological purposes.

Allowing that a timeless being can have some knowledge, some philosophers have argued that such a being nonetheless cannot be omniscient and therefore cannot be God. I turn to these arguments in the next two chapters.

Timelessness and Freedom

If God is not located in time, it follows that God does not change. In fact, as whatever is timeless is necessarily so, if God is timeless, God cannot change. Swinburne allows that God could happen in fact not to change but objects to the claim that God *cannot* change. For he holds that God is perfectly free, and he argues that "a perfectly free person could not be . . . unable to change. For an agent is perfectly free at a certain time if his action results from his own choice at that time and if his choice is not itself brought about by anything else. Yet a person immutable in the strong sense would be unable to perform any action at a certain time other than what he had previously intended to do. His course of action being fixed by his past choices, he would not be perfectly free."[32] On one reading, this argument is valid only if Swinburne is claiming that

> PF. an action at t is perfectly free *only if* it results from a choice
> at t.

32. Swinburne, *Coherence*, pp. 214–215.

But (PF) is counterintuitive. (PF) seems to entail, for instance, that if I uncoercedly and with full libertarian freedom decided yesterday to have eggs for breakfast today, then just because I decided that yesterday rather than this morning, I eat eggs unfreely or with imperfect freedom. More generally, (PF) seems to entail that no decision reached before one acts issues in a perfectly free action. Of course, Swinburne might intend (PF) to stipulate a necessary condition of an action's having a special attribute, perfect freedom. But if this is (PF)'s import, there seems no reason to prefer the claim that God performs perfectly free acts to the claim that God performs ordinarily free acts, and Swinburne gives us no reason to reject the latter claim. Further, suppose that we accept (PF). Even so, if we take eternity as a value of t, then if God is timeless, all of His actions satisfy (PF), for eternity is the only "time" at which God either wills or acts. Swinburne's argument is in fact directed solely to an immutable God who exists *in time:* its crux is that an unchangeable decision reached *temporally before* an action does not issue in a perfectly free action. A timeless immutable being's decision is always eternally simultaneous with its action. So a timeless immutable being's actions count as perfectly free even given (PF).

Still, there is a second way to read Swinburne's argument. He could mean to contend that

> R. an action at t is perfectly free only if its agent could have performed at t an act of refraining from it,

but an immutable agent, being unable to change, cannot change its intention to act and so cannot refrain. But refraining at t does not require changing one's intention at t or any other time. A person could refrain from action A at t because he or she had always intended not to do A at t. This intention would come to "count as" a refraining once the opportunity to do A at t actually arrived, but its doing so would not involve any real (as versus mere Cambridge) change in it. Thus even an act of a temporal but immutable God could count as perfectly free relative to (R). Moreover, if God is timeless, then since eternity is the only "time" at which He acts or could have refrained from acting, any divine act that God need not have done satisfies (R). If God is timeless, any divine action is simultaneous with His decision to act. So if God is timeless, He could have refrained from doing A just in case it is possible that He not have done A. Nothing in the doctrine of divine timelessness requires us to deny that a timeless God could have done other than He has in fact done. Thus Swinburne's argument does not tell against the claim that a timeless immutable God can be perfectly free.

Can a timeless God in fact be free? Philosophers have given us more than one account of the nature of freedom, but it is libertarian freedom that matters most to theists. Let us say that an agent S has libertarian freedom with respect to action A at time t just in case at t it is in S's power both to do A and not to do A. If God is timeless, the only t we need worry about is eternity. I now argue that nothing in the claim that God is timeless requires us to deny that a timeless God who eternally (say) creates universe A could have instead eternally created universe B.

We have already argued that a timeless God can have knowledge and intentions. We can therefore assume that divine actions are to be explained on a belief-intention pattern, i.e., that God does what He does because He intends to achieve certain results and believes that the means He chooses will do so.[33] In any possible world, logically before creating any contingent thing, God has almost the same beliefs. For if God is omniscient, God then believes all and only what is true then. What truths are true logically before God creates contingent things? There are, of course, the necessary truths. Given S_5, these are the same in all possible worlds. There are also truths about nonexistent entities. Given S_5, every possible world has the same cast of possible and impossible entities, each with the same character. Thus given S_5, before God creates, there are the same truths about nonexistent entities in all possible worlds. Finally, logically before God creates, there are truths about God. God has the same essential attributes in every world, and His beliefs about Himself in a world W_1 differ from His beliefs about Himself in W_2 only as He in W_1 differs from Himself in W_2. God is essentially omnipotent and morally perfect, so His power and basic character are the same in W_1 and W_2. It seems, then, that God in W_1 and God in W_2 can differ only with regard to their states of intention (and desire, though I have not spoken of divine desires) and that the beliefs of God in W_1 and the beliefs of God in W_2 will differ only in ways that reflect this difference.

Accordingly, a timeless God can create a world other than the one He in fact creates just in case He can have intentions other than those He actually has. But though a timeless God's state of intention cannot change, there just does not seem to be reason to deny that a timeless God could have intended other things than He has in fact intended. Of course, this raises a question: just *why* does God intend what He in fact does, if to do so is not essential to Him? Given that God creates a world iff He has the appropriate intentions and beliefs and that God's beliefs

33. I speak of God as having beliefs only to simplify the discussion.

are almost constant over worlds in the way described, this question is equivalent to the question of why God creates this world rather than any other possible world or no world at all. This is a thorny question indeed, but it is not thorny because God is timeless. His timelessness seems in no way relevant to it. Accordingly, barring the offering of further arguments, it appears that alternate actions are within the competence of a timeless agent: timelessness is compatible with full libertarian freedom. Though we cannot say that a timeless God deliberates and chooses what to do, we can say that such a God acts intentionally and willingly and could have done otherwise. We might add that such a God's creative action must be free from all external coercion, since any external force that might seek to influence His action exists only logically after He has acted.

Immutability and Timelessness

Traditional religious writings raise a problem for the claim that God is timeless by raising a problem for its consequence, the thesis that God is immutable. For the biblical tradition is full of cases in which God *appears* to change: for one instance, it is said that after the Flood, God repented what He had done and decided that He would not thus scrub the earth clean again. Let us call this the Change of Will Problem. Again, it is traditionally said that God is omnipresent, where this is understood to mean something like God's being present to all spaces. If this is what omnipresence is, though, then before there were spaces, God was not omnipresent: it seems, in other words, that God changed in virtue of creating spaces to which He could be present. Another traditional claim is that God is the Lord, the Ruler of creatures. But before there were creatures to rule, God could not in this sense be Lord. Hence it seems that God changed by having creatures over whom He could rule. Let us call this the Change of Property Problem.

These difficulties have rather well known countermoves. One can handle the Change of Will Problem by arguing that if a timeless God can create at all, as I have argued, such a God can interact with creatures without undergoing real change—for such a God can create a universe with His responses in a certain sense "built in." One can handle the Change of Property Problem via the well-known distinction between "real" and "Cambridge" change.

Change of Will

Let me first treat the Change of Will Problem. The question of whether a timeless God can have temporal effects (as is necessary for interacting with temporal beings) admits of two readings. It could be asking whether an atemporal God can act in an already-existing temporal universe, i.e., whether an atemporal being can produce a change in things. It could also ask whether an atemporal God can create the entire universe of temporal things.[34] We gain a decided advantage in dealing with the question on its first reading if we build God's intentions to respond to creaturely action into the divine intention to create the universe and time.

For suppose that we rephrase our two readings of the question "can a timeless God have temporal effects" in this way:

    i. can a timeless God act in time?
    ii. can a timeless God create time and all that is in time?

Question (i) is the harder of the two, because if time already exists and an effect is temporal, there is a presumption that its cause acts when or before the effect exists. As Pike has urged, "if we can assign a temporal location to what one produces, by the logic of 'produces' . . . we can assign relative temporal position to the productive activity itself."[35] But if the activity is located in time, then presumably so is its agent, and so its agent is temporal. So to defend on its own an affirmative answer to (i), one must try to explain why this "temporal effect-temporal agent" presumption does not apply and what sense one can make of the claim that an event is caused by a timeless agent if it does not. By contrast, the "temporal effect-temporal agent" presumption cannot apply where the act in question includes the creation of time itself. For in this case there is no time at which an effect can be located until logically "after" the action. So to speak, the activity of creating time must take place in eternity.

Thus if God's intention to create includes His intentions to respond, and His activity of creating includes His activity of responding, we can bypass several difficult issues.[36] For then if God's activity's having the temporal effect that is the universe does not itself locate Him in time, neither does the included activity of responding to creatures by includ-

34. Since we have already seen that a temporal God cannot create the entire universe of temporal things, this question is in effect equivalent to the question of whether God can create the entire universe of temporal things at all.

35. Pike, *God*, pp. 106–107; see pp. 97–120. As Pike continues, "if something is produced . . . it begins to exist. To produce something is to effect its beginning. Further . . . if something begins to exist, it has position in time. [So] a timeless individual could not produce, create, or bring about an object . . . or state of affairs" (ibid., pp. 107, 110).

36. Helm independently makes (but does not much develop) a similar suggestion, *Eternal God*, pp. 68–69.

ing specific events within the history of the world He produces. We have already seen that a timeless being cannot become temporal. Hence if a timeless being can create at all, such a being can create (and so respond) without thereby being located in time.

If God's act of creating includes His acts of response, then in creating, God brings into being a universe with the temporal effects of His eternal activity, including His responses to creaturely choices, "built in."[37] Suppose that God has middle knowledge, or knowledge before creating of what creatures definitely would do if placed in certain situations. If He does, He can timelessly will a universe within which Abraham will in fact choose to bring Isaac to the hill of sacrifice and make the universe such that when Abraham prays God to spare Isaac, a deep bass voice will be made to sound by sudden spontaneous quantum motions of the relevant physical particles, and this deep voice will tell Abraham where to find a ram.

Suppose, on the other hand, that a timeless God lacks middle knowledge. In this case, He knows what free creatures actually do and how their actions shape the history of the universe only logically "after" He has chosen which creatures and what initial conditions to create. But His initial act of creating free creatures and the initial conditions in which they act can create a universe with conditional responses to creaturely choices "built in." He can, for instance, will that if Abraham mounts Horeb, the voice will sound at Horeb, and if Abraham mounts Carmel, the voice will sound at Carmel, and so on.

Now this may not look like God's engaging in living dialogue with Abraham. Swinburne, for instance, says of this idea that "if God had thus fixed his intentions 'from all eternity' he would be a very lifeless thing; not a person who reacts to men with sympathy or anger . . . because He chooses to there and then."[38] But Swinburne is again directing his argument against a picture of God as temporal and immutable. His complaint is that if God has made up His mind how to deal with Abraham billions of years before Abraham's birth, He does not truly interact with Abraham. The fact is that if God is timeless, His willing the voice to sound at Horeb if Abraham mounts Horeb is *not*

---

37. Relatives of this move have been much discussed in recent literature. See, e.g., Huw Owen, *Concepts of Deity* (New York: Herder and Herder, 1971), p. 87; R. L. Sturch, "The Problem of the Divine Eternity," *Religious Studies* 10 (1974), 491; Swinburne, *Coherence*, p. 214; Sorabji, *TC&C*, pp. 240–242; Wolterstorff, "God," pp. 89–95; Thomas Morris, "Properties, Modalities, and God," *Philosophical Review* 91 (1984), 47–48; Alston, "Divine-Human Dialogue and the Nature of God," in *Divine Nature;* Creel, *Impassibility*, pp. 16–34. Sorabji traces the move back to the Patristic period and to Augustine; Creel cites its loci in Aquinas.

38. Swinburne, *Coherence*, p. 214.

before His hearing Abraham's prayer, let alone billions of years before it. What occurs in eternity occurs all at once; in eternity, God wills that the voice sound at Horeb if Abraham mounts Horeb *while* He "hears" Abraham's prayer. Nor is God's hearing or willing either before or after what occurs at any time, since whatever is before or after some time is itself a time or in time. Further, one can hold that God timelessly wills that the voice sounds under appropriate circumstances because He timelessly knows that one way the world may work out once created (or *the* way, if He acts from middle knowledge) will bring Abraham to this point of prayer, and He timelessly desires that this response be given should the world work out this way.

In short, one can hold that if Abraham does pray, the ram appears and the voice speaks *because* Abraham prays and *because* God timelessly wills that these things should happen in response. Nor need one say that on this picture, God responds only to a mere possibility of Abraham's action rather than the real living Abraham, even if one denies middle knowledge and holds that God builds in conditional responses. Rather, God possibly responds to Abraham's possible acts and actually responds to Abraham's actual acts. The only divine timeless intention to respond that is actually fulfilled is the one Abraham's act makes appropriate, and this intention is fulfilled *because* of what Abraham freely chooses to do. Consider these claims:

1. Eternally, God wills all of His conditional intentions, among them an intention that if eternally, God knows that Abraham does act A, then eternally, God wills that event E occurs.
2. Eternally, God knows that Abraham does A.
3. Eternally, God wills that event E occurs.

If God is timeless, then the truth of (1) and the truth of (2) are eternally simultaneous, and (1) and (2) jointly entail (3): which is true "when" they are not just because (1)–(3) are true in eternity but also because a validly entailed conclusion is true "as soon as" its premises are. That (3) is based on (1) and (2) and yet is not in any way really after them is no odder than a logical theorem's truth being in some sense based on the truth of a logical axiom even though the axiom is not true temporally before the theorem. Of course, in this case (1)–(3) do not express all that God knows and does. Presumably, the SOAs that render (2) true depend in part on some other divine conditional and unconditional intendings. But there seems no reason to suppose that these other dependences will involve temporal priority; they can all take place "when" the act of will (1) involves takes place.

If we do not assume that God has middle knowledge, we can logically order the relevant episodes of a timeless God's mental life as follows. First, God surveys all possible sets of initial conditions for the universe, i.e., all sets of SOAs that He can cause to obtain and that do not presuppose or involve any actions of created free agents. Some of these initial-condition sets will involve the existence of free creatures. Because they do, these will be smaller than one might think. For suppose that God is considering creating a stone, Peter, and that in some possible world, some free creature Paul moves Peter to a new place a microsecond after Peter comes to exist. In this case, only the first microsecond of Peter's existence is part of any set of initial conditions God considers which includes Paul's existing and being able to move Peter. For if Paul exists and can move Peter, then at any point after that first microsecond, Peter either is or is not where Paul might put it. If Peter is there, Peter is there (let us say) because Paul put it there. If Peter is not there, still Peter might have been there: Peter's being anywhere else presupposes that Paul did not freely put it there. In general, then, even if Peter is not free, if Peter's history possibly intersects the history of a free creature in an appropriate way, Peter's history after that possible point of intersection is not part of the initial conditions God considers.

Relative to each set of initial conditions, God also surveys all the possible histories that free creatures might enact within these conditions. As we are not assuming that God has middle knowledge, we are not assuming that He knows of any set of initial conditions what *would* happen if He actualized it. We assume only that He knows exhaustively what *might* happen. In surveying all the possible histories involving Abraham, God surveys all the actions Abraham might take *and* all the ways these acts might affect subsequent history, both if He responds to them in certain ways and if He does not. Knowing all this, for every possible Abrahamic action, God decides which of His possible responses that action would elicit: that is, He wills His conditional intentions involving Abraham. In and with this willing, God wills to create an actual world.

As God wills (in eternity) a world to exist, it exists. (Even if we leave aside the claim that both the will and its effect exist in eternity, theists will universally affirm that God's will is immediately effective; nothing can hinder the action of an omnipotent power.) As it exists, God knows—however His knowledge works—which actual actions Abraham performs. (Again, even if we leave aside the claim that both God's knowledge and its object exist in eternity, theists will universally affirm that God's knowledge is immediate, i.e., without temporal delay.)

Now while God knows that Abraham actually does climb Horeb, He is also willing a conditional intention such as

4. if eternally, God knows that Abraham mounts Horeb, then eternally, God wills that a voice sound at Horeb.

Given that God does in fact simultaneously eternally know that Abraham does mount Horeb, God's willing (4) entails His willing that a voice sounds at Horeb, and so there is a sense in which God's initial creative volition includes His response to Abraham on Horeb.

To strengthen the claim that God's response to Abraham is part and parcel of His creating the world, we could say that in creating, God eternally wills not a conditional like (4), but one like

4a. if eternally, God knows that Abraham mounts Horeb at t, then eternally, a voice sounds at Horeb at t.

On our Anselmian view, the consequents of claims like (4a) are true because it is the case in eternity that a voice sounds at Horeb at t. Other theories of divine timelessness may also be able to endorse (4a); these can perhaps say that its consequent means something like "it is fixed in eternity that in time, a voice . . ." Given that God wills (4a) rather than (4), His willing (4a) *constitutes* His willing that a voice sound at Horeb. The same intention that is conditional taken in abstraction from God's cognitive state is in effect unconditional in conjunction with God's cognitive state.

If God is timeless, all of these episodes, including Abraham's actual action, happen at once in eternity. Their order is *solely* logical. Now our representation of God's intentions may seem insufficiently complex. For in time, Abraham first does A, then E occurs in response, then Abraham does A2, in response to which E2 occurs, and so on: that is, certain divine responses presuppose other, temporally prior divine responses. But this is what is so *in time*. In eternity, God wills all His conditional intentions at once, including those whose antecedents include Abraham's having done certain acts and God's having made certain responses. In eternity, God knows at once all of Abraham's acts, including those that respond to His responses. And in eternity, God wills at once all of His unconditional intentions, including those that respond to Abraham's responses to God's responses.

We can render plausible the claim that God wills all of this at once by representing God's conditional intentions as in part multiply nested. Let "K" stand for "eternally, God knows that Abraham does act A,"

"E" for "eternally, God wills that E occurs," "K1" for "eternally, God knows that Abraham does act B," "E2" for "eternally, God wills that E2 occurs," and so on. Then our first simple model of God's conditional intentions can be symbolized as

5. K $\rightarrow$ E.

A second, more complex model can be symbolized as (5) plus

6. $((K \rightarrow E) \cdot K) \rightarrow (((((K_2 \rightarrow E_2) \cdot (K_3 \rightarrow E_3)) \cdot K_3) \rightarrow (K_4 \rightarrow E_4))$ ...

Such a chain of nested conditionals can be continued indefinitely. The logical relations between (5)-like statements plus (6), a statement specifying the content of God's eternal knowledge, such as

7. $K \cdot K_3 \cdot K_4$,

and a statement specifying the logically resultant divine unconditional intentions, such as

8. $E \cdot E_3 \cdot E_4$,

are just like the relations of (1)–(3). So if (1)–(3) can be timelessly simultaneous, so can (6)–(8). In this picture of God's inner life, God's intending how to respond if Abraham does A is logically prior to Abraham's doing A. But His actual intending to actually respond this way is logically posterior to Abraham's doing A. This could be because the very conditional intention that is prior to Abraham's action gains its unconditional effectiveness by conjunction with a divine cognitive state that presupposes Abraham's action. This is how things are if God's conditional intentions are of the form of (4a). But our picture of God's inner life can do without this feature.

On the account of God's acting and intending given here, if we individuate divine actions in part by their temporal effects, we can say that the divine act of responding to Abraham is a distinct action included in the overall action of creating the universe. God's timelessly willing His response is neither before nor after Abraham's action, in eternity. But if we speak loosely enough to allow ourselves improperly to date God's actions temporally by the time of their effects, we can add that God's response takes place after Abraham's action in time, even though it is part of an action that (dated by this means) began at the first moment of time (if there was one). So the conjunction of creation and timelessness allows a timeless God to interact with creatures in time. If a timeless God can create, He can will changes in the world in response to creatures without there being changes in His will. Let us turn, then, to the Change of Property Problem.

Change of Property

It has been standard at least since Augustine to handle the Change of Property Problem via the distinction between genuine and what have become known as "mere Cambridge" changes (or events, or processes).[39] This distinction is well established in recent literature. Genuine changes (etc.) are changes like gaining a pound or turning bright red, changes in which something "really happens" to something. Mere Cambridge changes are changes like Joan's becoming shorter than John solely because John grows an inch. In this case, a proposition about Joan is true which was not true before ("Joan is shorter than John"), but nothing "really happens" to Joan. There is a real physical process taking place in John which constitutes John's growing, but no second real physical process taking place in Joan which is Joan's becoming shorter. Further, when we are describing the physical process in John in terms of its linkage to the world's causal order, genuine-change descriptions such as "John's growing" are appropriate, and mere-Cambridge-change descriptions such as "Joan's becoming shorter" are not. We could describe the physical process in John as Joan's becoming shorter. But this description would be in a sense parasitic and ontologically obfuscatory. For had Joan grown when John grew, John would have grown without Joan becoming shorter, and this would have had no effect at all on John's growing. That process would have been in all respects as it in fact was, and the world's causal order as leading to and following from it could well have not been one whit different. Thus, Joan's becoming shorter is *irrelevant* to the world's causal order. An event's nature may be intimately tied to its place in the world's causal order.[40] If this is so, it specifies a sense in which the physical process we have discussed is "really" just John's growing, not

39. See Augustine, *De Trinitate* V, chap. 16, #17. For recent discussion, see Peter Geach, "What Actually Exists," *Proceedings of the Aristotelian Society* Supp. Vol. 42 (1968), 7–16, and "God's Relation to the World," *Sophia* 8 (1969), 1–9; T. P. Smith, "On the Applicability of a Criterion of Change," *Ratio* 15 (1973), 325–333; Paul Helm, "Are Cambridge Changes Non-Events?" *Analysis* 35 (1975), 140–144, and "Detecting Change," *Ratio* 19 (1977), 34–38; Lawrence Lombard, "Relational Change and Relational Changes," *Philosophical Studies* 34 (1978), 63–79; William Godfrey-Smith, "Change and Actuality," *Philosophical Quarterly* 30 (1980), 350–353.

40. This may account for some of the plausibility attaching to proposals to individuate events in terms of their causal antecedents and consequences.

Joan's becoming shorter. For the event has all its causes and effects qua
John's growing, not qua Joan's shortening.

There is no agreed criterion for sorting genuine from mere
Cambridge changes or events. But the distinction is clear enough, and
in most cases it is clear of which sort a given change or event is.
Further, for present purposes we do not need a criterion. For one thing
that is clear is that for a change to be real, the change's subject must
exist at and before the time at which the change occurs. It must actually
be at that time to be actually modified in some way at that time, and it
must actually exist before that time for the event to count as a change in
it. But a timeless being exists before no time and at only one "time,"
eternity. Hence no real change can befall such a being. All change in
such a being must be mere Cambridge change.

Let us apply the distinction between real and mere Cambridge
change to our specific cases. One can hold that God is eternally omnipresent in that there is not and cannot be a space from which He is
absent: call this God's negative omnipresence. When there come to be
spaces to which God is present, God is positively omnipresent. God's
becoming positively omnipresent involves a real change in the way
things are apart from Him, namely, the coming-to-exist of spaces to
which God is present. But God's becoming positively omnipresent is
only a Cambridge change in Him. For the situation is that He timelessly wills the existence of spaces, without in any way changing by
willing this, and spaces thus exist without His coming to be in any
further state. Spaces exist only as God timelessly causes them to exist.
Hence for them to exist is for God to be causally present to them.
God's timeless effective willing *is* His being present causally. So if
God's willing involves no change, neither does His omnipresence.
Again, in eternity, God is changelessly the Lord: He timelessly coexists
with His creatures. But in time, God is always negatively the Lord in
that there is not and cannot be any creature independent of His governance. This is so whether or not there actually are creatures subject to
His governance. God's positive Lordship is acquired much as His
positive spatial omnipresence is.

Examples could be multiplied, but the general strategy is clear
enough. I know of only one writer who has seriously challenged the
use of the real change/Cambridge change distinction to maintain divine immutability in the face of biblical evidence. Thomas Morris asks
us to

> consider a standard sort of story of merely relational change. A woman's
> husband is on an ambassadorial trip to a foreign land and dies at the hand

of a terrorist, unknown to her for some hours. At the moment of his death, she becomes a widow. But at that time, the change she undergoes is a merely relational change. The circumstances involve no real change on her part. Contrast this with an alternate story in which the murder occurs in her presence, or . . . she herself pulls the trigger. In neither of these cases is her becoming a widow a set of circumstances involving only merely relational change on her part. In light of this difference, we can isolate at least three features of any situation in which one object has undergone nothing more than merely relational change, reflecting some real change in a different object. First, the ongoing existence of the really changing object and its having at least most of the non-relational properties it has are matters in some sense causally and metaphysically independent of the object undergoing the merely relational change. Secondly, the real change in question involves no occurrent exercise of power on the part of the object undergoing merely the relational change. And thirdly, the real change is not registered as a piece of knowledge or belief on the part of the individual going through the merely relational change . . . But these are features which could never hold true of God and any of his creatures . . . Each of God's creatures depends on God moment to moment for its existence . . . Further, nothing can happen without at least the concurrent operation of God's conserving power. And nothing can come about without God's knowing it.[41]

Morris' argument seems to equivocate on the phrase "becoming a widow." This phrase can denote a complex causal process from which this unfortunate woman may or may not be causally isolated. It can also denote not the process, but the precise change that occurs as a result of this process. It is irrelevant to the precise change that occurs whether or not the woman is involved in the process. The real event that occurs when the precise change of becoming a widow occurs is the husband's dying, brought about by this causal process. The Cambridge change of becoming a widow has its Cambridge character solely because of its parasitic relation to the real event and regardless of the woman's participation in the process. Certainly God cannot be isolated from the causal processes by which creatures really change. But it does not follow from this that the precise "change" involved in His (say) becoming Lord is anything but a Cambridge change. And even this change exists (at most) only in *temporal* reference frames. In eternity, in which alone God is really located, not even this shadow of change exists. In eternity there is no such thing as God's *becoming* Lord or omnipresent. God is just eternally an omnipresent Lord.

41. Thomas Morris, *Anselmian Explorations* (Notre Dame, Ind.: University of Notre Dame Press, 1987), pp. 134–135.

Although I find it entirely adequate to dispel the Change of Property problem via the concept of mere Cambridge change, it may be worth noting that on our Anselmian theory of time and eternity, one need not do so. Suppose for the sake of argument that God had time begin and had a separate Newtonian space begin to exist at some point in time. On our Anselmian theory, this entails that in eternity, God timelessly coexists with time and with a space with a temporal extension shorter than that of time itself. In the only reference frame in which God is literally located, God is changelessly present to all things: there is not even the appearance of His changing in being omnipresent. Further, on our Anselmian theory, in any temporal reference frame, time exists before space exists, but God does not coexist with time before He coexists with space, else His existence would have a temporal relation to a temporal reality. Rather, it is always the case that God coexists with time without existing before, after, or temporally while it exists, and always the case that God coexists with space without existing before, after, or temporally while it exists. So on our Anselmian theory, there is not even the appearance within time that coming to be omnipresent involves a change in God.

The present view of time and eternity also generates a second distinctive way to dispel the Change of Property problem. Something undergoes even a mere Cambridge change only if some proposition P is true of it at some time t and false of it at some other time. But on the present view, no time t is such that something is true of God at t and false of God at some other time. Rather, if t = eternity, everything is true of God at t that is ever true of Him, and if t ≠ eternity, no proposition is true or false of God at t. So strictly speaking, the present view removes even the shadow of Cambridge change from God.

I take it, then, that these expedients can handle the Change of Will and Change of Property problems. Divine immutability thus appears defensible, and it does not seem that God's being timeless is incompatible with His living, being personal, having knowledge and will, being free, or responding to creatures.

[14]
Time, Actuality, and Omniscience

Many traditional theists hold that

    1. God is propositionally omniscient,

i.e., knows all truths.[1] I have argued that

    2. God is timeless,

i.e., that though God exists, there is no time at which He exists. Some recent philosophers, among them Arthur Prior, Robert Coburn, Norman Kretzmann, Nicholas Wolterstorff, Richard Gale, and Patrick Grim, have argued that

    3. There are truths to whose expression "now" is essential,

and that (1)–(3) compose an inconsistent set of propositions.[2] These writers argue that because of the semantics of "now," a timeless God

---

1. For instance, at *ST* Ia 14, 14, Aquinas states that "God knows all enunciations that can be formed" ("Deus sciat omnia enuntiabilia quae formari possunt," *ST*, vol. 4, p. 52).
2. Arthur Prior, "The Formalities of Omniscience," *Philosophy* 37 (1962), 114–129; Robert Coburn, "Professor Malcolm on God," *Australasian Journal of Philosophy* 41 (1963), 155–156; Norman Kretzmann, "Omniscience and Immutability," *Journal of Philosophy* 63 (1966), 409–421; Wolterstorff, "God Everlasting"; Patrick Grim, "Against Omniscience: The Case from Essential Indexicals," *Nous* 19 (1985), 151–180; Gale, "Omniscience-Immutability Arguments." This argument and its metaphysical congener have a long history. For their loci in medieval Arabic philosophy and in Aquinas, see Sorabji, *TC&C*, pp. 260–261 nn. 28–31.

cannot know what is happening now. To know what is happening now, it is claimed, one must be able mentally to token a proposition expressing what one knows.[3] Per (3), to token a proposition expressing the fact that something is happening now, one must token "now" or some relevantly similar term (e.g., a present-tensed verb). "Now" and relevantly similar terms inter alia locate those who use them in time: if one says truly that it is now 3 P.M., it follows that one exists at 3 P.M. So a timeless being cannot use "now" and relevantly similar terms and so (it is claimed) cannot know truths for whose expression "now" and its ilk are required.

This semantic timelessness–omniscience argument has been much discussed. Other philosophers, among them Delmas Lewis, Richard Creel, Bowman Clarke, William Craig, Stewart Sutherland, and William Hasker, have put forth or implicitly endorsed what I call a *metaphysical* timelessness–omniscience argument, or MTOA, one that has not been much discussed.[4] These writers argue that (1), (2), and

> 4. Time is tensed

make up an inconsistent triad. Some authors have not explicitly distinguished the metaphysical and semantic timelessness–omniscience arguments: Kretzmann's arguments in "Omniscience and Immutability" can be read either way, though the paper is usually taken as an example of the semantic argument. Other authors seem to have assumed that there are irreducibly tensed truths if and only if time is tensed and so have spoken as if the semantic and metaphysical arguments stand or fall together.[5] But though the semantic and metaphysical timelessness–omniscience arguments are related, they are distinct, because (4) and (3) are logically independent.

It could be the case that (3) is true while (4) is false. That is, it could be that time is not tensed and yet such propositions as "it is now 12 noon" have no acceptable paraphrases not involving tenses or indexicals. For perhaps tense and indexicality are ineliminable not because they represent some real feature of time but because our languages, conceptual schemes, or world views force us to introduce them into

---

3. Gale emphasizes this; see "Omniscience-Immutability Arguments," p. 322.

4. Clark, *Language*, p. 116; Stewart Sutherland, "Truth and God," *Proceedings of the Aristotelian Society* 56 (1982), 109; Delmas Lewis, "Eternity Again," pp. 78, 79; Craig, "Was Aquinas?" pp. 475–483; Creel, *Impassibility*, pp. 96–97, 111. See Delmas Lewis, "Eternity, Time," pp. 82–83. Hasker brings up this problem in his "Concerning the Intelligibility," pp. 190–194. In his "Yes, God Has Beliefs!" pp. 385–394, he uses it to reject the doctrine of divine timelessness.

5. See, e.g., Wolterstorff, "God Everlasting."

claims like "it is now 12 noon." Perhaps tense is an ineliminable feature not of time itself but of the way we represent time. John Perry's well-known "Problem of the Essential Indexical" more than acknowledges this possibility. This paper is a seminal defense of the claim that indexicals like "now" (and the related device of tense) are ineliminable parts of propositions like "it is now 12 noon." It also suggests that knowing indexical or tensed truths like "it is now 12 noon" is indispensable to human action. Yet Perry does not assume that time is tensed and even crafts a theory of propositions which seems tailored to a tenseless theory.

Again, it could be the case that (4) is true while (3) is false. For it could be that even if time is tensed, such truths as "it is now 12 noon" do have acceptable paraphrases not involving tenses or indexicals. It could be, for instance, that some token-reflexive analysis of indexicals will ultimately prove correct. If some such analysis is correct, the proper analysis of "it is now 12 noon" is something like "it tenselessly-is 12 noon at the time of this tokening." Yet time might nonetheless be tensed. For perhaps this token-reflexive analysis will prove correct not because of the nature of time but because of some peculiarity of our language. (4) and (3) are independent just because (4) is a thesis of metaphysics and (3) a thesis of semantics. There just is no tie between the expressive resources of our languages and the real nature of time.

This chapter discusses and dismisses both the semantic argument and MTOA. It concludes that a timeless God can be what I call factually omniscient.

The Metaphysical Argument Stated

Friends of MTOA find (1), (2), and (4) inconsistent because they hold that if God is timeless and omniscient, all events are timelessly present to Him. As chapter 10 showed, if God is timeless and omniscient, then

ST. God "sees" all temporal events happen at once.

As chapter 10 also showed, one can take (ST) as either

ST2. God's "seeings" of all temporal events all occur at once,

or else the conjunction of (ST2) and the claim that

ST1. what God sees is all temporal events occurring at once.

I have opted for the latter reading. So do partisans of MTOA, and they contend that on this reading, (1), (2), and (4) are jointly inconsistent, for if God sees all events as happening at once, He does not see which ones are really happening now. If we let the phrase "present-actuality" express that sort of actuality that according to tensed theories of time only presently occurring events have, then MTOA contends, as Delmas Lewis puts it, that

> there is an objective feature of reality (namely, the (present)-actuality of some temporal entities and events) of which an eternal entity who is supposed to know all of temporal reality by direct acquaintance . . . is ignorant . . . only some temporal events *are* (presently)-actual, and (in part) we know which they are; an eternal God, from whose viewpoint every temporal event is actually occurring, does not, [for] talk of locations on a linear continuum neither reflects nor captures (present)-actuality . . . an eternal entity . . . may know that temporal events occur sequentially and know the sequence and dating of them, but he cannot know which events are presently occurring (or) past and future . . . (So) an eternal entity cannot be omniscient, because . . . he does not . . . know . . . that Nixon's resigning of the Presidency is a past event and so not now (presently)-actual.[6]

The reference to "direct acquaintance" suggests that Lewis' target is a position that conjoins (ST1) and chapter 10's (ST2b). Hasker nicely expresses (without fully endorsing) the nub of MTOA when he asks us to

> assume that some temporal reality is literally immediately present to a timeless God . . . temporal realities are different from moment to moment, whereas a timeless God cannot experience things differently at different moments; in the life of such a being, there are no different moments. So . . . which momentary aspect . . . of the temporal entity is present to God? The answer . . . must be that all of the temporal aspects of the entity are present . . . to God, not successively but simultaneously. But for an entity to have a number of apparently temporally successive aspects present simultaneously is precisely what it is for that entity to be timeless rather than temporal. So if an apparently temporal entity is literally immediately present to a timeless God, that entity *really is* timeless,[7]

or, more cautiously, that entity really is temporal, but time is tenseless.

6. Delmas Lewis, "Eternity Again," pp. 78, 79.
7. Hasker, "Yes, God," p. 389.

I suggest, then, that the metaphysical timelessness–omniscience argument is basically this:

5. If time is tensed, then (T) a proper subset S of the set of temporal events, consisting of a, b, c, etc., now has present-actuality.
6. A timeless being knows about events in time only what it can know about them by perceiving them spread all at once along a linear continuum.
7. No perception of events spread all at once along a linear continuum is perception that (T).
8. Therefore a timeless being does not know that (T).
9. If God is omniscient and it is the case that (T), God knows that (T).
10. So if (T) is true, it is not the case both that God is omniscient and that God is timeless.
11. So if time is tensed, it is not the case both that God is omniscient and that God is timeless.

If (11) is true, then (1), (2), and (4) are indeed jointly inconsistent.

Recasting the Argument

Clearly, (6) and (7) are the key to MTOA. The friends of MTOA believe (6) because they model God's knowledge of temporal events on direct perceptual acquaintance. The direct-acquaintance model of God's knowledge has strong intuitive support. For one thing, many philosophers hold that God's mode of knowing is nonpropositional, and direct perceptual acquaintance is the only candidate we have for a nonpropositional mode of knowing. Second, God is thought to be a perfect being. Prima facie, then, if He has knowledge, He is a perfect knower. This surely entails that His true beliefs are justified in the best possible way. Arguably, where a contingent fact is in question, the best possible way to justify a belief that that fact obtains is to be acquainted with that fact itself.

Though (6) may rest on the direct-acquaintance model, it also presumes that

a. present-actuality is a feature or attribute of temporal realities.
b. present-actuality is an *observer-independent* feature of these realities.

    c. this feature can be apprehended by direct perception.
    d. God can apprehend this feature *only* by direct perception.

Assumption (d) is crucial, for if (d) is false, a timeless God's inability to perceive directly which entities are presently actual does not rule out His knowing this, as He might have other ways to know it. Assumption (d) presupposes (c), and (c) presupposes (a), since only features and things can be perceived, and present-actuality is not a thing. Unless (b) is true, further, there is no objective fact God is missing if He misses present-actuality. Assumptions (a)–(d) are one and all controversial. Philosophers fond of the adage that existence is not a predicate would dispute (a) and therefore (c) and (d). Opponents of tensed theories of time deny (b).

An argument leaning on (a)–(d) might seem too weak to deserve attention. But I think that (a)–(d) are peripheral to the problem MTOA poses and that we can reformulate MTOA without involving (a)–(d). MTOA urges, I think, that there are *facts* (rather than truths) that a timeless God cannot know. Its point is that a timeless God's not knowing such truths as (T) may be overdetermined: He may be unable to know these not just because of the semantics of "now" but also because God knows things by direct acquaintance with what is presented to Him, and facts like the fact that (T) cannot be presented to a timeless being. I read MTOA this way because talk of divine perceptual acquaintance in effect ascribes to God a direct access to facts not mediated by a grasp of propositions about those facts. Such talk thus can raise the question of *factual* omniscience without also raising the question of *propositional* omniscience: one can take MTOA to contest the claim that God is factually omniscient, or cognitively grasps all facts.

Factual and propositional omniscience are different matters because knowing facts and knowing propositionally expressed truths are different matters. For one thing, as I suggest below, facts and propositions are individuated differently. Again, if there are ineffable facts, e.g., what certain directly presented sense-contents look or sound or feel like, then these are known without our thereby knowing any propositionally formulable truths. Again, one can know a fact and a proposition expressing that fact in radically different ways. For instance, I can have direct perceptual acquaintance with some sorts of fact but with no sort of proposition. Now it is not possible to be propositionally but not factually omniscient, for to know a truth is to know the fact that truth expresses. But if there are nonpropositional ways to access facts, it may be possible to be factually but not propositionally omniscient.

Aquinas, for one, affirms that God's way to know facts is non-propositional. In discussing whether God knows "whatever is enunciable," Aquinas writes that "God knows all enunciations that can be formed . . . He knows these not in the way enunciations are known, as if there were composition or division of enunciations in His intellect, but He knows each thing . . . by understanding its essence . . . and whatever can be added to that."[8] Thomas here asserts that God knows all truths that propositions can state, knowing them not by knowing propositions, but by some sort of direct intuitive insight. (For Thomas, propositions, like other creatures, are *objects* of God's knowledge, but He does not know what He knows by affirming them.) What God sees into is described as things' essences and the attributes that can be added to them (accidents). What God sees, then, are presumably such facts as that a human is a rational animal or that a man can be pale-skinned: that is, the facts themselves that render propositions true. Thomas takes himself to be arguing for God's propositional omniscience. But if "what can be enunciated" are the facts that propositions express, then Thomas has in fact argued only that God is factually omniscient, which does not entail that He is propositionally omniscient. Thomas has, that is, argued that for every truth, God knows the fact which that truth expresses—a claim that does not entail that God knows every truth about every fact.

I suspect that Thomas is typical in being committed only to factual omniscience, for the claim that God's knowledge is nonpropositional is common medieval coin. He is also typical in his commitment to a tensed theory of time.[9] If this is so, MTOA is more important than the semantic timelessness–omniscience argument, because only MTOA can claim to find an inconsistency among commitments theists genuinely make. Recently, Alston has gone so far as to argue that the claim that God's knowledge is nonpropositional lets theists sidestep the semantic argument altogether: "If the knowledge of a timeless . . . deity is propositionally structured, we have to ask whether that deity knows just the proposition that I expressed by the words 'the sun is shining now' . . . But on the nonpropositional account of divine knowledge . . . God [has] no traffic with either indexical or nonindexical propositions concerning the current state of affairs. That being the

8. "Deus sciat omnia enuntiabilia quae formari possunt . . . scit enuntiabilia non per modum enuntiabilium, quasi scilicet in intellectu eius sit compositio et divisio enuntiabilium, sed unumquodque cognoscit . . . intelligendo essentiam uniuscujus-que . . . et quaecunque eis accidere possit." *ST* Ia 14, 14, in *ST*, vol. 4, p. 52.

9. See, e.g., *In I Perihermeneias*, lect. 5, ## 63–64.

case, we cannot specify some bit of knowledge that is unavailable to Him by focusing on indexical propositions."[10] I am not sure that Alston is right about this. For arguably, if an entity A has knowledge, and its knowledge is of a sort that can be expressed by uttering a truth, and A is of a sort that can express knowledge by uttering truths, then A can express its knowledge by uttering a truth.[11] If this is so, then arguably, if God has knowledge, God can express His knowledge by uttering a truth, and so one can still ask whether God's mental state is such as to be expressible by the utterance of an indexical truth. But Alston may be right, and even if he is not, given Aquinas' commitments and the way they may be typical of theistic tradition, it clearly is worthwhile to put MTOA in a more cogent form. We may do so as follows, using the phrase "essentially tensed fact" to refer to the sort of fact that obtains only if a tensed theory of time is true:

5a. If time is tensed, then (T) expresses an essentially tensed fact.
6a. A timeless being knows only facts that can in some way be presented to it.
7a. A timeless being cannot be presented with essentially tensed facts.
8a. Therefore, if time is tensed, a timeless being does not know the fact that (T) expresses.
9a. If God is factually omniscient and (T) expresses a fact, God knows the fact that (T) expresses.
10a. So if (T) expresses an essentially tensed fact, it is not the case both that God is factually omniscient and that God is timeless.
11a. So if time is tensed, it is not the case both that God is factually omniscient and that God is timeless.

This revised argument depends on none of (a)–(d), though it does incorporate the tensed view of time (b) involves. Nor does it model God's knowledge very closely on sense perception, as it leaves indefinite what "being presented with" facts involves. I dispute (7), (7a), and the reasoning behind them below, thus rejecting MTOA. But I would first like to make another point. The friends of MTOA seem to think that if (10) or (10a) is true, theists will inevitably opt to retain omniscience and reject divine timelessness. This may not be the case.

10. Alston, "Does God Have Beliefs?" in *Divine Nature.*
11. The second clause exempts Rylean knowledge-how. The third exempts the knowledge of nonspeaking animals like dogs.

Must God Know Whatever We Know?

If two claims conflict, one should drop the claim with less backing. The friends of MTOA evidently think that "God is timeless" has less to back it than "God is omniscient" does. The late-classical and medieval philosophers who developed and defended the doctrine of God's eternity might not agree. These writers took this doctrine to be a consequence of a well-supported overarching theory of God's perfection. So if faced by the inconsistency MTOA alleges, these philosophers might not reject divine timelessness. They might instead reject the claim that an omniscient being knows all truths or facts (thus allowing that a God who does not know [T] could still be omniscient) or simply drop the claim that God is omniscient.

The first alternative is not implausible. We call God omnipotent even though there are many things that we can do but God cannot, e.g., walking, breathing, and (some say) sinning. Whatever we mean by calling God omnipotent, then, it is not that He has every ability we possess or can conceive. Perhaps, then, we should not mean by calling God omniscient that He has every item of knowledge we possess or can conceive. Note that I am not pointing to the sort of "limit" on God's abilities which is involved in His being unable to create, e.g., a round square. Such logical "limitations" are not strictly speaking limits at all. The act of creating a round square just cannot be performed, for there just cannot be a round square. A so-called action that cannot be performed is not really an action, for what *is* an action save something that someone can do? So to claim that God cannot create a round square is not to specify some action that God cannot perform. On the other hand, walking, breathing, and sinning are activities we all engage in daily. When we say that God cannot do these, we are saying that there are quite doable actions that God cannot do.[12]

12. That God cannot do these things does not entail the falsity of the Christian doctrine of the Incarnation. If God is able to become incarnate, He is able to be able to walk, breathe, etc., because He is able to perform an action that will acquire for Him these abilities. But the logic of ability is not such that "able to be able" entails "able simpliciter." Socks are able to fit snugly around my feet merely by expanding in a shape they already possess. A ball of wool is able to be knitted into a pair of socks. Hence it is able to be able to fit snugly around my feet merely by expanding in a shape it already possesses. But it is not at present able to fit snugly around my feet, etc. A ball of wool does not fit my feet at all.

Now some might think a believer in both divine timelessness and the Incarnation (if these beliefs are cotenable) cannot say that at any time God is able to be able to walk but not able to walk. For the transition from ability to be able to actually being able constitutes a real change, and if God is timeless, He is unable to undergo real change: so

If God is to be called omnipotent although there are doable actions that He cannot perform,[13] it could similarly be that God is to be called omniscient despite there being knowable items that He cannot know.[14] But the connection between the range of God's abilities and the range of His knowledge is closer than mere analogy. If God really does lack the abilities mentioned, it *follows* that there are items of knowledge He also lacks. For instance, God does not know what it feels like to be, oneself, a walker, a breather, or a sinner. For all and only persons who can walk, breathe, or sin can know these things, and God cannot walk, etc. God may know what it feels like for *me* to be these things; He "sees the secrets of the heart," we know not how. Because of this, God may know what it feels like for *someone* to be himself a walker, etc. But that someone is himself a walker is not the same fact as that one is oneself a walker. A person can know that someone is himself a walker and that he himself (or she herself) is not a walker.

Again, God may know what it is like to *seem* to be a walker or an evildoer if, say, He can appear as a walker to people or if some possible divine actions can seem evil to certain people. But He does not know what it is like to Himself *be* these things. As there is something it is like to be, oneself, a bat,[15] so too there is something it is like to be, oneself, human, and something it is like to be, oneself, able to see, to sin, or to walk. We are acquainted with these experiences and God is not. Nor

---

if God is ever able to walk, He is always so. There is a truth in this. If God is timeless and at some time becomes incarnate, then since the incarnation cannot constitute a change in Him, He is from all eternity incarnate, notwithstanding that *in time* He becomes incarnate only at a certain date. (There is no paradox here, as will emerge in the penultimate chapter.) But it remains true that God qua nonincarnate remains eternally able to be able but not able. This being so, my earlier point about God's disabilities stands, suitably qualified, even for a believer in the Incarnation. Moreover, even if the Incarnation be held to eliminate inabilities to walk, breathe, etc., *tout court*, there will still remain God's inability to do moral evil, at least according to such traditional theists as Anselm (see *Proslogion*, chap. 7) and Aquinas (see *ST* Ia 25, 3 *ad* 2).

13. This does not entail that there is some distinct first-order power to do evil that we have and God lacks, as there is a distinct power to walk, breathe, etc. (see Thomas Morris, "Perfection and Power," *International Journal for Philosophy of Religion* 20 [1986], 167–168). An act of doing so-and-so is *also* an act of evildoing, in appropriate situations; its moral character supervenes on its other traits. If God is necessarily morally perfect, then in any circumstance C, He cannot perform any action A such that A would be an evildoing in C. What we have and a necessarily morally perfect God lacks, then, is a second-order power, the power to employ all one's first-order powers in all situations without regard for their moral character.

14. Thus limits on omniscience and limits on omnipotence seem fully parallel, counter to Jonathan Kvanvig, *The Possibility of an All-Knowing God* (New York: St. Martin's Press, 1986), pp. 23–24.

15. See Thomas Nagel, "What Is It Like To Be a Bat?" *Philosophical Review* 83 (1974), 435–450.

are these experiences wholly private. Each human being knows what it is like to be, oneself, a human being or a sinner.

This lack of experience affects God's knowledge of truths. Suppose that I want to show you how failure feels. I rig a test for you before a jeering throng, you fail miserably, the crowd hoots, and you slink away. I then say "being a failure oneself feels like *this*." This is a proposition we both grasp. Moreover, if I have been careful enough in setting things up, it is true—I have induced in you the feeling of failure. You and I can know that being a failure oneself feels like *this*, but if God cannot fail, God cannot (though He can know how failure feels *to you*). For if God cannot fail, God cannot have the kind of experience "this" picks out and so in a sense cannot even understand the proposition that "being a failure oneself feels like *this*."[16] So it seems that God's very perfection, by entailing that He cannot fail, entails that He cannot be propositionally omniscient—that there are knowable truths God cannot know.[17] God's lack of relevant abilities entails a lack of knowledge of certain truths.[18] It may also entail that there are facts with which He cannot be acquainted, e.g., the fact that being oneself a failure feels like *this*.

The limits on omnipotence we have discussed are reasonable and traditional. So the parallel limits on omniscience are equally reasonable and should have been traditional. If it does not detract from God's omnipotence to be unable to sin, forget, fail, feel pain, and so on, it does not detract from His omniscience not to know what it is like to do these things. Perhaps God is omniscient although there are things He is too perfect to be able to know, as He is omnipotent though there are tasks He is too perfect to be able to do.

Let us consider the second alternative introduced at the start of this section, that of just giving up the claim that God is omniscient. This move could be defended. Arguably, the controlling claim in philosophical theology is or should be the claim that God is a perfect being.[19] A reasonable decision-procedure for filling out the concept of a perfect

16. If God logically cannot fail, He cannot even try to grasp this proposition, for if He tried, He would fail.

17. The entailment between limits on God's power and limits on His knowledge runs in both directions. Suppose that we know and God does not know the proposition P. If we know P, we have an ability to express a proposition one knows by tokening "P." If God does not know P, God lacks this ability.

18. Again, this does not entail that there is some first-order ability to fail, which we have and God lacks. Rather, what we have and God lacks is a second-order ability, the ability to employ one's first-order abilities defectively.

19. "Process" philosophers can accept this, by interpreting "being" in a way reflecting a "process" metaphysics.

being, based on Anselm's,[20] might look something like this: isolate a set of attributes that prima facie ought to belong to such a being. (Just how one might determine what attributes these are is a long, hard story that does not need telling here.) If none of these are incompatible, assume that the being has all of them. If not all these attributes are compossible, then ascribe to that being a set of these attributes such that no possible set of these attributes could lend a greater degree of perfection to its possessor.[21]

Suppose that a set of attributes that results from the Anselmian decision-procedure includes that of having knowledge and also includes an attribute incompatible with that of having the maximum conceivable degree of knowledge. Arguably, if this is so, perfect knowledge is not omniscience but is instead the knowledge appropriate to an overall perfect being—i.e., is whatever knowing-attributes are members of this set. We have seen powerful reasons to embrace the claim that God is timeless. If we would have to qualify or give up some or all of the theistic commitments that led to this conclusion in order to secure God's knowledge of (T), perhaps the latter would not be prize enough to motivate this. Perhaps, that is, God would be more perfect without this knowledge than with it. If perfection does require time-lessness and MTOA is sound, then perhaps perfection simply precludes omniscience, by precluding knowing (T). That perfection precludes omniscience may sound paradoxical,[22] but philosophy is full of surprises.

There could be good reason to call God a perfect knower even if there were truths or facts He did not and could not know. Cognitive perfection need not involve having the greatest conceivable *range* of knowledge. It could instead be a multifaceted thing involving the necessary possession (say) of maximally continent doxastic habits, of the best possible grounds to justify any beliefs one does form, of the greatest *actual* range of knowledge, of the greatest possible range of knowledge of many important sorts (e.g., truths of ethics, mathematics, or future history), of all the knowledge it is possible that He have

20. See Anselm, *Monologion*, chap. 15; *Proslogion*, chap. 5.

21. Note that this procedure does not guarantee that just one such set of attributes will emerge. It may be that we are not that lucky. It *would* guarantee this if we legislated that if sets of attributes S and S* both lend their possessors the same degree of perfection, and no other set of attributes lends its possessors a greater perfection, the perfect being has neither S nor S*—for then in case of a tie, the sole set of attributes the procedure would warrant would be the null set.

22. Gale, "Omniscience-Immutability Arguments," p. 332.

(given that He can have a suitably large range of knowledge),[23] and/or of the greatest range of knowledge any single individual can have.

God's cognitive perfection could even involve having the greatest *possible* range of propositional knowledge, provided that propositional omniscience is impossible. But there is reason to suspect that propositional omniscience is not possible. For it may be that for each person, there is a truth that person alone knows: Herman alone knows the truth that he expresses by tokening "I am Herman," Hermione alone knows the truth that she expresses by tokening "I am Hermione," and so on.[24] It is true that when Herman says "I am Herman," Hermione can respond "I know that." But arguably, what Hermione knows is not exactly the same truth Herman knows. Hermione knows of Herman (*de re*) that he is Herman. But Herman could know this without knowing what he expresses by tokening "I am Herman."[25] Suppose that Herman acquires amnesia and forgets what his face looks like. Hermione then leads Herman into a room with some carefully arranged mirrors in it, so that Herman faces a reflection of himself in what *looks* like a window rather than a mirror: Herman sees the reflection but does not know that it is a reflection or a fortiori that it is *his* reflection. Hermione then points at Herman's reflection and says "this is Herman." In this case Herman knows of Herman that he is Herman but does not know what he would express by tokening "I am Herman." If such privately knowable truths as "I am Herman" exist, this is because each of us is one person rather than another.[26] God's not knowing these truths, then, might reveal no more than that He is one person rather than another, as are we all.

23. If one called it a cognitive perfection for any being to have all the knowledge it can have, regardless of the range of that knowledge, then if there were a being that could know only one proposition, this being would count as having a cognitive perfection in virtue of knowing just one truth—which is absurd.

24. See Kretzmann, "Omniscience," p. 376. This claim is contested in Kvanvig, *Possibility*, pp. 47–71. Kvanvig also cites some recent defenses of private truths.

25. My argument here depends on Perry, "Problem."

26. Were there no other hard cases for propositional omniscience lurking about, it would seem that had God not created other persons, He would be propositionally omniscient. It is also true that if God has created time, then if essentially tensed facts are a problem for His omniscience, they would not be so had God not created time. (I owe this point to William Alston.) Even if creating time or other persons did deprive God of an omniscience He would otherwise have, this would not entail that creating changes God. One could say rather that God always timelessly knows just what He in fact timelessly knows, but whether this knowledge counts as propositional omniscience depends on whether there are truths in addition to the truths God always timelessly knows.

326]   Time and Eternity

Strict propositional omniscience would include knowledge of all truths, including therefore knowledge of what Herman alone knows and Hermione alone knows, if there are such truths. Thus if there are such truths, someone can be propositionally omniscient just in case he or she can be both Herman and Hermione—which is impossible. Hence if there are such truths (as it seems there are), it cannot be the case that our world, which contains more than one knower, also contains a propositionally omniscient being.[27] A stronger argument against the very possibility of propositional omniscience may be based on Gödel's incompleteness results, but I cannot pursue this here.[28]

If propositional omniscience is impossible, it in no way impugns God's greatness that He lacks it. Again, if propositional omniscience is impossible, that God does not know some particular truth does not entail that He does not have the greatest possible range of knowledge. Finally, if propositional omniscience is impossible, this undercuts the semantic timelessness–omniscience argument's case that theists facing (10) should reject divine timelessness. For those who defend the semantic argument want theists to do this to preserve divine propositional omniscience. If this cannot be preserved regardless, there is no point to rejecting divine timelessness, unless (as I deny shortly) one can find some further reason that God must know temporally indexical truths. Parallel arguments could be made were factual omniscience to prove impossible as well. Suppose on the other hand that propositional omniscience is possible for God, though not in our world (since Herman exists and God ≠ Herman). Suppose, for instance, that there is a possible world in which neither time nor persons other than God exist, and that in this world, God is propositionally omniscient. If there is such a world, it does not affect my counter to the semantic timelessness–omniscience argument, for the semantic argument concerns whether God is timeless in *our* possible world, and it remains the case that denying that He is timeless in our world will not secure the claim that He is propositionally omniscient in our world.

If propositional or factual omniscience could not be salvaged, one would have to ask whether there is some other reason to say that a being must know (T) or the essentially tensed fact (T) expresses to be God. It would, for example, be a powerful objection to denying God knowledge of (T) or of this fact if this denial rendered God unworthy of worship. But if it makes sense to call God perfect though nonomniscient, then He can deserve our worship without knowledge of (T) or

27. This point was first made in Kretzmann, "Omniscience." Helm independently puts it to related use in *Eternal God*, pp. 75–76.
28. See Patrick Grim, "Logic and Limits," pp. 341–367, and "Truth," pp. 9–41.

this fact, for (I would argue) any perfect being deserves worship. Would denying that God knows (T) or the essentially tensed fact (T) expresses render God not unworthy but less worthy of worship? If a timeless, nonomniscient deity rather than a temporal and omniscient deity would be the most perfect possible being, God's knowing (T) or this fact would render Him less rather than more worship-worthy. So to press this objection, one would have to show that there can be no most perfect possible being or that the most perfect possible being would be temporal and omniscient—a tall order.

Again, it would be a powerful objection to denying God knowledge of (T) or the essentially tensed fact (T) expresses if this denial reduced the religious value of the concept of God. But this denial may well not do so, for as we have seen, God does not need to know which events have present-actuality to answer prayer or to act providentially or sal-vifically. Granted, *we* need to know this to guide our attitudes and actions. If I am told that a tornado strikes the Bronx at 10 A.M. on July 7, 1990, this will not motivate me to act unless I also am told that it is *now* 10 A.M. on that particular day (and I am in the Bronx). But suppose that God timelessly knows that on July 7, at 10:05, I pray to be spared death by tornado, and because He knows this timelessly ensures that on July 7, at 10:10, I make it safely to a tornado shelter.[29] In this case, God has heard my prayer and responded to it providentially, without having to know that it is now July 7.[30]

How God Perceives Present-Actuality

Let us return now to MTOA. The unrevised version of MTOA claims that

> 7. No perception of temporal entities spread out all at once along a linear continuum is perception of (T).

Delmas Lewis' justification for (7) seems to run this way. Present-actuality is differential actuality. It is part of the concept of present-actuality that not all things at all times have it at once. So some entities are perceived to have it only if some other entities are not perceived to have it. Thus, Lewis believes,

29. As was argued above, "because" does not imply that God acts *after* hearing me. It implies only that had it not timelessly been the case that God hears me, it would not have timelessly been the case that He saves me.
30. That God eternally responds to a prayer that takes place only on July 7, 1990, may sound paradoxical. But I have argued above that it is not.

12. for all x, if x perceives that all and only the members of S have present-actuality, x perceives only some, not all, temporal entities to be present now.

Lewis also holds that

13. for all x, if x perceives temporal entities spread out all at once along a linear continuum, x perceives them all as present now.

Given these premises, Lewis reasons that

14. If A perceives that all and only the members of S have present-actuality, A perceives only some, not all, temporal entities to be present now. (12, UI)
15. A perceives all temporal entities to be present now. (assumption for conditional proof)
16. A does not perceive that all and only the members of S have present-actuality. (14, 15, MT)
17. If A perceives all temporal entities to be present now, A does not perceive that all and only the members of S have present-actuality. (14–16, conditional proof)
18. For all x, if x perceives all temporal entities to be present now, x does not perceive that all and only the members of S have present-actuality. (17, UG)
19. For all x, if x perceives temporal entities spread out all at once along a linear continuum, x does not perceive that all and only the members of S have present-actuality. (13, 18, HS)

(19), of course, is equivalent to (7). Now for this argument to be valid, "now" must occur in the same sense in (12) and (13). But it does not. "Now" brings ambiguity to (12) and (13), as emerges when we consider STR's claim that simultaneity is framework-relative.[31] For the relativity of simultaneity entails a relativity of temporal presentness. This is because the predicable "____ is present now" has a token-reflexive aspect. Whatever else it may communicate, in normal circumstances

31. As we have seen, the relativity of simultaneity also entails a relativity of present-actuality. Lawrence Sklar argues further in "Time, Reality, and Relativity" that in STR there is an element of arbitrary convention in deciding to which distant events to ascribe simultaneity with present events; this conventionality may likewise infect ascriptions of present-actuality. If this is so, defenders of (4) must somehow come to grips with it. I need not try to, as I am merely granting (4) for the sake of argument.

the meaning of the assertion "A is present now" includes something like "A exists simultaneous with this time." So if temporal simultaneity is framework-relative, words such as "now" must in strict propriety be subscripted to indicate the framework of reference within which one is speaking. Thus in (12) and (13), "now" is ambiguous. It could indicate the now of any one of the infinitely many temporal reference frames. Or it could indicate the timeless "now" of the eternal reference frame.

Either "now" occurs in distinct senses (i.e., differently subscripted) in (12) and (13), or (13) is clearly false. According to (12), to perceive that all and only the members of a proper subset of S have present-actuality is to perceive only some, not all, temporal entities as present now. Presumably, "present now" is indexed to some temporal frame of reference in which all and only S's members *are* present now. Hence if "present now" in (13) is indexed to the same frame of reference, (13) asserts that a timeless being sees all events as occurring *at once in that frame of reference*. But Lewis himself denies this. On his view, what a timeless God sees is an extended four-dimensional continuum that suffices to inform him which events occur later than others (in each reference frame). Thus, again, either (13) is false or in it "present now" is used with reference to a different framework than that involved in (12). If the latter, Lewis' argument is invalid. For then (12) should actually read

12a. For all x, if x perceives that all and only the members of S have present-actuality, x perceives only some, not all, temporal entities to be present now$_1$,

so that (18) should read

18a. For all x, if x perceives all temporal entities to be present now$_1$, x does not perceive that all and only the members of S have present-actuality.

But (13) should read

13a. For all x, if x perceives temporal entities spread out all at once along a linear continuum, x perceives all entities as present now$_2$.

Clearly, (13a) and (18a) do not jointly entail (19). Thus Lewis does not manage to back (7). As (7a) and (7) are quite similar, I suggest that arguments for (7a) will rest on considerations like those backing (7) and so will also fail. So we are free to reject (7) and (7a), if we can offer a cogent alternate account of a timeless being's knowledge of essentially tensed facts.

The problem lurking beneath (12) and (13) points to more general difficulties with MTOA. In its unrevised version, MTOA ignores the framework-relativity of present-actuality. In its revised version, MTOA ignores the corresponding fact that even if they are objective, essentially tensed facts are framework-relative. I return to these points shortly.

Another Version

Lewis varies his argument in another article:

> In the eternal present in which God beholds all of temporal reality, there is no contrast between past, present and future with respect to existence . . . God is omniscient, and His knowledge is perfect and complete. Hence . . . God's view of things must be the correct view. Since God is unaware of [a] difference . . . with respect to existence . . . between . . . things present and . . . things past and future, there is no such difference . . . Otherwise . . . God has a false or inaccurate picture of temporal reality . . . Hence if God is eternal, the present does not differ with respect to existence from the past and the future, and the tenseless view of time is correct.[32]

Here Lewis' reasoning is this:

20. If God is timeless, then from His point of view all events are actual at once.
21. If all events are actual at once, time is not tensed.
22. If God is omniscient, then things are as they appear from God's point of view.
23. Hence if God is timeless and omniscient, time is not tensed.
24. So if time is tensed, it is not the case both that God is omniscient and that God is timeless.

(22) is a bit problematic. The claim that God is omniscient concerns the *range* of God's knowledge. It does not concern the way things appear to God; it entails at most that *however* things appear to God, they so

---

32. Delmas Lewis, "Eternity, Time," pp. 82–83.

appear as to allow Him to know some suitably large range of facts or truths. So it is not clear why (22) should be supposed to be true. Perhaps, then, Lewis means to assert not (22) but

22a. If God is a perfect knower, then things are as they appear from God's point of view,

and to adjust (23) and (24) accordingly. If (22a) is Lewis' real claim, then this argument is not actually a timelessness-omniscience argument. It might be stronger than a timelessness-omniscience argument, however, given the broader range of considerations that might support (22a). Another difficulty in this argument is that (20) is ambiguous, between at least

20a. The experience of a timeless being is such that all items that are ever in this experience are in it simultaneously, and
20b. A timeless being's experience involves perceiving all events as happening at once.

(20a) is clearly true. Were an item first not present in a timeless being's experience and then present there, the timeless being's experience would change, and so then would the timeless being. A timeless being cannot change. Thus items in a timeless being's experience cannot be there successively. But only (20b) will serve Lewis' purposes. (20a) does not entail (20b); on one perhaps viable but inelegant theory and one elegant but perhaps not viable theory of divine "perception," (20a) is true but (20b) is false.

(20a) could be true while (20b) is false if, for example, (ST2a) but not (ST1) is true, and God has a timeless equivalent of sense data. That God has a sense datum of temporally discrete events all at once does not entail that He forms the false belief that the events occur all at once or fails to form true beliefs about their temporal relations. Let us say that Betelgeuse is eight light-years from Earth and the star Stella is forty light-years away. I can have a single sense datum representing them both at once, if there are such things as sense data. Further, suppose some astronomer tells me about a certain light fluctuation that stars invariably produce one year before they explode. If I see Betelgeuse and Stella at once, and notice Stella producing this peculiar light pattern, I will form the belief that Betelgeuse exists and Stella no longer does, even if I see them both. If I can avoid believing that Stella and Betelgeuse both exist now although I perceive both now, God can. If I can, in addition, accurately judge the stars' distances, I can form accurate beliefs about the temporal relations of events on the stars.[33] If I can do this, surely a timeless God can. So divine sense data would let (20a) be true while (20b) is false.

The Stump-Kretzmann view of simultaneity offers materials for a direct-realist theory of divine perception.[34] On their version of (ST2b), a timeless God sees all events occur at once because

> 20c. the experience of a timeless being is ET-simultaneous with all successive temporal events, though they are not in any way simultaneous themselves.

On their view, that is, events really occur sequentially in time and also all at once *for God,* though they do not really occur at once and God has no eternal "sense data." Stump and Kretzmann hold that every divine perception of temporal events is ET-simultaneous with every temporal event, and so God coexists with the whole of time and perceives each event as it occurs in time. For Stump and Kretzmann, every divine perception is also eternally simultaneous with every other.[35] Thus every divine perception occurs at once in eternity. As all God's perceivings exist at once, all temporal entities exist at once *for God* although they do not do so in themselves and although God has no "sense data."[36] Nothing in this theory requires that God erroneously judge that all temporal entities really do exist at once. So this theory can deny that (20a) entails (20b). Moreover, on this theory God is directly acquainted with the very essentially tensed fact that (T) expresses and with all like facts. For every now, God "sees" what is happening now.

Either of these two theories might ultimately prove viable. If either is, one can reject (20b) and the claim that (20a) entails (20b), thus frustrating this version of MTOA.

The Anselmian Approach

The Anselmian theory of time and eternity cannot reject (20), since it explicitly affirms both (20a) and (20b). But this theory provides reason

33. At least, beliefs accurate relative to some perhaps-conventional specification of the one-way speed of light. For discussion of the problem of distant simultaneity in STR, see Wesley Salmon, *Space, Time,* pp. 93–127.
34. "Eternity," pp. 434–444. Hasker independently worked out basically the same position in "Concerning the Intelligibility."
35. Ibid., pp. 434–435.
36. One might want to argue that since God's seeing of event E is ET-simultaneous with E, God's seeing of later event E* is ET-simultaneous with E*, and God's seeings are eternally simultaneous, E and E* are in some manner simultaneous. But the fact that generic simultaneity is intransitive blocks this argument.

to reject (21). If the Anselmian is right, all events are actual at once, *in eternity*. But it does not follow that time is not tensed. Events also occur in temporal reference frames, and the time of these reference frames may be tensed. The Anselmian theory rejects as oversimple the conceptions of present-actuality and essentially tensed facts which motivate MTOA. Present-actuality, we have seen, is framework-relative. So too, then, are essentially tensed facts. The reason a timeless God does not know the essentially tensed fact that (T) is that in His framework of reference, eternity, *this is not a fact at all*. (T), again, is the claim that a proper subset S of the set of temporal events, consisting of a, b, c, etc., now has present-actuality. In eternity this claim is false. In eternity, *all* temporal events A-occur at once, and so all have present-actuality at once. Present-actuality is differential actuality *within temporal frames of reference,* and to perceive present-actuality requires perceiving not all events as actual at once *within temporal frames of reference*. But things are different in eternity.

All the same, the Anselmian theory in no way reduces time, change, succession, and nonsimultaneity to illusions. STR entails that *all* frameworks' distinctive judgments of local simultaneity are equally true. Even if an eternal frame of reference exists which contains its own simultaneity, present actuality, and essentially tensed facts, temporal frames of reference also exist, and these reference frames have their own equally real simultaneity, present actuality, and essentially tensed facts. Nor does the Anselmian theory render events' *occurrence* framework-relative. As we saw in chapter 10, on this theory, the very same occurrence occurs in all frameworks of reference. Only simultaneity, presentness, and present-actuality are framework-relative. The same events that A-occur in our temporal present A-occur in God's eternal present. They are there "in their presentness": the very A-occurrence that is B-simultaneous with certain events within temporal reference frames is A-simultaneous with a timeless being's existence and with all temporal events within an eternal reference frame. Thus God can timelessly perceive, all at once, the very A-occurring that we perceive sequentially, under the form of change.

This has a consequence that may seem startling. One traditional mark of "secondary" qualities has been a certain perceiver-relativity. Red, for example, is seen as a secondary quality because to be red is to be such as to look red to standard human perceivers in standard conditions.[37] If a timeless God can be presented with A-occurrences, but not with these as involving the sort of change we think them to involve,

37. See Colin McGinn, *The Subjective View* (New York: Oxford University Press, 1983), chap. 1, passim.

then this sort of change is itself perceiver-relative and a secondary quality. So, then, is spatial motion, which Locke called a primary quality. But this is actually as it should be. STR turns most or all Newtonian primary qualities into secondary qualities.

A factually omniscient being can only be required to grasp directly such facts as are genuinely facts within that being's framework of reference. Thus the fact that a timeless God grasps directly only the essentially tensed facts of eternity does not count against His strict factual omniscience, provided that he has some other access to the essentially tensed facts of other reference frames. But we have already seen that a timeless God can know all the facts of simultaneity that obtain in other reference frames. Thus He can know what the essentially tensed facts of these other frames *are*, though He cannot be directly presented with these facts: it is just not true that the only way God can know facts is by some sort of direct presentation. I suggest further that a timeless God's inability to be presented with the essentially tensed facts of other frameworks of reference is not a cognitive defect. For despite this, it can still be true that God has the greatest range of factual knowledge possible for any single individual. Further, that God cannot be presented with the essentially tensed facts of any temporal frame of reference follows from the claim that He is timeless (and so necessarily timeless) and the necessary truth that God cannot have as a reference frame a reference frame in which He is not located. Hence per our earlier argument, if our overall theory of divine perfection favors the doctrine of divine timelessness, we can just conclude that perfect knowledge includes being directly presented with only the essentially tensed facts of eternity.

If we now return to our revised version of MTOA, we can see that the Anselmian will consider this argument confused and unsound. To begin with, (5a) to an Anselmian is ambiguous between

   5a*. if time is tensed, then (T) expresses an essentially tensed fact *in the appropriate frame of reference,* and
   5a**. if time is tensed, then (T) expresses an essentially tensed fact *in eternity.*

Only (5a**) would cause problems for an Anselmian. But for an Anselmian, while (5a*) is true and harmless, (5a**) is false, since (T) is not true in eternity and so expresses no fact in eternity. Further, the Anselmian will reject (7a). On the Anselmian theory, God is presented with all the essentially tensed facts there are *in eternity,* and again, one cannot require a factually omniscient being to be presented with facts that are not facts in His framework.

On either the Anselmian or the Stump-Kretzmann view, God is directly presented with all essentially tensed facts. The two views differ chiefly over just what essentially tensed facts there are for God to grasp. I submit, therefore, that if either view is viable, there really is no problem about a timeless God's grasp of essentially tensed facts: the claim that God is timeless is compatible with the claim that God is factually omniscient.

Factual Omniscience

Let me try to flesh out the concept of factual omniscience. A fact is either the existing of a subject or a subject's exemplifying of an attribute. Ockham's Razor dictates parsimony not only in basic ontological kinds but in the number of entities of each kind we admit. If one adopts facts as an ontological category, then, it is reasonable to allow as few distinct facts as one can into one's scheme of things. (If one eliminates facts as otiose in a scheme that allows for subjects and attributes, the same point will apply to subjects and attributes.) I suggest, then, that we admit as real only the *most specific* fact or attribute needed to render a family of propositions true. For instance, suppose that Kermit is of the species bullfrog. That Kermit is of this species entails that he belongs to various other classes. We can say, then, that Kermit's being a bullfrog is a fact, but that Kermit is a frog or an amphibian or an animal are just truths which that fact goes to make true. These truths express aspects of that single fact but do not describe it as specifically as it can be described.

Families of truths need not be arranged in genus-species hierarchy. Perhaps only a knower at 3 P.M. can know the truth—let us call it (T*)—that one expresses by tokening at that time "it is now 3 P.M." The claim that

25. it is *then* (i.e., at 3 P.M.) 3 P.M.

is not identical with (T*). Nor is (25) just another way to express (T*), for one can know (T*) only at 3 P.M., but one can know (25) at all times or none, and if (25) were just another way to express (T*), then in knowing (25), one would know that it is now 3 P.M. All the same, I submit, (25) is true in virtue of the same fact that renders (T*) true, and expresses that fact. It is, I suggest, a member of the family of truths based on the (T*)-fact.

When I assert (25), I *mean* to point to the same fact that someone at 3 P.M. expresses by saying "it is now 3 P.M." There is no reason to think that I fail to do so, even if I at other times cannot know certain truths based on that fact, such as (T*). One fact can make true an indefinitely large family of propositions about that very same fact; conversely, many truths express the same fact. One could argue that such claims as (25) express the (T*)-fact as fully as can be done in non-3-P.M. contexts. One could contend, that is, that the difference in content between (25) and (T*) derives solely from the different modes of access differently located knowers have to the (T*)-fact.

Such writers as Nelson Pike, Richard Swinburne, John Perry, and Jonathan Kvanvig argue that when one tokens such tensed truths as (T*), two things are involved, a truth that anyone at any time (or no time) can know (say, that 3 P.M. = 3 P.M.) and a special mode of access to this truth which only someone located at 3 P.M. can use—namely, knowing this truth by knowing that it is now 3 P.M.[38] My position is not that of Pike et al., because these writers deny that there is a special truth to be known only at 3 P.M. and hold that there is just a special 3-P.M. mode of access to a truth knowable at all times. My position is rather that the (T*)-fact is accessible at all times in varying ways *and* that the various modes of access one can have to this fact generate distinctive truths that can only be known at various times.

If I never know that it is now 3 P.M., then, I never know all the truths about 3 P.M. But arguably, there is a sense in which even if I never know that it is now 3 P.M., if I know all other facts about 3 P.M. and also know that it was *then* 3 P.M. (and that for anyone existing then, this could be expressed by tokening "it is now 3 P.M."), I know all the facts about 3 P.M. For I know a truth based on and expressing the (T*)-fact which expresses it as fully, and is as close in content to "it is now 3 P.M.," as is possible at times other than 3 P.M.[39] Fully substantiating this claim would require a full treatment of intimacy to facts, which I cannot provide here. But the claim is plausible intuitively.

I suggest, therefore, that even if a timeless God cannot be propositionally omniscient concerning events in time, there is a case to be made that such a being can be factually omniscient about events in time. For a timeless God can directly grasp every fact about temporal events which is not essentially tensed, directly grasp every essentially tensed fact that is a fact for Him, and (on the Anselmian alternative) know in some other way all the essentially tensed facts of temporal frames of reference. A timeless God can also be fairly close to proposi-

38. Pike, God, pp. 87–96; Swinburne, Coherence, pp. 164–166; Perry, "Problem," pp. 18–20; Kvanvig, Possibility, pp. 27–71, 151–158.
39. Cf. Michelle Beer, "Temporal Indexicals and the Passage of Time," Philosophical Quarterly 38 (1988), 158–164. One need not use this fact, as Beer does, to argue for a tenseless theory of time.

tionally omniscient concerning events in time. Every family of temporal propositions contains some that use "now" or tense to express a temporal relation to a temporal A-occurrence. Such uses and only such uses of "now" or tense locate their user in time. So God's being timeless would be compatible with His knowing every member of every family of temporal propositions which does not so use "now" or tense. If my earlier arguments about omniscience and perfection hold up, this plus factual omniscience should be more than enough to preserve a strong sense in which a timeless God is cognitively perfect.

15

Omniscience, Change, and Epistemic Indexicals

Indexical terms like "I," "now," or "here" are semantically relative to their users and occasions of use: "now" always denotes the time at which the proposition in which "now" figures is uttered, and "I" always denotes the utterer of the proposition in which "I" figures. The previous chapter discussed the impact of personal indexicals on the possibility of omniscience and the impact of temporal indexicals on the compatibility of timelessness and omniscience. These matters have been much treated since the mid-1960s. To my knowledge, the debate over indexicality has not touched on what I call the epistemic use of indexicals.[1] A temporal indexical is semantically relative to its time of utterance, and so a truth essentially involving a temporal indexical can be known only at the appropriate location(s) in time. One makes epistemic use of an indexical if one uses an indexical to refer to something that can be known only to someone with certain epistemic abilities. If so, a truth essentially involving an epistemic use of an indexical can be known only by someone able to acquire information about the world in a certain way.

This chapter suggests that there are truths essentially involving epistemic uses of indexicals. If such truths exist, it can be argued that at least one cannot be known by a timeless, immutable deity, and others may be unknowable by a deity who cannot see. If there are such truths, they pose problems for the claim that an immutable, bodiless deity is

1. It has, however, come close. See John Lachs, "Professor Prior on Omniscience," *Philosophy* 38 (1963), pp. 361–364, and David Blumenfeld, "On the Compossibility of the Divine Attributes," in Thomas Morris, ed., *The Concept of God* (New York: Oxford University Press, 1987), pp. 201–215. Related matters crop up in Anthony Kenny, *The God of the Philosophers* (New York: Oxford University Press, 1979), pp. 27–37.

propositionally omniscient. If there are such truths, further, they suggest that there may be facts with which a timeless deity cannot be presented, and so they imperil the claim that such a God is factually omniscient.

I focus on one case, which can be taken as a case of an epistemically indexical truth or as a case of what Russell called knowledge by acquaintance. If it is the latter, it will suggest that knowledge by acquaintance is nonpropositional, or has a nonpropositional component. We will see that if there is such nonpropositional knowledge, there may be a fact with which an immutable deity cannot be presented.

What Can the Blind Know about Colors?

First, then, let us develop our example. Suppose that Caecus, blind from birth, decides that he wants to know all that he can about colors. He enrolls in courses on the physics of light. He listens to lectures on the colors of great paintings. He asks all his friends to compile lists of ordinary objects' colors. He also asks one particular friend, an inventor, to design a device that will enable him to give correct answers to questions about colors within the range of ordinary eyesight. The inventor obliges by wiring a narrowly focused and very discriminating color sensor to a small computer able to make musical notes. When the sensor is pointed at a green spot, the computer sounds middle C; for a lighter green, B; for a blue-green, C-sharp; and so on. By correlating musical notes with color terms, Caecus can use this machine to answer correctly any question about circumambient colors which a sighted person could answer.

By many more such expedients, let us suppose, Caecus acquires an immense range of true beliefs about colors and also becomes able to expand that range indefinitely. We may even suppose that Caecus, if asked for the information, could give directions for the production of a completely accurate map of the location of all patches of all colors. But there will still be at least one thing Caecus does not know. He will not know what colors *look like*. Let us now ask just what this ignorance involves.

By means of his sensor, etc., Caecus can create the complete color map just mentioned. So Caecus has access to a great range of color information that a sighted person can acquire by the use of vision. Can he know every truth a sighted person can know about colors, then, or is there some information Caecus cannot acquire? Consider truths of the form "red looks like this" or "this is what red looks like," where "this" picks out a red surface. Caecus's sensing device lets him know when claims of the form "this is red" are true. So he will also know when claims like "red looks like this" are true. The question, then, is whether in knowing that this claim is true, he will also know the truth it expresses.

One can maintain that he will. Let us first distinguish this claim's truth-conditions from its assertion-conditions. The proposition is about the surface, not the private, personal experience the surface may cause. Now truth-conditions, we are told, ain't in the head. What makes it true that this substance in my glass is water is a chemical makeup that is no part of my experience of it or my nonchemical thinking about it. Similarly, if it is true that this surface is colored in such a way as to make a normal perceiver in normal circumstances experience what red looks like, this is doubtless because of the peculiar makeup of the surface and its particles, their way of interacting with light of a particular wavelength and intensity, and the way such light would strike a normally disposed human eye at a suitable distance. All of these are matters we normally do not consider in thinking about colors. Blind and sighted are equally able or unable to ascertain that these conditions obtain. Where the blind and the sighted differ is in the assertion-conditions each will attach to the proposition "red looks like this" (and, of course, in the experience they will have on occasions when they are disposed to assert it). But as long as their diverse assertion-conditions would lead them to produce the same color map of their surroundings, perhaps it is acceptable to say that the blind and the sighted know the same facts about color, albeit that they learn them in different ways.

If the meaning of a proposition is a function of its truth-conditions, then perhaps we can even say that the blind and the sighted can know all of the same truths about those facts. (If meaning is a function of assertion-conditions, on the other hand, one may question whether the blind can know any of the same truths about color that the sighted may know. I find the claim that the blind can know nothing of what the sighted know of color implausible. If it is, perhaps this suggests that assertibility-based semantics are less than plausible.) If blind and sighted can know all the same truths, then what Caecus lacks is a form of nonpropositional knowledge. That is, suppose that Caecus can acquire every statable bit of color information in his own way. Even so, Caecus's way of acquiring all this information differs from a sighted man's. The difference in his mode of acquiring it may entail that he lacks another sort of knowledge of color, that which Russell would call nonpropositional knowledge of color by acquaintance.

If this knowledge exists, we cannot assimilate it to knowledge of how to apply color words or how to recognize colors. We are assuming that Caecus can do these things as well as a sighted person may (at least if by "recognizing colors" we mean an ability to acquire accurate information about colors and act and talk on the basis of that information). Again, we are assuming for the nonce that Caecus can acquire all the information a sighted person can have, meaning by that that Caecus can know all true propositions concerning colors. If we make this assumption, then what colors look like is not a piece of information or a truth. But still, it is something, and something knowledge of which Caecus cannot but lack. If there is such a something, then on this account it is not usually communicated by ordinary speech. For notoriously, inverted spectra at least *seem* possible, and color-blind persons may become fully competent users of color words and acquirers of color information even though the contents of their awarenesses of colors differ drastically from ours. Thus there are reasons to call what Caecus lacks nonpropositional knowledge.

But *is* what Caecus lacks really nonpropositional? Can we really be content to say that what red looks like is not a piece of information? A second approach to what Caecus can't know about color might be the following. Consider again such indexical-involving truths as "red looks like this." Wittgenstein argues in the *Investigations* that samples by reference to which the uses of color words are taught are in effect part of the language being taught—means of representation rather than things represented.[2] By extension, we could perhaps suggest that in "red looks like this," the indexical makes a sample presented to vision part of the proposition. If so, "red looks like this" is a proposition that Caecus can't understand: in effect, one of its terms is in a language he cannot comprehend. In this case, "red looks like this" is a proposition the understanding of which (and so the knowing of which) depends on having certain perceptual mechanisms. For "this" refers to something that can be presented only to sight. In this use, "this" is an epistemic indexical, tying the proposition to the sample bit of red. If all this is so, then even though Caecus knows when "red looks like this" is true, he does not know that red looks like this. In building up our description of the sort of color knowledge a blind person can have, we in effect took color terms as physical property terms.[3] But arguably, in such claims as "red looks like this," color terms express something about how objects visually appear. If so, such claims are unintelligible to someone to whom nothing can appear visually.

2. E.g., Ludwig Wittgenstein, *Philosophical Investigations* (New York: Macmillan, 1958), nos. 50, 53, pp. 24–26.
3. I owe this point to William Alston.

If all this is so, the next question becomes whether some proposition that a blind person can understand can express the same information that this proposition does. I am inclined to think that this is not possible. The precise information the proposition conveys is a comparison with the color of a particular visible surface under certain circumstances (or else the association of a color word with a particular sample surface). How can one grasp this comparison (or the example) if one cannot perceive that particular surface or any other relevantly like it?[4]

Omniscience and What the Blind Can't Know

The existence of epistemically indexical truths poses a problem for the claim that God is propositionally omniscient. For suppose that what the blind lack is not nonpropositional knowledge but the ability to understand a certain sort of indexical proposition. If understanding such propositions requires having the appropriate epistemic capacities, a God without vision may be no better off than the blind. If there are such propositions, a visionless God cannot be propositionally omniscient. If the information such propositions express cannot be expressed without epistemic indexicals, a visionless God cannot even possess nonpropositionally all truths expressible in propositions.

But we have already seen propositional omniscience to be unattainable regardless. What *is* worth worrying about is the fact that epistemically indexical truths express epistemically indexical facts. That there are such facts poses a problem for the claim that God is factually omniscient. For God is factually omniscient only if He can cognitively grasp all facts. That red looks like *this* may be a fact only a being with vision can grasp. If so, no visionless being can be factually omniscient.

Now secondary qualities like colors can be presented as such only to those who can acquire information about the world visually. So we might expect that if there are epistemic uses of indexicals, some truths about and facts involving colors may involve them. But there are also epistemic uses of indexicals which involve a Newtonian primary quality, motion. This fact lets one develop an argument that no deity can be both factually omniscient and immutable.

Knowledge of Change

Consider the claim that a change is occurring. There is more than one way to know that this is so. One may, for instance, know this by

4. This thesis does not depend on any claim about the incommunicability of sensation. Thus it escapes the response of Kenny in *The God of the Philosophers*, pp. 31–32.

knowing that speaking tenselessly, up to the time of this utterance, a proposition P is true, and from this time on, P is false. For this is true only if P is now changing. Nothing prevents an immutable deity from knowing in this way that changes are occurring. But obviously, this is not knowledge of change by acquaintance or by being directly presented with change.

What is it to be directly presented with change? Consider what you see as you watch a cue ball roll across a pool table. You see the ball occupying first place one, then place two, and so on, but you also see the ball changing its position. One can argue that an immutable deity can no more be directly presented with change than our blind man could be directly presented with color. This is because in watching the position of a pool-ball change, one has an experience that is itself a changing thing. As that of which I am aware changes, the content of my awareness changes. If it did not, I would no longer be aware of the changing thing as changing. But now consider my awareness as an entity in itself. My awareness has the property of having a certain content. Arguably this is a real (as versus merely Cambridge) property of that awareness, since it is caused by what I am watching. It may be an essential property of this awareness. That is, perhaps the awareness is made the awareness it is by its being my awareness of that particular content. If this last is true, then with every change in the content of my awareness, I have a new act of awareness. If this last is not true, it still remains that every change in that of which I am aware produces a change in the awareness I enjoy. Whether this change be accidental or substantial, it is real.

Now a change in my awareness entails that I change with respect to a real (because causally involved) property, the property of having an awareness of such and such a sort. If this is so, no form of real change can qualify the awareness of an immutable being. If *this* is so, no immutable being can be aware of change as occurring. If no aspect of an immutable God's experience can change, God must have a changeless experience of the world. It would seem to follow that God must experience the world as a static, four-dimensional, extensive continuum. If He perceives change, then, He perceives it only in the being-different of different segments of four-dimensional, static space-time worms. If we perceive a changing world three-dimensionally and God must do so four-dimensionally, there is something in our awareness of change of which God cannot be aware. For we are directly presented with the fact that change is like *this*. God is not.

Now this argument makes at least two debatable assumptions. First, it assumes that the awareness of change must itself be a changing awareness. But certain versions of the theory of an extended specious present deny this. Space precludes discussing the specious present here. But I do not myself find these versions of the theory convincing, and so I am prepared to let this first assumption stand. Second, this argument assumes that being of a certain content is always a real as versus a Cambridge property of an awareness. Even if this assumption holds for all human cases, it might not hold for God's, if one holds that the contents of God's awareness do not depend causally on the objects of which God is aware. As I do hold that the contents of God's awareness do not depend causally on their objects, I find this second assumption problematic.[5]

Still, if one grants this assumption, one can conclude that an immutable being cannot be directly presented with the fact that change looks like *this*, even if such a being can know all truths about change and changing things (as our blind man could perhaps know all truths about color). The fact that change looks like *this* may be epistemically indexical. If the reasoning above is correct, the epistemic ability needed to grasp this proposition is the ability to acquire information by undergoing real change. If something is immutable, it does not have this ability. Thus it seems that a timeless God cannot be factually omniscient.

Now if one asks whether a being without vision can be aware of what colors look like, or whether something that is not a bat can be aware of what it is like to be a bat, theists have at least one reply available. For perhaps someone who "sees the secrets of the heart" as God is said to do can be aware of the awarenesses of sighted persons and of bats. Being aware of these awarenesses presumably involves being aware of their content. If so, perhaps what color looks like and the unique qualia of being batty are not beyond the range of God's awareness. But arguably, theists cannot maintain that even if God cannot directly perceive change, He can perceive our awareness of change and so acquire awareness of change that way. For if our awareness of change is itself a changing thing, it alters as what we perceive alters. Hence our awareness, too, must appear to God, inaccurately, as an extended, static, four-dimensional thing.

The critic of divine timelessness can press this further argument: if God is cognitively perfect, nothing exists other than as it exists in God's experience—the way God sees things is the way they are. But then, if God is cognitively perfect and immutable, change as we have acquaintance with it does not exist: we are deluded in thinking that we perceive change. Here Creel chimes in: "even if the appearance of change on the part of every object is an illusion . . . still there is change

5. I hope to discuss this matter further in *Divine Simplicity*.

in our experience . . . it is self-evidently true that an experience of change involves change . . . change is occurring whenever we experience change to be occurring—even though the change be only in our experience . . . Hence if God is . . . eternal, then whenever our experience is changing, he cannot know . . . it as it is. But . . . God is omniscient; therefore God knows things as they are; therefore . . . God is not . . . eternal."[6] Creel's argument resembles an argument of Delmas Lewis' discussed in the preceding chapter. The Lewis-Creel argument can be represented as follows:

1. For all x, if x is timeless, x does not change.
2. For all x, if x is cognitively perfect, x knows all things as they are.
3. For all x, if x knows a changing thing as changing, x undergoes change.
4. Hence if changing things exist, no timeless being is cognitively perfect.
5. Changing things exist.
6. No timeless being is cognitively perfect.
7. God is cognitively perfect.
8. God is not timeless.

We have already seen some answers to the argument from cognitive perfection against timelessness. One *could* reply to it by ascribing to God a changeless divine sense datum distinct from the changing reality He perceives through it. For suppose that the direct object of God's awareness is not identical with the things themselves that God perceives. Then it can be the case that the direct object of God's experience is *de re* necessarily immutable and yet the things themselves that God experiences are not changeless. If this can be so, Creel's argument is blocked. An Anselmian can reply by observing that the objects of God's cognition *are* changeless in eternity—that it is *de dicto* necessary that an object in eternity is changeless even if that same object can change in time. The Anselmian who makes this move would simply say that the way God sees things is *a* way they are, but not the only way they are.

But another response is available which does not require the resources of the Anselmian or divine sense-datum theories. For in fact (3) is false: a changeless being can know what change looks like. Let me try to clarify the sort of change knowledge of which is problematic. We

6. Creel, *Impassibility*, p. 111. This argument derives ultimately from Peter Geach.

ordinarily think that the happening of an event involves sequence: first A is F, then A is not F. This is sequence *in the facts*. We also think that an event's happening involves a sequence *of* facts. We think not merely that it is timelessly true that first Fa, then not-Fa, but also that in some other sense, first the sole fact relating A and F is that Fa, and then the sole fact relating A and F is that not-Fa. That is, we think that first it is a fact that Fa, and then it is no longer in any sense a fact that Fa, but instead a fact that not-Fa. Our believing in this sort of sequence makes our ordinary view of time tensed rather than tenseless. It is sequence in this second sense, sequence *of* facts, which seems incapable of occurring in eternity.

Now whether reality contains not merely sequence in facts but sequence *of* facts is a matter of controversy; it is what separates tensed and tenseless theories of time. A defender of divine timelessness could make his or her lot easier by claiming that there really is no such thing as sequence of facts. But I am trying to deal with divine timelessness without assuming any particular theory of time. So I want to ask whether, if sequence of facts is a real feature of temporal frames of reference but not a real feature of an eternal frame of reference, sequence of facts is a feature of time that cannot be adequately represented by any entity or state of affairs existing in eternity. That is, is there really something about existence in time that a God existing only in eternity could not know or represent?

I want to suggest that static, eternal, 4D space-time worms adequately represent sequences of fact as well as sequences in fact. I offer the following as a model of how God's perception could work. I do not claim that if God exists, this *is* how God's perception works. There may be good reason to think that it is not. But so long as some model of timeless perception of sequence of facts is possible, one cannot claim that God's being timeless precludes His perceiving sequence of facts as such, or knowing what it is like, or that change is like *this*.

Let us suppose that God's awareness of the 4D worms of temporal things and events includes not just an awareness of their totality but all possible partial awarenesses of them. That is, let us suppose that God "sees" not just the whole of your life, but distinctly sees the distinct part of it which occurs from t to t + 1, etc. Temporal events and processes are continuous. Therefore, between any two points in time, such events and processes pass through an appropriate infinity of distinguishable states. Let us say that among God's partial awarenesses is a distinct awareness of exactly the state the world is in at each possible cut along the continuum of temporal processes.

Let us also say that God's states of partial awareness stand in an asymmetric ordering relation. Consider God's states C_1, C_2, and C_3.

These are related in such a way that C_2 is aware of C_1 but not vice versa, and C_3 is aware of C_2 (and so of C_1) but not vice versa. God's partial awarenesses are partial in content. They contain only what has happened up to one point in time. But they are complete in the sense that each awareness is relevantly like a distinct act of a distinct consciousness. In effect, God contains an infinitely multiple consciousness. God as a whole is always aware of all His conscious states; His awareness is not exhausted by these partial awarenesses. But if there are infinite divine partial awarenesses, no one of these is aware of all the others.[7] Nor is any aware of the divine total awareness in its totality, else it would involve awareness of all God's states of consciousness and so not be a partial awareness. C_2's relation to C_1 is relevantly as if C_2 were a personality split from C_1 within the same person and privy to all the contents of C_1. C_2 can so completely read C_1's mind, so to speak, that C_2 is at once the subject of its own awareness and C_1's, while C_1 is only the subject of C_1's awareness. This may sound bizarre, but something not wholly unlike it may be involved in certain mental disorders and may also be a consequence of traditional Christian beliefs about the Incarnation.[8] There is a distinct C-state for every point along the temporal continuum. Every $C_n + 1$ is aware of what all its included $C_1 \ldots n$ conscious states are aware of, and more besides, and is aware that no prior state was aware of this more. That is, $C_n + 1$ perceives as new what is new in its content relative to all prior $C_1 \ldots n$. $C_n + 1$ does not, however, perceive $C_n + 2$ and *its* new content. So these partial awarenesses provide God a way to be aware of what it is like to occupy a temporally limited standpoint. For at $C_n + 1$, propositions solely about the new content of $C_n + 2$ are true but not known (by $C_n + 1$).

When we perceive events as happening, or sequences *of* facts, one way to report this is to say that we perceive the flow or passage of events and time. But I think we report the same phenomenon if we say that we perceive the ever-new newness of what happens. That is, I think C. D. Broad was correct to describe the distinctive phenomenon of time's passage (granting for now that this does occur) as reality's growing by ever-new increments. To perceive passage is to perceive

7. If these acts of awareness must be really distinct, then this model of divine awareness cannot describe the inner life of a God who is wholly simple. But I am not claiming that this model does in fact describe God's inner life. Moreover, a defender of divine simplicity can hold that this is *only* a model and serves only to make the point that timelessness and awareness of change are not as such incompatible. With these provisos, perhaps even a defender of divine simplicity can make use of this model, at least dialectically.

8. See Thomas Morris, *The Logic of God Incarnate* (Ithaca, N.Y.: Cornell University Press, 1987).

what is new and perceive it *as* new—that is, to perceive it with a background awareness that it was not there before and against a background in which it was not present. It is to perceive the present as "added to" an immediate past that is somehow also given.

I suggest that timeless consciousness $Cn + 1$ perceives precisely this, in a timeless form. For it perceives its own content, and the addition this content makes to all the previously included contents of consciousness, and perceives this addition precisely *as* an addition, as something new. I suggest, then, that if we allow this sort of compounded consciousness to be possible, perhaps its content could provide an adequate atemporal representation of precisely the phenomena of newness and passage which we experience temporally as an objective feature of temporal frames of reference. In short, even if no object in eternity outside of God's awareness is a good atemporal model for sequence *of* facts, perhaps God's awareness of His awareness of these generates an adequate model. Moreover, as it is the intrinsic qualities of 4D worms which provide the matter for God's awareness, perhaps we can say that 4D worms can represent even the passingness of temporal events, to the appropriate sort of mind.

The key move in this suggestion is that the appropriate sort of juxtaposition of partial awarenesses can provide an experience of the temporal succession of awarenesses. In fact, if the Jamesian notion of the "specious present" is incoherent (as I think there is good reason to say), then *our* awareness of the ever-new present as ever new is of precisely this sort. Now we need not take the partial states of consciousness involved in all this to be God's. For God always eternally has awareness of all of our states of consciousness. He perceives these in eternity, of course—but if He includes in His single total awareness an awareness of my state of consciousness at t juxtaposed with a state of my consciousness that preceded t by an arbitrarily small time, He perceives its content as I do, i.e., as new relative to its immediate backdrop. So God *could,* after all, be aware of temporal passage and sequence of facts as such through an awareness of our awareness, as in the case of colors and what it is like to be a bat. I conclude, then, that we have at least two models on which it makes sense to say that a timeless God knows what change is like. Accordingly, sequence of facts does not provide a viable objection to the claim that a timeless God is factually omniscient. Divine timelessness and divine factual omniscience appear compatible.

16

Timelessness and
Religious Experience

A further challenge to the claim that God is timeless may arise from the question of whether one can perceive a timeless God. This question is important for preserving the "religious availability" of a timeless deity. Any religious experience whose object is God counts as some sort of observation or perception of God, if not an ordinary, sensory observation or perception of Him. If a timeless God cannot be observed, then, such a God must be unavailable to religious experience. A concept of God that renders Him inaccessible to religious experience is ipso facto unacceptable to Western theists. Further, the writers of the Old and New testaments claim to experience God in many ways. So if a timeless God cannot be experienced, the God of Western theism cannot be timeless. This chapter answers two arguments about perception of the timeless and sketches an account of how such perception is possible.

Does Perception Locate the Perceived in Time?

Delmas Lewis offers two arguments that we cannot observe timeless entities. The first is this: "How can a temporal observer observe anything without bringing that thing into the temporal series? The observations of temporal observers . . . occur in time, and the objects of those observations must also exist at some time, or there simply will not be any observation to be made . . . [this is because] the following is a necessary truth, in the sense of broadly logical necessity: (P) If O is observed by S at t, then O exists at t, or, if O has ceased to exist by t,

then O caused something observable to exist at t."[1] (P) is equivalent to
a conjunction of these claims:

> P1. If O is observed by S at t and has not ceased to exist by t, then
>   O exists at t.
> P2. If O is observed by S at t and has ceased to exist by t, then O
>   caused something observable to exist at t.

Only temporal things can satisfy (P2)'s antecedent, as a timeless being
cannot cease to exist. Suppose, then, that we look at the night sky and
seem to see a star, Stella, which no longer exists: Stella is forty light-
years away and exploded thirty years ago, though it will be ten years
before earthbound humans see its explosion and learn this fact. There is
at t something observable that Stella caused to exist, namely, the light
Stella emitted forty years ago. The light arguably is not *what we observe*
when we seem to see Stella. It is more plausible that we observe Stella.[2]
But (P2) does not entail that the light is what we see. It entails only that
the light (or some other entity) *exists* and is observable. The light is in
fact observable; its presence can be detected. More generally, any observed event is observed because some causal signal from the event
reaches an observer. Arguably, any causal signal able to cause an observation is itself observable. If so, (P2) is true.

Lewis, though, claims that (P) has broadly logically—i.e., absolutely—*necessary* truth. If (P) is equivalent to ((P1)·(P2)), (P) is necessary only if (P2) is. The argument for (P2) rests on current physical law
and so at most gives us reason to think that (P2) is *physically* necessary.
It does not support the stronger modal claim Lewis makes. That (P2) is
absolutely necessary is questionable. Certainly, it is not obvious that
current physical laws have this stronger modal status. Nor is it an
obviously necessary truth that signals that cause observations are themselves observable. As was mentioned, to observe *what* signals convey is
not to observe the signals themselves. It seems at least conceivable that
there be a sort of signal whose existence is not humanly detectable—
one that could be known to exist only by inference, e.g., from the
premises that human experiences of physical events are caused by physical events and that all physical events cause effects by sending the
appropriate signals. It also seems conceivable that there be a physical
universe in which it is not true that all physical events cause effects by
sending appropriate signals—in which, for instance, some thing acts

---

1. Delmas Lewis, "Eternity Again," p. 75. Helm concurs in *Eternal God*, p. 34.
2. See Roderick Chisholm, *Perceiving* (Ithaca, N.Y.: Cornell University Press,
1957), pp. 153, 156.

directly on another thing at a distance, with no physical intermediaries.

If these things are conceivable, then conceivably it is false that all experience is caused by a detectable or inferrable signal, or by any signal. That this SOA is conceivable is a good (though defeasible) reason to call it possible. It also seems possible that this SOA be conjoined with the nonexistence of sense data. So it appears possible that some object O has ceased to exist by t and is observed by S at t, but not in virtue of having caused something observable (either a signal or a sense datum) to exist at t. If so, arguably (P2) is contingent, and so then is (P).

If (P2) is true, (P) is true iff (P1) is. But (P1) may be false, for arguably, we observe mirages. For instance, if Frederic sees a mirage of a lake, and Frederica fears lakes, it is perfectly legitimate to say "what Frederic saw was the very kind of thing Frederica fears."[3] In this true statement one quantifies over a lake, not a mirage of a lake (Frederica does not fear mirages), and it is not clear that one can adequately paraphrase this statement in a way that does not refer to a nonexistent object.[4] So arguably, in seeing a lake mirage, one observes a nonexistent lake. But then the lake Frederic sees is observed at t and has not ceased to exist by t (since it does not exist, it cannot cease to exist), and yet it is false at t that that lake exists. This falsifies (P1). Still, many people are not comfortable with nonexistent lakes, and to these (P1) will still seem plausible.

It also seems plausible that

P3. If O is observed by S at t and has not ceased to exist by t, then it is true at t that O exists.

It is because (P3) seems so obvious, I suggest, that (P1) looks so plausible, for (P1) *appears* to be just a harmless rephrasing of (P3). But it is not. As we have seen, there can be a significant difference between its being true at t that O exists and its being true that O exists at t (i.e., that O's existence is located at t).

If its being true at t that O exists does not entail that O exists at t, (P3) and (P1) are not equivalent. Rather, (P3) entails (P1) only in conjunction with

P4. If it is true at t that O exists, then O exists at t.

3. See Roderick Chisholm, *Brentano and Meinong Studies* (Atlantic Highlands, N.J.: Humanities Press, 1982), p. 66.
4. Ibid., pp. 37–67.

If the semantic machinery and examples assembled earlier are reasonably clear, (P4) is questionable. The main reason one would accept (P4), I suspect, would be that one could get no handle on the idea of timeless existence. But if the machinery set out in earlier chapters is in working order, it is not much harder to get a handle on timeless truth than it is to get a handle on the idea of a proposition's not being a member of any of a certain set of sets of propositions (namely, the sets correlated with moments of time). Similarly, then, one can see timeless existents as those that are not members of any of a certain set of sets (namely, the set of entities that exist during each moment of time).

As there are significant likenesses between space and time, a spatial analogy will provide some positive reason to reject (P4). If S observes an existing O while S is located at place p, it is true at p that O exists, but it does not follow that O exists at p, i.e., that O has p as its spatial location. O could be elsewhere, while being observed by S, who is at p. Nor does it follow that O exists at any p, i.e., has some p as its spatial location. I can observe that Rodney is a rodent. But that-Rodney-is-a-rodent or Rodney's-being-a-rodent has no spatial location.

Perhaps one could reply that in (P4)'s spatial analogue, "O" ranges over only concrete particulars, thus excluding that-Rodney-is-a-rodent, which as a fact is abstract. But even with "O" thus restricted, that O is observed does not entail that O has any spatial location. If we can observe mirages, we can observe concrete particular things that do not actually exist and so do not actually have any spatial location. Still, perhaps one cannot say that we observe mirages. It can be argued that all we really observe are (say) the spatially located conditions that produce mirages. So instead, consider telepathy, the perception of others' thoughts.

Thoughts exist, are particulars, and are concrete (qua involved in causal relations of some sort), yet they *appear* not to be located in space.[5] Telepathy, if it exists, is direct observation of others' thoughts, without observing brain-events with which they may be identical or connected or bodily phenomena they cause. I cannot see that telepathy is conceptually impossible: it seems conceivable. It is also conceivable

---

5. I stress this "appear." I have argued that whatever is in time is also in space, and I have claimed that there are no nonmaterial things in space. So I am committed to claiming that thoughts are or involve only material things with spatial locations. Some might argue that I should not assert that thoughts appear not to be located in space and should confine myself to the weaker claim that they do not appear to be located in space. But our pre-analytic thinking about our thoughts rebels at any suggestion that any particular place is a place at which one of our thoughts is located. To say that our thoughts appear to us such that no place is their place is to say that they seem to us to have no spatial location.

that thoughts are, as they seem, not located in space. If so, there is reason to say that conceivably thoughts are observable but nonspatial.

In making this move I am not relying on a general principle to the effect that if conceivably P and conceivably Q, then conceivably P and Q. This inference is clearly invalid: it is conceivable that my car is red all over throughout 1988 and conceivable that my car is green all over throughout 1988, but not conceivable that my car is both red and green all over throughout 1988. My point is rather that in the absence of explicit reason to think that P entails ~Q, the conceivability of P and of Q is good evidence that conceivably P and Q. But if conceivably thoughts are observable but nonspatial, this is reason to say that possibly thoughts are so.[6] If possibly thoughts are so, then even with the range of "O" restricted, the spatial analogue of (P4) is false. If the spatial version of (P4) is false, then given the significant likenesses that exist between space and time, (P4) is likely false.

There are, of course, also disanalogies between space and time. The question is whether any of these defeat the analogy with spatial-(P4) just offered. The chief or only germane disanalogy one might allege is that what does not exist now or at some time does not exist, whereas (allegedly) it is not the case that what does not exist here or at some place does not exist. The Minkowskian picture of space and time, however, gives good reason to say that this disanalogy does not actually exist.[7] According to Minkowski, actual time can be represented as a fourth dimension of a four-dimensional continuum whose other dimensions are spatial—that is, there can be a coordinate system with four axes which maps the actual world, generating three spatial coordinates and one temporal coordinate.[8] Now as we have seen, an object that has a coordinate relative to one axis of a coordinate system ipso facto has one relative to all axes. If anything located relative to one axis of a coordinate system is located relative to all of its axes, then something exists at some time iff it exists at some place. But then it is true that whatever exists exists at some time only if whatever exists exists at some place. The disanalogy mentioned in the last paragraph is not really there, provided only that (as has been overwhelmingly con-

6. Of course, they are so only in a possible world in which time is not just one abstracted aspect of a spacetime continuum (if at all).

7. This is not to say that it does not *possibly* exist. Perhaps in some possible world, time is *not* representable as a fourth coordinate axis, as Minkowski says it actually is. In this possible world, the disanalogy would exist.

8. Saying only this does not commit one for or against the reality of "becoming" or to any particular theory of time. See Milic Capek, "The Myth of Frozen Passage," in R. S. Cohen and M. Wartofsky, eds., *Boston Studies in the Philosophy of Science* II (New York: Humanities Press, 1965), pp. 441–463.

firmed in contemporary physics) one can map actual time and space within a four-dimensional coordinate system. Thus my argument against (P4) stands.

If (P4) is false, (P3) does not entail (P1) and so does not support (P). But there may be another reason to accept (P1). For an experience to count as an observation of O, the experience must have O among its causal conditions. So O is observable at t only if O can have effects at t. Thus if a timeless being cannot have effects in time, (P1) is true. However, Lewis' only argument that a timeless being cannot have temporal effects is this: "consider some temporal event E that God has brought about at t by an atemporal action. Would a list, compiled at t, of what there is include both the cause of E and E? If so, then the cause of E exists at t, and cannot be eternal. If not, then the cause of E does not belong to the objective order of things when E occurs."[9] This argument assumes either that there is no distinction between existing at t and existing during t or that (P4) is true. Thus we have already denied its suppressed premise. Further, we have already argued that a timeless being can indeed have effects in time.

Having shown this also obviates one last way to defend (P1) and (P). My discussion of (P2) premises that one can observe an event that actually occurred thirty years ago. In so doing, it rests implicitly on a Newtonian conception of time, according to which events have absolute dates by their inclusion in sets of distant events that occur in absolute simultaneity. Relativity theory renders simultaneity relative to a frame of reference, rather than absolute. According to William Godfrey-Smith, this dictates a "causal theory" of the present.[10] Rather than taking the present as the class of events simultaneous with now in absolute time, Godfrey-Smith argues, we must take the present as the class of events such that causal signals from those events arrive *now* and so can be observed now, i.e., locally simultaneously with the act of observation.[11] Given *this* understanding of the present, it appears necessarily true that what I observe now exists now, and consequently it appears impossible to observe a timeless being. But to appeal to a causal theory of the present in arguing that one cannot observe a timeless being now would require showing that a timeless being cannot have effects now. So by showing that a timeless being can have temporal effects, I block this last route to (P1). So once more, we have no reason to accept (P1).

9. Delmas Lewis, "Eternity Again," p. 77.
10. Godfrey-Smith, "Special Relativity and the Present."
11. Ibid., pp. 240–242.

The situation, then, is this. Any direct counterexample to (P1) will have to be a case of observing something that does not exist, or observing something that exists, but only either before or after t, or observing something that exists timelessly. Our mirage example was of the first sort and likely convinced few. If an observed object exists only before t, or before t and then (after a temporal gap) after t, it has ceased to exist by t and so is no problem for (P1). Objects in the future at t cannot be observed, for an observed object is among the causal conditions of an observation, and (I submit) backward causation is impossible.[12] Hence the only sort of counterexample to (P1) left is experience of something timeless. Such experience occurs just in case (P1) is not true. Now we have stripped (P1) of all the backing it seemed to have. I suggest, therefore, that if an experience occurs which one has good reason to think is an experience of a timeless being, (P1) constitutes no reason to deny that it is just that. Nor therefore does (P).

A Second Argument against Observing the Timeless

Lewis' second argument against temporal things' being able to observe timeless entities is this: "if temporal y observes eternal x at t, x exists at one and the same time as y . . . This becomes clearer when one considers that the event of y observing x at t is identical with the event of x's being observed by y at t."[13] Lewis' argument resembles one by Wolterstorff: "The event consisting of my referring to X is a temporal event [and] is identical with the event of X's being referred to by me. And this event is an aspect both of X and of me. So if X is a being which lasts longer than my act of referring to X does, then for a while X has this aspect and for a while not. And thus X would [undergo] succession . . . And so X would not be eternal."[14] We may unpack Lewis' argument as follows.

1. The phrases "the event of x's being observed by y at t" and "the event of y observing x at t" both name events.
2. These phrases are mere grammatical transforms.
3. If phrases are mere grammatical transforms and name events, they name the same event.
4. If these phrases name the same event, the event of y observing x at t = the event of x's being observed by y at t.

12. This does not rule out precognition. It entails only that if precognition occurs, it is not a form of observation.
13. Delmas Lewis, "Eternity Again," p. 75.
14. Wolterstorff, "God Everlasting," p. 95.

5. The event of y observing x at t occurs at t. Therefore
6. The event of x's being observed by y occurs at t.
7. If an event occurs at t, then that to which the event happens exists at t.
8. Thus if x's being observed by y occurs at t, x exists at t.
9. Thus nothing is both timeless and observed by temporal beings.

(8) entails (P), and so I am committed to (8)'s being false. Hence I must show that at least one of (1)–(7) is also false. I submit that (6) is.[15] (6) entails that there is a genuine event that is x's being observed by y. I suggest that there is not, so that what (6) entails is false and so therefore is (6). I contend that even if there is a genuine event which is y's observing x, and the description "x's being observed by y" applies to this event, there is no genuine event of x's being observed by y. The event to which both descriptions apply is really just y's observing x. Let me explain.

We have already discussed the distinction between genuine and mere Cambridge changes (or events). Now it just seems intuitively plain that y's being observed by x is a mere Cambridge event (even though if y did not exist, the event of x's observing y could not exist). If argument is nonetheless requested, I offer this. It is plausible that any real change imparts some causal power that its subject previously lacked. For even a mere shift in spatial position enables a billiard ball to interact with other billiard balls in ways in which it previously could not (because it was out of position to do so), and any macrophysical alteration at least imparts the ability to cause different sorts of experience. (Beyond offering these examples, though, I am unsure how to argue for a claim so general.) Being observed by someone imparts no causal power. If so, it is no real change, and so in Lewis' case no event of being-observed occurs at t.

If (6) is false, (4) is false if it is read to entail that the event of x's being observed by y at P is a real event. But (3) is also questionable. According to one popular theory, events are exemplifyings of attributes.[16] This cannot be the whole truth about events; events are happenings, and states in which nothing happens can also be exemplifyings of

---

15. Or is at least not true. If (6) *presupposes* that an event exists, and (as I argue) that event does not exist, then perhaps (6) is a case of presupposition failure and is not false but truth-valueless. I continue to speak only of falsity in the text to simplify the discussion.

16. See Jaegwon Kim, "Events as Property-Exemplifications," in Myles Brand and Douglas Walton, eds., *Action Theory* (Dordrecht: Reidel, 1976), pp. 156–177.

attributes. But if this is at least part of the truth about events, then two event-descriptions denote the same event only if they pick out the same subject and the same attribute. "The event of x's being observed by y at t" picks out x and the attribute of being-observed-by-y. "The event of y observing x at t" picks out y and the attribute of observing-x. These two event-descriptions pick out the same event, then, only if x = y and observing-x = being-observed-by-y. But Lewis will hardly claim this. Hence the two descriptions pick out distinct events or, more precisely, one event and one pseudoevent.

Now Lewis could object that (4) need not involve ascriptions of prima facie distinct monadic properties. Rather, he can say, in (4) we use two nonsynonymous descriptions to pick out a single event in which two items come to exemplify jointly the relation that any x and any y bear iff x observes y. If this is so, though, to claim that this event occurs only at t is simply to beg the question against the claim that this event genuinely involves a timeless being, for there is an alternate way to describe the event. It could be held that if S observes a timeless O during t, the event of S's observing O occurs in both eternity and time. We could say that this event has two locations or that it has a single location "scattered" over eternity and time. Either way, to presume that the event is located solely at t is to presume that it does not involve a timeless being, which is the point at issue.

Lewis could rejoin that this alternate description of the event entails a paradox. For if O is observed by S, then O has a property, being-observed-by-S. If O is timeless, O has this property timelessly. If O timelessly is observed-by-S, and a timeless entity cannot change, then at every moment, it is true (though in no sense true *then*) that O timelessly is observed-by-S. If so, that O timelessly is observed-by-S is true prior to t. Yet only during t does S observe O. So it seems to follow that O is observed by S before S observes O and that during some time, O is observed by S and yet S does not observe O.

But is this really paradoxical? On this second description, it is time-lessly true that O is observed by S *at t* and it is also timelessly true that S observes O *at t*. It is not the case in eternity, then, that S does not observe O, but O is observed by S. In time, S observes O only at t— and at t, when S observes O, it is also timelessly true that O is observed by S. There is no time during which S does not observe O and yet O is observed by S, *for there is no time at all during which O is observed by S: O is observed by S, but not during any time.* Now at times other than t, S does not observe O, but it is timelessly true that O is observed by S at t. I do not think that this is paradoxical, for at these same times it also is timelessly true that S observes O at t.

There may seem to be another problem here. Eternity, I have suggested, is logically speaking another "time." So to say that S observes
O at t while O is observed by S in eternity is to say that the time at
which S observes O ≠ the "time" at which O is observed by S. This
seems counterintuitive; certainly it would be strange to say that S
observes O at 2:00 but O is not observed by S until 2:05. Here, however, there is a relevant difference between eternity and a time. The
problem with S observing O at 2:00 and O being observed only at 2:05
is that in this case, time elapses between the obtaining of logically
inseparable states of affairs. It is not the distinctness of the times in
question but the fact that they are separated by a temporal interval
which makes this example odd. Now necessarily, times are distinct if
they are separated by a temporal interval. But as eternity is not located
in time, no time can elapse between S's temporally observing O and
O's being observed by S in eternity. This suggests that there is no real
problem in the fact that the time at which S observes O ≠ the "time" at
which O is observed by S. Eternity is a distinct "time," but no time
elapses between S's observing O and O's being observed by S, and so
the logical inseparability of S's observing O and O's being observed by
S is respected.

Now all of this establishes only that Lewis has not shown that an
observer's being temporal rules out his or her observing a genuinely
timeless entity. It does not entail that nothing else rules out such observation. But let me suggest one way observation of a timeless entity
might take place.

The term "observation" can bear many senses. In the strictest, nar-
rowest sense, x observes y just in case y is directly present to one of x's
senses and x notices y. ("Directly" here has a commonsense rather than
a philosophical meaning. It rules out such alternatives as being observed in a mirror, not such alternatives as being observed via sense
data.) In slightly looser senses, x observes y if y is directly present to
one of x's senses and x does not notice y, or if y is indirectly present to
one of x's senses (as in a mirror) and x notices y.

Again, perceiving certain images on an electron-microscope screen
amounts to observing atoms, in an appropriately loose sense of "observing." Suppose, then, that a timeless God exists and sustains the
starry heavens above and that Herman, gazing on said heavens, has an
overwhelming sense that the heavens are sustained by God. In this case,
arguably, Herman acquires a true belief by becoming perceptually
aware (though by what mechanism we do not know) of the very state
of affairs that renders his belief true. If perceiving the effects of atoms
can amount to perceiving atoms, then a fortiori perceiving the effects

of God as the effects of God amounts to perceiving God. Could we really deny that in this case, Herman has in some sense observed a timeless God? An experience is an observation of O only if O is among that experience's causal conditions. So we could deny that Herman has observed a timeless God if we could maintain that a timeless God is not among the causal conditions of Herman's experience. But we have already seen that a timeless deity can have temporal effects, i.e., that we can make sufficient sense of God's sustaining of the universe to grant that an atemporal God can create the entire universe. If this is so, then such a God can create the universe with the occurrence of special creaturely experiences under certain circumstances "built in." If God does this, God is among the causal conditions of these experiences. So it appears that God can create a universe within which occur experiences of a timeless God. If so, a timeless God can be perceived.

17

Vale et Salve

This book has presented and sought to defend one picture of the relations between a timeless God and His temporal creation. On this picture, God is the absolute source of absolutely everything that is not Himself. Thus God creates time and all that is in it. But God can create time only if He exists and acts in eternity. Thus God is timeless, and God's act of creation exists in eternity. That act's product exists "when" that act occurs: as the two are causally connected, they cannot be discrete or incommensurable, and as that act is timeless, nothing can exist before or after it takes place. I have suggested that we understand this simultaneity to imply that not just God and His creative act, but also time and the temporal, exist in eternity.

All at once, in eternity, God knows all that He ever knows, including events that to us are future, and God wills all that He ever wills, including His responses to prayers we have not yet prayed and decisions we have not yet made. All at once, in eternity, our acts meet His responses, and His responses elicit our further acts, and our lives are played out. We and all we do exist in eternity with God. Despite this, I have argued, God's creatures are indeed temporal beings. They really are dreamlike and evanescent in contrast with the absolute stability of God, and they and time may or may not literally "pass"—nothing in our picture of God and time precludes the claim that time is tensed. Events all occur in the frozen simultaneity of eternity. But that is just one way they occur. They also follow one another in time.

In fact, nothing in our picture of God and time rules out any claim that common sense or metaphysics might incline one to make about time and temporal things. Nor does this picture go that far beyond at least a theist's common sense. Ordinary theists are wont to say that God sees all events at once. I have agreed and just inferred that in one reference frame, events are as God sees them.

The present picture of time and eternity does not belie the tenets and experience of ordinary religious believers. God as I have depicted Him can be in a strong sense omniscient; for all that His timelessness involves, one can hold that no temporal fact escapes His gaze, and for all I have said, He understands all temporal facts more fully than we ever will. God as I have depicted Him can answer prayer, act providentially, reveal Himself in human experience, and perform all the rest of the acts the Western religions ascribe to Him. The God who creates time can also act within it and is closer to spatial and temporal creatures than any spatial or temporal creature can be. Yet paradoxically, He is with all times "at once," and so (speaking loosely) both our past and our future are now and ever before Him: I have argued that God can have knowledge of actions that for us are future and that if God is timeless, this is compatible with our having libertarian freedom.

I have argued that God is beyond and in a sense above time. But I have also argued that this does not diminish His efficacy within it. The God I depict can have the greatness both of the philosophers' transcendent source of all and of the believers' living Lord. If my arguments are sound, there is just no need to choose between the two.

References

Adams, Ernest. "The Logic of Conditionals." *Inquiry* 8 (1965), 166–197.

Adams, Marilyn. "Is the Existence of God a 'Hard' Fact?" *Philosophical Review* 76 (1967), 492–503

Adams, Robert M. "Actualism and Thisness." *Synthese* 49 (1981), 3–41.

——. "Middle Knowledge and Evil." *American Philosophical Quarterly* 14 (1977), 109–117.

Allen, R. E. "Participation and Predication in Plato's Middle Dialogues." In Gregory Vlastos, ed., *Plato I: Metaphysics and Epistemology* (Garden City, N.Y.: Doubleday, 1971) 167–183.

Alston, William P. *Divine Nature and Human Language*. Ithaca, N.Y.: Cornell University Press, 1989.

Anscombe, G. E. M., and Peter Geach. *Three Philosophers*. Ithaca, N.Y.: Cornell University Press, 1961.

Anselm. *Proslogion, Monologion, De concordia*. In Franciscus Schmitt, ed., *S. Anselmi: Opera omnia*. Edinburgh: Thomas Nelson, 1946. Vols. 1, 2.

Aristotle. *De interpretatione*.

——. *De caelo et mundo*.

——. *De generatione et corruptione*.

——. *Metaphysics*.

——. *Physics*.

——. *Posterior Analytics*.

——. *Prior Analytics*.

Augustine. *Oeuvres de Saint Augustin*. Paris: Desclée de Brouwer, 1955.

——. *S. Aur. Augustini: Opera omnia*. Paris: Gaume Fratres, 1836.

Austin, J. L. *Sense and Sensibilia*. New York: Oxford University Press, 1964.

Beer, Michelle. "Temporal Indexicals and the Passage of Time." *Philosophical Quarterly* 38 (1988), 158–164.

Blumenfeld, David. "On the Compossibility of the Divine Attributes." In

Thomas Morris, ed., *The Concept of God* (New York: Oxford University Press, 1987), pp. 201–215.

Boethius. *De Trinitate, Philosophiae consolationis.* In H. F. Stewart and E. K. Rand, eds., *Boethius: The Theological Tractates* (New York: G. P. Putnam's Sons, 1926).

Bonaventure. *QD de mysterio Trinitatis.*

Capek, Milic. *The Philosophical Impact of Contemporary Physics.* Princeton, N.J.: Princeton University Press, 1961.

———. "The Myth of Frozen Passage," In R. S. Cohen and M. Wartofsky, eds. *Boston Studies in the Philosophy of Science* II (New York: Humanities Press, 1965), pp. 441–463.

———. "Time and Eternity in Royce and Bergson." In Eugene Long and Bowman Clarke, eds., *God and Temporality* (New York: Paragon House, 1984), pp. 133–154.

Chandler, Hugh. "Plantinga and the Contingently Possible." *Analysis* 36 (1975–76), 106–109.

Chisholm, Roderick. *Brentano and Meinong Studies.* Atlantic Highlands, N.J.: Humanities Press, 1982.

———. *Perceiving.* Ithaca, N.Y.: Cornell University Press, 1957.

Clarke, Bowman. *Language and Natural Theology.* The Hague: Mouton, 1966.

Coburn, Robert. "Professor Malcolm on God." *Australasian Journal of Philosophy* 41 (1963), 143–162.

Cook, Robert. "God, Time, and Freedom." *Religious Studies* 23 (1987), 81–94.

Cox, John. "Must Mental Events Have Spatial Location?" *Pacific Philosophical Quarterly* 63 (1982), 270–274.

Craig, William L. "God, Time, and Eternity." *Religious Studies* 14 (1978), 497–503.

———. "Was Aquinas a B-Theorist of Time?" *New Scholasticism* 59 (1985), 475–483.

Creel, Richard. *Divine Impassibility.* New York: Cambridge University Press, 1986.

Davis, Steven. *Logic and the Nature of God.* Grand Rapids, Mich.: Eerdmans, 1983.

Dummett, Michael. *Frege: Philosophy of Language.* 2d ed. London: Gerald Duckworth, 1981.

Duns Scotus, John. *Ordinatio.*

Falkenstein, L. "Spaces and Times: A Kantian Response." *Idealistic Studies* 16 (1986), 1–11.

Fischer, John M. "Freedom and Foreknowledge." *Philosophical Review* 92 (1983), 67–79.

Fitzgerald, Paul. "Stump and Kretzmann on Time and Eternity." *Journal of Philosophy* 82 (1985), 260–269.

Flint, Thomas, and Alfred Freddoso. "Maximal Power." In Thomas Morris, ed., *The Concept of God* (New York: Oxford University Press, 1987), pp. 134–167.

Freddoso, Alfred. "Accidental Necessity and Logical Determinism." *Journal of Philosophy* 80 (1983), 257–278.

Gale, Richard M. "Has the Present Any Duration?" *Nous* 5 (1971), 39–47.

——. "Omniscience-Immutability Arguments." *American Philosophical Quarterly* 23 (1986), 319–335.

Geach, Peter. "God's Relation to the World." *Sophia* 8 (1969), 1–9.

——. *Providence and Evil*. Cambridge: Cambridge University Press, 1977.

——. "What Actually Exists." *Proceedings of the Aristotelian Society* Supp. Vol. 42 (1968), 7–16.

Geroch, Robert. "Space-Time Structure from a Global Viewpoint." In R. K. Sachs, ed., *General Relativity and Cosmology* (New York: Academic Press, 1971), pp. 71–103.

Godfrey-Smith, William. "Change and Actuality." *Philosophical Quarterly* 30 (1980), 350–353.

——. "Special Relativity and the Present." *Philosophical Studies* 36 (1979), 233–244.

Goodman, Nelson. *The Structure of Appearance*. 3d ed. Dordrecht: Reidel, 1977.

Grim, Patrick. "Against Omniscience: The Case from Essential Indexicals." *Nous* 19 (1985), 151–180.

——. "Logic and Limits of Knowledge and Truth." *Nous* 22 (1988), 341–367.

——. "Some Neglected Problems of Omniscience." *American Philosophical Quarterly* 20 (1983), 265–276.

——. "There Is No Set of All Truths." *Analysis* 44 (1984), 206–208.

——. "Truth, Omniscience, and the Knower." *Philosophical Studies* (1988), 9–41.

Grünbaum, Adolph. "The Resolution of Zeno's Metrical Paradox of Extension for the Mathematical Continua of Space and Time." In his *Philosophical Problems of Space and Time*, 2d ed. (Dordrecht: Reidel, 1973), pp. 158–176.

Guleserian, Theodore. "God and Possible Worlds: The Modal Problem of Evil." *Nous* 17 (1983), 221–238.

Harris, James. "An Empirical Understanding of Eternality." *International Journal for Philosophy of Religion* 22 (1987), 165–183.

Hartshorne, Charles. *Creative Synthesis and Philosophical Method*. London: SCM Press, 1970.

——. "Real Possibility." *Journal of Philosophy* 60 (1963), 593–605.

Hasker, William. "Concerning the Intelligibility of the Claim 'God is Timeless.'" *New Scholasticism* 57 (1983), 170–195.

——. *God, Time, and Knowledge*. Ithaca, N.Y.: Cornell University Press, 1989.

——. "Yes, God Has Beliefs!" *Religious Studies* 24 (1988), 385–394.

Helm, Paul. "Are Cambridge Changes Non-Events?" *Analysis* 35 (1975), 140–144.

——. "Detecting Change." *Ratio* 19 (1977), 34–38.

——. *Eternal God*. New York: Oxford University Press, 1988.

——. "Timelessness and Foreknowledge." *Mind* 84 (1975), 516–527.

Hesse, Mary. "Action at a Distance and Field Theories." In Paul Edwards, ed., *The Encyclopedia of Philosophy*, vol. 1 (New York: Macmillan, 1967), pp. 9–15.

Hintikka, Jaakko. *Time and Necessity*. New York: Oxford University Press, 1973.

Hoffman, Joshua, and Gary Rosenkrantz. "Hard and Soft Facts." *Philosophical Review* 93 (1984), 419–434.

Hollis, Martin. "Box and Cox." *Philosophy* 42 (1967), 75–78.

———. "Times and Spaces." *Mind* (1967), 524–536.

Holt, Dennis C. "Timelessness and the Metaphysics of Temporal Existence." *American Philosophical Quarterly* 19 (1981), 149–156.

Hopkins, Jasper. *Anselm of Canterbury*. Vol. 4. Toronto: Edwin Mellen Press, 1976.

Hume, David. *Dialogues on Natural Religion*. In *The Empiricists* (Garden City, N.Y.: Doubleday, 1974).

Jackson, Frank. "On Assertion and Indicative Conditionals." *Philosophical Review* 88 (1979), 565–589.

James, William. *Essays in Radical Empiricism and a Pluralistic Universe*. New York: Dutton, 1971.

———. *Principles of Psychology*. Vol. 1. New York: Dover, 1890.

Jantzen, Grace. *God's World, God's Body*. Philadelphia: Westminster Press, 1984.

Kapitan, Tomis. "Agency and Omniscience." Unpublished.

Kaplan, David. "Dthat." In P. Cole, ed., *Syntax and Semantics: Pragmatics* (New York: Academic Press, 1978), vol. 9.

Kenny, Anthony. *The God of the Philosophers*. New York: Oxford University Press, 1979.

Khamara, E. J. "Eternity and Omniscience." *Philosophical Quarterly* 24 (1974), 204–219.

Kim, Jaegwon. "Events as Property-Exemplifications." In Myles Brand and Douglas Walton, eds., *Action Theory* (Dordrecht: Reidel, 1976), pp. 156–177.

Kneale, Martha. "Eternity and Sempiternity." In Marjorie Grene, ed., *Spinoza* (New York: Doubleday, 1973), pp. 227–240.

Kneale, William. "Time and Eternity in Theology." *Proceedings of the Aristotelian Society* 61 (1960–61), 87–108.

Kovach, Francis. "The Enduring Question of Action at a Distance in St. Albert the Great." *Southwestern Journal of Philosophy* 10 (1979), 161–235.

Kretzmann, Norman. "Omniscience and Immutability." *Journal of Philosophy* 63 (1966), 409–421.

Kripke, Saul. "Naming and Necessity." In Donald Davidson and Gilbert Harman, eds., *Semantics of Natural Language* (Dordrecht: Reidel, 1972), pp. 253–355.

Kvanvig, Jonathan. *The Possibility of an All-Knowing God*. New York: St. Martin's Press, 1986.

Kvanvig, Jonathan, and Hugh McCann. "Divine Conservation and the Persistence of the World." In Thomas Morris, ed., *Divine and Human Action* (Ithaca, N.Y.: Cornell University Press, 1989), pp. 13–49.

Lachs, John. "Professor Prior on Omniscience." *Philosophy* 38 (1963), 361–364.

Leftow, Brian. "God and Abstract Entities." *Faith and Philosophy* 7 (1990), 193–217.

———. "Individual and Attribute in the Ontological Argument." *Faith and Philosophy* 7 (1990), 235–242.

———. "Simplicity and Eternity." Ph.D. diss., Yale University, 1984.

Lewis, David. *Counterfactuals* (Cambridge, Mass.: Harvard University Press, 1973).

———. "Causation." In David Lewis, *Philosophical Papers*, vol. 2 (New York: Oxford University Press, 1986), pp. 159–172.

———. "Counterfactuals and Comparative Possibility." In David Lewis, *Philosophical Papers*, vol. 2 (New York: Oxford University Press, 1986), pp. 3–31.

———. "Probabilities of Conditionals and Conditional Probabilities." In David Lewis, *Philosophical Papers*, vol. 2 (New York: Oxford University Press, 1986), pp. 133–152.

Lewis, Delmas. "Eternity Again." *International Journal for Philosophy of Religion* 15 (1984), 73–79.

———. "Eternity, Time, and Tenselessness." *Faith and Philosophy* 5 (1988), 72–86.

———. "God and Time." Ph.D. diss., University of Wisconsin 1984; Ann Arbor, Mich.: University Microfilms, 1985.

Lockwood, Michael. "Einstein and the Identity Theory." *Analysis* 44 (1984), 22–25.

Loinaz, J. *Praelectiones E Theologia Naturalis.* Turin: Marietti, 1929.

Lombard, Lawrence. *Events.* London: Routledge and Kegan Paul, 1986.

———. "Relational Change and Relational Changes." *Philosophical Studies* 34 (1978), 63–79.

Lucas, J. R. *A Treatise on Time and Space.* London: Methuen, 1973.

Mabbott, J. D. "Our Direct Experience of Time." In Richard Gale, ed., *The Philosophy of Time* (N.J.: Humanities Press, 1968), pp. 304–321.

———. "The Specious Present." *Mind* 64 (1955), 376–383.

MacBeath, Murray. "God's Spacelessness and Timelessness." *Sophia* 22 (1983), 23–32.

McGinn, Colin. *The Subjective View.* New York: Oxford University Press, 1983.

Maimonides, Moses. *The Guide for the Perplexed.* Translated by M. Friedländer. New York: Dover, 1956.

Malcolm, Norman. "Anselm's Ontological Arguments." In Alvin Plantinga, ed., *The Ontological Argument* (New York: Doubleday, 1965), pp. 136–159.

Mann, William E. "Divine Simplicity." *Religious Studies* 18 (1981), 451–471.

——. "Epistemology Supernaturalized." *Faith and Philosophy* 2 (1985), 436–456.

——. "God's Freedom, Human Freedom, and God's Responsibility for Sin." In Thomas Morris, ed., *Divine and Human Action* (Ithaca, N.Y.: Cornell University Press, 1988), pp. 182–210.

——. "Simplicity and Immutability in God." In Thomas Morris, ed., *The Concept of God* (New York: Oxford University Press, 1987), pp. 253–267.

Mavrodes, George. "Is the Past Unpreventable?" *Faith and Philosophy* 2 (1983), 131–146.

Mellor, D. H. *Real Time*. Cambridge: Cambridge University Press, 1981.

Menzel, Christopher. "On Set-Theoretic Possible Worlds." *Analysis* 46 (1986), 68–72.

Migne, J. P., ed. *Patrologia Latina*. Paris, 1841.

Molina, Luis de. *De concordia*, pt. IV. Translated by Alfred Freddoso. Ithaca, N.Y.: Cornell University Press, 1988.

Morris, Thomas V. *Anselmian Explorations*. Notre Dame, Ind.: University of Notre Dame Press, 1987.

——. *The Logic of God Incarnate*. Ithaca, N.Y.: Cornell University Press, 1987.

——. "Perfection and Power." *International Journal for Philosophy of Religion* 20 (1986), 65–68.

——. "Properties, Modalities, and God." *Philosophical Review* 94 (1984), 35–56.

——. *Understanding Identity-Statements*. Aberdeen: Aberdeen University Press, 1984.

Mundle, C. W. K. "Consciousness of Time." In Paul Edwards, ed., *The Encyclopedia of Philosophy*, vol. 8 (New York: Macmillan, 1967), pp. 134–138.

——. "How Specious Is the Specious Present?" *Mind* 63 (1954), 26–48.

Nagel, Thomas. "What Is It Like To Be a Bat?" *Philosophical Review* 83 (1974), 435–450.

Nelson, Herbert. "Time(s), Eternity, and Duration." *International Journal for Philosophy of Religion* 22 (1987), 3–19.

Newton-Smith, W. H. *The Structure of Time*. London: Routledge and Kegan Paul, 1980.

Nussbaum, Martha. *The Fragility of Goodness*. New York: Cambridge University Press, 1986.

Owen, Huw. *Concepts of Deity*. New York: Herder and Herder, 1971.

Padgett, Alan. "God and Time: Toward a New Doctrine of Divine Timeless Eternity." *Religious Studies* 25 (1989), 209–215.

Pendlebury, Michael. "Facts as Truthmakers." *Monist* 69 (1986), 177–188.

Perry, John. "The Problem of the Essential Indexical." *Nous* 13 (1979), 3–19.

Pike, Nelson. *God and Timelessness*. New York: Schocken Books, 1970.

Plantinga, Alvin. *Does God Have a Nature?* Milwaukee: Marquette University Press, 1980.

——. *The Nature of Necessity*. New York: Oxford University Press, 1974.

——. "On Ockham's Way Out." *Faith and Philosophy* 3 (1986), 235–269.

Plass, Paul. "Timeless Time in Neo-Platonism," *Modern Schoolman* 55 (1977), 1–19.

Plato. *Parmenides*.

———. *Phaedo*.

———. *Republic*.

———. *Timaeus*. In Edith Hamilton and Huntington Cairns, eds., *Plato: The Collected Dialogues* (Princeton, N.J.: Princeton University Press, 1961).

Plotinus. *Enneads*. Cambridge, Mass.: Harvard University Press, 1966–88.

Plumer, Gilbert. "The Myth of the Specious Present." *Mind* 94 (1985), 19–35.

Pollock, John. *The Foundations of Philosophical Semantics*. Princeton, N.J.: Princeton University Press, 1984.

———. "Plantinga on Possible Worlds." In James Tomberlin and Peter van Inwagen, eds., *Alvin Plantinga* (Dordrecht: Reidel, 1985), pp. 145–186.

Post, John. *The Faces of Existence*. Ithaca, N.Y.: Cornell University Press, 1987.

Prior, Arthur. "The Formalities of Omniscience." *Philosophy* 37 (1962), 114–129.

Putnam, Hilary. "Time and Physical Geometry." In Hilary Putnam, *Mathematics, Matter, and Method* (New York: Cambridge University Press, 1979), pp. 198–205.

Quinn, Philip. "Divine Conservation, Secondary Causality, and Occasionalism." In Thomas Morris, ed., *Divine and Human Action* (Ithaca, N.Y.: Cornell University Press, 1989), pp. 50–73.

Quinton, Anthony. "Spaces and Times." *Philosophy* 37 (1962), 130–147.

Royce, Josiah. *The World and the Individual*. New York: Macmillan, 1901.

Salmon, Nathan. "Existence." In James Tomberlin, ed., *Philosophical Perspectives I: Metaphysics* (Atascadero, Calif.: Ridgeview, 1987), pp. 49–108.

———. "The Logic of What Might Have Been." *Philosophical Review* 98 (1989), 3–34.

———. *Reference and Essence*. Princeton, N.J.: Princeton University Press, 1981.

Salmon, Wesley. *Space, Time, and Motion*. Minneapolis: University of Minnesota Press, 1980.

Sanford, David. "Borderline Logic." *American Philosophical Quarterly* 12 (1975), 29–39.

Simons, Peter. *Parts*. New York: Oxford University Press, 1987.

Sklar, Lawrence. *Space, Time, and Spacetime*. Berkeley: University of California Press, 1976.

———. "Time, Reality, and Relativity." In Richard Healey, ed., *Reduction, Time, and Reality* (Cambridge: Cambridge University Press, 1982), pp. 129–142.

Smith, Quentin. "A New Typology of Temporal and Atemporal Permanence." *Nous* 23 (1989), 307–330.

Smith, T. P. "On the Applicability of a Criterion of Change." *Ratio* 15 (1973), 325–333.

Sorabji, Richard. *Time, Creation, and the Continuum*. Ithaca, N.Y.: Cornell University Press, 1983.

Spinoza. *Ethics*. Translated by R. Elwes. New York: Dover, 1955.

Stump, Eleonore, and Norman Kretzmann. "Absolute Simplicity," *Faith and Philosophy* 2 (1985), 353–382.

——. "Atemporal Duration." *Journal of Philosophy* 84 (1987), 214–219.

——. "Eternity." *Journal of Philosophy* 79 (1981), 429–458.

——. "Eternity Examined and Extended," forthcoming.

Sturch, R. L. "The Problem of the Divine Eternity." *Religious Studies* 10 (1974), 487–493.

Suarez, Francisco. *Opera Omnia*. Paris: Vives, 1856–66.

Sutherland, Stewart. *God, Jesus, and Belief*. Oxford: Blackwell, 1984.

——. "Truth and God." *Proceedings of the Aristotelian Society* 56 (1982), 99–115.

Swartz, Norman. "Spatial and Temporal Worlds." *Ratio* 17 (1975), 217–228.

Swinburne, Richard. *The Coherence of Theism*. New York: Oxford University Press, 1977.

——. "Conditions for Bi-temporality." *Analysis* 26 (1965), 47–50.

——. *Space and Time*. New York: Macmillan, 1968.

——. "The Timelessness of God." *Church Quarterly Review* 166 (1965).

——. "Times." *Analysis* 25 (1964), 185–191.

Taylor, Richard. *Metaphysics*. 3d ed. Englewood Cliffs, N.J.: Prentice-Hall, 1983.

Thomas Aquinas. *Compendium theologiae*.

——. *In I Librum Sententiarum*.

——. *In VIII Libros physicorum*.

——. *In Perihermeneias*.

——. *QD de veritate*.

——. *Summa contra Gentiles*.

——. *Summa theologiae*.

Tomkinson, L. J. "Divine Sempiternity and Atemporality." *Religious Studies* 18 (1982), 177–189.

van Inwagen, Peter. "Ontological Arguments." *Nous* 11 (1977), 375–396.

——. "The Place of Chance in a World Sustained by God." In Thomas V. Morris, ed., *Divine and Human Action* (Ithaca, N.Y.: Cornell University Press, 1988), pp. 211–235.

von Wright, G. H. "Time, Change, and Contradiction." (London: Cambridge University Press, 1968).

Ward, Keith. *Rational Theology and the Creativity of God*. Oxford: Blackwell, 1982.

Weingard, Robert. "Relativity and the Reality of Past and Future Events." *British Journal for the Philosophy of Science* 23 (1972), 119–121.

——. "Relativity and the Spatiality of Mental Events." *Philosophical Studies* 31 (1977), 279–284.

White, Michael. *Agency and Integrality*. Dordrecht: Reidel, 1985.

Whitehead, Alfred N. *Process and Reality*. New York: Macmillan, 1929.

——. *Science and the Modern World*. New York: Macmillan, 1925.

Whitrow, G. J. *The Natural Philosophy of Time*. London: Thomas Nelson and Sons, 1961.

Widerker, David, and E. M. Zemach. "Facts, Freedom, and Foreknowledge."
Religious Studies 23 (1987), 19–28.

Wolterstorff, Nicholas. "God Everlasting." In Steven Cahn and David Shatz,
eds., *Contemporary Philosophy of Religion* (London: Oxford University Press,
1982), pp. 77–98.

Zalta, Edward. "On the Structural Similarities of Worlds and Times." Read at
the American Philosophical Association Pacific Division meeting, San Francisco, April 1987.

Zemach, E. M. "Many Times." *Analysis* 28 (1968), 145–151.

Index

absolute modality, 10–14
  warranted claims about, 14–17
abstract-concrete distinction, 33–34, 43, 205–209
abstract entities, 205–208
acquaintance. *See* perceptual acquaintance
action at a distance, 186–191, 350–351
actualism, 9–10, 56
actuality, relativity of, 232–235, 328–330
Adams, Ernest, 259
Adams, Robert M., 9n, 14n, 55n
Adams, Marilyn, 160n
Allen, R. E., 126
Alston, William, 19, 145n, 159n, 220–221, 243n, 255n, 280–281, 304n, 319–320
Anselm, 2, 4, 54, 61, 68, 148, 152–153, 156, 183–217, 228, 269, 321n, 324
antirealism, 37, 141
Aquinas, 4, 52, 57, 61, 77–78, 87, 188, 211, 228, 260n, 269, 290n, 321n
  on divine foreknowledge, 160–161, 163, 169–170, 181–182
  on divine simplicity, 30n, 68–69, 149–151, 204–205
  on eternality, 118n, 147, 149–151, 156–158, 201–202, 235–236
  on mode of divine knowledge, 219, 220n, 243, 244n, 319
  on talk about God, 19, 129
Aristotle, 1n, 55n, 64–65, 86, 93, 95n, 136n, 183, 187–188, 199n
atoms, 137–140
  of time, 140–142
Augustine, 4, 61, 64n, 73–112, 116n, 149n, 183, 189, 199, 211, 260n, 278, 290, 309

Austin, John L., 101
author-character analogy, 162, 263–265

B-series, 238–241
Beer, Michelle, 336n
beginnings, 27–28, 31, 32, 65, 77–78, 132, 268–269, 286, 290
  and ceasings, 65, 76, 79–80, 200–201, 202
Big Bang, 28–29, 32
Blumenfeld, David, 338n
Boethius, 51, 61, 83–84, 86n, 182n, 189, 213, 278
  on divine foreknowledge, 160, 169–170, 250–255
  on divine simplicity, 64n, 68, 149–150
  on eternality, 2, 112–150, 157–158, 201–202, 209–210, 243
  on time-eternity relations, 162–164, 181–182
Bonaventure, 65n
Broad, C. D., 347

"Cambridge" changes or attributes. *See* real vs. "Cambridge"
Capek, Milic, 142n, 221n, 353n
Castañeda, Hector-Neri, 55n
causation, 22–23, 29–30, 43, 145–146, 162, 173–175, 177–178, 186–191, 245, 291–295, 309
Chandler, Hugh, 14n
change, 42, 76–77, 79, 85, 238–239, 286–287, 333–334, 342–348
character (nature), 257
  explains consents, 257–259
  grounds divine foreknowledge, 259–262

Chisholm, Roderick, 350n, 351n
Cicero, 189
Clarke, Bowman, 230–231, 314
Coburn, Robert, 313
color, knowledge of, 339–342
consents to action, 256–260
contiguity
    of a cause, 186–191
    spatial, 190–191, 224–226, 271n
    temporal, 53–54, 62, 190, 215, 225–226
Cook, Robert, 113n, 278–279
counterfactuals of freedom, 9
Cox, John, 213n
Craig, William L., 40n, 52, 230, 314
creation of the universe, 275, 290–295,
    302–309
Creel, Richard, 171, 230–231, 304n, 314,
    344–345

Davis, Steven, 41n, 171
Dedekind, R., 136n
discrete time series. See time: unity of
divine sense-data, 220–221, 331–332, 345
divine simplicity. See God: simplicity of
divine timelessness
    as atemporal duration, 112–146
    and divine simplicity, 2, 4, 151–157
    as everlasting temporal existence, 1, 63,
        65, 112–113, 268
    and God's agency, 3, 5, 291–297
    and God's life, 2, 114–115, 147–158,
        278–279, 287–288, 290
    and God's omniscience, 3, 5
    and God's personhood, 3, 5, 283–312
    as nunc stans, 112–113, 116, 146
    and religious experience, 5
dream and reality, 100–110
Dummett, Michael, 34
Duns Scotus, John, 2, 19, 228, 229, 230,
    239n
duplication argument, 258–259

eternal tense, 61–62, 66, 253–254
eternity
    contains temporal entities, 183–184,
        212–245, 253–254, 306–307, 310,
        333–335, 345
    contiguous with times, 52–54
    as a dimension, 183, 211–216
    and divine simplicity, 2, 66–67, 134–
        137, 139–140, 147, 149–158, 183,
        255, 261–262
    as a duration, 112–150, 199–203, 209–
        210, 267n, 270
    as a frame of reference, 54n, 167, 219,
        226–228, 239–240, 251, 265–266, 333

and God's life, 114–115, 140, 147–158,
    183, 209–210
as a locational property, 209
as a modal property, 201–202, 209,
    236–241
quasi-temporal, 120–146, 157–158, 237,
    267, 290n, 299
superior to temporality, 73–111, 278
as a "time" (date), 51, 61, 65, 215, 234,
    284, 292, 296, 297, 300, 310, 358
existence
    degrees of, 73–111, 278
    genuine, 82–90
    immutable, 73, 74, 87–88, 89, 131
    necessary, 270–271
    and unity, 92–96
extension. See points vs. extensions
extrinsic timelessness, 22, 62

facts, 6, 318, 335, 336
factual omniscience, 318–319, 334–337,
    342, 344, 348
Falkenstein, L., 21n
Fischer, John, 160n, 250n
Fitzgerald, Paul, 113, 116, 123–126, 145,
    147–149, 171
fixity of facts, 87–89, 160, 163–164
Flint, Thomas, 273n
foreknowledge, divine. See freedom and
    divine foreknowledge; God: knowl-
    edge of
Freddoso, Alfred, 194n, 228n, 273n
free agency, 256–265, 281–282, 299–300,
    306
freedom and divine foreknowledge, 159–
    160, 163, 179–180, 221n, 246–266,
    280

Gale, R. M., 221n, 297, 313, 314n, 324n
Geach, Peter, 309n
Geroch, Robert, 38n
Ginet, Carl, 281n
God
    agency of, 3, 5, 161, 175, 186–191, 245,
        293–297, 301–302, 306
    freedom of, 299–302
    how God knows, 169–171, 173, 218–
        222, 243–244, 272, 279–280, 306
    immutability of, 79–80, 149–150, 254–
        255, 299–312, 343–348
    knowledge of, 3, 159–160, 179–180,
        235, 246–266, 280–282
    life of, 2, 113–147, 196
    omnipotence of, 273, 277, 321–323
    omnipresence of, 54, 183–194, 210–211,
        214–215, 228, 271, 302, 310

God (*cont.*)
  omniscience of, 5, 313–348
  perfection of, 270–271, 277, 279–280,
    317, 321, 322n, 323–327, 331, 337,
    344–345
  personhood of, 3, 5, 283–312
  response to creatures, 280–281, 303–
    309, 327
  simplicity of, 2, 67–72, 93–94, 99, 134–
    137, 147, 170–171, 183, 185–186,
    189, 197–198, 204–208, 222, 255,
    261–262, 280n, 292n, 347n
Godfrey-Smith, William, 233n, 309n, 354
Goodman, Nelson, 142n
Grim, Patrick, 8n, 313, 326n
Grünbaum, Adolph, 192n
Guleserian, Theodore, 271n

hard vs. soft
  facts, 160n, 194n, 249–250
  processes, 194
Harris, James, 221n
Hartshorne, Charles, 34–35
Hasker, William, 9n, 36, 171, 181, 220n,
  221n, 247n, 249n, 250n, 262n, 272,
  279, 314, 316, 332n
Helm, Paul, 45, 55n, 78–80, 161–162,
  163n, 171, 267–270, 298–299, 303n,
  309n, 326n
Hesse, Mary, 187n
Hintikka, Jaakko, 34n, 55n
history, intrinsic vs. extrinsic, 155–157
Hoffmann, Joshua, 194n
Hollis, Martin, 21n
Holt, Dennis, 152n, 196n
Hume, David, 284

immutability, 73, 77, 80–81, 85, 89, 92,
  98, 138–139, 184
Incarnation, 19, 321n, 347
indexicals, 313–315, 327, 338, 341
  epistemic, 338–339, 341, 342, 344
  and knowledge of the present, 313–337
  personal, 322–323, 325–326
  temporal, 313–315, 327, 335–337, 338
intuitive knowledge, 260–264

Jackson, Frank, 259
James, William, 143
Jantzen, Grace, 40, 221n, 284n

Kant, Immanuel, 38n
Kapitan, Tomis, 281n
Kaplan, David, 55n
Karmo, Toomas, 58n
Kenny, Anthony, 338n, 342n

Khamara, E. J., 296n
Kim, Jaegwon, 356n
Kneale, Martha, 1n, 20n, 41, 44–46, 113n
Kneale, William, 40, 63, 113n, 290n, 296–
  297
knowledge by acquaintance. See perceptual acquaintance
Kovach, Francis, 188n
Kretzmann, Norman, 4, 151, 161, 219,
  332, 335
  on eternality, 113–134, 148n, 149
  on indexicals and omniscience, 313–314,
    325n, 326n
  on time-eternity relations, 164–182,
    216–217, 221, 231, 235–238, 240,
    252, 266
Kripke, Saul, 10
Kvanvig, Jonathan, 192n, 194n, 322n,
  325n, 336

Lachs, John, 338n
LaCroix, Richard, 281n
Lewis, David, 156, 258n, 259, 293, 294,
  295
Lewis, Delmas, 40n, 156n, 171, 212, 228–
  231, 235, 314, 316, 327–333, 345,
  349–358
Lockwood, Michael, 213n
Loinaz, J., 244n
Lombard, Lawrence, 197n, 309n
Lombard, Peter, 112
Lucas, J. R., 283–284

Mabbott, J. D., 221n
McCann, Hugh, 192n, 194n
McGinn, Colin, 333n
McTaggart, J., 238
Maimonides, 64
Malcolm, Norman, 40, 63
Mann, William E., 251n, 255n, 280n
Mavrodes, George, 160n
Mellor, D. H., 144n, 152n
Menzel, Christopher, 55n
middle knowledge, 247–249, 262, 304
Minkowski, H., 39, 353
Molina, Luis de, 61, 247–249, 262n
moments, 51, 55, 112–113, 190–191, 193–
  194
Morris, Thomas, 304n, 310–311, 322n,
  347n
motion, 23–25, 226–227, 334, 342–343
Mundle, C. W. K., 221n

Nagel, Thomas, 322n
Nelson, Herbert, 22n, 118n, 124n, 138n,
  146n, 167–168

Newton-Smith, W. H., 21n, 26n
numbers, 40–49
Nussbaum, Martha, 111

observation, 169, 349–352, 358
    divine, 160–161, 163, 169, 170–171,
        219–221, 316–318, 331–333
    eternal-temporal, 169–172, 245, 349–
        359
Owen, Huw, 304n

P-series, 232–233
Padgett, Alan, 272n
Parmenides, 64
parts, 94–96, 98, 135–136, 142, 151, 195–
        196, 222
    of eternal duration, 121–122, 124–125,
        135–136, 145, 148, 237
    vs. points, 124
    temporal, 135, 151–152, 191–192, 195–
        196, 237
past, fixity of, 160, 163–164, 246, 249–
        250
Pendlebury, Michael, 8n
perceptual acquaintance, 169, 219–221,
        243–244, 279, 316–318, 339–341,
        343–344
permanence, 86–89, 131–133
Perry, John, 55n, 315, 325n, 336
Philoponus, John, 115n–116n
Pike, Nelson, 3n, 40, 63, 284n, 289, 291–
        292, 295, 303, 336
Plantinga, Alvin, 10, 69n, 163–164
Plass, Paul, 120n
Plato, 64, 82, 83, 100, 108n, 113n, 118,
        213
Plotinus, 63, 93, 113n, 146, 149n, 198
Plumer, Gilbert, 221n
Plutarch, 119n
points vs. extensions, 112, 123–125, 128,
        130–131, 133–135, 149, 158, 287
Pollock, John L., 10n, 292n, 295
possible worlds, 7–9
    times as like, 55
Post, John, 7n, 21, 32n, 38n, 40
present-actuality, 316–318, 327–328, 330,
        333
presentness, 84, 89–90, 162
    character-presence and existential pres-
        ence, 85–89
    measured by permanence, 86–89
    specious. See specious present
Prior, Arthur, 313
propositional omniscience, 313, 318–319,
        323, 325–326, 336–337, 342
Putnam, Hilary, 7n, 233n

quasi-Molinism, 257–262
quasi-temporal eternity. See eternity:
        quasi-temporal
Quine, W. V., 7n
Quinn, Philip, 192n
Quinton, Anthony, 21n

real vs. "Cambridge"
    attributes, 67–68, 154, 343–344
    changes, 300, 302, 309–312, 356–357
Rosenkrantz, Gary, 194n
Royce, Josiah, 284n
Russell, Bertrand, 55n, 339, 340

Salmon, Nathan, 10n, 14n, 95n
Salmon, Wesley, 172n, 176n, 332n
Sanford, David, 80n
sense-data, divine. See divine sense-data
simultaneity, 161, 172, 217–245
    A- and B-, 239–241
    causal theory of, 177–178
    eternal, 162, 179, 184, 217, 219, 234,
        251–255, 265–266, 300, 332
    eternal-temporal, 161–162, 165, 167–
        182, 184, 216–217, 221, 231, 238,
        240, 242, 252, 266, 332
    generic, 179
    and God's knowledge, 218–222
    relativity of, 165–167, 172, 176, 232–
        235, 239n, 272, 328–330
    somehow-, 166–167
    temporal, 165–167, 179
Sklar, Lawrence, 172n, 233n, 328n
Smith, Quentin, 26n, 33n, 39n, 131n,
        133n, 275n
Smith, T. P., 309n
Sorabji, Richard, 1n, 40, 113n, 115n,
        119n, 124n, 125n, 140, 142n, 295,
        296–297, 304n, 313n
space, 23–25, 34, 38–39, 41, 120, 137–
        141, 144–145, 212, 224–225, 352–
        354
space-time, 24–25, 32, 34, 36, 38–39, 47,
        98, 138n, 213–214, 275, 353–354
special theory of relativity, 145–146, 165–
        167, 172, 176, 213–214, 226, 234,
        272, 291–292, 328–329, 330, 333,
        334
specious present, 143–144, 220–221, 284n,
        343–344
Spinoza, 63–64
STR. See special theory of relativity
Strawson, Peter, 287
Stump, Eleonore, 4, 151, 161, 219, 332,
        335

Stump, Eleonore (*cont.*)
  on eternality, 113–134, 148n, 149
  on time-eternity relations, 164–182,
    216–217, 221, 231, 235–238, 240,
    252, 266
Sturch, R. L., 304n
Suarez, Francisco, 95n
Sutherland, Stewart, 295n, 314
Swartz, Norman, 21n
Swinburne, Richard, 19n, 21n, 26n, 39–
    40, 47n, 113n, 129n, 239n, 249n, 278,
    296, 299–301, 304, 336

Tarski, Alfred, 6
Taylor, Richard, 42
temporality, 316
  as a locational property, 236–237
  as a modal property, 236, 238–241
  as a prerequisite of mind, 283–297
time
  beginning (and ending) of, 32–33, 132–
    133, 275–277, 289–290
  compared with space, 120–121, 144–
    145, 212, 352–354
  contiguity in, 52–53, 57–58
  contingency of, 32–39, 273
  creation of, 191–194, 203, 273–278
  as a dimension, 35–36, 38–39, 47, 144,
    227, 272
  division of, 26–28
  as relational, 77–78, 275, 277–278
  tensed vs. tenseless, 17–18, 42, 48, 83–
    84, 89, 91–92, 120, 122, 184, 191–
    194, 229–231, 233–234, 314–315,
    317, 320, 330, 346–348

  travel, 23n
  unity of, 21–31, 57–58, 62, 168, 175,
    269n, 272, 273
timelessness-omniscience arguments
  metaphysical, 314, 315–320, 327–335
  semantic, 313–314, 319–320, 326
Tomkinson, L. J., 278
truth, 6–7, 37–38, 51, 55–57, 59–61, 62,
    164, 180, 351–352
  conditions, 340–341
  degrees of, 80
truthmakers, 6–7, 8n, 59–60

understanding, timeless, 285–290
unity
  and divine simplicity, 93–94
  and existence, 92–100
  of material objects, 97–98

van Inwagen, Peter, 33n, 263n

Wang's Law, 95
Ward, Keith, 29–30, 35n, 218
Weingard, Robert, 213n, 233n
White, Michael, 34n, 55n, 87n
Whitehead, A. N., 141, 143
Whitrow, G. J., 141n
Widerker, David, 160n, 250n
Wittgenstein, Ludwig, 341
Wolterstorff, Nicholas, 40n, 41n, 156n,
    304n, 313, 314n, 355

Zalta, Edward, 55n
Zemach, E. M., 21n, 160n, 250n
Zero Thesis, 222–228, 271n

Library of Congress Cataloging-in-Publication Data

Leftow, Brian, 1956–

    Time and eternity / Brian Leftow.
      p.   cm. — (Cornell studies in the philosophy of religion)
    Includes bibliographical references and index.
    ISBN 0-8014-2459-3 (alk. paper)
    1. God—Immutability—History of doctrines.   2. Time—Religious aspects—Christi-
    anity.   3. Eternity.   I. Title.   II. Series.
BT153.I47L43   1991
212'.7—dc20   90-55890

CPSIA information can be obtained at www.ICGtesting.com
Printed in the USA
BVOW080819280213

314259BV00001B/3/P